Studia Fennica
Historica 12

THE FINNISH LITERATURE SOCIETY (SKS) was founded in 1831 and has, from the very beginning, engaged in publishing operations. It nowadays publishes literature in the fields of ethnology and folkloristics, linguistics, literary research and cultural history.

The first volume of the Studia Fennica series appeared in 1933. Since 1992, the series has been divided into three thematic subseries: Ethnologica, Folkloristica and Linguistica. Two additional subseries were formed in 2002, Historica and Litteraria. The subseries Anthropologica was formed in 2007.

In addition to its publishing activities, the Finnish Literature Society maintains research activities and infrastructures, an archive containing folklore and literary collections, a research library and promotes Finnish literature abroad.

oa.finlit.fi

EDITORIAL OFFICE
SKS
P.O. Box 259
FI-00171 Helsinki
www.finlit.fi

Modernisation in Russia since 1900

Edited by Markku Kangaspuro & Jeremy Smith

Finnish Literature Society • Helsinki

Studia Fennica Historica 12

The publication has undergone a peer review.

VERTAISARVIOITU
KOLLEGIALT GRANSKAD
PEER-REVIEWED
www.tsv.fi/tunnus

A digital edition of a printed book first published in 2006 by the Finnish Literature Society.

Cover Design: Timo Numminen
EPUB: Tero Salmén

ISBN 978-951-746-854-1 (Print)
ISBN 978-951-858-021-1 (PDF)
ISBN 978-951-858-020-4 (EPUB)

ISSN 0085-6835 (Studia Fennica)
ISSN 1458-526X (Studia Fennica Historica)

DOI: http://dx.doi.org/10.21435/sfh.12

A free open access version of the book is available at http://dx.doi.org/10.21435/sfh.12 or by scanning this QR code with your mobile device.

Contents

List of Figures

List of Tables

List of Illustrations

Foreword

The research project "The Conditions for Constructing New Russia. Inter-actions of Tradition and Europeanness in the Development of 20th Century Russia" examined developmental processes in contemporary Russia and the conditions delimiting its choices in the light of the central turning points in its twentieth century history. The central theme of the project concerned the interaction of Russia and Europe. Our aim has been to explore from a multi-disciplinary perspective what is new in post-1991 New Russia and what is a continuation of Russia's own historical and cultural tradition. In other words, what in the tradition of Russia's culture and history has set the conditions for its developmental and political choices? The project concentrated in particu-lar on the changes in Russia's relationship with Europe in the 20th century. The issue of the meeting of Europeanness (advocated by the Zapadniks) and traditional Russianness (the Slavophiles) shows concretely the two central factors that have affected Russia's development. The question of European-ness and its ideals of the Enlightenment, often interpreted as universal, has divided Russian society for centuries. Ultimately the question is whether Russian development leads towards modernisation in the European sense of the term or whether Russia will continue on its own developmental path, unifying, once again, European influences with Russian specificity. This also touches on the question of the aims of the West's politics towards Russia and how realistic their aims are. Thus, what are the conditions stemming from and determined by the reality of Russia, its history and culture that affect fundamentally its future development and political choices?

This volume results from the collaboration between the Finnish participants in our project, and researchers at the University of Birmingham's Centre for Russian and East European Studies, which has a long tradition of exploring modernisation in Russia, especially in Soviet industry. This collaboration resulted in two conferences, one in Helsinki in 2002 and one in Birmingham in 2003, which drew in additional international scholars. I would like to thank all the important people who have contributed to this publication without mentioning them individually. In particular I would like to thank Dr. Markku Kangaspuro and Dr. Jeremy Smith, the editors of this volume and the per-sons who carried the main responsibility in organizing the two conferences. For me personally, our joint conference and the publication derived from it has been a valuable experience, and the publication itself is an important contribution to the academic community. The Academy of Finland awarded a significant grant for the project's work in 2000–2003.

Antti Laine
PhD, Senior Researcher
Karelian Institute
University of Joensuu
Project Leader

Further Acknowledgements

The editors would like to thank Professor Antti Laine and the Academy of Finland for the financial and academic support to the conferences which lay behind this volume, and to the volume itself. The Aleksanteri Institute and its director Professor Markku Kivinen made an important contribution to realizing the first conference at the University of Helsinki in 2002. The Birmingham conference, held at the European Research Institute in October 2003, could not have happened without the tireless efforts of the Centre for Russian and East European Studies' Marea Arries and Patricia Carr. Elizabeth White made essential contributions to the running and content of the conference, and in addition to the authors of this work, we would like to thank the other historians and social scientists who participated in discussion in both Helsinki and Birmingham, many of whose ideas have found their way into the final volume. Laura Quist has been of enormous assistance in the final stages of editing the book in the fall of 2006. Finally, we would like to thank SKS, especially Rauno Endén and Johanna Ilmakunnas, for their patience and enthusiasm in making publication of this volume possible.

Markku Kangaspuro
PhD, Head of Research
Aleksanteri Institute
University of Helsinki

Jeremy Smith
PhD, Senior Lecturer in
Russian History
Centre for Russian and East
European Studies
University of Birmingham

MARKKU KANGASPURO AND JEREMY SMITH

Introduction: Modernisation in Russian History

From at least the time of Ivan the Terrible up to the present day, it has been a major concern of Russia's rulers to overcome the perceived lag in development between Russia and her neighbours and global competitors. The gap between relative levels of production with the leading western powers has never been overcome, and the need to bridge this gap has preoccupied successive regimes. Until quite recently, the emphasis had been on the need to achieve military parity or superiority. Modernisation therefore included finding ways of making the economy more productive generally, and deploying more effective technologies. While economic and military needs may have lain at the heart of Russian drives to modernise, the project included, of necessity, important elements of social and political modernisation. In a direct sense, Peter the Great's reorganisation of the state bureaucracy, Alexander II's emancipation of the serfs, Stalin's collectivisation of agriculture and industrialisation, the emphasis on social equality and the welfare state after World War II, and the spread of democracy and institutional reform during and after *perestroika* have been part of the modernisation project. Indirectly, deliberate economic, social and political modernisation has led on to other elements of modernisation, often with unintended consequences. In the 20th century, industrialisation and modernisation had a major impact on all areas of life, dramatically changing the overall social structure, the position of women and non-Russians, and the welfare needs of society.

For much of Russian history, modernisation has been almost synonymous with westernisation. Russian backwardness has always been measured against the standard of the leading powers in Western Europe and, later, North America. This was particularly true of certain historical periods: Peter the Great's time, the aftermath of the Crimean War, after the Bolshevik revolution, during Stalin's industrialisation drive, and in the transition from communism to a free market. Russian liberals and westernisers in the nineteenth century explicitly advocated the adoption of western norms and institutions as the answer to Russia's problems. The same can be said for the European-oriented Russian Marxists from the founding father of Russian Marxism, G. V. Plekhanov, to V. I. Lenin. As several of the contributors to this volume point out, many of the efforts at modernisation in the 20th century were based on imitation of foreign models.

11

But modernisation has not been pursued purely by direct imitation of the West. While Peter adopted western forms in many symbolic spheres, his actual reform programmes were largely original, and elements of his military reform anticipated measures which were later adopted in the West. Catherine the Great introduced notions into the education and legal systems which were ahead of their time, while Alexander II's judicial reform gave Russia, for a while, one of the most advanced legal systems on the planet (at least on paper). Numerous Russian scientists, writers, and composers were world leaders in their fields from the late eighteenth through to the twentieth centuries. On a darker note, the police systems developed by Ivan IV, Nicholas I and Alexander III in many ways foreshadowed what was to become globally commonplace only in the 20th Century. Certainly Russian thinkers and political figures have, for the most part, advocated Russia's place as a world leader, not as an imitator. The semi-official doctrine of Moscow as the Third Rome assigned Russia the task of saving Christendom from moral and spiritual decay, setting up the Empire as the global guardian of spiritual values. Geoffrey Hosking has argued that similar messianic impulses were at work in the twentieth century, albeit in a spirit that was fundamentally alien to the Russian character, expressed in the doctrine of international communism. And even with the loss of the Superpower status enjoyed by the Soviet Union, the Putin administration has asserted in both ideological terms and in practise Russia's destiny to be the leading light in her part of the world. Thus modernisation in Russia has been based not just on recognition of Russia's backwardness, but on an equally strong conviction of Russian superiority and destiny.

The ultimate Russian visionary modernisers were the Bolsheviks. Marxism was a stepbrother to the ideas of the European Enlightenment at the time of industrialisation, and Russian Marxists shared the vision of a 'modern industrialised world' and enlightened society with their western 'modernist' counterparts. While competition with the West became a driving force, the Bolsheviks' utopian vision also led them to look beyond existing models – socialism was, after all, supposed to be superior to anything that existed under capitalism. The chief paradox facing the Bolsheviks was that they sought to implement this visionary programme in conditions of economic and cultural backwardness. Although the Soviets rarely used the term 'Modernisation', Lenin insisted that the central task of the Bolsheviks was 'to catch up and surpass the capitalist countries economically'. Stalin was even more explicit in his celebrated phrase 'We are fifty or a hundred years behind the advanced countries. We must make good this distance in ten years. Either we do it, or we shall go under.' While Lenin and Bukharin were certainly interested in the application of western models to Russian conditions, Stalin's industrialisation drive, while deploying imitation of western models and imported technology, used an original framework for the solution to backwardness – the planned economy. In the later Soviet period Khrushchev (implicitly) and Gorbachev (explicitly) were concerned to overcome the evident technology gap between the USSR and the West, particularly the United States. In certain spheres modernity now meant original innovation, which was pursued in particular in culture, education, and the extension of personal and political rights. The conditions of socialism also allowed for the pursuit of original economic policies in an effort to modernise not just up to but beyond existing western levels. Modernisation by any means was a constant imperative in Soviet policy, but it could be achieved by a variety of means. Borrowing ideas and technology from the West and the development of original ideas and technology were aims which were frequently linked. As Sari Autio-Sarasmo puts it in this volume 'the aim of transferring technology was to absorb and diffuse western technology in order to create local innovations. The task of imitation was to transform the imitator into a pioneer…'

The innovatory aspect of Khrushchev's period in office was characterised by his adoption of a series of widely derided 'hare-brained schemes'. After Khrushchev, however, the visionary and innovative Russian tradition seemed to die out. In the transition from communism, modernisation remained an imperative, but the emphasis was again on imitating western models, some would say slavish and misguided imitation. As a number of chapters in this book testify, post-Soviet Modernisation based on western models has met with mixed fortunes, with negative outcomes resulting from either inappropriate or incomplete imitations. In other cases, as Richard Sakwa points out, we find the paradoxical situation where the model of modernity being pursued is itself anachronistic.

Rapid transformation from a predominantly rural to an industrial society caused a social and cultural upheaval almost without precedent in the modern world. The transformation of peasants into workers, an increasing role for women in the workforce, and the physical displacement of large parts of the population all presented challenges for which the state was not altogether prepared and which resulted in substantial changes to culture, living practises, identity, and beliefs. The economic and social difficulties following this forced, poorly prepared and top-down process at a time of increasing international tensions undermined the credibility and legitimacy of the Soviet government and led it finally to resort to the use of force instead of reform politics in governance. Stalin's Purges can be seen as an example of a modern 20th century ruler's unprecedented access to resources and technology which enabled him to wage external and internal wars, to control and if needed suppress his subjects. Although special treatment is not devoted to Stalin's Purges in this volume, it is necessary to emphasise that the consequences of this tragedy were longstanding and drastic to society, as we can see from various chapters.

Educational and welfare modernisation also affected the social structure of the USSR, posing new challenges and creating unstable imbalances. Indeed, one of the central paradoxes of the Soviet system was that social and cultural modernisation ultimately outstripped economic modernisation, for which the centrally planned economy proved effective at one stage but obstructive later on. This imbalance between an educated and aware population on the one hand, and a stagnant economy and political system on the other, was one of the chief factors in the downfall of Soviet communism.

The Russian/Soviet approach to modernisation was very much top-down:

modernisation was a government aim and policy. Certainly in the economy, Russia has historically been characterised by a lack of initiative and a wariness of new technologies and methods from the shop-floor or the farm. A partial exception is the Internet, where development has been driven to some extent by young people, businesses and newspapers, presenting an alternative model for modernisation from below. While it is clear that the Russian security services have been keen to extend control over the Internet, they have, for reasons discussed by Cooper, failed to do so effectively. While the Internet may, therefore, provide a possible space for 'modernisation from below', at other times popular conservatism, which can be traced back to Russian peasant attitudes, has led to resistance to new technologies, which may have hampered the modernisation project. On the other hand, popular expectations have played an important role in pushing forward modernisation in areas such as welfare.

The linear pursuit of modernisation by Russian governments has been held back at various times by more than just popular conservatism. The fact that it took until 1861 for Russia to abolish a system of serfdom whose equivalents had long since disappeared throughout most of Europe is just one indication of the obstacles that prevailed for much of Russian history. Determination on the part of Russia's rulers to preserve a system of autocracy which rested on a social system established in the sixteenth century, the entrenched interests of the landowners and military elite whose positions depended on that system, and an almost constant state of warfare and territorial expansion all conspired to reinforce top-level resistance to modernisation, even when it was most needed. It took a unique tsar – Peter the Great – to first of all break this mould, and the shock of defeat in the Crimean War to provoke the most significant round of modernising reform in the nineteenth century. But Russia failed to go beyond the Great Reforms of the 1860s and 70s at a time when Germany was raising the stakes even higher in developing streamlined forms of economic, political and military organisation, and when demographic and societal change inside Russia was outstripping the political framework which controlled it. The consequence was a series of political and social revolutions which in the end overturned the old system and its conservative tendencies. A return to the old ways in the Brezhnev 'years of stagnation' led to similar consequences.

The pattern of reform and reaction which has so often been observed in Russian history can be illuminated by reference to the competing pressures of modernisation. Russia's size and geo-strategic position, its rigid social hierarchies, and the insulation of its peasant communities combined to both expose it to technologically superior and better organised foes, and to give rise to internal discomfort at the apparent lower level of civilisation enjoyed by Russia in comparison to some of her competitors. At the same time, these factors reinforced the autocratic tendencies of the state and the resistance to change of its bureaucratic apparatus. Russia's ability to rely on huge reserves of manpower further reduced the urgent pressures for change which were being felt elsewhere. At no time were the contradictory pressures more evident than during the reign of Catherine the Great who, after Peter, seemed the monarch most likely to embrace a radical and europeanising agenda. Simultaneously inspired by the Enlightenment and fearful of the ripples of the French Revolution, urged on by advisers pushing for change while having to placate the entrenched nobility, expanding the frontiers of the Empire towards their largest extent while dealing ruthlessly with a series of peasant revolts at home, Catherine embarked on a number of fundamental reform programmes which aimed at least to bring Russia in line with advanced European countries, but few of which ever amounted to much. Russia aspired to be among the most modern European nations, but did not know how to get there except by the old methods. What Catherine's reign illustrates is how, under the specifically Russian conditions of a state exercising control over a large country while interacting only minimally with its society, contradictions arise from the uneven development of the different facets of social, public and economic life. This same contradiction has been in evidence in different ways since 1900, and constitutes one of the major themes of this book.

***

This volume is concerned directly with economic, technological, social and political modernisation understood as either catching up with existing models or original innovation. Six broad themes have clearly emerged in the preparation of the volume and the discussion of early drafts:

- 'Catching up' with or imitating the West
- Utopian visionary projects
- Technological innovation
- Social consequences of modernity
- Structural obstacles to modernisation
- Popular attitudes to innovation

In the past forty years, an often heated debate has been conducted, principally among social scientists, as to the meaning of modernisation and its usefulness as an analytic tool, some of which is summarised in Peter Gatrell's chapter. From the historical perspective, however, these complexities are of marginal significance in the Russian context given the prevalent theme of modernisation as an end to be pursued in itself or, in the eyes of some, to be resisted. In the traditional sense of catching up and surpassing competing models the concept here is treated as a straightforward one.

Understanding the historical context of modernisation in Russia is of great relevance to the study of contemporary Russia. The disintegration of the Soviet Union in 1991 and its new Western orientation caused a wave of enthusiasm in the West. It appeared that the centuries-old dispute of the Russian intelligentsia on the appropriate developmental model for Russia was solved. In the course of Russia's transition she had abandoned the Slavophile model of separate development. History was over, and what was left was the Western developmental model and Russia's *zapadniki* (westernisers). The West began to believe that one day it might remake Russia in its own image.

This optimistic evaluation generated a set of transition discourses in social sciences. As a consequence, in the late 1990s there has been a common sense of disappointment in the West. Change has not happened as soon as was expected and the results have not been as hoped. Instead of a Western type of civilised society, it appeared that Russia had given birth to her own type of capitalism with unforeseen results. Instead of speaking of transition it might be more accurate to speak of a certain kind of modernisation in Russia. It has had its ups and downs and its direction has not been so self-evident at some times as at others. The conditions of Russia's development are rooted in its history, which has laid the particular foundations of modernisation.

The process of modernisation in the late tsarist period set the tone for what was to follow, and this is the subject of Peter Gatrell's chapter. From this study the links between economic and social modernisation are immediately apparent – however much the state was involved as the instigator of industrialisation, the process itself gave rise to new social actors, new forms of discourse, and hence new sources of opposition. Markku Kangaspuro then examines how the Bolsheviks rose to the challenge of modernisation, highlighting the contradiction between ideology and social reality. This contradiction ultimately was expressed in an educational and social system which was well in advance of its economic base, a situation which, David Lane argues, was ultimately the main reason for its downfall.

The economy plays a large role in the exploration of modernisation in this volume, and R. W. Davies and Mark Tauger introduce in broad overview the Soviet experience in industry and agriculture respectively. Both find that, in spite of obvious weaknesses and obstacles, the rapid development of the Soviet economy under Stalin, and even to some extent the stable progress of later years, owed much to the successful pursuit of a modernisation strategy based in part on Marxist ideas and in part on western models. This last aspect is developed by Sari Autio-Sarasmo, who finds that the level of technological inter-action between East and West was much higher than might be expected in spite of the Cold War, and that the successful 'borrowing' of technology from the West also served to spur on domestic research and development efforts. Even stronger West-East influences were at work in the post-Communist transition but here, as Philip Hanson demonstrates, it was the development of institutions and models that counted more than technology. After a slow start, he argues, the development of these institutions and a modern business culture laid the foundations for further economic progress.

While Lane highlights the way that social modernisation outstripped economic and political development, Melanie Ilič shows that the impact of modernisation on Soviet women was somewhat more mixed: in spite of idealistic plans, economic modernisation did not bring the position of women up to western levels across a range of indicators. This lag between different sectors is also touched on by Richard Sakwa, who suggests that political modernisation, as expressed in styles of leadership, has failed to keep pace with the developing social, economic, and global environment. This is a familiar situation in Russian history, and the studies in the second part of the book highlight some of the problems arising from this basic contradiction, as well as the different contradiction, already introduced by Kangaspuro, of a regime whose thinking is ahead of the social and material situation in which it finds itself. For the early Soviet regime, nowhere was this more obvious than in the visual arts, as is illustrated by Tomi Huttunen's study of 1920s montage culture. The inability (or unwillingness) of the regime to sufficiently prioritise in investment the social modernisation which might have begun to overcome this particular contradiction is shown by Chris Williams' study of health care reform. Like Ilič, he finds that it was the precedence of more pressing priorities rather than lack of understanding of the problems involved that hampered progress. While this was also a factor in the reform of education, Jeremy Smith examines a case where Khrushchev appeared determined to lay the basis for a modern, technology-based, economy in a modern education system, only to fall foul of structural inertia and bureaucratic resistance. Katri Pynnöniemi and Linda Trautman examine transport policy, an area meeting with mixed success in both the Soviet and post-Soviet periods, as grand designs and sufficient prioritisation went some way to overcoming structural and financial constraints.

Stefanie Harter and Julian Cooper look more closely at developments in the 21st century. Harter examines the area where state and society most frequently interact – the reform of public administration. She identifies two kinds of approach at work – one based on new attitudes linked to ideas of a market and a shifting political culture, themselves the product of the process of modernisation as already shown in earlier chapters; and the other the top-down centralised approach which has characterised reform in the past, the problems associated with which are apparent from the studies of the Soviet period. At the time of writing, the readiness of Putin's administration to modernise the system of administration is demonstrated by the legislation passed and reorganisations carried out to date, but what is not yet clear is whether a corresponding shift in attitudes has taken place which will give these changes real substance, on the part of both the providers and consumers of administration – the civil service and the citizens of the Russian Federation. Cooper explores how the latest technological development may be opening up a space for large sections of society to be able to operate outside of the structures of the state and its administration, through the Internet. While young people in Russia are avid users of the Internet, it is apparent that even this area suffers from some of the problems common to other areas of modernisation – the development of the Internet is still, in European terms, at a relatively low level in terms of infrastructure and use.

The comparison of the challenges of modernisation in the tsarist, Soviet, and post-Soviet periods yields some interesting conclusions for contemporary Russia. Chapters by Davies, Tauger, Williams and Smith underline some of the problems with modernisation associated with autocratic regimes and a state-centric system which some would say is characteristic of all three periods. The top-down approach to reform (at periods when the need for reform is recognised) suffers from structural problems, a resistant bureaucracy, and conservatism among both elites and the population, and is hampered by a lack of prioritising in resource allocation to those areas in which modernisation is an essential prerequisite for long-term economic modernisation (welfare, education, family policy). The chapters by Sakwa, Pynnöniemi and Trautman show how serious lags in structural modernisation can further hamper progress, while Harter demonstrates that democratisation in itself does not automatically overcome these structural obstacles. On the other hand, Gatrell highlights an important cycle in the modernisation process – any process of economic modernisation itself creates forces operating outside of the immediate orbit of the state, which in turn present new possibilities and impulses for modernisation. While Gatrell is referring to the emergence of professional associations in the late tsarist period, Lane identifies the analogous evolution and growth of a middle class in the late Soviet period, and Hanson sees the basis for profound modernisation lying in the emerging Russian business culture, while Cooper identifies another possible source of change from below among users of the Internet. This cycle ought to lead to a spiralling modernisation, as the new social forces and ideas resulting from earlier change push forward their own agendas. But history shows that this cycle is itself prone to interruption, and modernisation, as well as developing the forces in favour of progress, also serves to stimulate the conservatism of entrenched interests. Modernisation in late Imperial Russia was cut short by War and Revolution; in the Soviet Union, Lane argues, it was this very process that brought about the demise of the political and economic systems and the need to build them anew. Although the Russian Federation is relatively young, it would seem we are at a similarly critical juncture in the first decade of the twenty-first century. Much depends on whether the political leadership and society can work hand in hand in achieving aims which appear to be common to both – in short, modernisation. The imperfect democracy which has been established in Russia ought to facilitate this cooperation if it is allowed to develop. If it is not, then the lessons of Georgia and Ukraine demonstrate what may happen when regime and society are set in opposition. While Russia is a long way from such a situation, the lessons of history should not be ignored if Russia is really to regain its place as a leading power in the world while avoiding the painful experiences of her past.

I
Perspectives

PETER GATRELL

Modernisation Strategies and Outcomes in Pre-Revolutionary Russia

Introduction

Many attempts have been made to offer a working definition of the vexed term 'modernisation'. Notwithstanding the barrage of criticism that the term has attracted over the last half century, it continues to resonate, perhaps because its very vagueness summarises the rapidity of social and economic change under the impact of industrialisation.[1] For Cyril Black, who helped bring the term into scholarly usage, modernisation meant a broad 'process of change from an agrarian to an industrial way of life that has resulted from the dramatic increase in man's knowledge of and control of his environment in recent centuries'. In Black's lexicon, modernisation entailed social changes, including the spread of education, the rise of the nuclear family and the emergence of a welfare state. He also drew attention to the role of government intervention, and thus to the social and political forces that supported modernisation as well as those opposed to it. Although he did not confine himself to Russia, much of Black's argument was designed to illuminate developments in Russia and the Soviet Union. In Black's view, Russia's economic transformation created intolerable strains that led to the collapse of the entire social order in 1917. (The triumph of Soviet communism and the 'problem' of the Third World invested this debate with enormous political significance in post-1945 American academic circles.) After the revolution, according to Black, modernisation continued along an inexorable path, albeit with distinctive Soviet features.[2]

1   For a careful early critique that retains much of its force see Dean C. Tipps, 'Modernisation theory and the comparative study of societies: a critical perspective', *Comparative Studies in Society and History*, vol.15, 1973, 199–226. To be sure, the modernisation debate encouraged a great deal of high quality original research. Just as serious historical scholarship in Soviet Russia continued notwithstanding overt ideological constraints, so too research in the USA survived the crude framework imposed by a highly politicised modernisation theory.
2   Cyril Black, 'The modernisation of Russian society', in C. E. Black, ed., *The Transformation of Russian Society: Aspects of Social Change since 1861*, Harvard University Press, 1960, 661–80.

Much of the historiography on modernisation in pre-revolutionary Russia tends to focus on deficiencies and obstacles, with the main yardsticks of comparison (as in Black's work) being Western Europe and the USA. This approach invited a discussion of the actions needed to remedy Russia's relative backwardness. In the hands of outstanding economic historians such as Alexander Gerschenkron, modernisation gave rise to a powerful set of reflections about the conditions of economic backwardness and the 'substitutes' for factors of production that were in short supply. Elements in Gerschenkron's story have been challenged: thus he neglected regional differences in peasant welfare, understated autonomous industrial growth before 1900 and discounted the impact of state-financed rearmament in asserting that the state's role diminished after 1905. Although Gerschenkron parted company with other theorists, such as von Laue and Rostow, over the path to modernity, nevertheless he shared a common vision of the final destination. His overall interpretative framework has proved remarkably stimulating and durable.[3] More recently Paul Gregory, following in the footsteps of Simon Kuznets, has sought to place Russian economic growth on a more secure quantitative footing. Gregory has shed a great deal of light on such key matters as government policy and foreign investment, and to dispute some of Gerschenkron's findings about the pattern of Russian industrialisation. One of his main contributions has been to propose a more upbeat assessment of tsarist economic growth than many previous commentators, something that is consistent with the doctrine of progressive economic modernisation.[4]

In a different vein, and in reaction against modernisation theorists, the sociologist Teodor Shanin prefers to treat Russia as a 'developing society', in which opposing visions of development were being played out against the background of concerns about state security and of international rivalry. Shanin's approach has a number of merits. First, he questions the helpfulness of measuring development against a 'western' yardstick, particularly when it ignores the vitality of peasant society and its interaction with other socio-economic formations. Thus, Shanin regards the increased rate of labour migration before 1914 not as a hallmark of proletarianisation but as indicative of a peasant strategy to generate remittances in support of the family farm. Second, he directs attention to social and political conflicts as constitutive features of development, not as a pathological 'failure of integration', which is how they appear in much of the modernisation literature. Shanin demonstrates how, out of the grand political and social crisis in

---

3   Alexander Gerschenkron, *Economic Backwardness in Historical Perspective*, Harvard University Press, 1961. See also Theodore von Laue, *Sergei Witte and the Industrialisation of Russia*, Columbia University Press, 1963; W. W. Rostow, *The Stages of Economic Growth: A Non-Communist Manifesto*, Cambridge University Press, 1960. For an informed discussion of the continued relevance of Gerschenkron's work, as well as some critical reflections, see the essays in Richard Sylla and Giovanni Toniolo eds., *Patterns of European Industrialisation*, Routledge, 1991. His grandson has written an illuminating biography: Nicholas Dawidoff, *The Fly Swatter: How My Grandfather Made His Way in the World*, Pantheon Books, 2002.

4   Paul R. Gregory, *Russian National Income 1885–1913*, Cambridge University Press, 1982.

1905–1907, development debates in Russia crystallised around competing visions of progress, associated respectively with Lenin, the revolutionary, and Stolypin, the conservative statesman. This was an important contribution to the historiography.[5]

Recent work has taken the debate in yet another direction. In a collection of essays on Russian modernity, Yanni Kotsonis and David Hoffmann argue in favour of examining the paradoxes inherent in modernity rather than establishing a trajectory of modernisation or measuring Russia against a western European benchmark of development where it is then found wanting. According to Kotsonis and Hoffmann, Russia did not constitute an aberration. Instead, it exemplified processes and practices that were similar to those evident elsewhere, including the intelligentsia's misgivings about 'backward' elements in society and the articulation of claims to be able to 'civilise' them. This stimulating body of work helps problematise the notion of modernisation itself rather than taking it as given.[6]

In this chapter I outline key features of the modernisation debate in pre-revolutionary Russia. In a short space it is only possible to deal in cursory fashion with important points, but I do emphasise the deeply embedded process of debating 'modernisation'. I then indicate some of the ways in which it might be said that Russia had become 'more modern' prior to the October revolution. Here I focus largely on the extent to which industrialisation transformed Russia before 1917. This seems to me preferable to seeking to package a multiplicity of changes within the unwieldy framework of modernisation. Most of my comments on development indicators are confined to the period between 1900 and 1917, whereas my discussion of contemporary debates offers a longer temporal perspective.

Contemporary debates about modernisation

A sustained and rich discussion of modernisation took place among Russia's pre-revolutionary intelligentsia against the backdrop of rapid change in western Europe. Contemporary thinkers did not use the term modernisation, which only gained currency after the Second World War. Nonetheless, like Molière's Monsieur Jourdain, who spoke prose without knowing it, they voiced concerns about the implications of Russia's status vis-à-vis its western neighbours and how economic backwardness might be overcome. Even before the abolition of serfdom in 1861 the renowned nationalist historian Mikhail Pogodin had proclaimed Russia's potential as 'a country that contains all kinds of soils, all climates ... a world in itself, self-contained. Independent ... What is it that we cannot obtain at home? What, that we could not furnish to others? ... Where is the country more fit for the establishment of factories

---

5   Teodor Shanin, *Russia as a 'Developing Society'*, Macmillan, 1985. Also at http://ruralworlds.msses.ru/eng/shanin-develop/glava2.html.

6   See the contributions to Yanni Kotsonis and David Hoffmann, eds., *Russian Modernity: Politics, Knowledge, Practices*, Macmillan, 2000.

... Everything is within reach ... and could be ordered tomorrow if necessary by supreme command'. However, he hoped to forestall the manifestations of poverty, inequality and social turmoil that characterised western Europe. Pogodin thus anticipated an important strand of thinking about the costs as well as benefits of modernisation.[7]

As Pogodin indicated, Russia's rulers had the capacity to bring about an acceleration in the rate of economic growth. In 1840 the progressive thinker Vissarion Belinskii had famously praised the creative genius of Peter the Great in dragging his reluctant subjects towards modernity. In pinpointing the need for reform 'from above' Belinskii introduced a recurrent theme:

> With us everything had to be started from the top downwards, for at the time when we felt the need to shift from the spot on which we had been dormant for centuries we found ourselves on a height that others had already taken by storm.[8]

The modernisation debate became even more agitated during the later nineteenth century. Partly this was a consequence of the abolition of serfdom in 1861, a measure that formed part of an extraordinary package of 'great reforms' following the debacle of the Crimean War. The reform era encouraged debates about the desirability or otherwise of longstanding legal and institutional arrangements and devices, such as estate (*soslovie*) banks and courts and the peasant land community. Here the Russian bureaucracy constituted a key sphere in which these arguments were played out. Inevitably there were tensions within the bureaucracy between those who advocated major institutional reform and those who adopted a more conservative stance. Although the reforms put paid to non-economic forms of coercion and introduced a crucial element of 'self-government' to Russia's towns and provinces – with long term consequences for education and public health – they left intact the peasant commune as the cornerstone of local administration.[9]

Another important element was international power politics. Russia's reputation as a great power was founded upon its territorial extent, resource endowment and the size of its armed forces. But its prestige suffered badly as a consequence of the Crimean War. Subsequent engagements – against Turkey in 1877 and against Japan in 1904 – reinforced a sense that Russia's international ambitions outstripped its economic capabilities. The emergence of powerful European nation-states such as Britain, France and Germany demonstrated that claims to political primacy were established not just on the basis of manpower but also hinged upon modern industries such as iron and steel. As Witte put it in 1899, 'Russia is an independent and strong power.

---

7   Cited in Hans Kohn, *Pan-Slavism: Its History and Ideology*, Vintage Books, 2nd edn., 1960, 142.

8   V. G. Belinsky, *Selected Philosophical Works*, Foreign Languages Publishing House, 1956, 142.

9   Ben Eklof et al., eds., *Russia's Great Reforms 1855-1881*, Indiana University Press, 1994.

She has the right and the strength not to want to be the eternal handmaiden of states which are more developed economically'.[10]

Other elements also entered into the equation. They included the emergence of a stratum of professionals who embodied a self-conscious ethos of obligation towards society. Educational change helped create a professional stratum – lawyers, doctors, teachers, engineers, chemists, economists, agronomists, accountants and others – whose members were committed to social and economic modernisation. These professionals regarded the land commune, estate banks, merchant assemblies and noble courts as exclusive and outmoded institutions that should be replaced by inclusive bodies. They looked around and did not like what they saw. They demanded reform, and reform implied modernisation.[11] Another reason has to do with a conscious belief in the politics of social welfare. Reform-minded bureaucrats understood that living standards in Russia were low and needed to be improved. The grounds for seeking an improvement were in turn linked to ideas about social instability, although a more immediate preoccupation had to do with maintaining the capability of the population to supply military manpower and to pay direct and indirect taxes. Russia was not alone in reflecting these concerns.

'Traditional' Russia under attack

As already stated, the adherents of modernisation held up 'traditional' features of Russian society to a west European mirror and found them in need of reform. Many examples could be chosen. For the sake of simplicity, we shall identify two sets of concern. One related to the maintenance of long-established juridical categories, which were seen as a stumbling block to modernity. Another related to the persistence of the land commune and its consequences for peasants' willingness or capacity to 'adapt' to change.

Each subject of the tsar was ascribed to a specific juridical category or estate (*soslovie*, plural *sosloviia*). Ascription to *sosloviia* reminded subjects of their rights and obligations, of where they belonged in the social order. From the government's point of view, they were 'valuable self-regulating administrative units in preparing legislation, regulating social mobility, maintaining public order and apportioning rights and privileges in relationship to state service'. The system of estates had become embedded in law and social practice.[12] Even while rapid economic and social change began

---

10 T. H. Von Laue, 'A secret memorandum of Sergei Witte', *Journal of Modern History*, 26, 1954. There are strong similarities with the stance adopted by Dmitrii Mendeleev, for whom protection was a means to establish capital goods industries.

11 Harley D. Balzer, ed., *Russia's Missing Middle Class: The Professions in Russian History*, M. E. Sharpe, 1995; Gregory Guroff, 'The legacy of pre-revolutionary economic education: St. Petersburg Polytechnic Institute', *Russian Review*, 31 no.3, 1972, 272–81.

12 Alfred J. Rieber, 'Sedimentary society', in E. Clowes et al., eds., *Between Tsar and People*, Princeton University Press, 1990, 343–66 (here p. 356).

to create a more complex and fluid social reality, many individuals and corporate groups retained their official affiliation, deploying it tactically in order to gain or enhance political leverage. To be sure, the persistence of *sosloviia* failed to capture the emergence of new social groups such as the working class, industrialists, the creative intelligentsia and educated professions, all of which began to establish their own organisations albeit in difficult conditions. Dramatic social and economic changes associated with industrialization made it more difficult to maintain the integrity of existing status boundaries. Nevertheless, traditional practice still had the capacity to mobilise particular groups, such as the landed gentry, clergy and some members of the merchantry, who felt threatened by economic modernisation and reasserted their traditional rights and privileges.[13]

The status and integrity of the land commune (*mir*) aroused even more passion. Until the revolution of 1917 and beyond, most peasant-held allotment land continued to be cultivated by peasant households who belonged to a village community, one of the functions of which was to reallocate arable plots periodically in accordance with changes in family size and composition. (It is sometimes forgotten that an increasing number of peasants also acquired privately-owned land over which the commune had no formal jurisdiction.) Peasants' attachment to the commune gave grounds for concern, partly because it was believed that traditional methods of cultivation condemned successive generations to poverty by restricting the scope for the improved productivity of land and labour. Particular attention focused on the custom of redistributing allotment land, which was believed to act as a disincentive to innovate, and on the fragmentation of peasant allotments. The commune also attracted attention because it was associated with the persistence of patterns of behaviour and belief in rural society that were held to be at odds with 'rational' conduct. The commune placed a premium on peasant custom; for example, members of the community were taught to value village healers rather than 'modern' medical practitioners. On the other hand, some proponents drew attention to the commune's role as a collective device to protect peasants against hardship.[14]

Against this background of anxieties about backwardness Russia did not lack apostles of economic modernisation. Within government circles the most famous statement originated with Minister of Finances Sergei Witte, in a secret memorandum to Tsar Nicholas II in 1899. It deserves to be taken seriously not only because of the coherence of its argument but also because Witte was uniquely well placed to realise his vision. He wrote as follows:

13 Gregory L. Freeze, 'The *soslovie* (estate) paradigm and Russian social history', *American Historical Review*, 91, 1986, 11–36.
14 Boris Mironov, 'The Russian peasant commune after the reforms of the 1860s', *Slavic Review*, 44, 1985, 438–67; Shanin, *Russia as a 'Developing Society'*.

Russia was and to a considerable extent still is a hospitable colony for all industrially developed states, generously providing them with the cheap products of her soil and buying dearly the products of their labour. But there is a radical difference between Russia and a colony...

We need capital, knowledge and the spirit of enterprise. Only these three factors can speed up the creation of a fully independent national industry...

The influx of foreign capital is ... the sole means by which our industry can speedily furnish our country with abundant and cheap goods. Each new wave of capital ... knocks down the immoderately high level of profits to which our monopolistic entrepreneurs are accustomed and forces them to seek compensation in technical improvements, which in turn will lead to price reductions ...

We have at our disposal cheap labour, tremendous natural riches, and only the high price of capital now stands in the way of getting cheap goods. So why not let foreign capital help us to obtain still more cheaply that productive force of which alone we are destitute?[15]

This is a classic statement of the case for deliberate and sustained programme of economic modernisation, in which capital investment in industry would play a prominent part, in order to realise Russia's assets of labour and natural resources. In order to create the right conditions for direct foreign investment Witte acknowledged that Russia's population could not escape short-term sacrifices of output and personal consumption as a result of tariff protection and a restrictive monetary policy.

Witte's opponents were vocal and vicious. Typically they tended to come from the landed gentry. They denounced the gold standard that Witte introduced in 1897. They resented the tariff on manufactured and luxury goods. They feared that industrialisation would increase the cost of agricultural labour. Above all they disliked the prospect of nouveaux riches who threatened to become socially – and also politically – more influential. The terms of the contemporary debate around Witte's economic policy have been remarkably resilient. Historians continue to debate the extent to which Russian consumers did or did not suffer from Witte's fiscal and monetary policies. There is notoriously little agreement about the extent to which the Russian peasantry did or did not 'pay' for industrialisation.[16]

It is important not to exaggerate the impact of officialdom. In the first place, divisions within the tsarist bureaucracy make it impossible to speak of any coherent government policy. A resolute minister might get his way, but the lack of collective cabinet responsibility meant that he found it difficult to count on colleagues' support.[17] In any case, the tsarist government did not control the direction of the entire economy. Officials bemoaned the

15 Von Laue, 'A secret memorandum'.
16 Peter Gatrell, *The Tsarist Economy 1850–1917*, Batsford, 1986; P. R. Gregory, *Before Command: An Economic History of Russia from Emancipation to the First Five-Year Plan*, Princeton University Press, chapters 3&4.
17 Tim McDaniel, *Autocracy, Capitalism and Revolution in Russia*, University of California Press, 1988.

intrusion of 'spontaneous' factors such as poor harvests (using this, of course, as further justification for 'modernising' Russia). They knew that the course of economic activity was influenced by private enterprise, for example by powerful agencies of intervention in production and distribution. Officials disliked the forces of 'organised capitalism', but accepted that it could contribute to economic modernisation. However, some of them – along with some professional economists and engineers – argued in favour of state 'planning', in particular of railway building, not least as a means of overcoming the periodicity of business cycles. Nothing much came of these proposals before the war.[18] Meanwhile, other contemporaries regarded Russia as a potential laboratory for experimental forms of industrial organisation and social practice. The radical theorist Aleksandr Bogdanov, famous subsequently for his role in Proletcult, anticipated a world in which science and technology would emancipate humanity from the constraints of 'nature'.[19]

Of course, some contemporary observers valued precisely Russia's backwardness and 'tradition'. Foreign visitors, such as the German poet Rainer Maria Rilke, came to Russia precisely because it was pastoral, romantic and 'authentic'.[20]

We cannot leave this discussion of modernisation without reflecting on its meaning for non-Russian populations in the empire. Here the process of economic transformation aroused misgivings on the part of Russian intellectuals. For example, in the Siberian branch of the Imperial Geographical Society, debated the prospects of nomadic peoples within the expanding economy. One important strand of thinking bemoaned the impact of capitalist economic penetration on 'traditional' economic culture, threatening the survival of the *inorodtsy*. From their point of view, the government had an obligation to 'preserve' traditional ways of life.[21]

Modernisation, movement and space

Economic progress entailed a new conception of space. We can think of this in a fairly conventional sense, as the exploration and conquest of new territory. The rapid expansion of the Russian railway system was one of the hallmarks of economic change in the generation before the outbreak of war. As a large sprawling empire, much of whose population and natural resources

18 L. E. Shepelev, *Tsarizm i burzhuaziia v 1904–1914gg.*, Nauka, 1987; Ruth A. Roosa, *Russian Industrialists in an Era of Revolution: The Association of Industry and Trade 1906–1917*, M. E. Sharpe, 1997, 68–84.

19 Aleksandr Bogdanov, *Red Star* (first published 1908), ed. Loren Graham & Richard Stites, Indiana University Press, 1984.

20 Yevgeny Pasternak et al., eds., *Letters: Summer 1926, Boris Pasternak, Marina Tsvetaeva, Rainer Maria Rilke*, New York Review of Books, 2001.

21 Vera Tolz, 'Orientalism, Nationalism and Ethnic Diversity in Late Imperial Russia', *The Historical Journal*, vol. 48, no.1, 2005, 127–150; Yuri Slezkine, *Arctic Mirrors: Russia and the Small Peoples of the North*, Cornell University Press, 1996; Susan Laycock?

were scattered in far-flung corners, Russia had developed a transport system appropriate to its size. The total length of railway track increased by around one third between 1900 and 1913, and stood at 71,000 km on the eve of war. Total traffic (freight and passengers) grew at a much faster pace.[22]

The transport revolution encouraged migration. Belinskii recognised the symbolic significance of space to the modernisation project. Speaking of Peter the Great's foundation of a new capital city he wrote:

> For such a haven he required an entirely new and traditionless soil, where his Russians would find themselves in an utterly new environment in which they could not help but recast their customs and habits of their own accord.[23]

This is a very remarkable statement. The transformation of space allowed for a mental revolution as well. Lenin had much the same idea when he spoke at the century's end of urbanisation as a stimulus to the acquisition of 'literacy … understanding and … civilised habits and requirements'. But migration to other rural areas, such as Siberia, could also have a transformative effect on economic activity and cultural life.[24]

Other thinkers were more cautious. An influential body of opinion held firm ideas about the need for the maintenance of traditional attachments to place. These ideas were closely linked to considerations of social and political security. The state sustained an elaborate system that sought to tie peasants to the land commune, even after their formal emancipation in 1861. In exchange for their freedom, peasants were obliged to accept a plot of land and a share of their debts incurred to the state. The state guaranteed a flow of revenue by forcing fresh administrative controls on a revitalized land commune. The commune monitored peasant movement, lest individual peasants shirk responsibility to pay their share of the combined tax levy by moving out of the village for good. Conscription also loomed large in government thinking; knowledge of the whereabouts of potential conscripts reinforced the need for administrative controls over population movement. Much power was conferred on the head of the peasant household, without whose approval passports could not be issued to individual members. Meanwhile, the community was able to monitor the movement of peasants who were in arrears with their tax liabilities. These administrative functions, whilst devolved upon the peasant community by an 'absentee government', nevertheless formed part of a much more widespread supervision and regulation of peasant economy and society.[25] Land played a crucial role in the overall strategy of the state;

22   Railways accounted for three fifths of all freight transport in 1913, with river and sea transport making up all but a tiny fraction of the remainder. John Westwood, 'The railways', in Davies, ed., *From Tsarism to NEP*, 172–5.
23   Belinsky, *Selected Philosophical Works*, 147.
24   V. I. Lenin, *The Development of Capitalism in Russia*, Progress Publishers, 1977, 582.
25   A. J. Rieber, 'The sedimentary society', in Edith W. Clowes, et al., eds. *Between Tsar and People: Educated Society and the Quest for Public Identity in Late Imperial*

by guaranteeing each peasant household access to a plot of land, the state intended to instil in peasants a sense of place and a primary allegiance to a specific locality.[26]

In 1894 the government introduced a new passport law, which liberalized existing regulations to a degree. The new law allowed peasants to have a passport for up to five years, provided the village community agreed. In addition, peasants were allowed to travel up to 50 km. without a passport, unless they worked in factories (for 270 years the limit had been fixed at 30 km). Passports could be recalled if the remaining family members were at risk of becoming destitute, or if the head of the household revoked it by application to the peasant court. There was thus no automatic entitlement to a passport. Only in October 1906 did the state declare that peasants were free to come and go, since the redemption payments had been cancelled and fiscal motives no longer made it necessary for the village community to control the movement of its members. Yet, even after the 1905 revolution, many powers over population settlement remained intact.[27]

Migration did not necessarily entail permanent resettlement. Instead, millions of villagers made regular short visits to towns and cities. In 1900, up to one-fifth of the resident population of Moscow and St.Petersburg 'had either just arrived or would leave before the end of the year...one might envisage these urban centres as great revolving doors through which passed a significant proportion of the population of large regions of Russia'.[28] Others who found jobs in trade, transport, construction, mining and manufacturing stayed on for several months or even years, but eventually went back to their villages to take up farming, to find a partner or simply to retire. Estimates for the 1890s indicate that close on seven million passports and other travel documents were granted each year to peasants throughout European Russia. By 1906–10 this figure had risen to an annual average of 9.4 million.[29]

Seasonal labourers posed a particular challenge to tsarist officialdom. Sometimes living on the river bank, without any prospect of more comfortable or permanent accommodation, these workers appeared most likely to turn into a 'mob' that threatened public order. Indeed, the perceived threat did not require any direct action on the part of the migrant population; it was enough that they lived on the margins of urban society. Many of them 'appear to have dispensed with proper documentation', but were left in peace, provided they did not disturb public order and, in some cases, so long as

Russia, Princeton University Press, 1991, 343–66 (quotation at p. 345).

26 Roger Bartlett, ed., *Land Commune and Peasant Community in Russia*, Macmillan, 1990; and Timothy Mixter and Esther Kingston-Mann, eds., *Peasant economy, culture, and politics of European Russia, 1800–1921*, Princeton University Press, 1991.

27 N. I. Ananich, 'Iz istorii zakonodatel'stva o krest"ianakh', in Voprosy istorii Rossii XIX-nachala XX v., LGU, 1983, 34–45.

28 Daniel Brower 'Urban revolution in the late Russian empire', in Michael F. Hamm, ed., *The City in Late Imperial Russia*, Indiana University Press, 1986, 319–53, here 327.

29 L. E. Mints, *Trudovye resursy SSSR*, Nauka, 1975, 118–19.

they bribed the police. As Daniel Brower shows, however, what looked like disorder and depravity to the outside observer could conceal a 'cultural creation' that maintained rules and customs, easing the passage of the migrant from one world to another and back again.[30]

Women began to shape their own lives in the city, unconstrained by traditional rules that defined what conduct was appropriate. Migrant workers came into contact with men and women from different villages, and exchanged stories of displacement and dreams of economic betterment. Some in-migrants were insulated from the urban milieu by communal living arrangements, such as by the *zemliachestva* that grouped together men from the same district or village. Migration also changed the ways in which villagers thought about peasant life. The impact of such changes needs to be set in the context of traditional norms and customs of the village. Mention has already been made of the role of the peasant commune in regulating the temporary departure of its members. Even when the formal responsibilities of the commune disappeared, the mir retained the potential to regulate peasant behaviour. It was precisely the threat to this cultural "shell" in wartime that alarmed educated society. What would become of women and children who lacked the discipline imposed by the household and village community? Increased spatial movement between country and town had other, more troubling consequences for pre-war Russian observers. Liberal physicians and social commentators believed that the urban environment tended to deprave the virtuous peasant in-migrant, who forfeited the ties of family and community for the dubious privilege of 'freedom'.[31]

Economic progress

We have considered the causes and character of debates around issues of economic modernisation in pre-revolutionary Russia. What, in quantitative terms, did Russia's pre-revolutionary modernisation entail? By 1914 Russia had experienced more than a quarter century of rapid economic growth. True, this spurt was interrupted by a sharp downturn between 1900 and 1908, a period coinciding with the revolutionary upheavals of 1905–1906. Yet the long-term trajectory was unmistakable. Total output grew by around 3.4 per cent per annum between 1885 and 1913, and 5 per cent per annum between 1909 and 1913.[32]

Most dramatic of all was the transformation of large-scale industry, marked by the emergence of a more modern fuel economy, a modern iron

---

30 Daniel Brower, *The Russian City between Tradition and Modernity, 1850–1990*, University of California Press, 1990, 90–1

31 Barbara Engel, *Between the Fields and the City: Women, Work, and Family in Russia, 1861–1914*, Cambridge University Press, 1994; Laura Engelstein, *The Keys to Happiness: Sex and the Search for Modernity in Fin-de-Siecle Russia*, Cornell University Press, 1992, 272–4.

32 Gregory, *Russian National Income*, 56–7.

and steel sector, as well as new industries such as chemicals and electrical engineering. The process of industrial and technological modernisation was sustained in part by direct and indirect foreign investment, primarily from British, French, Belgian, and German sources. Some of this investment also fuelled the expansion of the infrastructure, including urban utilities and port facilities. To be sure, new industrial enterprises coexisted alongside a plethora of technically quite primitive small-scale enterprises. Even supposedly modern factories relied upon a mixture of new technology and traditional methods and techniques. Labour productivity left much to be desired; factory managers had access to abundant cheap labour and maintained a large labour force. Most factories produced a bewildering array of product types, reflecting the small production runs and frequent changes demanded by capricious customers, including the Russian government. Some attempts were made to impose control over the market, notably by the formation of sales syndicates, but these were confined to a limited number of industrial syndicates such as coal, iron and steel, whose existence prompted intense public debate before the war.[33]

We have already noted the growth of the railway network. Here, too, development was uneven. Although the length of the track grew rapidly before 1914, the age of the capital stock gave grounds for concern. One in four Russian locomotives was more than 20 years old, and only one-third was less than 10 years old. Most wagons took the form of enclosed vans that were awkward to load and unload. Locomotives had no automatic brakes. Switching and signalling were carried out by hand. The fuelling and cleaning of locomotives were cumbersome procedures. Many lines were single-track.[34]

Russia's large and notoriously unstable agricultural sector developed at a less dizzying speed. Agriculture was dominated by the production of cereals for household consumption as well as for the domestic and export markets. The chief crops produced on peasant farms were rye, buckwheat, potatoes and flax, although in the years immediately preceding the war Russian peasant farmers had begun to cultivate more wheat and barley, particularly in the southern provinces. Rye and potatoes were typically grown for the household's own consumption, either as food or in a distilled form. Unpredictable meteorological conditions continued to induce the volatility of grain production, threatening disaster as occurred during the famine of 1891–2. This remained a painful moment in Russia's pre-revolutionary history.[35]

Here too there were signs of change. The half century since the emancipation of the serfs witnessed a steady transfer of land from the gentry to the peasantry, confirming their position as the chief element in rural society and

33 Peter Gatrell and R. W. Davies, in Davies, ed., *From Tsarism to NEP*, Macmillan, 1990; J. P. McKay, *Pioneers for Profit: Foreign Entrepreneurs and Russian Industrialisation 1885–1913*, University of Chicago Press, 1970.

34 N. Vasil'ev, *Transport Rossii v voine 1914–1918gg.*, 1939, 15.

35 M. E. Falkus, 'Russia's national income in 1913: a re-evaluation', *Economica*, 35, 1968, 52–73 (here p. 59); R. W. Davies & S. G. Wheatcroft, *The Years of Hunger: Soviet Agriculture, 1931–1933*, Macmillan, 2004.

agricultural production. By 1917 peasants owned around 47 per cent of all land, including forests, meadows and arable land. The state and other public bodies such as the zemstvos owned a further 37 per cent. Private proprietors other than peasants owned 16 per cent of the total. (A quite different picture emerges if we confine ourselves to arable land, nine-tenths of it farmed by peasants and the remainder by the owners of private estates.) The rural economy was diversifying, as peasants exploited the opportunities available by supplying new urban centres with fresh meat, fruit, vegetables and dairy products. Peasants who had taken a significant risk migrating to western Siberia found prosperity in livestock farming and in the co-operative marketing of dairy products.[36]

All this activity was underpinned by the growth of other services such as retail trade and a more sophisticated financial services sub-sector. The financial services sector played an important part in the modernisation of Russia before the war. Commercial banks performed a vital role. Called upon to accept government securities that the public were averse to holding, they fulfilled this function provided they could preserve their normal distribution of assets, that is a mixture of long-dated and short-dated assets, such as Treasury bills. At the same time, Russia's commercial banks continued to juggle the various demands made by the state with the demands of their clients in the private sector.[37]

Russia also acquired a somewhat more sophisticated urban infrastructure. Writing in 1919, a well-informed economist summarised the results of a generation of urban progress. By 1913 Russia officially recorded a total of 1,231 towns and cities. Of these, 1,068 had street lighting, although most relied on kerosene lamps rather than electricity. Only a small number boasted motorised forms of transport. Around one quarter had a telephone service, and half of them 585 contained libraries. Two hundred had a permanent theatre, and 136 contained a museum of some description. Most had either a bank or a mutual credit association, as well as savings societies and insurance institutions. Much of this urban infrastructure had been financed by means of loans floated in St. Petersburg as well as in France, Germany, and Britain.38

Imperial Russia had enjoyed more than a generation of monetary stability, the result of the momentous decision in 1897 to take the country on to the Gold Standard.[39] Even the Russo-Japanese War did not disturb fundamental confidence in the currency. This helped to underpin the surge in foreign investment before 1914 to which reference has already been made. To be sure, the years immediately prior to the outbreak of war witnessed a sustained upsurge in prices, but most observers took this as a sign of underlying

36 A. N. Antsiferov, *Russian Agriculture during the War*, Yale University Press, 1930, 22–3, 354.

37 Olga Crisp, *Studies in the Russian Economy before 1914*, Macmillan, 1976, chapter 5.

38 E. M. Kayden, 'An economic study of Russia before and during the war', War Trade Board, Washington D.C., manuscript, 1919, 11.

39 Crisp, *Studies*, chapter 4.

economic well-being rather than of crisis. Successive tsarist ministers of finance, notably Witte, were also credited with innovations in the tax system, substituting indirect taxes as well as a selective and more discriminating portfolio of direct taxes for pre-modern devices such as the poll tax, from which members of the privileged estates had been exempt.[40]

Budget revenue doubled between 1900 and 1913. Witte's successor Vladimir Kokovtsev took much of the credit for balancing the budget after the turbulence of 1904–06. The increase reflected sustained population growth, increased incomes and (after 1909) rising outlays on defence and rearmament. Much of the growth in revenue was generated by long established items, such as excise duties and receipts from the spirits monopoly and from state-owned property. Attempts at fiscal innovation had relatively little impact. In 1913 expenditure was distributed as follows: 27.0 per cent to state enterprises, 26.6 per cent to defence, 16.9 per cent to productive purposes (education, agriculture etc.), 16.4 per cent to general administration, and 13.1 per cent to debt payments.[41] Spending on state enterprises had patchy results; critics complained that the Urals ironworks absorbed huge amounts of cash to little effect. Defence spending led to the creation of an imperial navy whose rationale was unclear; it did much less to modernise the army, whose troops continued to supply their own needs in respect of footwear and foodstuffs. Spending on education and health was quite modest when set against a rapidly growing and youthful demographic profile.

The growing integration of Russia in the international economy was signalled by the inflow of foreign capital and the expansion of foreign trade. Germany was an important trade partner and source of foreign investment. German investors favoured utilities, steel, electrical engineering, chemicals and the financial sector. Russia's trade with Germany amounted to around 47 per cent of its total foreign trade by value. More generally, Russia was vulnerable to a decline in overseas trade, even though some observers believed that it would be far less exposed than more advanced economies.[42]

Following widespread peasant unrest in 1905 and 1906 Prime Minister Stolypin targeted the traditional land commune, in the expectation of replacing it with a class of 'sturdy and strong' farmers with full title to the land. The edict of 9 November 1906 enabled peasant heads of household to petition for communal allotment land to be transferred into their personal ownership. Where such a household had more land than would be allotted at the next redistribution, its head was entitled to purchase the excess on very favourable terms, with the help of a Peasant Land Bank. The commune was obliged to comply with any such request within one month. Furthermore, the head of a

40 A. M. Michelson, *Russian Public Finance during the War*, Yale University Press, 1928, 246. See also Yanni Kotsonis, '"Face-to-Face": the state, the citizen, and the individual in Russian taxation, 1863–1917', *Slavic Review*, forthcoming 2004.
41 A. Raffalovich, *Russia: Her Industries and Trade*, P. S. King, 1918, 331; Iu. N. Shebaldin, 'Gosudarstvennyi biudzhet tsarskoi Rossii v nachale XXv.', *Istoricheskie zapiski* 65, 163–90.
42 Michael Dohan, 'Foreign trade', in Davies ed., *From Tsarism to NEP*.

household was entitled to demand the consolidation of scattered strips. Provision was also made for the entire commune to embark on land consolidation, provided two thirds of its members agreed. Where a commune appeared to resist, the government was entitled to intervene on behalf of the 'separator'.

The reformers faced an uphill struggle to convert – the word is used advisedly, since so many embarked on their task with missionary zeal – Russian peasants from subsistence farming to a capitalist ethic. Much of their analysis overlooked the fact that the land commune governed all aspects of peasant life, from the allocation of scattered strips of land (itself a kind of insurance against risk) and the use of communal pasture to the maintenance of rural infrastructure and the apportionment of taxation. Thus a householder's request to privatise his plot had far-reaching consequences, which the government sought to minimise by insisting that the household retained other rights of membership of the commune, such as access to meadows and pasture. Many peasants resented the claims of their neighbours who sought to take advantage of the new legislation, and there were stories of intimidation. Besides, subordinate members of the separating household begrudged the new powers vested in the hands of the paterfamilias. Nor did the reformers dissuade the majority from the view that their prospects would be greatly enhanced by a revolutionary redistribution of the land privately held by noble landowners.

The reform impulse amongst a new generation of Russian agronomists swept all before it, and these enthusiasts themselves did not shrink from intimidation. Much publicity attended the creation of independent farms (*khutora*), idealised and actively promoted by government Land Organisation Committees. More than one million households took advantage of consolidation between 1907 and 1915; this implies that around 8 per cent of peasant communal land underwent full re-organisation. Particular enthusiasm for enclosure was demonstrated in the southern provinces of European Russia where cereal production became increasingly commercialised. Nevertheless, neither these purchases nor the land reforms introduced after the 1905 revolution fundamentally altered the grip of the village community and the tightly-knit households that underpinned it.[43]

The reforms themselves are of considerable interest, because they reveal a concerted willingness to impose modern patterns of land organisation as well as new kinds of behaviour upon a sceptical peasantry. These grand ambitions (like the land commune itself) persisted into the Soviet period. Yet, in economic terms, the direct results of the Stolypin land reforms were quite modest. As Esther Kingston-Mann and others have pointed out, the reformers refused to accept that the land commune was quite compatible with improved cultivation on peasant farms. In truth, of much greater consequence for the advance of Russian agriculture before the war was the growth of new markets and the improvement in the terms of trade for food producers, which

43 Dorothy Atkinson, *The End of the Russian Land Commune, 1905–1930*, Stanford University Press, 1983.

enabled farmers to diversify into new products and to invest in agricultural equipment. Institutions such as co-operatives helped to sustain this activity. For many observers the co-operatives constituted instances of 'modernity, distinct from the 'archaic' land commune.[44]

Modernisation and war

Very few contemporaries believed that the war contributed to the emergence of a more modern agricultural sector – rather, the reverse, since commercially oriented larger landowners tended to suffer from conscription and a shortage of hired labour. In other sectors the story was more positive. Some observers maintained that the war enabled Russia to seize important opportunities to modernise industry, by introducing new branches of industry, by introducing new methods of manufacture and by investing in modern capital equipment. Others disputed the magnitude or significance of these gains.

It is, however, certain that the war helped encourage a belief (not confined to Russia) in the need for 'planning'. Influential professional elites now found a bigger platform from which to voice the need for further modernisation. One such group crystallised around the Academy of Sciences' 'Committee for the Development of the Productive Forces of Russia'. Other groups, including engineers, statisticians, agronomists, doctors and social workers also gained confidence. They asserted the desirability of institutional change, whether in advocating the creation of new government departments (such as a Ministry of Health), in pressing the case for electrification of the whole country or in improving the resources at the disposal of local authorities.[45]

To give one example, technical specialists took the view that economic reconstruction needed to begin with massive investment, particularly in extractive industries, in transport, and in electrification. In the view of Vladimir Grinevetskii, this meant in the first instance a policy of attracting fresh foreign investment on a massive scale – 15 or 20 billion rubles over the next decade. Foreign investors did come forward, but many of them entertained fantastic ambitions. They fed Russian fantasies as well. The CWIC negotiated with American banks for a massive loan to rebuild the railway network between Moscow and the Donbass, hoping that American investors would provide up to 18 billion rubles to support capital projects. Such projects echoed the industrialisation drive that Witte had masterminded during the 1890s, emphasising foreign investment as the motor for a sustained increase in industrial production. Grinevetskii attached particular importance to improvements in labour productivity, which he envisaged from a combination of foreign investment and 'scientific organisation'.[46]

44 Yanni Kotsonis, *Making Peasants Backward: Agricultural Co-operatives and the Agrarian Question in Russia, 1861–1914*, St. Martin's Press, 1999.
45 Peter Gatrell. *Russia's First World War: An Economic and Social History*, London: Pearson Longman, 2005.
46 V. I. Grinevetskii, *Poslevoennye perspektivy russkoi promyshlennosti*, Khar'kov,

Conclusions

Russia made rapid strides in the generation before 1914. The industrialisation drive during the later 1880s and 1890s, and an economic revival after 1907, enabled Russia in aggregate terms to begin to close the gap on Western Europe. Development indicators portrayed a dynamic society. Literacy rates rose rapidly and a massive growth in publishing took place.[47] Infant mortality rates were beginning to fall, and new urban centres were springing up. Even if the political system remained sclerotic, particularly at a national level, Russia had major achievements to its credit, leading the way in experimenting with new artistic, literary and musical forms, and making scientific and technological advances.

Russia's industrial modernisation sparked controversy at the time, and its welfare consequences have been debated ever since. Conservatives bemoaned the intrusion of a modern financial sector and foreign investment in Russia, and charged Witte with the neglect of agriculture. However important their strictures were in political terms, they did not interrupt the course of economic progress. Even if Witte's successors, Kokovtsev and Bark, lacked his clear-sightedness they did not reverse his achievements.

Whatever conclusions one reaches about the pace of change in pre-revolutionary Russia, modernisation established itself as an important way of thinking about change. It became a myth that (in the words of a leading anthropologist) 'gives form to an understanding of the world, providing a set of categories and premises that continue to shape people's experiences and interpretations of their lives'.[48] In this sense one important hallmark was the efflorescence of numerous professional associations that asserted their claim for greater autonomy from the bureaucratic state and campaigned for social and economic 'improvement'. Their role increased during the war, thereby promoting yet further the modernisation agenda. The war did not bring the debate about modernisation to an end; it leant new vitality to claims on the part of educated society to do a better job than tsarist officialdom.

1919, pp. 105, 184, 202–4; Jonathan Coopersmith, *The Electrification of Russia 1880–1926*, Cornell University Press, 1992, 139–50.

47 N. S. Timasheff, 'Overcoming illiteracy: public education in Russia 1880–1940', *Russian Review*, 2 no.1, 1941, 80–88; Jeffrey Brooks, *When Russia Learned to Read: Literacy and Popular Culture 1861–1917*, Princeton University Press, 1985. By 1912–13 Russia published 1,132 newspapers and 1,656 magazines.

48 James Ferguson, *Expectations of Modernity: Myths and Meanings of Urban Life on the Zambian Copperbelt*, University of California Press, 1999, 14. Ferguson's work on the 'crisis of meaning' in modern Zambia carries important connotations for students of post-Soviet Russia.

MARKKU KANGASPURO

The Bolshevik Modernisation Project

Introduction

The most significant question facing Russia during the Soviet era and post-communism has been what is the way forward to the future? During the 1990s, Russia underwent a "transition" bringing it more in line with Western society. The common expectation was that the combination of "free-market capitalism", which in fact does not correctly characterise even a modern capitalist system, and an "American model" are what the future of Russia must look like. However, one can ask whether it is self-evident that both economic growth and political and social change are driving Russia along the same route as the "West"? And on the other hand, it is possible to argue that Russia and the Soviet Union have been all the time in "transition", on a path to modernisation. Russians have interpreted modernisation in the framework of their intellectual and societal realities. It is possible to conclude that Soviet modernisation, completed by the 1980s, created the diverse and differentiated society and educated population that gradually grew out from the pre-modern political system. This contradiction between the well-educated and socially diverse population and the old-fashioned political system and ineffective economy established a gap between the rulers and the ruled, the people and the power.

This contradiction was the central agent of political change at the turn of the 1980s and 1990s. The new modern divergent society, which had emerged from the bowels of Soviet modernisation, conflicted with the common Bolshevik aim of creating a homogenous and harmonic socialist society. This fundamental contradiction triggered the general political (and economic) crisis of the 1980s. General Secretary Mikhail Gorbachev's *perestroika* and his new attitude to the intelligentsia and especially to the former Zapadnik dissident, Andrei Sakharov, were some of the first indications that the Soviet leadership was reconsidering the relationship between government and citizens. The educated Soviet intelligentsia provided a broad range of people who kept society running and yet were ousted from political power. In December 1986, Gorbachev personally phoned Sakharov and invited him to return to Moscow from the closed city of Gorky, to where he was exiled in 1980. It has often been noted that some of the premises of Gorbachev's "new thinking" were very close to the ideas of Sakharov, particularly in the sphere of foreign policy (inadmissibility of nuclear war), democracy and the convergence of socialism and capitalism.[1] Gorbachev's attempt to establish new relations with the Soviet intelligentsia was an expression of understanding the consequences of modernisation. He aimed to overcome the alienation of the new middle class and to integrate it somehow with the governance of Soviet society. The task was not easy, not least because of the enclave of the educated elite and the post-Stalinist and, in many cases, poorly educated political leadership. Gorbachev made the first attempts to take into account the divergent needs of the diverse society and its classes.

In this chapter the idea of modernisation is discussed in general and some suggestions concerning modernisation in Soviet society in particular are made. In this respect, the antipodes of continuity and a break in history, universalism and particularism, 'Other' and 'Us', the 'Western' and the 'Eastern' development models, progressive and conservative, and finally Soviet and Western interpretations of Enlightenment deserve attention.

Westernisers and Bolsheviks

Without discussing details, I suggest that modernity understood as a time dimension has played a central role both in the ideological premises of the Bolsheviks and in the *Realpolitik* that they employed. Here, the time dimension means interplay of past, present and future. The future is an essential and significant premise of the politics and the development models, which are based somewhat on the idea of modernity. Consequently, the future has been explicitly present in the Bolsheviks' everyday politics, but concurrently this future-driven decision-making has also been embedded in the past.

Historians – both totalitarian and revisionist schools – have had a long-standing argument on how much the burden of the Russian past has determined the development of Soviet society, and what has been the role of the future-directed Bolshevik policy. We might also interpret this future-driven policy as an ideological dimension of the Bolshevik policy, which is inherited from and based on the particular interpretations of the tradition of the Enlightenment and the tradition of "Russian Messianism".

Ideological universalism has always been an essential feature of the Enlightenment and the modern. Concurrently, it can be seen that ideological universalism might contain the seeds of totalitarianism, which is another issue regarding the Bolshevik ideology and politics. Generally speaking, however, the universal development models based on modernity have been common in all societies, in particular after the French Revolution. In Russia, discourse on the modern has been an inextricable part of the definition of Russia's

---

1   Alexander Chubarov, *Russia's Bitter Path to modernity. A History of the Soviet and post-Soviet Eras* New York-London: Continuum, 2001, 161–163.

identity, a part of the debate on what constitutes Russia's relationship with Europe since the rule of Peter the Great. Vera Tolz has pointed out that the first features of the divide between the cosmopolitans of the Enlightenment and the (proto-)nationalists occurred during Peter's time and that this divide has dominated the intellectual debate ever since. One of the peculiarities of Russian historical and cultural traditions was that often the division between liberal cosmopolitans and conservative nationalists was rigid. Representatives of both groups continued to operate within a framework of set stereotypes, determined by the comparison between Russia and 'the West', without being able to transcend them. In this comparison with 'the West', the liberal cosmopolitans, those who paid attention to Russia's own traditions, felt the urge to argue for Russia's superiority. Tolz has suggested that in the 1840s some Westernisers had already come to the conclusion that in fact Western political institutions failed properly to represent the Western ideals of liberty, equality and fraternity. Contemporary Europe was understood to be a false Europe, and the true Europe was to be found elsewhere.[2] This comes very close to the Bolshevik's idea of Russia's own, self-sufficient modernisation project.

Iver B. Neumann has suggested that for Russia, and in the framework of her identity-building process, Europe has represented the main 'Other'.[3] Antipodes in the Russian discourse have been Westernisers and Slavophiles. The Westernisers' policy was based on the idea that in borrowing from the West the modern development model clashed with the Slavophiles' policy in departing from national romantic traditionalism, which emphasised Russia's historical and organic uniqueness, distinguishing her from the rest of Europe. As Tolz puts it, the Slavophile model resembled those colonial and post-colonial societies in Asia and Africa in which nationalism derives its power by distinguishing itself sharply from the West as an anti-model.[4]

The Russian 'Zapadnik' Marxist, G.V. Plekhanov, disagreed with the populist-Slavophile attempt to avoid the western development model and capitalism. Plekhanov argued that the great mission of the working class was to complete the Westernisation of Russia begun by Peter the Great. Plekhanov warned that the seizure of power by revolutionary socialists would only hinder this, and would indeed be a disaster that in the end could only be viewed as a major step backwards. "Without the Westernisation of Russian society, Russian socialism organised by the authorities from above in a backward country would be forced "to resort to the ideals of patriarchal and authoritarian communism; the only change would be that the Peruvian 'sons of the Sun' and their officials would be replaced by a socialist caste."[5]

2   Vera Tolz, *Russia: Inventing the Nation*. London-New York: Arnold, 2001, 65, 94.
3   e.g. Iver B. Neumann, *Russia and the Idea of Europe. A study in identity and international Relations*. London and New York: Routledge, 1996, e.g. 1.
4   Tolz, *Russia*, 70.
5   Andrzej Walicki, *A History of Russian Thought from the Enlightenment to Marxism*. Stanford, California: Stanford University Press, 1979, 414–415.

However, the definitions of modern and modernisation – not to speak of modernism in terms of culture - are both somewhat blurred and many. It is possible to approach modernity from different points of view. Usually modernity is distinguished in four main spheres, namely cultural, social, economical and political. Historically, modernisation is connected with the French and Industrial Revolutions.[6]

Time dimension of the modern and Bolshevik Policy

As a result of this modern development model, progress has been very western. Ronald Schleifer argues that the assumption and conception of continuous development through time are at the heart of the bourgeois and Enlightenment order of the 18th and 19th centuries, and within this absolute temporal continuity the necessity of the full consciousness of an atemporal subject of knowledge and experience can be discerned. Regarding the economy – the core area of Marxism – Schleifer points out that both for Adam Smith and Marx, production constantly and infinitely expands, just as for Newton time is an unending expansion of an ongoing sequence. John Maynard Keynes represents this firm faith in the linear development of a technological and productive modern in his last essay of 1930 in which he argues that technological and scientific development open up the way to overcome the material poverty of the human race for the first time in history.[7] This is a usual promise of the Enlightenment, a promise of the future for a temporal world, a "modern" dream of the brighter world by means of future-driven politics.

As a result of this, modern holds both time dimension and "Otherising" characters. "Modern" can be understood as a counterpart of "ancient", and in this respect, modern contains strong features distinguishing it from the past or even represents a revolutionary break in historical continuity. Moreover, sometimes modern has represented a messianic aspiration to a new present, to the future. Indeed, from this viewpoint the Bolshevik revolution and the Bolshevik mission for a world revolution were very modern ideas, which also laid the foundations of the new Soviet revolutionary identity. The Soviet "modern" distinguished new rulers from the oppressive past, from former reactionary regimes as well as from the conservative ("ancient") West, who did not follow the route of progress from capitalism to socialism. This time dimension has been very crucial both in the ideas of modern and in Bolshevik politics.

6 Ronald Schleifer has written a profound and inspiriting study of modernism. Ronald Schleifer, *Modernism and Time. The Logic of Abundance in Literature, Science, and Culture, 1880–1930.* Cambridge: Cambridge University Press, 2000.
7 Schleifer, *Modernism and Time* 30, 43, 47.

Figure 1. Time Dimension of Politics

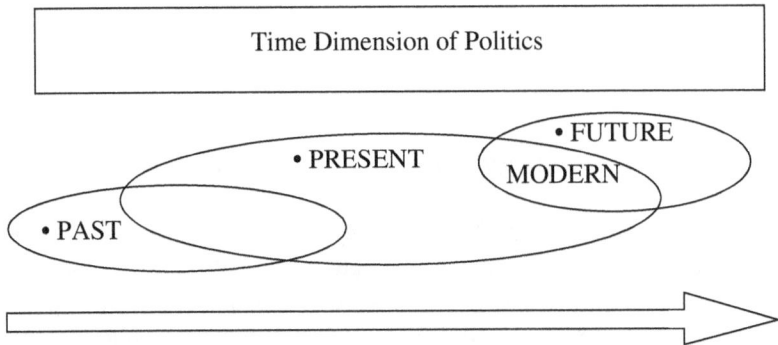

Thus, we can say that the "modern" Soviet identity in a way established a part of the legacy of the Bolsheviks' revolutionary policy in Russia and abroad. This future-driven mission also revitalised ideas of Russian Messianism.[8] Stalin's 'socialism in one country' policy represented the isolationism and the 'eastern' or, in other words, the voluntarist development model, revolution from above. Indeed, this was exactly the development model against which Plekhanov warned the Russian socialists in the late 19th century. Another question is whether the Bolsheviks had any other means of holding on to power than running the economy in a somewhat autarchic way. In terms of the time dimension, it is worth noting that the autarchic model was the traditional manner in which all vast Empires of the 19th century engaged in economic activity.[9]

Enlightenment and futurity

Following the heritage of Enlightenment, "Otherising" features are also a part of the modern. Modernisation can be understood as a "universal" project to civilise "the uncivilised", "the Orient", "the East", "the West", peasants, the proletariat, children and women. And vice versa, otherising is one precondition for the identity-building policy of a state and its people. Accordingly, therefore, since modern contains features of holistic and even totalitarian interpretations of the future, it is used for different political purposes. In this

8   Peter Duncan has written a splendid book on Russian messianism. Peter J. S. Duncan. *Russian Messianism. Third Rome, revolution, Communism and after.* London and New York: Routledge, 2000.

9   Dominic Lieven. *Empire. The Russian Empire and Its Rivals.* New Haven and London: Yale University Press, 2000, 18–19.

context, those who are in a position to define what is modern and progressive also have a strong argument for justification of the policies carried out.

The consequence of modern's 'universality' is internationalism, which prohibits particular, national characteristics and even heritage. Various values are defined characteristics of modern regardless of people's specific (local) cultures or traditions. Therefore modern's universality and the above-mentioned break in history are connected to demands of futurity. The missionary philosophical and religious tradition of Russian society matched perfectly with the idea of the proletariat's political vanguard , the Bolshevik party. The idea of the party as a present embodiment of the future occurs explicitly both in Lenin's 'What is to be done' (1902) and Karl Marx's and Friedrich Engels' 'Communist Manifesto' from 1848. For them, the civilised and educated world's proletariat represents the future in the present. It was also thus for the Russian Marxist westernisers such as Plekhanov and Lenin in contrast to the narodniks.

Iver B. Neumann distinguishes two major traditions in Russia: the Russian narodnik-voluntarist and the Slavophile-Bolshevist, which contradicted the liberal and Marxist European style behind the evolutionary way of modernisation. The big issue for the Russian revolutionaries was whether they should try to stage a coup before capitalism became firmly entrenched, or whether they should resign themselves to the necessity of copying European capitalism in order to reach socialism. There were crucial differences between the Marxist-Slavophile debate and the Menshevik-Bolshevik debate, however, and it hinged on one, single move. Revolutionary populists such as Peter Tkachev had wanted to stage a coup in order to keep industrialisation out of Russia. The Bolsheviks, on the other hand, wanted to seize power so that they could surge ahead with industrialisation. The revolutionary populists and the Bolsheviks were both voluntarists in that they thought it was possible to will a transfer of power. The populists, however, had wanted to use that power to steer Russia clear of decadent Europe and its perverted course of development. The Bolsheviks wanted to save Russia from the clutches of bourgeois Europe and to plunge it directly into the final stage of historical development – socialism.[10]

The third tradition was that of the western Marxists, such as Plekhanov, to whom Lenin and his like owed much, and who represented perhaps the purest modernisation tradition in Russia. Plekhanov wrote that Russia must choose the 'long and difficult capitalist way'. He believed that a sufficiently long time must elapse between the political revolution (i.e. the overthrow of tsarism) and the future socialist revolution to enable the capitalist forces of production to become fully established and the Russian proletariat to receive political training in a law-abiding parliamentary state. However, Plekhanov also believed that the capitalist stage might be shorter in Russia than in the West, but that it should not be too brief – it was possible to shorten a 'natural' process, but every attempt to shorten it too much or to replace it with an

10 Neumann, *Russia and the Idea of Europe,* 73–74.

'artificial' process entailed the risk of an undesirable 'chemical change'.[11] This westernisation and modernisation of the society was one of the major dilemmas in which the Bolsheviks performed a balancing act. One attempt to resolve it was the NEP policy launched by Lenin in 1922. The NEP was understood as a concept of the transition period from capitalism to socialism, from an Asiatic empire to a western civilised society, as Lenin had opined. In this process, the western experts or specialists recruited in the 1920s and the 30s had a central role. The imitation of the West and the implementation of its best practices and production methods were the route by which Russia would be modernised.

The New World and Russian Messianism

Bolshevik ideology was constructed as a Janus-faced ideology originating from two main components: from ideas of modernisation and the linear development of the World (a sort of Bolshevist zapadnism) and from the traditional Russian Slavophil ideas on community 'sobornost' and 'narodnost'. The Messianic idea of Russia's role as a saviour of the World is directed from Russian philosophy. The revolutionary romanticism of the Soviet Union's foreign policy, which can be seen as an inheritance of Messianism, was particularly prominent in certain periods of Soviet history: especially immediately after the Revolution, in World War II, and in Khrushchev's foreign policy on the Third World and his support for national liberation movements in particular.[12]

According to Nikolai Berdyaev, Russian Marxism had become a cover for the traditional narodnik "cliquishness" of the intelligentsia. Thus, the intelligentsia was not interested in whether a theory was true, but only in whether it served the proletariat. In particular, the Russian Marxist had an "exceptional belief" in the possibility of achieving socialist objectives in Russia earlier than in the West.

The group that most fully represented socialist Russian messianism in 1917 was the Left Socialist Revolutionaries (SRs). For this party of romantic revolutionaries and narodnik populists, Russia's suffering in the war was akin to the Crucifixion, and the October Revolution represented redemption. Russia was the instrument for the creation of a New World.[13]

Many of the members of the SRs later joined the Bolshevik party and consequently brought their own ideas along with them. These ideas matched very well the Soviet Patriotism that had evolved from the tense international relations and from the internal struggle against 'local nationalism' of the 1930s.

---

11 Walicki, *A History of Russian Thought,* 415.
12 On Khrushchev's revolutionary-imperial paradigm and his commitment to support 'movements of liberations' see Vladislav Zubok and Constantine Pleshakov. *Inside the Kremlin's Gold War. From Stalin to Khrushchev.* Cambridge, Mass., and London: Harvard University Press, 1996, 206–209, 281.
13 Duncan, *Russian Messianism,* 52.

The messianic idea of Russia can be found in the patriotic discourse on World War II and the Stalinist post-war period of the Soviet Union in particular. This discourse emphasised how Russia had rescued, through enormous self-sacrifice, the rest of Europe from the Nazi onslaught as it had already done during the Mongol Yoke in the 14th century. The heavy burdens borne by the Soviet Union and her population during World War II bestowed a plausibility on this rhetoric. As usually happens, war established one of the basic elements of the justification of the Soviet Union from the late 1940s. It was a deliberate decision of Stalin to invoke Russian nationalism and Russia's 'heroic' war history. In 1941, he told Arvell Harriman, the American Ambassador, that the Russian people were not fighting for the Party, but for Mother Russia.[14] The ancient messianic tale of the eternal destiny of Holy Russia matched perfectly with the new discourse of the Great Patriotic War and the interpretations of Russia's role in Europe.

The Mikhail Gorbachev era represents a new opening into Europe and discussion about the modernisation of the Soviet Union within the framework of Europe. The economy of the Soviet Union was in trouble and the new leadership of the country turned its face to the West and the reduction of the armament costs. The Soviet economy and especially technology were second to those of the West and the arms race appeared to be an excessive burden for the Soviet Union. This constituted a significant change in the Soviet discourse on Europe in the context of Slavophile and Zapadnik disputes. Gorbachev's new line, 'new thinking', was the most prominent change in the mentality of the Soviet leadership regarding the West since the short period in the late 1940s when it realised the consequences of the nuclear era. Actually, Georgi Malenkov was in this sense the first Gorbachevian, when he drew the first far-reaching conclusions[15] about the nuclear threat, and which Nikita Khrushchev partially adopted after coming to power. Khrushchev adopted the idea of a 'peaceful co-existence' instead of 'messianic revolutionary romanticism'.[16] In addition to the shift in foreign policy, the American nuclear capability and the threat of war, which were taken very seriously, also had significant consequences for Soviet domestic policy.[17] The leadership was forced to improve the conditions and societal status of the creative intelligentsia to whom the Bolsheviks had paid special attention since the era of Lenin's rule. In 1946, Stalin significantly increased the salaries of scholars and professors. For the next two decades, they were among the wealthiest people in the Soviet Union.[18]

14 Duncan, *Russian Messianism,* 56.
15 In a speech on March 12, 1954 Malenkov said that the 'new world war... given modern weapons, would mean the destruction of world civilisation.' Zubok and Pleshakov, *Inside the Kremlin's Gold War.*, 166.
16 Zubok and Pleshakov, *Inside the Kremlin's Gold War.* 188–189, 297.
17 Vladimir Shlapentokh, *A Norman Totalitarian Society. How the Soviet Union Functioned and how It Collapsed.* New York: M. E. Sharpe, 2001, 21.
18 Shlapentokh, *A Norman Totalitarian Society.* 68.

Space, Nationality and Modern

Russia was a vast continental-scale empire, whose geopolitical heritage the Bolsheviks and the Soviet Union had inherited. By the last quarter of the 19th century, both industrial and agricultural protection were the norm in most great powers. Protectionism and autarchy inevitably put a heavy emphasis on direct control over the maximum amount of territory and raw materials, if only to stop rival powers grabbing colonies and excluding others from their markets. By the end of the 19th century, it was widely assumed that colonies were a key source of present wealth and future power. However, by the second half of the 19th century the continental-scale empires such as Russia met a new and unexpected threat – rising nationalism.

Dominic Lieven has pointed out that this was the great dilemma for all empires in the century following 1850. One, and perhaps the most ambitious, solution was to seek some new supra-ethnic identity, perhaps linked, as had sometimes been the case in the past history of empires, with a universal religion of salvation. Russia and the Soviet Union took this path.[19]

Obviously no ruler of the Russian Empire and the Soviet Union who valued its political stability could scorn the interests, prejudices and values of the Russians and Russia's emerging new middle classes (nomenklatura and intelligentsia) and, increasingly, the masses. The societies of the 20th century were modern mass societies where regimes had to seek the consent of people and especially of ideologically decisive intelligentsia and other branches of the middle class. In this framework, nationalism has played a crucial role in the integration policy of all regimes.

Consequently, the Soviet nationality policy was an important device in organising relations between centre and periphery. The Soviet Union's federative structure, comprising the Soviet Republics, autonomies, and districts, established an institutional framework for the new vertically determined administration. There were two main objectives to involving the representatives of the minority nations into their 'own' Republic's governance: first, to obtain the (minority) population's consent for the new regime and integrate it into the state building process[20]; and second, to transform the old social and political relations and establish a new Soviet order. The Soviet integration policy utilised nationalism of both Russians and of the minority nationalities. The Soviet nationalities and state building policies varied from the *korenizatsiya* policy of the 1920s and 1930s to the utilisation of the nationalism of Russians as the core nation of the Soviet Union in the 1930s and 1940s. However, the major direction was to rely on civic nationalism, a politically defined Soviet supra-identity. From the beginning of the Soviet power, state identity politics were based on the *korenizatsiya* policy, which

19 Dominic Lieven, *Empire. The Russian Empire and Its Rivals*. New Haven and London: New Haven University Press, 2000, 51.

20 In an article published in Pravda at the end of 1921, Stalin emphasised the inevitable task of driving the peasant closer to socialism. Jeremy Smith, *The Bolsheviks and the National Question 1917–1923*. London: Macmillan, 1999, 27.

explicitly contained a task to modernise society and civilise the 'backward' peasant minority nationalities. The model of this new civilisation was the urban Russian working class.[21] As is widely known, the Bolsheviks held that peasants were one of the major restraints of Russia's development.[22]

The Soviet distinction of peoples into four categories established a hierarchy for the state structure, which was based on the ethnically determined administrative areas. The hierarchisation began from Russia, from the highest status of the nations with some other nations[23], and continued to the fourth, underdeveloped ethnicity (*ethnie*) or nationality without the features of statehood. This view represents the modernist time dimension, which originates from the expectation that all nations develop along the same direction in the process of modernisation.

The Soviet industrial policy also took this purpose into consideration. Establishing new plants in distant peripheral regions among the minority peoples, it was possible to create a modern national working class and transfer the more advanced Russian civilisation with its allied Russian industrial work force to the less prosperous nations..This is a typical policy of "Otherising", which inevitably generates the notion of nationalism in the core and minority nations.

Social mobility

The Soviet system had various integration techniques in use. Shlapentokh has argued that in a way it had succeeded in involving a relatively large section of the population in networks and activities within the society. The system included many millions of people in various state organisations. In 1982, there were 17.7 million party members, 41.3 million people in the Komsomol, 2.3 million deputies in the soviets at various levels, 7 million members of trade union committees, 131.2 million "ordinary" trade union members, and 10.4 million volunteers in the 'system of people's control'.[24]

Moreover, millions of people were involved in middle and low-level managerial work. The system employed millions of factory foremen, chiefs of laboratories, managers of educational, financial, and research institutions, and supervisors of collective farms. Up to one-third of the adult population belonged to the stratum of "little bosses", who had minimal privileges or real authority yet maintained a sense of "belonging" to the dominant class.[25] According to data from the Russian Centre for Public Opinion Research (VTsIOM), 43 per cent of the population reported themselves as belonging to the

21 The Tenth Congress of the Russian Communist party in March 1921, e.g. Smith, *The Bolsheviks and the National Question,* 26.
22 It is known that e.g. Maxim Gorky also shared this opinion.
23 Poland, Georgia and Finland were also included.
24 ThsSU SSSR 1982, 47–51. In Shlapentokh. *A normal totalitarian society* 6–8, 167.
25 Shlapentokh, *A normal totalitarian society*, 101.

"middle class". With a growing population, technological progress, and the increasing complexity of Soviet life, it became necessary for the leaders to delegate more and more of their power to the nomenklatura.[26] This specialisation and differentiation of the middle class with its estrangement from the political framework caused one of the major unintended consequences of Soviet modernisation. Alexander Chubarov has pointed out that contrary to the ideological claims that it developed in the direction of a socially homogeneous society, the social structure that emerged by the early 1980s was increasingly diverse and varied and was dominated by distinctive groups of urban populations with their own interests, way of life, and mentality.[27]

Shlapentokh has distinguished three apparatchik generations. He characterises the last[28] one (1950–1960s), which emerged after Stalin's death, as careerists, absorbed only in securing promotions by any legal means. In a way, they might be described as Soviet consumers.

However, the idea of a state-regulated economy was quite fashionable at the time, even outside the socialist movement, in the early 20th century until the late 1970s. After World War I, the prestige of the state as an active economic agent increased in the world, with the help of John Maynard Keynes's theory and Roosevelt's New Deal. Many politicians and scholars considered the state-regulated economy across the globe as the best instrument for rapid modernisation and the prevention of economic crises. In the Russian context, the highly centralised economy was considered not only by Bolsheviks but also by many Western experts as vital for the modernisation of the country.[29]

Regardless of the real flaws in the system and the pessimistic prognoses in the 1920s, the Soviet economy functioned until 1989–1990. Indeed, the economy helped the leaders achieve their primary goals: modernisation and geopolitical tasks. The ability of the system to mobilise its human and material resources, while ignoring the costs, made it possible to implement many gigantic projects, from the creation of several new industries in the late 1920s and 1930s to the development of nuclear weapons and missiles.[30]

Conclusions

The political and social development (differentiation) of Soviet society forced the regimes to also develop and modernise their governance. A monopoly of power and the capability to use and show it are one of the prerequisites of every normal state. This stage was reached after the Stalinist purges, and

26 Yurii Levada, *Sovetskii prostoi chelovek*. Moscow: Intercentr, 1993, 53. In Shlapentokh, *A normal totalitarian society*, 43, 68.
27 Alexander Chubarov, *Russia's bitter path to modernity. A History of the Soviet and Post-Soviet Eras*. New York- London: Continuum, 2001, 13.
28 Shlapentokh, *A normal totalitarian society*, 90.
29 Shlapentokh, *A normal totalitarian society*, 104.
30 Shlapentokh, *A normal totalitarian society*, 117–118.

it created a solid foundation for the integration policy of the Soviet government, relative political agreement and the consent of Soviet citizens to the ruling power. However, in order to be functionally effective the governance must obtain as wide consent of the citizens as possible. In this respect, the intelligentsia and middle class play an important role and their relationship to governance proved to be one of the core problems of the modernised Soviet Union. The closer the Bolsheviks reached the goal of modern society, the further the goals of an egalitarian, homogenous and classless society, without social and interest contradictions, diverged. The interests of the ruling elite and those of the intelligentsia were in many spheres of life far removed from each other.

Besides the traditional nationalistic (Soviet patriotism) justification of the power, the regime had to find new and more developed ruling methods to gain the consent of the population. In this respect, progress and modernisation played a crucial role in Soviet propaganda. The new and progressive were represented by socialism, which was interpreted as a way to overcome backwardness, and above all, to modernise the economy.

In this respect, the enormous task, which Vladimir Ilyich Lenin set for the new Soviet Russia, is illustrative: uncivilised 'Asian Russia' is to be Europeanised 'not shrinking barbarous methods of struggle against barbarism' and the whole country is to be electrified. In other words, the mission of the Bolsheviks was to overcome the uncivilised 'Oriental' characters of society and to modernise the underdeveloped economy. The obsession of all Russian leaders, from Peter the Great to the current leaders, has been to overcome Russia's backwardness, to modernise society and to catch up with the West. As Lenin put it, 'it is our task to teach ourselves the state capitalism of the Germans, to imitate it with our strength not to spare dictatorial methods in order to hasten the copying of Westernism by barbarous Russia even more than did Peter'.[31] In principal all the Soviet leaders have pushed forward quite unanimously the modernisation of the Soviet economy. Even the most prominent 'political' isolationist J. V. Stalin proved to be a consistent supporter of economic modernisation of the Soviet Union. Actually the imitation of western modern economy and production techniques started during Stalin's era and continued steadily throughout the years of Brezhnevian *stagnation*.of the 1970s.[32] The broader variety of the attitudes of the Soviet leaders can be found from their orientation to Europe and common European legacy of Enlightenment and modernity. In this respect it is easy to name two European oriented leaders, namely V. I. Lenin with his policy of European revolution and Mikhail Gorbachev with his idea of the common European home. Both of them made practical conclusions of the Europeanism and it had also explicit consequences within the Soviet Union. Nikita Khrushchev opened Soviet society after Stalin's era of fear and repression, but Khrushchev's view was directed to Russia's own history, 'Leninism' and

31 V. I. Lenin, 'O "levom" rebyachestve i o melkoburzhuaznosti'. In V. I. Lenin, vol. 27, 302.
32 See Sari Autio-Sarasmo's article in this volume.

its authentic legacy. On the other hand Khrushchev's government had very ambitious programmes on developing economy, technology and education as a way to reach communist society.[33] In this respect he did not differ from the other Russian and Soviet modernisers whose aim was first to catch up and finally to pass the West. The only ones who really held fast to the ideas of modernisation due to the convergence of Russia and the West were Lenin and Gorbachev. Lenin believed that the West would follow the Russian way to modern socialist society and Gorbachev engaged in a constant but gradual reassessment of Western societies and the necessity of the convergence of the Soviet Union and West. He and his policy of 'New Thinking' owes a lot to European social democracy and liberalism.

However, Western liberalism and Soviet socialism were sister ideologies. Both had their roots in the European 18th-century Enlightenment and in the 19th-century British political economy. Both believed that history was a tale of human progress and would continue to be so. Both took it for granted that happiness would result from science, the conquest of nature and the creation of great material wealth.[34] When we are considering why the gravity of the Soviet Union was so big among the masses of the European working class and the left movements, it is important to keep in mind that, in spite of Stalin, the Soviet Union has had three essential features, which have determined its development. The first and perhaps foremost feature was a promise of a better material future for all workers in Russia. It was a promise of a new welfare society based on the experience and aspirations of the European working class movement.

The second feature was its promise of political and social equality among all nations and people. This had been one of the main motives of many minority nations' political movements to overthrow tsarist rule. And after the horrors of World War I, this was an especially attractive view and widely understood as a precondition of peace.

The third feature was hope in the future, the future-driven politics of the Bolsheviks. The new state ideology of the Soviet Union (world revolution, patriotism and marxism-leninism) offered a comprehensive world view and established a sort of belief framework for the people. The Soviet Union had a mission, and the people had a task and a better future to come.

Very many features and processes of the social and political history of the Soviet Union have resembled very much the history of its Western counterparts. The roots of the Russian revolutions and their ideas, ideas of modern and socialism as a higher stage of modern society obviously originated from Europe.[35] As a conclusion, we can sum up that the the Bolshevik Revolution is a stepbrother of European Enlightenment and the birth of modern societies The Bolshevik project to build up the Soviet Union was a Russian experiment of the modern state building project after the fall of the Russian Empire. And

33   See Jeremy Smith's article in this volume on Khrushchev's commitment to the cause of modernisation.
34   Lieven, *Empire,* 66.
35   Mark Sandle, *A Short History of Soviet Socialism.* London: UCL Press, 1999, 9.

the Soviet depression of the late 1920s and the early 1930s and its societal and political consequences including Stalinism (dictatorship) were basically not anomalies but rather almost universal processes of Europe. In many ways, the response of Stalinist rulers reflected the essential and universally well-known mechanisms of power policy. What makes this case different from most of the other cases was the obvious extension of violence.

DAVID LANE

Modernisation and the Changing Social Structure of State Socialism [1]

Modernisation is a type of social change involving an increase in social differentiation in a society. The chapter considers the effects and consequences of induced change in urbanisation and industrialisation which have taken place since the Bolsheviks took power. It is contended that these changes have led to social and structural differentiation which in turn changed the political support system and put strain on the political leadership. State socialist societies were command societies but there was a form of social pluralism consequent on the process of modernisation. The social structure was one of the most important determinants of political change (*perestroika*) and consequently the subsequent disintegration of the state socialist system.

Modernisation is a form of social change. In sociology and political science it is associated most strongly with the theorising about developing countries which was fashionable in the 1960s. Unlike Marxism, which viewed social change as being driven by the contradiction between the productive forces and the ownership of means of production, modernisation is an evolutionary theory, best known in the work of Talcott Parsons.[2] Societies develop, it is contended, not through class struggle, but through the action of people striving to adapt to, and to improve, their economic, political and social environment. The process of modernisation in sociology has three major components: *differentiation*, in which social units become more specialised, *adaptation* – the process of improvement of the (economic) environment. As differentiation (e.g. occupational change) and adaptation (economic development) proceed, the greater social and economic complexity requires a third dimension in the modernisation process: ideological and political legitimation. Modernisation through industrialisation involves the development of industry and commerce, modernisation of social structure gives rise

---

1 Some of the empirical data used in this paper was also used in my article, 'The Roots of Political Reform', in C. Merridale and C. Ward, Perestroika in Historical Perspective, London: Edward Arnold, 1991. Reprinted here with permission of the publisher.
2 Talcott Parsons, Societies: Evolutionary and Comparative Perspectives. Englewood Cliffs, NJ: Prentice-Hall, 1966.

to urbanisation, waged occupation, education and finally modernisation of political culture leads to participatory democracy.

Modernisation theory of the 1960s and 1970s focused on explaining the conditions in which democracy had arisen in the twentieth century and the prospects for democracy in the communist and non-democratic societies. It attempted to explain the conditions of, and to identify social and psychological pre-requisites for, modern democracy. (The major writers are S. M. Lipset, Neil Smelser. Pye, Verba. Rustow. Almond and Verba.)

Modernisation theorists contended that stable democracy was associated with certain economic and social requisites. The most important of these were high per capita income, widespread literacy, enrolment in higher education, and urban residence. The methodology of these writers was to consider social and economic variables associated with stable democracies, unstable democracies, and dictatorships[3]. This theorising gave rise to optimistic conclusions: as the economy develops, it leads to higher literacy, a greater degree of urbanisation, an employed labour force which in turn promotes a stable democratic polity. This was a kind of economic dependency theory (though notably property relations were not included as independent factors) of modern democracy, which was considered to be the most appropriate shell for the development of a modern economy.

The modernisation approach has only exceptionally been applied to Soviet-type societies[4]. Political domination expressed in the paradigm of 'totalitarianism', effectively precluded the rise of social institutions, groups, classes and ideologies with any independent influence on the political system. Politics, it was contended, controlled all aspects of societal life: culture, values, social relations and institutions. The social structure was ignored as an explanatory tool in the analysis of stability and change. The peculiar feature of the state socialist societies was that modernisation was imposed by the state: the state, led by a dominant Communist political party, had a mission to 'build communism'. In doing so it acted as a comprehensive modernising force. However, the effects of policy wrought significant changes on society – the social structure was transformed – and, it is contended in this chapter, these changes led in turn to demands and pressures on the political leadership.

In this collection, the state-led process of modernisation is analyzed in the context of pressures given not only by history (the weight of the peasantry) geography (the vast land mass) and culture (the values of autocracy) but also in the context of the effects of industrialisation on the structure of the population. There are then two major topics to be addressed: first, the extent and relative success of a state-led modernisation policy and second,

---

3   See Seymour Martin Lipset, "Some Social Requisites of Democracy, Economic Development and Political Legitimacy", American Political Science Review, LIII (March 1959).
4   See articles by T. Anthony Jones, Alex Inkeles (who was a pioneer of this approach) in Mark G. Field, *Social Consequences of Modernisation in Communist Societies*, London and Baltimore: Johns Hopkins Press, 1976.

the reciprocal effects of changes in the social structure on the political order. The second problem is the topic of this chapter.

A Social Structural Approach

By the term 'social structure' we mean an array of positions or statuses, the conditions that shape them and a network of relationships between people and groups. Statuses give rise to patterns of behaviour, to norms and expectations; they are foci which give people a sense of social and individual identity. Statuses include occupations and social groups which may be divided into many categories – such as by sex and age, urban and rural, ethnic and religious, manual and non-manual, professionals and collective farmers. The sheer size and differentiation of Soviet society as it developed made it impossible to control 'from the top down'. Rather than modern society providing the means for ubiquitous control as entailed by totalitarianism, it leads to considerable differentiation. The diverse forms of administrative organisation, the specialised division of labour, the heterogeneity of urban life gave rise to a social pluralism.

Analysis of 'real existing socialism' in the USSR and the 'real existing transformation' in the Russian Federation has to take account of historically determined role structures which provide 'resistances' to changes introduced from above and modify them in line with practical possibilities. A process of osmosis takes place whereby orientations, practices and procedures socialised under the old regime gradually modify the policies and practices of the political elites seeking to institute a new social system. Study of this process shows that various institutional structures have some autonomy and may be able to 'resist' changes which take place in others, or at least be able to deflect them.

The ethno-national culture inherited by revolutionary elites plays a large part in determining the extent and character of modernisation. This occurred not only under Stalin in the USSR but continues to have effects in the contemporary Putin era. The effects of a modernisation policy on the social structure need reciprocal changes in the political and economic. If incompatibilities arise between the various sub-systems constituting a society, then 'regression' may occur. One example is the 'fall' of the western Roman Empire and the reversion of its territories to more or less 'archaic' social conditions in the 'dark ages'.[5] In this chapter I shall show how changes in the social structure were conditioning factors in the rise of perestroika.

I do not claim that social structural factors are the only, or even the major, determinants of the changes in the regime which have taken place. They are though necessary precipitating factors. My own preference would be for a multiple causal model: this entails that several variables (ideology, economic conditions, external global constraints) act concurrently to promote the de-

---

5   Parsons, Societies, 4.

velopment of a new regime. The changing social structure, my subject here, is one of these crucial variables in providing support for, or opposition to, a given political leadership and system of rule. A change in social structure influences norms, values, institutions and processes.

Changes in Social Structure

The social structure of Soviet society confronting the leadership of Gorbachev was of a qualitatively different type to that associated with the regimes of Stalin and Khrushchev. Major changes had occurred in the social formation of the Soviet Union. These have to be seen as providing the major social and political supports and inputs into the political system. Gorbachev might be viewed not as 'changing society' from the top but as an expression of new social groups and interests which developed in the post Second World War period. The role of the reform leadership was not only to propel change and react to demands but, in addition, it created an alternative vision of new ways of doing things. Hence the approach adopted here is not a form of sociological reductionism, as in some of the earlier modernisations theories, but the role of a creative political leadership is important.

Figure 2. USSR Population 1917–1989

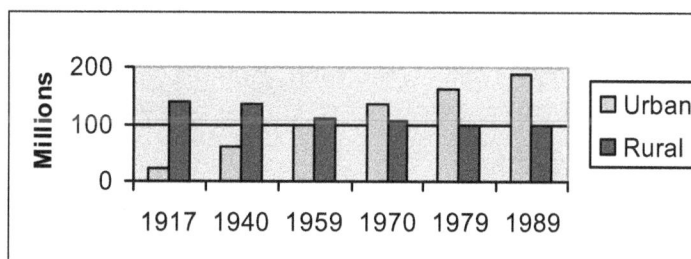

I shall outline only two major developments in the social structure. First, differential rates of urbanisation and population growth and second, changes in the occupational and class structure. These changes, in conjunction with other factors, led to the growth of groups which have been predisposed to dissatisfaction with the processes of Soviet society and have been responsive to calls for reform. Thirdly, I shall show how these changes affected the political class.

Study of the urban and occupational composition of the population establishes that by the 1980s the USSR was an urban industrial society comparable in many respects to the advanced Western states. Figure 2 shows the growth of population for the USSR between 1917 and 1989 (from 163 millions to 286.7 millions); the urban population in 1989 comprised 66 per cent of the population.[6] One must also bear in mind the great regional diversity of the USSR with the Western European republics being more highly urbanized, whereas the Central Asian republics even in 1990 were predominantly rural. In 1989, for example, the Russian Republic had an urban population of 74%, Latvia 71% and the Ukraine 67%, whereas Tadzhikistan had only 33%, and Uzbekistan 41%.

Only in the early 1960s did the USSR become mainly urban – a condition reached in Britain before the mid nineteenth century. The rate of growth of the urban population in the second half of the twentieth century is remarkable. The total number of urban dwellers rose from some 22 million in 1922 to 186.8 millions in 1989 and between 1959 and 1989 the urban population nearly doubled from 100 million to 186.8 million. Clearly, this urban population explosion put great strain on the supply of commodities (especially food) and services. Any government would have been hard pressed to meet the demands on food supply and the provision of social services and housing.

Figure 3. USSR Employment by Sector 1913–1987

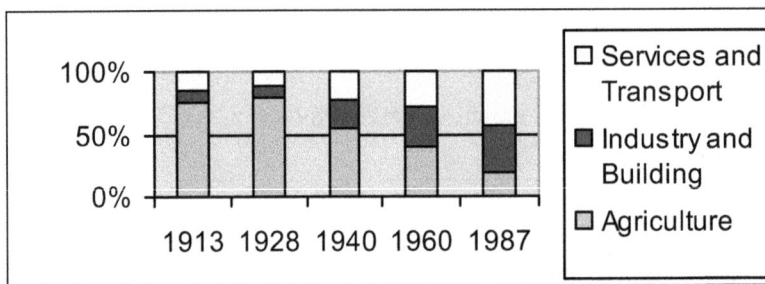

The movement of population from countryside to town has been accompanied by important changes in employment, both by economic sector and by occupation. Figure 3 illustrates the major changes that have taken place in employment by economic sector: as late as the 1960s agriculture was the major employer, losing its prime place to industry and building in the seventies. The final twenty years of the twentieth century witnessed another

6   Population data are given in the yearly publication: *Naselenie SSSR*, and in *Narodnoe khozyaystvo SSSR*, the volumes for 1988 published in 1989 have been used in this article. Data for the 1989 census appear in Pravda 29 April 1989.The definition of "urban" varies between different republics of the USSR. In the Russian Republic, towns are defined as contiguous populations not less than 12,000 with non-manuals and manual workers forming 85 per cent or more of the population, and urban area has to be settled by 3,000 people with at least 85 per cent of the population being composed of manual and non-manual workers). in the Ukraine, urban areas on the other hand are defined as 2,000 people with a majority outside of agriculture. *Naselenie SSSR*, 1983 :22–3 fn.

major transformation: employment in agriculture in 1987 was only 35 per cent of that of 1940; by 1987, the largest economic sector was services and transport (42%).[7]

The manual working class grew tremendously: employment was as follows: 1928 4.628 millions; 1940 12.543 millions; 1960 17.864 millions and 1987 38.259 millions.[8] An important change took place in the character of the urban working class. The recruitment of workers in the 1930s involved a very high proportion of young peasants new to the town: the culture of the factory was strongly influenced by peasant mores.[9] These young men and women received their rudimentary training on the shop floor. From about the 1950s, a critical proportion of the manual working class had began to reproduce itself. For instance, a study of Leningrad workers in the mid 1970s found that 83 per cent hailed from an urban background and 39 per cent were the children of industrial workers; only 28 per cent of the skilled workers came from an agricultural or unskilled manual worker background.[10] With the replenishment of the working class, aspirations changed considerably and the levels of skill and education significantly improved. For instance, to the workforce between 1960 and 1986 were added 20 million graduates of trade schools (an annual output of 2.6 million in the late 1980s).[11] There arose a significant stratification of the working class, with a younger generation of workers being more skilled and educated than their older colleagues.

Figure 4. Soviet Republics Employment by Sector 1987

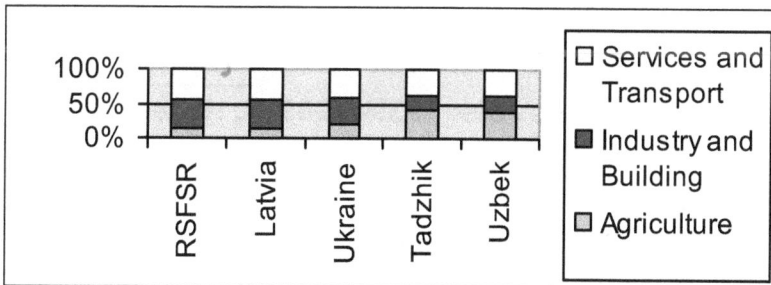

---

7   *Trud v SSSR* 1988,14.
8   *Trud v SSSR* 1988, 47, 55.
9   For further details see: David Lane and Felicity O'Dell, *The Soviet Industrial Worker: Social Class, Education and Control*, Oxford: Martin Robertson, 1978, chapters 1 and 2.
10 N. P. Konstantinova, O. V. Stakanova , O. I. Shkaratan, 'Peremeny v sotsial'nom oblike rabochikh v epokhu razvitogo sotsializma', *Voprosy istorii*, 1978, No 5:11.
11 Ibid, 95.

There were significant differences between republics: on Figure 3 are data representing five republics in 1987: the industrially and economically advanced republics of European Russia (Latvia and the Ukraine,) the Russian Republic, one of the most backward (Tadzhikistan) and one of the more advanced though unevenly developed Asian Republics (Uzbekistan).[12] The RSFSR and Latvia had very similar occupational structures and it is noteworthy that in 1987, the largest sector was in services. The Ukraine had somewhat larger industrial and agricultural sectors and the two central Asian republics had sizable agricultural ones. Perhaps surprisingly their service sector is relatively substantial and greater than that of the industry and building sectors combined. This indicates the presence of a large non-manual class in public fields: teaching, medicine and administration.

Linked to these sectoral changes in employment were developments in cultural levels and a changing occupational structure. Such advancement led to the growth of a competent and literate citizenship and to the formation of a middle class. One measure of such improvements is the standard of education. In 1926, the Soviet authorities claimed that 51.1 per cent of the population aged over nine years was literate and by 1939, the figure reached 81.2 per cent.[13] This figure probably errs on the side of charity: according to the census of 1937, of 98 million people aged over nine, 37.3 million (38 per cent) were illiterate. [14] The social base on which the Stalinist regime developed was largely composed of poorly educated people and a large number of illiterates infused with superstition. As late as 1937, only 43 per cent of adults (over 15) were self defined as non-believers and in the census of that year 42 per cent professed allegiance to the Orthodox Church. [15]

Figure 5. USSR Educational Levels 1939–1989

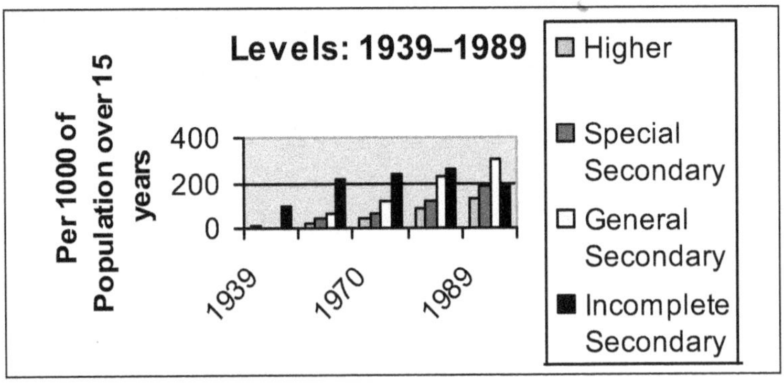

---

12   Based on statistics from *Trud v SSSR* 1988: 16,17.

13   *Narodnoe obrazovanie v SSSR*, Moscow: Akademia pedagogicheskikh nauk 1957: 733.

14   Calculated on census data published in Yu. A. Polyakov, V. B. Zhuromskaya and I. I. Kiselev, 'Polveka Molchaniya', *Sotsiologicheskie issledovaniya*, no 7, 1990, 67.

15   Data calculated on table cited in Polyakov et al., 69.

Under Brezhnev, as a consequence of the social policies adopted earlier, this social base had changed remarkably. Comparative data for the years 1939,1959, 1970, 1979 and 1989 are given in Figure 5.[16] Even in 1959, by far the bulk of the population had no more than an 'incomplete secondary' (mainly primary) education. The graph illustrates the spectacular rise in educational standards during the post 1970 period. Some of the major indices are as follows: in 1939, there were only 1.2 million people with a complete higher education (only 911,790 were recorded in the census of 1937), [17] in 1959, there were 8.3 millions and by 1989 the number had risen to 23 millions.[18] By the 1970s, the density of the professional non-manuals had given them a 'demographic identity'. There was a massive growth in the numbers of engineers and technicians, vets, economists, lawyers, physicians and medical specialists, teachers and other personal services employees.[19] These professionals were people with a higher or specialist secondary education. By 1987, their number had grown to over 35 million people from a mere 2.4 millions in 1940. A significant proportion of this skilled non-manual group were women. (Thirty-six per cent in 1940 rising to 61 per cent in 1987).[20]

Such developments were not restricted to the Russian Republic but also characterised the Republics. Educational achievements broken down by republic are shown on Table 1. These data indicate the higher levels of tertiary education in the European areas of the country. The strata of upper professionals are to be found in the capital cities of the European areas. But the differences are not as marked as one might have expected. Indeed, the figures for full general secondary education give both Tadzhikistan and Uzbekistan higher ratios than the USSR as a whole. The main reason for this was that the Central Asian republics did not have the large number of older people educated before 1959 when facilities were poor. Nevertheless, levels of higher education in Latvia and the Russian Republic were significantly higher than in the Central Asian republics.

Such figures suggest a linkage between levels of urbanisation and higher education and political support for a new style of leadership: the Central Asian republics have not been particularly prominent in the drive to establish a new type pluralistic polyarchic political system – rather the contrary. Higher education was probably the more important variable to act as a 'push' factor in favour of reform of the traditional Soviet political system. In addition, however, one must add to such predisposing factors those of knowledge and a vision of an alternative political regime. In the Baltic republics (as in the East European socialist states) this vision was sustained by a history of independence and the proximity of the advanced affluent counties of the

---

16 *Chislennost' i sostav naseleniya SSSR*, 1984, 23; *Narkhoz v 1989g*, 1990, 187. Figures here for 'higher education' include incomplete higher, the latter being approximately 20 per cent of the total.
17 See table in Polyakov et al., 'Polveka Molchaniya'.
18 *Trud v SSSR*, 1988, 119. *Narkhoz v 1989*, 187.
19 *Trud v SSSR*, 1988, 113.
20 Ibid, 119.

West. These were lacking in the central Asian republics. Since the fall of the Soviet system, it seems likely that the young non-manual groups will have become the basis for a heightened national consciousness.

The Social Support of Leadership

On the basis of these data we may make a number of inferences. The rapid growth of the urban population, particularly after 1959, had put considerable stress on the resource mobilisation system to supply goods to the towns. Urban dwellers have higher levels of consumer expectations than rural ones: the aggregate demand schedules for goods and services shifted to the right, straining the provision of consumer goods and the heightened need for services. Hence population growth, as well as the often cited military competition, put stress on the government.

By the 1980s there was a large educated non-manual urban population. Numerically, the manual working class replaced the peasant population of the inter-war years and in a qualitative way, the working class had come to possess an urban culture: it was no longer formed of *muzhiks* wearing boiler suits. One might hypothesise that the social base of politics had changed. Under Stalin, the peasantry was a major social prop to the regime; at the beginning of the Second World War the Soviet Union had a large illiterate peasant population. Even in the towns the typical resident had only a primary education. The white collar middle class was small and undereducated. Under Brezhnev and Khrushchev diffuse political backing was provided by the manual worker. By 1950, employment of manual workers had outstripped that of any other group and by 1980 it was nearly 80 million in size making it the largest single agglomeration of manual workers in the world.

Under *perestroika*, the professional non-manuals became the ascendant groups and, it may be hypothesised, provided a social base which both pushed and was attracted to Gorbachev's policies. The number of non-manual workers between 1960 and 1987 more than doubled in size to over 36 million employees. These social strata made demands to which the leadership responded. One should therefore qualify the widely held and correct view that *perestroika* was a 'revolution from the top'. It had also been 'pushed' by the demands of these new social forces. In turn, however, the reform leadership had 'pulled' to it the non-manual groups with higher education.

Such developments have to be interpreted in the context of the presence of more traditional interests and groupings (the unskilled manual workers still formed a very large group). The cultural legacy of previous epochs of Soviet history also made its particular impact. Furthermore, national identification became a latent force in the Central Asian republics. The growth of a young intelligentsia in the Central Asian republics may indicate a future post-socialist development of nationalist sentiment. The rise of independence movements in the republics overwhelmingly led by the nationalist intelligentsia has to be analyzed in the light of traditional dispositions which give rise to a vision of an alternative political and social order.

Table 1. Educational Levels of the Population in the USSR, RSFSR, Latvia, Ukraine, Tadzhikistan, Kirgiziya, and Uzbekistan (1959, 1970 and 1979).

(Per 1,000 Of The Population Aged 10 And Above)

	1959	1970	1979
RSFSR			
All Higher	35	57	86
Full general sec.	58	108	188
Latvia			
All Higher	39	67	95
Full general sec.	75	119	187
Ukraine			
All Higher	31	52	78
Full general sec.	64	139	225
Tadzhikistan			
All Higher	24	41	61
Full general sec.	48	112	220
Uzbekistan			
All Higher	30	52	74
Full general sec.	67	141	275
USSR			
All Higher	34	55	83
Full general sec.	61	119	207

Source: Census data, *Chislennost' i sostav naseleniya SSSR* (1984): 26–41.

Much study of political support in the West has related voting behaviour to social class and in this fashion has depicted the social basis of politics. In the absence of competitive elections in the Soviet period, one can only have cruder linkages between the leadership and the population. One may hypothesise that to ensure diffuse supports, the policies of a regime need to be congruent with the interest and culture of salient social groups. (By 'salient' I mean that a given social group may have significant and widespread political effects).

In this sense, I would contend that the social ballast of the political leadership had changed from the manual working class under Brezhnev to the non-manual strata which was a stanchion to the reform leadership.[21] This may be illustrated by consideration of the social composition of the leading institutions of power. Under Brezhnev, the density of manual workers in the membership of the Communist Party of the Soviet Union rose considerably. In the period 1956 to 1961 (under Khrushchev) workers made up 41.1 per cent of *new* Party members, their share rising to 59.4 per cent in the late Brezhnev period (1981–85). [22] This gave a solid working class membership to the Communist Party: manual workers constituted 43.4 per cent of membership in 1981 and 45.4 per cent in 1989. [23]

However, manual workers and collective farmers had been increasingly excluded from positions of power under the Gorbachev leadership which was dependent on the non-manual and professional social groups. Since the mid-fifties there had been a massive increase in the numbers of Party members with higher education: in 1957 only some million members had a higher education; by 1971 it had risen to 2.81 million (19.6 per cent) and to 6.8 million (31.8 per cent) in 1989. Density of people with higher education was even greater at crucial levels of the Party apparat: of the Party's leading cadres (members and candidates of central committees and auditing commissions of Union Republican parties and Province (obkom) and territories (krai) committees) 69.4 per cent had higher education. Even at the level of cities, districts (raykom) and areas (okrug) 56.7 per cent had a complete higher education. [24] These changes in social composition entailed a different world view on the part of the Party leadership: authoritative positions in the Party were increasingly occupied by people with higher education and they were respondent to a similar constituency in the Party's membership.

Another measure which indicates the changing political base for the new leadership was the social background of the membership of the Supreme Soviet and the Congress of People's Deputies of the USSR. In 1974, workers constituted 32.8 per cent of the members of the Supreme Soviet of the USSR.[25] This figure rose slightly to 35.2 per cent in the Supreme Soviet elected before the reform leadership was in command. Similarly, women constituted 31 per cent of the delegates in 1974 and 33 per cent in 1984. These high figures were secured by notional 'quotas' from various social groups which ensured their symbolic representation. The massive decline of working class and female representation may be gauged from the social background of membership of the deputies to the Supreme Soviet in 1974 and 1984 with those nominated and elected to the Congress of People's Deputies in 1989. The share of workers among the deputies in the 1989 election came to 18.6% compared to 34 per cent in 1974, collective farmers fell to

21 For a comparison with Britain, see J. Goldthorpe, 'On the Service Class, its Formation and Future', in A. Giddens and G. Mackenzie, Social Class and the Division of Labour, Cambridge 1982: 171–2.
22 'KPSS v tsifakh', *Partiynaya zhizn'*, No 21, 1987, 8.
23 'KPSS v tsifrakh', *Izvestiya Ts.K. KPSS*, 1989, No 2: 140.
24 Sources: 'KPSS v tsifrakh', *Partiynaya zhizn'* no 4 1986, 23,29; 'KPSS v tsifrakh', *Partiynaya zhizn'* no 21 1987, 10; *Izvestiya Ts.K. KPSS* No 2 1989, 140.
25 *Verkhovny Sovet SSSR* (1974).

only 11.2% (compared to 16.1%) of the seats and the proportion of women dropped considerably from 33 per cent to 17.1%.[26] The number of deputies in the professional classes with higher education rose from 7.8 per cent to 15.7 per cent. [27]

These data are illustrative not only of a symbolic but also a real shift in the basis of power of the leadership towards the non-manual professional strata. A problem here is how the system of class stratification related to the system of political power and influenced political change under Gorbachev.

Social Class and Political Class

Under state socialism, the major criteria for class stratification were political control and market position, though both had operated (until the post-socialist period) in ways different to capitalist societies. In state socialist bureaucratic systems, political and economic power were combined. There was a hierarchy of political position which gave control of the economy as well as the cultural, police and military apparatuses: such rights of control of property were analogous to the bourgeoisie under capitalism. This group might be termed an administrative class.

However, this class operated in the context of a market for labour and a consumer market for commodities. People sold their services and they were rewarded with money income with which commodities were purchased. Labour productivity was encouraged through the incentive of monetary reward. In addition, many services were provided through state forms of distribution and had no price (medical services) or a nominal one (rent for apartments). The relationship between market and administrative forms of distribution was a major difference between state socialism and capitalism and it was also one of the major tensions in the state socialist system. By combining administrative control and marketability, class boundaries may be determined.

In order to capture the distinctive way in which administrative control operated under state socialism, the stratification order is divided vertically into 'nomenklatura' positions and others. A nomenklatura position was a post the occupancy of which is controlled formally by the political authorities, the Party. It indicates that a particular role had some strategic importance, particularly control over people, institutions and property. Recruitment of personnel was under the command of executive bodies of the Party apparatus: e.g. the 'nomenklatura of the politburo' for very top positions (such as government ministers) and local Party executives for more lowly positions (trade union functionaries).

The nomenklatura affects not only elite positions, but also ones of authority at lower levels. Hence one may note a vertical linkage of members of the nomenklatura, with movement between nomenklatura posts (illustrated in Figure 6).

26   For election results see: *Izvestiya* 5 May 1989, *Moscow News* 16 April 1989.
27   *Izvestiya*, 6 May 1989.

Figure 6. Linkage of Nomenklatura and Social Strata

1. Ruling elite
2. Upper intelligentsia
3. 'Spetsialisty'
4. Private enterprise
5. Skilled Manual
6. Routine Non-Man
7. Semi-skilled Man
8. Agricultural Wks

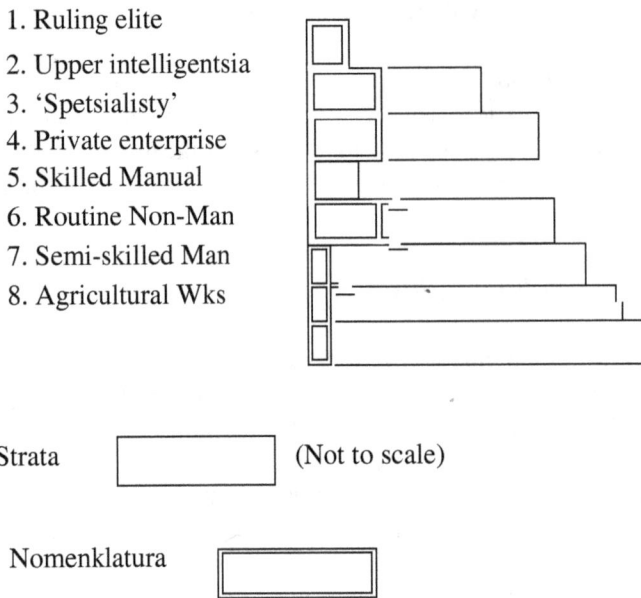

Strata ☐ (Not to scale)

Nomenklatura ☐

This was a vertically structured power system. These positions were also not only forms of paid employment as they also include political positions which may be associated with the work process (trade union secretary) or with political organization in any association (Komsomol secretary). Hence the 'political elite' is not to be confused with the nomenklatura as a whole, but is a special stratum of it. The nomenklatura had the character of a political class, not a political elite, as some people believe. The political elite is recruited from the political class.

The other systemic form of class stratification was linked to the market. This was similar to the process of Western capitalism though there were important differences. Market relations exist in the sense that employees had to sell their labour for a wage. Income and status derived from employment were important in the determination of life chances. The population was then stratified by market position in a similar way as in other industrial societies with a hierarchical status ranking. The modernisation process increased significantly the number of persons in groups 2, 3 and 5 in the diagram. (Group 4, 'cooperatives' were introduced under Gorbachev). This also increased the density of these occupational groups in nomenklatura positions, especially at elite levels as noted above.

One of the differences from capitalism was that the labour market operated in the context of a planned economy and protection of manual labour: this effectively eliminated unemployment (until the reforms of the early 1990s) and considerably strengthened the position of the working class against management. The absence of professional associations and independent trade unions had the effect of preventing the use of monopoly power by groups with skills and severely depressed their wages compared to similar groups under capitalism. The low pay of physicians, accountants and lawyers under state socialism was not due to the absence of a market, as is usually assumed, but to the absence of combination by professional groups. Obviously, a 'market' relationship in which their skills could be valorised would be much to their interest and accounts for the support of many strata for the reform movement. These two systems of class stratification (political and economic) have to be considered to operate conjointly. An occupation may be combined with a nomenklatura position; for instance, almost any occupation may be associated with position of Party or trade union secretary. Hence occupational mobility and career has to be understood in the context of other positions held (membership of nomenklatura posts in the local Soviet or Party organization). Under the traditional system of state socialism, one may conceptualize two overlapping blocs in the stratification and political order: one derived from nomenklatura position and the other determined by occupation and the market. Changes consequent on the industrialisation programme greatly increased the numbers of people which were intertwined with the political class (particularly in groups 1, 2 and 3). Sections of the middle classes and sectors of the nomenklatura became disenchanted with their conditions and were a dynamic of social change. As Przworski has aptly put it: 'If they are self-interested, people who have little chance to earn a high income under capitalism prefer socialism; people whose earning potential is restrained under socialism prefer capitalism. Hence, preferences about economic systems have class bases[28]'.

Allocative Politics

Above I contended that under Brezhnev the political leadership had a particular affinity with the working class. The working class acted as an effective 'veto group' on the political elite. By this, I mean that the working class as a collectivity had the power to frustrate any action by the government or their direct employers unless it was perceived to be in their interests. This was interpreted by western commentators such as Echols and Bunce and Hough as a type of corporatist politics. A number of cogent reasons have been put forward in support of this view: the working class had high job security, the worker was cushioned by overfull employment and a labour shortage, there was lax labour discipline and low labour productivity. Hence, even if the working class did not have independent political organisations representing its 'interests', it was able to exert pressure on the shop floor by slackening the activity of work. It was also capable of articulating its interests through the Party organisation and also through the unions. An outburst of worker unrest was regarded as a serious failure of local political leadership and hence in various ways manual workers were able to secure significant advantages from the regime.

28 Adam Przeworski, *Democracy and the Market*, Cambridge: Cambridge University Press, 1991, 104.

Figure 7. Wage Ratios 1932–1986: Managerial/Technical, Non-Manual Office, Manual Workers

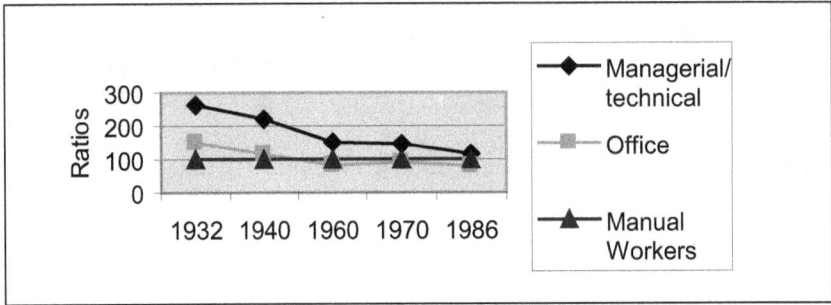

There had been a slow but constant rise in manual workers' wages coupled to low price inflation, and a steady decline of non-manuals': the index of real income for manual and non-manual workers rose from 100 in 1970 to 155 in 1986; and it rose 17 percentage points between 1980 and 1987.[29] But labour productivity was falling and technological advance required the re-location of personnel.

Unlike under capitalism where unemployment and the price system are levers of change and the working class is relatively weakly organized relative to management and capital, in the Soviet case it was the other way around. It was very difficult to legitimate the laying off of workers which was nec-essary to improve productivity when technology improves. Unlike under capitalism, participation in the increased wealth accrued disproportionately to the manual working class. This may be illustrated by the changing wage differentials between three main groups (workers, managerial/technical and office workers) in Soviet society. While these are wide social categories, they show clearly the trends and are corroborated by other qualitative evidence on differentials. The trends between 1932 and 1986 of three occupational groups are shown on Figure 7. These figures based on official Soviet wage statistics have the advantage that they show trends over a long period and they are confirmed by other qualitative and anecdotal evidence of income disparities between professionals and manual workers. Complaints about salary 'injustices' were frequently aired in the press in the post-Khrushchev period. Wage relativities for manual workers in industry had improved dra-matically during the last fifty years or so: by 1986, they received on average 20 per cent more than office workers (sluzhashchie) whose income was 50 per cent greater in 1932. Taking 1932 as a base, the managerial/technical staff wage ratio was 2.1 times greater in 1940, but only 1.1 times in 1986; the office workers' (sluzhashchie) differential fell even more, from 1.09 to only 0.79 times between these two dates. [30]

29 *Narkhoz za 70 let*, 441; *Narkhoz v 1987g*, 402.
30 *Narkhoz v 1979g*. (1980), 394. *Narkhoz v 1984g*. (1985), 417.

While these scales apply to wages in industry, they are also true of wage differentials generally. They had led to feelings of injustice by white collar employees in the USSR, not only by upper professionals but also by other lowly paid non-manual workers such as nurses, teachers, and clerks. Physicians, teachers, engineers, research personnel often received salaries less than those of skilled manual workers[31] (though, of course, their forms of consumption, particularly of transfer services, and life style were not necessarily inferior).

Moveover, during the leadership of Gorbachev, external comparisons became more prominent. Modernisation is conceptualised as a global process. In the socialist bloc, there was a qualitative rise in the levels of mass communications which directly and indirectly changed people's perceptions of life in the West which became for them an ideal. Television became widespread and Western programmes became directly accessible in the German Democratic Republic, Czechoslovakia, Hungary and the Baltic areas; video recorders gave access to Western films on a wide scale. The population's expectations rose: there was a development of a consumer mentality and a bourgeoisification of aspirations.[32]

These developments all led to a population more open to a move to a market economy. In the 1980s, the intelligentsia was a stratum receptive to an alternative conception of socialism (which in practice embraced many of the practices of contemporary capitalism), to a vision of a future different from that of their parents. As Millar concludes from a study of Soviet immigrants to the United States, 'A long term trend toward privatization is evident, which shows up not only in the evasion of mobilization effort.. but also in the economic realm. The study reaffirms the pervasiveness of illegal as well as private economic activity'.[33] An underlying cause of this consciousness was the market relationships on which these strata could capitalise (or believed they could capitalise) their skills. The consumption of commodities in exchange for effort was not in equilibrium: this was expressed in the growth of corruption (behaviour which deviates from accepted public norms to serve private ends). The failure of the loyalty-solidarity-commitment nexus led to moral decay.

Field studies conducted in 1991 confirm that, on the part of the intelligentsia in the post-communist countries, there was a significant negative attitude to socialist principles and a positive attitude to capitalist ones. (i.e. opposition to: income being determined by need rather than merit, government provi-

31 See the discussion in T. Zaslavskaya, *The Second Socialist Revolution: An Alternative Socialist Strategy*, London:Tauris,1990, 120–1.

32 Studies of émigrés, for example, showed a consistent pattern of pattern of changing support: in the 1980s, the young were much more critical of state socialism, whereas in the early post-war generation, youth had been more supportive. See J. R. Berliner, 'The Harvard Project and the Soviet Interview Project', in F. J. Fleron Jr. and E. P. Hoffmann, *Post-Communist Studies and Political Science*, Boulder and Oxford: Westview Press, 1993, 177–182.

33 J. R. Millar, 'History, Method and the Problem of Bias', in Fleron and Hoffmann,187.

sion of employment, egalitarianism of income distribution, limits on earned income). One study shows that there was a 'steady decline in support for socialist principles from those with low education to those with higher educations. Across all the East European countries, the correlation coefficient between the socialism index and education level is -.33. .. [N]on-egalitarian reforms are supported by the more highly educated minority in those societies, who, as it happens, also have the most to gain from such reforms'.[34]

These changes in the loyalty and solidarity of the population are evidence of increasing levels of dissatisfaction by the growing professional classes. It is not being argued here that these demographic changes directly led to challenges to the system of state socialism, rather they created predispositions towards change.

The greater use of the market was a strategy which the leadership adopted not only to meet such demands but also to use as a means of disciplining the workforce to raise productivity and to change the pattern of differentials to the disadvantage of the unskilled manual workers and to the benefit of those with skills and education, particularly the intelligentsia. Ideologically, this involved the delegitimisation of planning and the command system. In more intangible ways, the processes of 'glasnost' and decentralisation of power enhanced the authority of the intelligentsia.

In his discussion of the 'service class', Goldthorpe pointed to the autonomy of this group and the advantages of employment in this sector. In the West, it is a class which has consolidated its position. [35] The Soviet equivalent of the service class (the higher and middle intelligentsia), however, lacked autonomy of work situation and salaries were depressed compared to the working class. While it grew in size and become more heterogeneous in social composition, it lost in status. It was a group which became disgruntled with the 'command system' and was increasingly conscious of an alternative in the market societies of the West. Its members were frequently spellbound by Thatcherite and Friedmanesque rhetoric. Curbing the power of the bureaucracy would lead, it was believed, to the fragmentation of power and professions would develop independently under the market. There were good reasons for the intelligentsia to believe that their work situation and market situation would improve under the conditions of economic and political pluralism. *Glasnost'*, *demokratiya* and *khozraschet* would raise considerably the autonomy of the work situation of the intelligentsia.

Hence the 'support-exchange' theory of allocative politics would suggest that the intelligentsia had much to gain from *perestroika*, and the manual working class much to lose. One might expect opposition to the Gorbachev, and subsequent market reforms, to have a material basis among many strata

34 David S. Mason, 'Attitudes toward the Market and Political Participation in the Postcommunist States', *Slavic Review*, vol. 54, no 2 (Summer 1995), 393–395. Mason points out that, '... in many of these countries the new governments are dominated by the highly educated, because the revolutions swept into power intellectuals who had previously opposed the communist system.'
35 Goldthorpe, 'On the Service Class', 178.

of the manual working class. As in Western market economies, the heaviest burden of redundancy is carried by the unskilled. The large stratum of older unskilled, poorly educated manual workers are particularly prone to unemployment, and more so as welfare support had not been developed in the state socialist societies.

Conclusion

This chapter addresses the problem of the role of social differentiation on political change. Developments in the social structure (in the sense of the enlargement, and formation, of new social groups and strata) have multiple effects - influencing norms, values and processes. But changes in social structure have to be considered also in the context of other variables. The relative economic decline of the socialist states was also an important precipitating factor of change and so have been changes in the nature of the world economic and political order.

The type of Soviet society inherited by Gorbachev was significantly different from that of Khrushchev. A modernisation process had occurred. A major feature of social structural development had been the growth and differentiation of the population and a steep rise in levels of urbanisation. Changes in the social composition of the population led to diffuse support for policies of perestroika. Levels of education had risen considerably and there was a substantial mass of young people with higher education. A 'demographic identity' developed among groups of the Soviet intelligentsia which facilitated the rise of a new political consciousness. Modernisation indirectly led to support for political and economic change.

Under Gorbachev, the Soviet political culture contained a significant number of individuals and groups having a positive conception of their own interests; this gave rise to a critical mass which could evaluate the government's actions. Soviet society changed from one with a significant passive peasantry under Stalin, to one dependent on the participation of the intelligentsia and on the rising productivity of the skilled manual working class. Such individuals and groups were receptive to an alternative conception of socialism (which in practice embraced many of the practices of contemporary capitalism), to a vision of the future different from that of their parents.

In the wake of social modernisation, the population came to expect a rising standard of living and a better quality of life. This changing value system became a 'push' factor for perestroika. 'Moral' incentives and commitment to work as a collective duty were not regarded by the reform leadership of Gorbachev as being effective and higher differentials linked to greater productivity were favoured. Demands for 'social justice' in the USSR called for greater earned income differentials. A contented working class had been at the basis of the political stability of the Soviet system. The cost of stability had been in terms of absenteeism, poor labour discipline and quality of production: in short, low labour productivity. But in terms of 'allocative politics', the manual working class benefitted disproportionately from the rising standard of living. It had been a mainstay of the centralised command economy.

The falling levels of economic growth and the non-fulfilment of plans led to widespread consumer dissatisfaction despite the fact that living standards had improved. Reform policy involved a recalibration of the differentials between various groups and the ways that they were calculated. Gorbachev's recognition of 'deficiencies' and 'shortcomings' in policy had been triggered particularly by the lack of fulfilment of the aspirations of groups of intellectuals. The policy of glasnost' was a recognition of a surge of individual and group demands. If one assumes that the political leadership was dependent on the loyal support and creativity of the intelligentsia, as this stratum grew in size and maturity, the opinions of its sub-groups, particularly with respect to their professional expertise, were increasingly taken into account. To challenge technologically the West, a competent, creative and contented intelligentsia was required.

It is undoubtedly the case that the reform leadership under Gorbachev tilted the political fulcrum of diffuse and specific support away from the manual working class and the traditional Party and state bureaucracy to an alliance with the more technologically inclined and modernizing forces among the political elite and the intelligentsia. This threatened the traditional alliance between the Party executive, government administrators and their supporters among the manual working class. The maintenance and replication of their own positions would be undermined by the rise of market forces. But the reform leadership under Gorbachev not only refracted social grievances and aspirations, it also unintentionally created them. It revived old (nationalistic) and stimulated new (market) political ideals. These brought down Gorbachev and led to a new era, that of the transformation of state socialism, and a move to capitalism.

A social structural analysis alone cannot explain the salience of support for an alternative conception of the Soviet political regime, nor can it explain the mechanisms which promoted system change. The context of relative economic decline, proximity to the West, the role of external political powers (particularly the USA), and traditional forms of national identity are important variables which give rise to new political ideals and to support for a new regime. But the modernisation of Soviet society, in the sense of a more differentiated, highly educated and urbanised population, had profound effects on political stability. The reform movement of Gorbachev was supported by a 'push' from the professional non-manual groups in the social structure which in turn were attracted by the ideological promise of perestroika. The consequences of modernisation were not only a cause of the eventual fall of state socialism, but also led to the quest for continuing modernisation under the post-socialist leadership in the form of markets and support for private property.

R. W. DAVIES

The 'Modernisation' of the Soviet Economy in the Inter-War Years

The term 'modernisation' was rarely used by marxists, including Soviet marxists. Elementary Soviet marxist assumptions about economic and social development were their equivalent to 'modernisation', and all the economic disputes and decisions of the 1920s and 1930s took this ideological framework for granted.

Marx held that human progress was achieved by the growth of productive resources, the 'forces of production', which included not only capital in the form of buildings and machinery, but also labour skills. The advance of the forces of production meant that at each stage of history the existing social and political order – which rested on the dominance of a ruling property-owning class – became a hindrance to economic development and was overturned by the new social class which had emerged within the old order. Slavery was replaced by feudalism, feudalism by capitalism, capitalism by socialism.

The capitalist system enabled a vast development of the forces of production, characterised by large-scale production socially organised but owned by private individuals or companies who exploited the wage-earning working class or proletariat. The political and social order, based on the private ownership of capital, increasingly hindered the further growth of the forces of production. In the most advanced capitalist countries the proletariat would overthrow the capitalist order and replace it by a system based on social or collective ownership. As Marx wrote in a famous passage in volume one of *Capital*:

> The monopoly of capital becomes a fetter upon the mode of production, which has sprung up and flourished along with, and under it. Centralisation of the means of production and socialisation of labour at last reach a point where they become incompatible with their capitalist integument. This integument is burst asunder. The knell of private property sounds. The expropriators are expropriated.[1]

---

1 K. Marx, *Capital*, vol. 1 London: Allen and Unwin, 1946 (reprint of 1889 edition), 789.

Social ownership would involve a further even more rapid development of the forces of production. Socialist or communist society would be a classless society, and the state – whose main function historically was to maintain the power of the ruling class and repress the exploited classes – would disappear. In Engels' words 'administration over persons would be replaced by administration of things', and society would 'reorganise production on the basis of a free and equal association of the producers'.[2]

However, the first successful proletarian revolution took place in October 1917 not in an advanced capitalist country but in the largely peasant Russian Empire. As Lenin put it soon after the revolution, the material or economic half of socialism had been realised in Germany, the political half in Russia in the form of the dictatorship of the proletariat.[3] At first, the Bolsheviks hoped that the rapid spread of the Russian revolution to the advanced capitalist countries would bring the economic and political halves of socialism together. By 1921, this expectation had not been realised. The solution – eventually embodied in the slogan 'Socialism in One Country' – was to use the power of the proletarian state to develop the productive forces of peasant Russia. The State Planning Commission, Gosplan, was established in February 1921. Its first head, Krzhizhanovsky, an electrical engineer and close associate of Lenin, declared that the 'economic October' in Russia would 'bring our economic front level with our political front'. In December 1926 Stalin formulated this strategy in the doctrine that the dictatorship of the proletariat had 'created the *political* base for the advance to socialism'; the possibility now existed of 'creating the *economic* base of socialism'.[4]

The aspects of socialism embodied in Engels' dicta were eroded under Lenin and vanished under Stalin. On the assumption that 'political' socialism had already been achieved, the economic tasks of the regime became paramount. They were always posed in the context that the international revolution had failed, and capitalism dominated everywhere but Soviet Russia.

Lenin had already insisted that the task of the Bolsheviks was not to bring about economic development in general but 'to catch up and surpass the capitalist countries economically'. In November 1928, on the eve of forced industrialisation, a plenary session of the Central Committee of the CPSU expanded this slogan by one significant word: the goal must be 'to catch up and surpass the capitalist countries both technically and economically'.[5]

The contentious issues were the methods and the speed by which the capitalist countries could be surpassed. The overwhelmingly predominant view among the Bolsheviks was that, even though some 80 per cent of the population were engaged in agriculture, economic progress must take place

2   F. Engels, *Herr Eugen Dühring's Revolution in Science (Anti-Dühring)* New York: International Publishers, 1939, 315, and *The Origin of the Family, Private Property and the State* London: Lawrence and Wishart, 1940, 198.
3   See E. H. Carr, *The Bolshevik Revolution, 1917–1923*, vol. 2, London: Macmillan, 1952, 363.
4   I. V. Stalin, *Sochineniya*, vol. ix, Moscow: Gosizdat, 1948), 22–4 (address to the executive committee of the Communist International).
5   *KPSS v rezolyutsiakh*, vol. ii, Moscow, 1954, 526.

though the development of industry itself.[6] Moreover, in the context of the dangerous world capitalist environment, the Soviet economy must be liberated from dependence on capitalist countries – it must become broadly 'self-sufficient'. As early as December 1925, the XIV party congress declared that the Soviet Union must be transformed 'from a country which imports machinery and equipment into a country which produces machinery and equipment'.[7]

These general decisions were closely connected with the debates in the 1920s on the nature of planning. How far should it be 'genetic', based on forecasting or prognosis, and how far should it be purposive or 'teleological', based on programming the future in terms of specific goals. Even the strongest advocates of the importance of forecasting accepted that successful forecasting would make it possible for the state to pose certain goals.[8] Even enthusiastic advocates of purposive planning, such as the Gosplan economist Strumilin, recognised that the goals must be realistic. Strumilin commented acidly about the extreme advocates of purposive planning that an approach based on the acceptable rather than the feasible would result in a planned iron output four times the volume of the earth.[9]

The crucial issue at the end of the 1920s was of course the speed of industrialisation. In 1921, the adoption of the New Economic Policy assumed that the peasants must not be coerced into delivering their products to the state, but must be offered prices and other incentives which would lead them to sell their products voluntarily. Bukharin, Rykov and other party leaders, together with the majority of the economic advisers to the Soviet government, assumed that this restriction must hold throughout industrialisation. Stalin, Kuibyshev and other party leaders, supported by a minority of their advisers – including Krzhizhanovsky and Strumilin, did not admit that the pace of industrialisation they proposed would undermine the market. But Stalin spoke of exacting a tribute from the peasants. (The word *dan'* was traditionally used for the Mongol tribute taken from Muscovy.) And he insisted that rapid industrialisation was of overwhelming importance. Speaking at the November 1928 plenum of the party central committee, he asked rhetorically:

6   The main exception was the People's Commissar for Finance Sokol'nikov, who argued that agricultural production and agricultural exports should be afforded priority, in order to pay for the import of machinery (G. Sokol'nikov, *Finansovaya politika revolyutsii*, vol. 3 (Moscow, 1928), 69–81.

7   *KPSS v rezolyutsiakh*, vol. ii, Moscow, 1954. This approach was resisted by the prominent non-party Gosplan economist Bazarov, who advocated the concentration of effort on industries in which mass production for sale at home and for export was immediately possible – see *O planirovanii razvitiya narodnogo khozyaistva SSSR*, Moscow, 1928, 75, and E. H. Carr and R. W. Davies. *Foundations of a Planned Economy, 1926–1929*, vol. 1 London: Macmillan, 1969, 788–9.

8   See for example L. N. Yurovskii, *Denezhnaya politika sovetskoi vlasti* Moscow, 1928, 372 ff. (Yurovskii was responsible until 1928 for currency planning).

9   *Planovoe khozyaistvo*, no. 3, 1930, 156.

Can we not manage without strain? Surely we could do the job at a slower rate, in a 'calmer' context? Is not the rapid rate of industrial expansion which we have adopted to be explained by the restless character of the members of the Politburo and Sovnarkom? Of course not. The people in the Politburo and Sovnarkom are sober and calm. ... But the point is that, first, it is wrong to reason independently of the environment abroad and at home, and secondly, if one thinks in terms of the environment in which we are placed, then it must be recognised that this environment compels us to adopt a rapid rate of growth for our industry.

It was urgent to 'catch up and surpass' the advanced countries of the capitalist world in which technology was 'simply rushing ahead'; 'either we achieve this, or they will destroy us'. This was a matter of 'life and death for our development'. It was essential for defence, and to provide the machinery to support the reconstruction of agriculture on a collective basis.[10]

By this time Soviet economic policy assumed that rapid industrialisation could and should embody the latest achievements of western technology. Modern technology, freed of the fetters of private ownership, would enable an unprecedented rate of progress. Even during the civil war Krzhizhanovsky cited the physicist Soddy to support his vision of the atomic age of the near future:

We are approaching the last frontier. Behind the chemical molecule and the atom, which were the primary foundations of the old chemistry, there are taking shape more and more clearly the ion and the electron, the fundamental substances of electricity; dazzling prospects are opening up in connection with radioactive materials. Chemistry is becoming a branch of the general science of electricity. Electrical engineering is leading us to the internal store of energy in atoms. A completely new civilisation is dawning.[11]

Krzhizhanovsky saw these developments as the foundation for the victory of socialism:

The proletariat will closely integrate itself with the prerequisites of the twentieth century's immense potentials for technical progress; it will actively make use of the powerful prospects of the new energy techniques of the world, and in this way it will be able to accomplish its mission.[12]

10 I. V. Stalin, *Sochineniya*, vol. xi, Moscow: Gosizdat, 1949, 246–8, 252–3.
11 G. M. Krzhizhanovskii, *Izbrannoe* Moscow: Gosizdat, 1957, 39. Towards the end of the end of the first five-year plan, Krzhizhanovsky was overruled in a dispute about the relative importance which should be attached to investment in electric power and in the machine-building industry (see R. W. Davies, *Crisis and Progress in the Soviet Economy, 1931–1933*, Basingstoke and London: Macmillan, 1996, 136–7)
12 G. M. Krzhizhanovskii, *Sochineniya*, vol. 2, *Problemy planirovaniya* Moscow, 1934, 33 (memorandum dated April 1921 responding to the less optimistic view of Groman, a non-party (ex-Menshevik) economist in Gosplan).

There was no agreement, however, on the optimum path for introducing advanced technology into the semi-developed economy of the late 1920s. An economist working in Vesenkha, the commissariat for industry, summed up the two main approaches:

> There are two approaches to capital construction. In the conservative English approach, improvements are introduced with difficulty, extra buildings are added to every existing factory, and individual shops are re-equipped; in one enterprise, you can trace the whole history of industrial progress. The other approach is the American one: a new factory is really built from scratch, in a new place without harmful traditions; the old works carries on as long as it can make a profit, and is then scrapped.[13]

The economic case for the less radical approach was strong. The small size of the industrial economy, the scarcity of capital and the abundance of labour meant that capital should be used sparingly. The advocates of the more radical approach argued, however, that modern technology was so productive that if introduced in sufficient quantities it would sweep aside the limitations imposed by the peasant environment and the market:

> We have in front of us [a supporter of this approach wrote in 1926] a process like that by which a young capitalist nation, in undertaking the mechanisation of its production, borrows machines, appliances and productive methods which are the last word in capitalist practice from the arsenal of its capitalist neighbours, and does not go through the preliminary stages of mechanisation.[14]

Aleksandrov, the designer of the Dnepr dam hydro-electric project, insisted that American mechanisation could not be transferred in part: '*it is necessary that at a given enterprise everything from beginning to end should be mechanised*'. The first major schemes would serve as an attractive force, 'an example proving the possibility of adopting American technology in our conditions'.[15]

At first even those party leaders who supported industrialisation were uncertain about the extent to which investment should be concentrated on large American-type factories. The shift of view towards the more radical approach was dramatically symbolised in 1926 when Stalin changed his assessment of the Dnepr project. In April he sceptically compared it with a peasant buying a gramophone instead of repairing his plough.[16] By the end of the year the project had been endorsed by the Soviet government on the initiative of Kuibyshev, Stalin's close ally.[17]

---

13 *Predpriyatie*, no. 6, 1928, 19 (M. I. Birbraer).
14 *Planovoe khozyaistvo*, no. 2, 1926, 15.
15 See Carr and Davies (1969), 907–8.
16 See E. H. Carr, *Socialism in One Country, 1924–1926*, vol. 1, London: Macmillan, 1958, 355, 535. A political factor in Stalin's hostility was the close association of Trotsky with the early stages of the Dnepr project.
17 See Carr and Davies (1969), 903–7.

In the course of the preparation and revision of the first five-year plan this strategy was gradually put into effect. Iron and steel provides a characteristic example of a high-priority industry in which there was an increasing effort to switch to the most advanced technology. When the five-year plan was prepared at the end of 1928, only 1.3 million of the proposed increase in production of 5.7 million tons in the basic draft of the plan was planned to come from new (what are nowadays called 'greenfield') works. But the revised plan prepared by the end of the year proposed an increase in production during the plan of as much as 13.1 million tons – and nearly half of this (6.1 million tons) was to come from new works.[18]

In enlarging the capacity which was to come from new works, the Soviet authorities (and the US corporation providing them with technical assistance) increased the planned size of the plants, and of their individual units, so that it equalled or even exceeded that of the most advanced North American models.[19] The cast of mind among leading Politburo members was dramatically indicated in a speech by Ordzhonikidze:

> Cde. Stalin asked about the capacity of factories in America, and the reply was that large factories in America gave 2½ million tons of pig iron a year. Cde. Stalin said that we must build such a factory here, in the first place for 2–2½ million tons, and then for 4 million tons.[20]

To enable these developments the design of the major plants in the key industries was concentrated in large project institutes responsible for inculcating new technology throughout their industry. The director of the institute for designing iron and steel plants claimed that his institute was 'resolving the extremely complicated task of inculcating into our industry the most novel methods of production on the basis of the achievements of Europe and America'.[21] The Soviet authorities, unlike the Chinese Communists at an equivalent stage of their development, unambiguously took the view that the most advanced American technology must be borrowed with the assistance of the best American engineers, and overruled objections from Russian engineers with the assistance of the OGPU.

The iron and steel industry was already well established in Russia before 1917. Other major industries – such as the tractor and tank industries, which were closely associated – were almost starting from scratch. Here the case for copying the most advanced American plants was accepted by the political authorities with even greater alacrity. The Stalingrad tractor factory, planned in 1927 as a fairly small-scale affair, was constructed with a capacity equal

18 See R. W. Davies, *The Soviet Economy in Turmoil, 1929–1930,* London: Macmillan, 1989, 199.

19 See M. G. Clark, *The Economics of Soviet Steel*, Cambridge, Mass.: Harvard University Press, 1956, 64, 321–2.

20 G. Ordzhonikidze, *Stat'i i rechi*, vol. 2, Moscow: Gosizdat, 1957, 481 (speech of July 1933).

21 *Byulleten' Gipromeza*, no. 7–8, 1929, 87.

to that of the equivalent International Harvester factory in Milwaukee.[22] Stalin, in a message to the factory on its completion, thanked 'our teachers in technology, the American specialists and technicians'.[23]

It was recognised, however, that this far-reaching scheme could not be applied universally. In engineering, the five-year plan acknowledged that the industry would remain 'to a considerable extent at only the initial change of development'.[24] In the infant machine-tool industry, 'only the most *popular* machines' would be manufactured, and more complex special machine tools would be produced only in small quantities in order to gain experience.[25]

In the course of the 1930s, important parts of Soviet industry underwent an unprecedented rapid technological transformation. No systematic study of this transformation has been undertaken either in the Soviet Union or in the West. The developments in certain major industries were aptly summed up in the popular Soviet saying that the growth of industry was like the sewing of a coat on to a button rather than a button on to a coat. By 1941 the Soviet Union produced tanks and aircraft, and tractors and combine harvesters, the best of which were equal in performance to the most advanced Western models. And industries already established before the revolution underwent revolutionary changes in their type of production. In 1928 less than 3 per cent of steel production was in the form of 'quality steel'; by 1940 the proportion had reached 25 per cent, and during the war it increased to almost two thirds.[26] Even more significant: in the early 1930s, the Soviet Union depended largely on imports for the equipment for its iron and steel plants and its power stations, and for the machine tools which equipped its engineering and armaments' factories.[27] But in the later 1930s most of such equipment was manufactured in the USSR. By the eve of the war, the machine-tool industry was able to produce many automatic and semi-automatic machine tools, and other complex models.[28] Similar developments took place in some consumer goods' industries, notably in meat processing and bread baking.[29]

This impressive technological advance is, however, only part of the story. Other consumer industries continued to use manufacturing processes which had hardly changed since the 1920s. Even when large-scale production was introduced the models were not updated. As late as 1956 the standard new

---

22 See N. T. Dodge, 'Trends in Labor Productivity in the Soviet Tractor Industry: A Case Study in Industrial Development', unpublished PhD thesis, Harvard University, 1960, 355.

23 *Pravda*, June 18, 1930. This phrase was omitted when Stalin's collected works were published in the very different atmosphere of 1949 (*Sochineniya*, vol. 12, 234).

24 *Pyatiletnii plan narodno-khozyaistvennogo stroitel'stva SSSR*, Moscow: Planovoe khozyaistvo, 1930, vol. 1, 47–9, vol. 2, part i, 156.

25 See J. M. Cooper, 'The Development of the Soviet Machine-Tool Industry, 1917–41', unpublished Ph. D. thesis, University of Birmingham, 1975, chapter 3.

26 See Clark, 1956, 21.

27 For example, between January 1, 1931, and April 1, 1932, 81 per cent of additional machine-tool horse power was obtained from imports (see Davies, 1996, 495).

28 Cooper, 1975, 332.

29 See Davies, 1996, 480–81.

Soviet bicycle included features (such as the application of the brake to the outside of the tyre!) which had been abandoned in Britain after the first world war. Soviet attention was concentrated throughout on certain priority industries and products.

In the priority industries the intention of introducing factories which were the same or better than the most advanced American equivalents was soon drastically modified. The experience of constructing the Stalingrad tractor factory in 1930 immediately showed that the weakness of the industrial infra-structure in the Soviet Union meant that the factory could not obtain essential supplies. Stalin's message of congratulations in June 1930 was decidedly premature. The builders of the Khar'kov tractor factory, which produced the same tractors on the same scale as the Stalingrad factory, took this experience into account, and adapted the factory to Russian conditions, for instance by establishing in-house facilities for the production of parts which were not easily obtainable from elsewhere in Soviet industry.[30]

More generally, in all industries the variant of American or European technology adopted in the Soviet Union in practice used far more labour per unit of capital than in their Western equivalent. Capital rather than unskilled labour was the scarce factor of production; and Soviet planners and engineers compromised by using more labour per unit of capital, particularly on aux-iliary processes. On the iron and steel industry, Gardner Clark commented:

> One would expect the Soviets to devote their primary energies to maximizing the productivity of capital, not labour, and this is exactly what they have done. The productivity of Soviet blast furnaces and open-hearth furnaces is higher than our own, but the productivity of these same furnaces per worker is much less.[31]

It should be added, however, that this adaptation to Soviet economic condi-tions, though rational and inevitable, was not an optimum one: it was not planned, but took place pragmatically, especially in the early years.

In the armaments' industries, and in the major 'modernised' civilian in-dustries, technical innovation was imposed by induced competition from the West. The Soviet authorities ensured that 'catching up the capitalist countries technologically' was kept in the forefront of the minds of Soviet planners and engineers. In the defence sector the general level of Soviet technical competence was systematically measured by the planners. Thus in May 1937 Gosplan prepared an elaborate comparison of Soviet technical equipment per 1,000 soldiers with six major capitalist countries, using indicators such as the number of bullets which could be fired per minute, the availability of lorries, tractors and horses, and the number of tanks and artillery pieces of different types.[32] The central authorities continuously confronted the priority

30 See Dodge, 1960; Dodge's material is conveniently summarised in D. Granick, *Soviet Metal-Fabricating and Economic Development: Practice versus Policy,* Madison, Milwaukee and London: University of Wisconsin Press, 1967, 117–9.
31 Clark, 1956, 247.
32 The countries were France, Germany, Poland, Great Britain, United States and Japan:

industries with the necessity of reaching Western technical levels. The latest Western military aircraft and tanks, for example, were purchased whenever possible, and then dissected in detail.

For example, in 1934, when the Soviet Union was offered a loan by Germany for the purchase of German goods, the Politburo decided that 'orders should be placed mainly for chemical equipment, and for aviation and the needs of defence'.[33] In 1935 a commission headed by the aircraft designer Tupolev visited the USA, placed orders for military equipment, and proposed further orders which were immediately approved by the Council of Labour and Defence.[34] In the following year the Defence Commission resolved to construct a new type of American aircraft at factory no. 1, and for this purpose 'immediately send to America from factory no. 1 a further 20 engineers...and designers to speed up the receipt of technical assistance and materials, and to study production'.[35] In 1940 the fighter aircraft designer Yakovlev paid an extensive visit to German aircraft factories and arranged the purchase of their most advanced aircraft.[36]

Thus the centralised system on the whole successfully introduced advanced technologies from above in the high-priority sectors or products which were under close control and support from the political authorities in Moscow. Even in the second half of the 1930s and on the eve of the Second World War a technological gap remained between the Soviet Union and the advanced industrial countries even in high-priority industries. The system of inculcating advanced technology from above remained appropriate (with the important qualification, however, that miscalculations at the centre also tended to be reproduced throughout the industry concerned.[37])

Behind the scenes, and occasionally in public, the technological gap was frankly acknowledged. Thus in 1937, at a conference discussing the expansion of the Chelyabinsk tractor factory (ChTZ), a top-priority factory intended for wartime conversion to the production of tanks, the senior industrial administrator A. D. Bruskin frankly stated:

> I think it is necessary to copy the [United States] Caterpillar tractor...
> In relation to the design of the diesel engine, it must be designed, but I must say that at ChTZ we had several difficulties when we departed from Caterpillar principles. We thought we were cleverer in diesel production,

RGAE: 4372/91/3217, 131–128, dated May 22, 1937.

33 RGASPI, 17/162/17, 88–89 – art. 97, dated December 5. See also *Stalin i Kaganovich: perepiska, 1931–1936*, ed. O. Khlevnyuk et al. Moscow: Rosspen, 2001, 471, where Stalin insists that all German factories should be accessible to the Soviet purchasing commission (cipher dated September 3, 1934).

34 GARF, 8418/28/7, 85–86 (art. s-109ss dated August 25, 1935).

35 GARF, 8428/28/10, 200–203 (STO decree dated December 28, 1936 – art. OK 245ss).

36 A. Yakovlev, *Tsel' zhizni* Moscow: Izd-vo politicheskoĭ lit-ry, 1967, 217–26, 236.

37 For examples, see R. W. Davies, M. Harrison and S. G. Wheatcroft (eds) *The Economic Transformation of the Soviet Union, 1913–1945*, Cambridge: Cambbridge University Press, 1994, 146–7.

but we are taking only the first steps in this production – we are pupils, and we don't understand much about it, so we must learn from Caterpillar.[38]

The Soviet Union remained dependent on the West for much of the most sophisticated production. For example: in spite of the progress of the machine-tool industry, desperate efforts were made to produce all machine tools in the USSR. In 1936, following a visit to the United States by Alperovich, the head of the industry, the People's Commissar for Foreign Trade proposed a comprehensive programme to this end based on Alperovich's findings.[39] But the Soviet Union continued to import more complex machine tools throughout the 1930s.[40]

Soviet designers and Soviet industry did not, however, confine themselves to merely copying the most advanced Western products. During the 1930s they also developed the art of adapting Western models to Soviet conditions and improving their performance. For example, the best Soviet pre-war tank, the T-34, was manufactured to a simple design suitable for mass production using semi-skilled labour.[41] It was also substantially improved in its design and its battle capability as compared with the BT (Christie) series of tanks on which it was originally based.[42] In high-priority industries, the Soviet designers proved capable of innovative engineering thought. In these industries, centralised research and project institutes were combined with the establishment of development facilities at major factories, and innovation was encouraged by competition between design bureaux and the provision of strong material incentives.[43]

However, in the rest of the economy, which was not subject to pressure to innovate from the central authorities, already in the 1930s the system inhibited the development of new types of production and new technological processes by factories and enterprises, and by scientists and engineers as individuals and in groups. Even in the case of lorries, which were near the top in the priority list but rarely discussed by the Politburo, the main lorry produced at the automobile works in Gor'kii (Nizhnii Novgorod) was out

---

38   RGAE, 7622/1/1369, 29–30 (dated April 19, 1937). Bruskin was director of ChTZ from 1933–6, and was appointed a deputy people's commissar of heavy industry on August 7, 1936.

39   See Rozengol'ts' memorandum dated June 30, 1936, and Ordzhonikidze's reply: GARF, 5446/16/86, 7–1.

40   See *Vneshnyaya torgovlya SSSR za 1918–1940gg.: statisticheskii obzor,* Moscow: Vneshtorgizdat, 1960, 344, 368, 398 and Cooper, 1975, Appendix Tables XVIII and XIX. The numbers imported underestimated the importance of imports, because the imported machines tended to be more complicated and expensive.

41   See D. Holloway in R. Amann, J. M. Cooper and R. W. Davies (eds), *The Technological Level of Soviet Industry,* New Haven and London: Yale University Press, 1977, 420, and in R. Amann and J. M. Cooper (eds) *Industrial Innovation in the Soviet Union,* New Haven and London: Yale University Press, 1982, 384.

42   For the major features introduced by Soviet designers, see Holloway, 1977, 420.

43   See the account of the aircraft industry in R. Lewis, *Science and Industrialisation in the USSR,* London and Basingstoke: Macmillan, 1979, 132–142.

of date as compared with relevant Western models as early as 1936.[44] In a famous example, Academician Kapitsa – one of the most influential Soviet scientists – described how he was unable to secure the satisfactory development of his process for producing liquid oxygen at a factory before the war in spite of the support of the economic council, because the time and effort required interfered with the basic plan of the factory.[45]

The inhibitions on innovation and the diffusion of new technology in the Soviet system are the subject of a vast literature.[46] Throughout the inter-war years, attempts were made to overcome these inhibitions. Laboratories and design bureaux were established at factories. To encourage closer links between research and the needs of industry, contracts were introduced between industrial customers and suppliers of research. Bonuses to encourage innovation were introduced both in research institutes and for the factories. But all these measures had a very limited effect.[47] The pressure to carry out the central production plans was overwhelming.

The disincentives for innovation were amplified by several political factors. First, the growing dual threat from Nazi Germany and Japan, which led highly-trained personnel and physical resources to be increasingly concentrated on the armaments' industries. Other sectors of the economy were deprived of resources. Secondly, the repressions, and particularly the Yezhovshchina of 1937–8. In these two years a very high proportion of the senior staffs of the economic commissariats, and of the major enterprises, were arrested and executed.[48] The purges also seriously damaged the project institutes and design bureaux responsible for new products and processes. Some major lines of development – for instance, radar – were halted for some years. Others were continued under prison conditions by those members of staff who had not been executed or exiled to remote regions (for example, Tupolev's famous aircraft design bureau).

The Yezhovshchina also had a longer-term effect which it is impossible to quantify. It resulted in the prevalence of a conservative culture of avoiding risk in the bureaucratic elite. From the Politburo downwards all officials understood that they were exercising a degree of autonomy only within very narrow limits, and that it would be dangerous for their careers to step outside them.

Thirdly, these limits were reinforced by censorship, and by the regime of secrecy. The range of issues which were treated as secret was far wider than in other industrialised countries. The principle of 'need to know' meant that scientists and engineers were unable to obtain information about activities

---

44 See G. D. Holliday, *Technology Transfer in the USSR, 1928–1937 and 1966–1975* Boulder, Col.: Westview, 1989, 122, 130–2.

45 P. L. Kapitsa, *Teoriya, eksperiment, praktika*, Moscow: Izd-vo znanie, 1968, 42–4.

46 See, for example, E. Zaleski et al., *Science Policy in the USSR*, Paris: OECD, 1969, and J. S. Berliner, *The Innovation Decision in Soviet Industry,* Cambridge, Mass., and London: MIT Press, 1976.

47 See Lewis, 1979, 91–4, 114–132.

48 See chapter by Oleg Khlevnyuk in M. Ilič, ed. *Stalin's Terror Revisited,* Basingstoke: Palgrave, 2006.

in fields quite closely related to their own. As a result of the restrictions on travel and communication scientists and technologists were ill-informed about foreign innovations in their field, and particularly in neighbouring fields. The establishment of an elaborate intelligence network overcame these difficulties only for a small number of people in a limited number of fields.

After the Second World War, the defects of the innovation system emerged more strongly with the increasing size and complexity of the economy. Military research and development continued to be the favoured child of the regime. The culture of avoiding risk, and the regime of secrecy, largely remained in force, even though the worst features were removed after the death of Stalin. Between 1955 and 1990 heroic efforts were made to combine central planning and strong incentives to innovate, but were fundamentally a failure.

****

So far this chapter has discussed only the technological aspects of the Bolshevik drive for economic and social progress. But great importance was also attached to the development of 'labour skills' – education – an inherent part of all concepts of modernisation. In the world at large, the social infrastructure grew more rapidly in twentieth-century industrialisations than in their classic predecessors. But the expansion of education was particularly rapid in the Soviet Union.[49] It is not generally realised that the drive for mass and higher education had the result that the number employed in the education services expanded more rapidly than the number employed in industry between 1928 and 1940. Between the 1927/28 and 1940/41 school years the number of children at school increased from 12 to 35 million. The Bolsheviks certainly did not start from scratch. In 1927/28 most children, including those in rural areas, were already attending school for four years. But only a small proportion remained at school above the age of ten, and the number attending school above the age of fourteen was minute. By 1940/41 two-thirds of all children attended school from eleven to fourteen – nearly all the urban children, and about half the rural children. And about one-third of urban children attended school to the age of seventeen.

Higher education also expanded rapidly, from a low initial level. The total number of specialists with higher education quadrupled between 1928 and 1940, increasing more rapidly than the non-agricultural labour force as a whole. This provided the basis for the huge expansion in higher education after the Second World War.

In important respects, however, the quality of education deteriorated. In higher education, a broader technical education gave way to narrow specialisation, and the humanities were confined in a strait jacket of conformity. Education in schools and universities became much more formal. Neverthe-

49 For the sources of the information in the following paragraphs see *Economic Transformation*, 1994, 339, notes 12–14.

less, this was an educational revolution. It provided the preconditions for *perestroika* and may prove to have been the most enduring positive consequence of Soviet industrialisation.

MARK B. TAUGER

Modernisation in Soviet Agriculture

Introduction

This chapter reviews some of the literature and some of the important aspects of Soviet agricultural history from the perspective of evaluating whether or not Soviet agriculture was "modern". The use of this term inherently and explicitly implies a comparison between the agricultural system and conditions in the USSR and those in an unambiguously "modern" country. Soviet leaders were quite conscious of this comparison and undertook to transform Soviet agriculture mostly on the model of agriculture in the United States, which in the early 20th century was very self-consciously the most modern agricultural system in the world.

On the basis of these considerations, I seek in this chapter first of all to make these comparisons explicit, and second to propose a number of alternative perspectives on some well-known features of Soviet agricultural history usually seen as signs of its backwardness or limited modernisation. The chapter begins with certain points in the historiography, and then addresses historical issues chronologically. I do not seek to be exhaustive but to discuss unquestionably important points.

Historiography

The proposition that Soviet agriculture underwent a process that could be described as modernisation would be controversial in many perspectives. Much of the recent historical literature, for example, is skeptical of and often rejects any possibility of "modernisation" in the genuine intentions of Soviet leaders and the planning or realization in Soviet agriculture. The best that the Soviet regime could do was to leave peasants alone, which is what these scholars consider that the regime did during NEP; the worst was the attempt to remodel agriculture to the needs of Soviet industry and armaments through collectivisation from 1930 onward.

We can categorize some of the main arguments in these "non-modernising" interpretations as follows. The most common and important of these arguments in historical scholarship is the claim that collectivisation represented not modernisation but a turn backwards to a type of serfdom. A leading historian openly accepts, for example, the comparison frequently made by peasants between collectivisation and serfdom, and even attempts to support the analogy point by point. Among other points, this author compares work in the kolkhoz to *barshchina* (the obligation that Russian landlords imposed on serfs to perform forced labor on landlords' farmland during the period of Russian serfdom), the passport system introduced in the 1930s to serfdom's constraint on peasant movement, and peasants' behavior in the kolkhozy – resistance, deception, and a "dependent psychology" – to their presumed attitudes under serfdom.[1] Another leading scholar derives a similar backward-looking view of the collective farm system from the survival of the private plot and the "absolute priority and superiority of the interests of the state over the interests of the producers" to argue again for parallels between collectivisation and serfdom. This author agrees with certain other Western scholars that the kolkhoz became "a system of forced labor". He argues that peasants distinguished between work for their families and work "for them" in the same way that serfs distinguished between labor for the landlord and labor on their own allotments, and he emphasises the backwardness of rural life in the 1930s and for many years afterwards: inadequate roads, no guaranteed income but only the "residual principle" imposed by the laborday system, no social security, and heavy taxation.[2]

The main points in the interpretation of collectivisation as serfdom, then, are:

1. The passport system as a constraint on peasant mobility represented a recreation of the peasants' confinement to the estate under serfdom.

2. Peasant labor in the kolkhoz system recreated peasants' forced labor (*barshchina*) on serf estates because the kolkhoz system represented a type of forced labor, which peasants distinguished from their work on their own allotments, the "private plot", and to which the government, as the ultimate manager of the farms, ascribed priority.

3. Peasant life in the kolkhoz was like serfdom because the countryside suffered from lack of investment, peasants received little pay, faced high prices for items they purchased and heavy taxation, had no safety net, and developed dependent attitudes.

Many writings by social scientists and others about the Khrushchev and Brezhnev years also argue that Soviet agriculture continued to retain backward characteristics, never realized the optimistic plans that the regime set for it, absorbed vast investments yet produced little improvement, and became dependent on growing and ultimately enormous subsidies. At the same time, some of these writings deplore the "disappearing villages" of the Soviet countryside and the depeasantisation of the country, which in the view of

1   Sheila Fitzpatrick, *Stalin's Peasants*, Oxford and New York: Oxford University Press, 1994, 129.
2   Moshe Lewin, "The Kolkhoz and the Russian Muzhik", in Lewin, *The Making of the Soviet System*, New York: Pantheon, 1985, 184–86.

for example the writers of the "village school" or of Ukrainian nationalists represents the destruction of established traditions of personal commitment to the land that underlay the presumed higher productivity and marketability of Russian agriculture before the revolution.[3]

This argument against Soviet agricultural modernisation thus rests on two points:

4. The Soviet agricultural system was inefficient and relatively underproductive, and these problems resulted not only from the agricultural system itself but also from its involvement in a socialist planned economy. This argument holds that the relatively higher productivity of the private plot economy indicated the fundamental problem with the socialist sector.

5. The Soviet agricultural system destroyed the established structures and relations of agriculture that were progressive in the past, and was insufficiently responsive to and considerate of the attitudes and needs of its people and the environmental needs of the land.

While all of these arguments against the claim that Soviet agriculture was modern or modern enough make some valid points, in general they are flawed because they derive from one or both of two problematic approaches. Either they assume a kind of idealised version of modern agriculture that does not correspond to reality, or they generalize about the Soviet system from evidence and examples that cannot be taken as representative and that misrepresent the character of Soviet agriculture and its conditions of operation. The following section discusses each of these categories.

1. The comparison between the passport system and serfdom misunderstands the Soviet passport system. One of the basic defining characteristics of Russian serfdom was the right that the lord had to reclaim peasants who left his estate. The stipulation allowing this without any constraint in the 1649 Ulozhenie is accepted as one of the defining documents of serfdom.[4] The object of the system, in other words, was to keep the peasant on the land. The object of the passport system imposed in 1933–1934, by contrast, was to regulate the movement of peasants out of the villages and into the cities. To achieve this goal, the passport system that the Soviet government introduced in 1933–1934 allotted passports only to legitimate urban residents; peasants could obtain passports legally only from certain rural officials or through the intervention of urban agencies such as factories or military units when these agencies wanted to retain the individual in the town. The author who wrote that the passport system made the kolkhoz like serfdom also argued and presented evidence that the passport system constrained peasant movement relatively little, and that the regime want-

3   For example, L. H. Denisova, *Ischezaiushchaia derevnia Rossii: Nechernozem'e v 1960–1980-e gody*, Moscow: IRI RAN, 1996; Alec Nove, Economic History of the Soviet Union, New York 1992.

4   See for example Jerome Blum, *Lord and Peasant in Russia from the Ninth to the Nineteenth Century*, New York: Atheneum, 1969, ch. 14, and the documents in R. E. F. Smith, *The Enserfment of the Russian Peasantry*, London: Cambridge University Press, 1968.

ed peasants to move out of the farms under the passport regime, just in a controlled manner.[5]

During the decades after the imposition of the passport system, the Soviet regime oversaw massive movements of millions of peasants off the farms, into the army, cities, and industry, and the passport system never served as a serious obstacle to this movement. In fact, the passport system unexpectedly encouraged movement out of the villages. Young people became eligible for passports at the age of 16, and many rural adolescents would leave villages for towns at that age in order to qualify for a passport in order to be able to leave their villages. As a result, the government recognised a pattern of de-population of villages, and finally introduced passports for peasants in 1976 to stop this. One of the results of this extension of the passport system was in fact to reduce slightly the continuing outflow of people from the villages.[6]

2. Some documentary sources have peasants comparing work in the kolkhoz to *barshchina*, apparently because they thought that they would not be paid for it. It is clear, however, that peasants did receive payment in kind and money for their work in the kolkhoz. These payments varied from place to place and year to year. Kolkhozniki earned more, sometimes much more, on farms with good harvests or better management than on farms with poorer harvests or worse management. Any kind of evaluation of this has to be based on more evidence than isolated complaints from disgruntled peasants recorded in OGPU reports in 1932 and 1933, the worst years of the system, because OGPU reports are simply not valid representative samples of popular attitudes.[7]

The comparison between the private plot and the kolkhoz fields is extreme-ly problematic and misleading. First, the items that peasants produced on the private plots, usually vegetables and livestock products, were much more suited to such small-scale production than the crops grown on the kolkhoz fields. This difference was recognized in the early stages of collectivisation and the kolkhoz system was designed to accommodate both types of pro-duction. Second, the same distinction between high yielding small plots and lower yielding large farms can be found in any agricultural system, at least up to the time of genetically-modified crops. For example, in 1951 a study was conducted in Britain of 600 private gardens in London suburbs, which found that the financial output of food per unit of area from the average garden plot was close to that for the best farmland and significantly higher

5   Fitzpatrick, *Stalin's Peasants*, 96.
6   Zhores Medvedev, *Soviet Agriculture*, New York: Norton, 1987, 323. On peasant movement out of the villages, see among many other sources, A. A. Nikonov, *Sprial' mnogovekovoi dramy: agrarnaia nauka i politika Rossii (XVII–XX vv.)*, Moscow: Entsiklopediia rossiiskikh dereven', 1995, 280–281.
7   For examples of the use such sources, see Fitzpatrick, *Stalin's Peasants*, and Lynn Viola, *Peasant Rebels Under Stalin*, New York: Oxford University Press, 1996. On the limitations of the OGPU reports, see M. B. Tauger, "Soviet Peasants and Collectivisation, 1930–1939: Resistance and Adaptation", *Journal of Peasant Studies*, vol. 31, no. 3–4, April–July 2004, 427–456, reprinted in Stephen Wegren, ed., *Rural Adaptation in Russia*, London: Routledge, 2005.

than the average for all farmland in Britain. The study found that the average output of these plots, of 250 square meters, was sufficient to provide all the protein needs and one-third of the energy needs of the average Briton, albeit on a vegetarian diet.[8] A similar study in the 1970s in the United Kingdom found that the home/garden allotment was the most energy efficient of all methods of growing and supplying food. Numerous studies conducted in many countries have consistently shown that small farms have higher yields than large farms.[9]

The higher land productivity of the private plot compared to the kolkhoz grain fields, thus, is no more a criticism of Soviet agriculture than it is of any other modern large scale farming system. To attack Soviet collective farms by saying that the private plots were more productive is a purely political attack against "socialism" and does not hold up because the same attack can be made and has been made by comparing small garden plots and the relatively lower yields of large "capitalist" farms.[10] The issue is one of crops and labor distribution: large farms may not have as high yields, but they can be farmed with many fewer people and still produce vast amounts of grain or other crops, freeing the rest of the population for other activities, and this is what happened in the U.S., Europe, and the USSR.

3. The argument that rural areas and kolkhoz peasants were not modern because they received the short end of the stick in investments and pay again reflects an unrealistic image of modern agriculture. One observer of world agriculture wrote that "cheap food means poor farmers", explaining that farmers the world over are poorer than their urban counterparts. He demonstrated these points both in terms of markets – competition among farmers producing surpluses will drive prices down – and in terms of urban needs for low prices and a secure supply.[11] Lipton generalised this argument to a theory of "urban bias", according to which an entire complex of ideologies, policies, and practices in developing countries, and even advanced countries, conspire to keep farmers and rural people poor.[12] It is of course true that infrastructure development proceeded significantly faster in the U.S. than in the USSR, but this distinction has to be seen in perspective: rural areas were "behind" urban areas in these respects in both countries. As regards income, in com-

8   Colin Tudge, *The Famine Business*, London, 1977, 5–6, citing Gerald Leach, *Energy and Food Production*, Guildford: IPC Science and Technology Press, 1976.

9   Agricultural specialists and economists have published a vast literature on the complex relationships between farm size and productivity; one place to start is David Grigg, *The Harsh Lands*, London: MacMillan, 1970, 133–139. A case study of a pattern similar to the Soviet one is Graham Dyer, *Class, State, and Agricultural productivity in Egypt: A Study of the Inverse Relationship between Farm Size and Land Productivity*, London: Frank Cass, 1997.

10 See for example Eric T. Freyfogle, *The New Agrarianism: Land. Culture, and the Community of Life*, Washington, D.C.: Island Press, 2001.

11 Sir Joseph Hutchinson, *Farming and Food Supply*, Cambridge: Cambridge University Press, 1972, 135.

12 Michael Lipton, *Why Poor People Stay Poor: Urban Bias in World Development*, Cambridge: Harvard University Press, 1977.

paring Soviet and U.S. farmers we have to distinguish in the U.S. between the incomes earned by "farm operators" and those earned by farm laborers, whose work was often more comparable to the work many kolkhozniki did. While many kolkhozniki did not have the incomes that many U.S. farmers had, particularly in the post-World War II period, those same kolkhozniki had conditions and incomes that were better, and sometimes much better, than those of the millions of farm laborers who actually produced most of certain crops in the U.S.[13]

The argument that collectivisation destroyed initiative and made the farmers sullen, resentful, and in essence like servile peasants, is again problematic on several points. First of all, collective and state farms became highly mechanised, certainly by the 1960s if not before in many cases. As a result, relatively few people performed most of the farm work. This was already evident at the beginning of collectivisation, when in 1930 studies found that collective farms increased their area under crops yet needed only a fraction of their populations to do so.[14] Most of the rural population had little to do. Descriptions by outside observers (including security police officials) of "inertia", "lack of initiative", and peasants standing around doing nothing, were a reflection of this major technological change. Second, this argument again raises the issue of the degree to which particular sources are representative. The historical and memoir literatures, and archival sources, contain a number of descriptions of sullen peasants; they also contain different descriptions which scholars often do not cite because they would like to portray Soviet agriculture as plagued by resistance. Yet if the picture of sullen resistance was actually as representative as these scholars claim, it is difficult to conceive how the USSR existed after 1930, let alone that it could have endured the Nazi invasion and produced any of the good harvests that it actually did. We will examine this point in more detail below.

4. The criticism that the Soviet system did not show a sufficient response to agricultural investment assumes that agricultural production should increase production commensurately with the scale of investment. First of all, farmers around the world can demonstrate that large investments far from always result in large returns. In Britain, again, during 1900–1970 farms increased their use of nitrogen fertilisers by a factor of eight, and potassium

---

13 A large literature spanning decades documents the low wages, extremely poor living conditions, abusive treatment and political subordination endured by U.S. farm laborers. One such study is Truman Moore, *The Slaves We Rent*, New York: Random House, 1965.

14 An investigation in April 1930 found that kolkhozy in the North Caucasus would employ only 60 percent of their available labor, and those in the Urals only 50 percent; an extensive survey at the end of the year found labor utilization in kolkhozy in the Middle Volga, Central Blackearth oblast', and Ukraine even lower, from 25 to 31 percent; *Sots. zem.*, 2 April 1930, 3; 16 December 1930, 2. This low labor use in 1930 does not appear to have reduced farm work done. For example, a nearly-complete survey in mid-1930 in the Middle Volga found that sowings in kolkhozy increased more than six-fold over 1929, and included one-third of the region's sown area even though kolkhozy had only 22 percent of the region's households. RGAE 7486 .37 .49: Decree of the biuro of the Middle Volga kraikom, 21 Sept '30, ll. 138–47.

and phosphorus by a factor of thirty, but agricultural output increased only by a factor of two. Even this increase was misleading because it was based on a decreased crop area that resulted from mechanisation and decreased use of horses. Taking all farmland into account, the increase was only 50 percent.[15]

Second, many factors can delay returns to investment in agriculture. Crop yields can vary for many factors, some of which may not be recognised for some time after they occur. Canada, for example, has as modern an agricultural system as the U.S., uses the same equipment, has comparable soils, and has a free-market economy with subsidies like the U.S. Yet Canada's grain yields are significantly lower than U.S. yields, simply because Canada is located further north and has colder weather and a shorter growing season.[16] In other words, in these cases, comparable investments had significantly different returns.

5. Other types of agricultural modernisation have also had the same effect of destroying traditional rural social and economic relations and allegedly replacing the traditional concern for the land with purely economic values. This is one of the main themes in the history of U.S. agriculture, repeatedly noted during its modernisation in the 20th century. In the U.S., the increasing introduction of large-scale, mechanised modern farms even in the 1920s, with their decreased need for rural labor, early on had the effect of decreasing rural populations, closing schools and shops. Towns began to disappear.[17] This situation has worsened dramatically in the U.S. concurrently with and because of the intensive modernisation of U.S. farming. Despite decades of immense farm subsidies, rural areas in the U.S. have much higher concentrations of poor people than urban areas, especially children. Rural residents earn on average only about two-thirds of urban incomes, and they lag behind in access to communications, transport, and other basic services. Certain parts of the U.S., the Southwest and the Appalachians, are in even worse condition in these respects.[18] Agricultural modernisation in developing countries has had even more serious effects.

One conclusion from this discussion would be that the criticisms leveled against Soviet agriculture derive from what appears to be either ignorance or a state of denial about agricultural modernisation elsewhere in the world. Agricultural development is a complex and multisided process, and like any such process inevitably has unanticipated and negative consequences; as one respected agricultural educator who helped implement the Green

---

15 Tudge, *Famine Business*, 5.

16 For example, Canada's grain yields in 1983–85 averaged 2.15 metric tons per hectare, while those of the U.S. averaged in the same period 4.28 tons per hectare. Their respective average yields in 1990–1992 were 2.5 and 4.88 tons. World Resources Institute et al., *World Resources 1987*, New York: Basic Books, 1987, 276, and *World Resources 1994–95*, New York: Oxford University Press, 1994, 292.

17 Deborah Fitzgerald, *Every Farm a Factory*, New Haven: Yale University Press, 2003, 123ff.

18 Joel Kotkin, "The Withering of Rural America", *Washington Post Weekly*, July 29–August 4, 2002.

Revolution in India in the 1960s liked to say: "Every time you solve one problem, you create two more."[19] To note a narrow and biased approach in the literature on Soviet agriculture is not to defend Soviet policies any more than such a comparison would be meant to rationalise the often similar problems in other agricultural systems. For example, the poverty and decline of rural areas in the U.S. and Russia are both serious issues that some in both countries have seen as "the price of progress" and others in both countries have seen as "the destruction of a way of life". The point is that the Soviet events were not the uniquely disastrous results of a uniquely irrational system, but rather a somewhat distorted version of patterns of agricultural modernisation applied widely in the 20th-century world, with often similar deplorable effects. Descriptions of the Soviet case as so unique, without at least an acknowledgement that similar patterns occurred in other times and other places, inherently must misinterpret the Soviet case and must lead to unbalanced and unfair conclusions about it.

Another conclusion that could be drawn from these considerations is that scholars dealing with the Soviet case have to be careful about the sources they use and the conclusions they draw from them. The fact that the Soviet press and Soviet archival documents contain so many references to problems in agriculture (as in other aspects of the country's economy) does not mean that there were only problems. A number of scholars have written studies of Soviet peasants and resistance to collectivisation, using archival sources, and have created a picture of a uniformly resistant peasantry that lived only to avoid work. These depictions cannot explain, however, the incontrovertibly facts that those same peasants produced many large harvests both in the 1930s and afterwards, that agricultural production overall increased from the 1930s to the 1980s, and that Soviet food consumption improved significantly over the same period. Part of the problem here is that these scholars used sources in illegitimate ways: they assumed that the archival documents, especially OGPU reports, were actually representative of all or even most peasants, when any objective statistical approach to these sources would show immediately that they were not representative at all, and were recognized as such by Soviet officials and later scholars.[20] These scholars also lost their objectivity, identifying with the peasants sufficiently that they completely rejected all statements by Soviet officials from Stalin on down that could have led them to reconsider their sources and conclusions.

With these caveats in mind, the rest of this chapter examines certain aspects of modernisation in Soviet agriculture to suggest an alternative perspective.

19 Dr. Layle Lawrence, Davis College of Agriculture, West Virginia University, personal conversation.
20 On this see Tauger, "Soviet Peasants and Collectivisation".

The Problem: Backwardness and the Famines it caused

The main interpretation in most works on Soviet history and especially on Soviet agriculture is that Soviet leaders viewed agriculture and the peasants as a kind of resource to exploit. According to this interpretation, the Soviet leadership ultimately decided to carry out collectivisation because these leaders thought only that collectivisation would enable the government to extract more grain, taxes, and other assets from the peasantry.[21] This interpretation oversimplifies the motivations of Soviet leaders, overemphasising one important concern while ignoring many others. In particular, advocates of this perspective either minimise or completely omit the most important context of Soviet agricultural decision-making: the famines of the 1920s.

The Soviet regime came to power in part because of a famine in the towns, a crisis that Stalin described in 1917.[22] As this famine worsened during 1918–1920, the Bolsheviks, like their "White" opponents, requisitioned food from peasants to feed soldiers and townspeople.[23] The urban famine of the civil war merged into the even larger famine caused by two years of severe droughts in 1920–1921, for the relief of which the USSR obtained more than 718,000 tons of food from the American Relief Administration, and other substantial imports.[24] Soon after recovery began, another serious drought struck in 1924, and the regime again imported hundreds of thousands of tons of grain. The 1925 and 1926 harvests were better, but those of 1927–1929 were worse, leading to a famine in Ukraine in 1928–1929, for which the government organized relief, and to shortages and rationing in towns by 1929. This crisis again forced the regime to import food despite the needs of the Five-Year plan.[25]

21 See for example Lewin, "The Immediate Background of Soviet Collectivisation", in Lewin, *Making of the Soviet System*, 91–120; Robert Conquest, *Harvest of Sorrow*, Ch. 4–5; Fitzpatrick, *Stalin's Peasants*, 37ff; Viola, *Peasant Rebels*, ch.1. These are recent works; this interpretation can be found in many older publications.

22 I. V. Stalin, *Sochineniya vol.3* Moscow: Gosizdat 1946–51, 331–34. The food crisis in 1917 is well documented in the secondary literature on the Revolution, for example Lars Lih, *Bread and Authority in Russia, 1914–1921* Berkely, Stanford University Press, 1990.

23 The Bolshevik requisition policies are better known than the similar or harsher policies by the Whites; see Peter Kenez, *Civil War in South Russia, 1919–1920: the defeat of the Whites*. Berkeley: Published for the Hoover Institution on War, Revolution, and Peace: University of California Press 1977; and Jonathan Smele, *Civil war in Siberia: the anti-Bolshevik government of Admiral Kolchak, 1918–1920*. Cambridge: Cambridge University Press 1996.

24 Harold Fisher, *The famine in Soviet Russia, 1919–1923: the Operations of the American Relief Administration* New York: Macmillan 1927, 554; E.M. Khenkin, *Ocherki istorii bor'by sovetskogo gosudarstva s golodom: 1921–1922* Krasnoiarsk: Izd-vo Krasnoiarskogo universiteta 1988.

25 Mark B. Tauger, *Natural Disaster and Human Actions in the Soviet Famine of 1931–1933* Pittsburgh, Pennsylvania: Center for Russian and East European Studies, University of Pittsburgh 2001.

Soviet leaders interpreted these famines in ways that resemble present-day views.[26] They blamed the urban famines of 1914–21 on "speculators", traders and peasants withholding food in order to obtain a higher price, who thereby created famine without a shortage. They viewed famines that developed from crop failures, however, as results of the backwardness of traditional peasant agriculture. Aleksei Rykov, the then-head of the Soviet government, writing on the 1924 famine, described its causes as follows:

> The backwardness of peasant farming, its inadaptability to climate, and the lack of culture and poor organisational character of the peasant population are guilty first of all for the destruction of the harvest by drought. As a result of the unified efforts of Asiatic pomeshchik-tsarist despotism, which held the population in ignorance, and the arid Asiatic winds, the Republic of Soviets acquired in these regions a source of grandiose shocks of the entire state organism. And the first, and most important of what is necessary to achieve in organising the post-October government of the toilers, is – to make such shocks impossible.[27]

This viewpoint rested on certain assumptions shared by most Soviet leaders about modern agriculture, in particular that it can adapt to climate, and is "organized" and the product of "cultured" people. In describing their country's agriculture as backward, Rykov and other leaders were always conscious of how Soviet agriculture compared to farming in other more advanced countries. Hrihorii Petrovskii, for example, as head of government in Ukraine, wrote in1928 during the famine of that year that unlike French or American farmers, who fed their countries and exported, Soviet peasants could not even reliably feed themselves. And Soviet leaders connected improvement in Soviet agriculture with general industrial modernisation. Stalin pointed out in 1926 that Soviet agriculture could not grow without industrial development to provide necessary equipment.[28]

Behind this high-level official perspective on Soviet backwardness, however, lay a variety of proposals for improving peasant farming, and several disputes among agricultural specialists about these proposals. All agreed that Soviet agriculture needed to be improved and modernised in technology and methods, but they disagreed over how these changes could and should be

26   Their attribution of famines to speculators has much in common with Amartya Sen's concept of "exchange entitlements", in which increased prices make it impossible for poor people dependent on the market to purchase the food they need, A. Sen, *Poverty and famines: an essay on entitlement and deprivation.* Oxford: Clarendon Press 1981. For analyses that discuss crop failures and backwardness see S. Devereux, *Fieldwork in developing countries.* Boulder, CO: Lynne Rienner 1993; D. Arnold, *Famine: social crisis and historical change.* Oxford: Basil Blackwell 1988; and A. T. Golkin, *Famine, a heritage of hunger: a guide to issues and references.* Claremont, Calif.: Regina Books 1987.

27   A. I. Rykov, "Na puti k usoichivomy krest'ianskomy khoziaistvu", in Rykov, ed., *V bor'be s zasukhoi i golodom*, Moscow: Gosizdat, 1925, 6.

28   Rykov "Na puti...", 1; Petrovskii, cited in Tauger, *Natural Disaster*, 170; Stalin, *Sochineniya*, v. 8, 117–119.

brought about. Like the official viewpoints, these disputes involved comparisons between Soviet agriculture and pre-Revolutionary agriculture, and also between Soviet peasant farming and farming in other countries, most of the United States. During NEP several Soviet specialists traveled to the U.S. to study U.S. farming and farm policies.

An important dispute for the present topic developed over the issue of the relative efficiency and rationality of small peasant farms versus large-scale farms, which continued a dispute in between Marxists and peasant specialists (whom the Marxists often called "narodniki", sometimes inaccurately) in late Imperial Russia and elsewhere in Europe. This dispute in NEP took on an almost apocalyptic quality because it was often phrased in terms of whether or not the small peasant family farm had a future. Advocates of the peasant farm, such as the economist Evgenii Varga, A. V. Chaianov, N. D. Kondrat'ev, L. I. Litoshenko and others, argued that the peasant farm had demonstrated a basic superiority over large-scale farms during the late Imperial period, the Civil War, and NEP. These researchers argued that the peasant farms had adapted to the dramatic economic changes and difficulties from emancipation to 1917 much more flexibly than had the large noble estates, which had sold most of their lands to peasants. They noted that the peasant farm was serving as the basis for the recovery during NEP, and argued that peasant farms had considerable potential to develop given supportive policies.[29] Some of these scholars in particular warned against policies that assumed that any successful peasant was a kulak and subjected to harsh taxation that discouraged him and other peasants from expanding their farms.[30]

Their Marxist opponents insisted that small peasant farms were an anachronism and doomed to be displaced by large, industrial farms. These writers emphasised the primitive methods, ignorance, and conservatism of peasant farmers, the limitations on their productivity that small interstripped farming imposed, particularly since this farm layout made use of farm machinery like tractors practically impossible, and the limited surplus above their own needs that these farms produced.[31] These writers held that sooner or later large scale farms would replace the small peasant farms. Even Bukharin, who advocated movement to socialism at a snail's pace, stated repeatedly that large-scale farming would ultimately and inevitably replace small farms, as did Rykov. And these writers and politicians were always ready to jump to the conclusion that "kulaks" sought to undermine the Soviet government, especially by demanding higher prices for food products.[32]

29 V. I. Mel'nikov, *Istoricheskaia subd'ba krest'ianstva i melkotovarnogo proizvodstva: polemiki i diskussii perioda NEPa (1921-konets 20-kh gg.)*, Nizhnii Novgorod, 1999, 46. See also Litoshenko, L. N. *Sotsializatsiia zemli v Rossii*. Novosibirsk: Sibirskii khronograf, 2001 (actually written in 1923); A. V. Chayanov, *The Theory of Peasant Economy*, Madison: University of Wisconsin Press, 1986.

30 For example, Kondratiev; see Vincent Barnett, *Kondratiev and the Dynamics of Economic Development*, New York: St. Martin's, 1998, 70–71.

31 Mel'nikov, *Istoricheskaia sud'ba*; D. J. Male, *Russian Peasant Organization before Collectivisation*, Cambridge: Cambridge University Press, 1971.

32 Mel'nikov, *Istoricheskaia sud'ba*, 98.

Marxists, and Soviet leaders, thus could not accept the idea that peasant farms as such could be modernized. They saw such farms as structurally incompatible with modern farming. Their ideal of modern farming was U.S. farms, especially the larger U.S. farms that used the new tractors and combine harvesters. These farms were increasing in number rapidly during the 1920s, and U.S. Department of Agriculture officials, agricultural experts, farmers themselves, and of course companies who produced and distributed farm equipment, all advocated the new mechanised methods to foreign visitors as they did to U.S. citizens.[33]

On another level, of course, the dispute over the future of the peasant farm had a different and what many have seen as a more sinister meaning. Advocates of the peasant farm were also advocates of policies that would allow such farms to exist and work more or less as they wished. During NEP, Marxists and Soviet leaders, especially in the wake of the extremely intrusive policies of the Civil War years, implicitly and sometimes explicitly advocated policies in which the Soviet government would actively intervene in the villages in a manner that would induce the peasants to change they way they managed the land and performed farm work.

As far as I have been able to determine, no scholars writing about the USSR in this period have ever noticed that this Soviet debate echoed similar debates taking place in other countries, above all in the U.S. In that country, as increasing numbers of farmers purchased tractors, as increasing numbers of specialists in the new field of agricultural engineering met with farmers to advise them on reconstructing their farms, the character of farming changed from the traditional family farm to an industrial pattern. The Secretary of Agriculture in his 1926 report to Congress stated, "agriculture must follow the example of industry", and specifically referred to large-scale farms managed by competent executives. As a result of these efforts, by 1930 the U.S. had more than 21,000 large-scale farms, meaning farms at least five to eight times as large as those typical in the locality, and producing the same products.[34]

Remarkably, in this context, the same arguments emerged as in the USSR in the 1920s. Critics of the industrialising-enlarging farms evoked the threat that "corporate farms" posed to small farmers. These critics emphasised the problems of industrial farms, in particular the fact that even though they were more productive, their costs were still too high, with the result that they were not flexible enough to adjust to market downturns, while family farms could return to subsistence. On the other hand, advocates of industrial farming scoffed at the idea of defending the family farm, with its low standard of living. Why continue a system with those results, they asked. They argued that the small farmer cannot survive against the flood of technology: "his race is run", one wrote. Another asked, which farmer would not trade his independence for a comfortable living and a steady job working for Tom

---

33   Fitzgerald, *Every Farm a Factory*.
34   Fitzgerald, *Every Farm a Factory*, 107–108.

Campbell, who operated a vast farm in Montana that as we will see influenced the Soviet leaders greatly.[35]

This issue of independence is central to the problem of modernisation and to the Soviet case. One of the main criticisms of collectivisation has been that it took away the peasants' independence, making them instead poorly paid employees on state-run enterprises; some who make this criticism have added derogatory statements alleging that governmental employees inherently have less incentives to work well than employees of private firms, referring to a stereotype of "listless state employees". Aside from the easily document-ed evidence of "listless private employees" and hard-working government employees, this stereotype overlooks the reality of farming in the U.S. and elsewhere in the 20th century. One U.S. farmer in the late 1920s, in response to the discussion described above about small farmers and industrial farms, laughed at the prospect of "losing his independence;" he called it a cruel myth for farmers who owed banks so much that they could only do what the banker said.[36] By the 1990s, farmers – even if they own their own land and farm as legally independent operators – are subordinated to input providers, buyers of their products, and banks who finance their operations, all of which are usually very large corporations. Farmers are thus "price takers", and often if not mostly dependent on government subsidies for their economic survival.[37] We will return to this point.

In the 1920s, then, Soviet specialists and government officials wrestled with similar, and often the same, ideas and problems as U.S. specialists, officials, and farmers. Taken as a whole, among the Soviets more special-ists, and of course many more farmers, were skeptical of the prospect of modernisation for a number of reasons, took more seriously the farmers' commitment to independence, and saw greater prospects for small farming. Soviet political leaders were much more uniform, though not completely, in their basic distrust of peasants and peasant farming; their attitudes were more like those of U.S. agricultural engineers.

Grain crisis, sovkhoz plan, and collectivisation

Soviet leaders shifted their views increasingly toward policies that would encourage collectivisation in 1925–27. In December 1927 the Fifteenth Party Congress set collectivisation as a goal of Soviet policies, though without setting a definite deadline. After the Congress, however, a shortfall in food supplies to the towns, the "Grain Crisis", led officials to accelerate their policies. Much of the literature contains a kind of conventional wisdom that Stalin saw the grain crisis as caused only by "kulaks" withholding grain. In fact, in his statements during the crisis, when he went to Siberia to try to

35 Fitzgerald, *Every Farm a Factory*, 123–125.
36 Fitzgerald, *Every Farm a Factory*, 125.
37 Geoff Tansey and Tony Worsley, *The Food System: A Guide*, London: Earthscan, 1996, 85–100.

extract more grain, he explicitly blamed the crisis on the backwardness of peasant agriculture:

> We must realize that we can no longer make progress on the basis of small individual peasant farms, that what we need in agriculture is large farms capable of employing machines and producing the maximum marketable surpluses.[38]

One of the most important steps the regime took in this area was the "sovkhoz project", a plan that Stalin proposed in February to establish dozens of large-scale mechanised state farms in the open lands of southern Siberia, northern Kazakhstan, and certain other regions. In the discussion over this project at the June 1928 Central Committee plenum, Kalinin (who introduced it) emphasized that the problem was due to shortage of food, not to withholding by peasants, and his claim elicited no protests the audience at the Central Committee plenum. The sovkhoz project proposal explicitly referred to the large farm of Thomas Campbell in Montana, which covered more than 60,000 acres and was completely mechanized in its operations, as the model for the new sovkhozy.[39] In the course of the discussions of this project at the plenum, the economist and high-level statistic official V. V. Osinskii challenged the proposal on the grounds that the large American farms had mostly failed, and that the Campbell farm was just an advertising vehicle for tractor producers. He reached this conclusion on the basis of conversations with apparently resentful farmers and did not visit the farm himself.[40] In response, Stalin cited a description of the Campbell farm by the agronomist N. M. Tulaikov, who did visit it and described its successful operations.[41]

Up to this point, these policy measures were not that distant from the policies in the U.S. to open up the great plains for farming in the previous generation. The sovkhoz plan did not involve coercion or remodeling of peasant farms, but was basically a socialist version of the breaking of the plains, and some specialists who met to discuss the project in May 1928 acknowledged this.[42] Soviet leaders assumed, however, that enlargement and elimination of interstripping was "scale neutral": if it worked with a 10,000 hectare farm in Siberia, it would work with a 500 acre village. It was in part based on this assumption that they undertook collectivisation.

Much recent research has brought to light many details about collectivisation, especially the coercion employed during the first campaign of December 1929 to March 1930, the peasant rebellions that followed, the disorganisation

38 Stalin, *Sochineniia*, v. 11, 4–9. I explain the arguments put forward here in more detail in "Stalin, Soviet Agriculture, and Collectivisation", in F. Just and F. Trentman, eds., *Food and Conflict in Europe in the Age of the Two World Wars*, London: Palgrave MacMillan, 2006 (forthcoming).
39 RGASPI f. 78., o. 7, d. 109, ll. 1–8.
40 V. P. Danilov et al., eds., *Kak lomali NEP: Stenogrammy plenumov TsK VKP(b) 1928–1929 gg.*, Moscow: Rossiia XX Vek, 2000, v. 2, 481–484.
41 *Kak lomali NEP*, v. 2, 514–16.
42 RGASPI f. 78, o. 7, d. 108, l. 98.

and other problems in the kolkhozy during the first years, and the major crop failures and famines that resulted from them. All of these aspects could be addressed from the standpoint of modernisation, but I believe the best and most all-encompassing way to approach them is to focus on an aspect of this situation that has received little attention: the ways in which the new kolkhoz system recovered from famine crises.

Grain harvests in the USSR, as in Russia before, varied greatly from year to year as a result of weather and other natural disasters. Much recent scholarship on the social aspects of collectivisation, however, deals extremely superficially and presumptuously with production data, at best dismissing it as untrustworthy without any discussion of its sources. Yet these same studies claim that peasants expressed their hostility and resistance to collectivisation by working to reduce harvests.[43] If, however, we examine the grain harvest data in a careful and legitimate way, using a consistent source base, a pattern emerges that at least does not fit recent scholarly views that focus exclusively focus on resistance. That pattern is that the bad harvests were in all cases the result of natural disasters, and were followed by years of good or even excellent harvests. So the harvests of 1931 and 1932 were very low (respectively approximately 55 and 48 million metric tons) because of drought (in 1931) and a complex of natural disasters (in 1932), but were followed by a much larger harvest in 1933 of approximately 69 million tons. Similarly the harvest of 1936 was also reduced by drought, and was followed by the excellent harvest of 1937 (respectively 56 and 97 million tons).[44] These data derive from a consistent source base, the annual reports of the collective and state farms, which derive from actual harvest results and were the basis for the corrections of the "biological yields" in the years after Khrushchev.[45]

These data demonstrate that at least a large proportion of the peasants, most of whom were farming in collective or state farms, worked despite disastrous conditions of shortage and famine to produce good harvests and overcome the crises. In Ukraine, for example, yields increased sixty percent from 1932 to 1933 (from five to eight centners per hectare), despite the severity of the famine in that region. In the Urals harvests increased from 2.6 million tons in 1936 to 13.2 million tons in 1937, or almost five times. In that province the average able-bodied kolkhoznik earned 204 labordays in 1936 and 245

43 Fitzpatrick, *Stalin's Peasants*, 71; also Lewin, "The Kolkhoz and the Russian Muzhik", in *Making of the Soviet System*, and Viola, *Peasant Rebels*, Penner, "Stalin and the Ital'ianka".

44 S. G. Wheatcroft, R. W. Davies, J. M. Cooper, "Soviet Industrialization Reconsidered: Some Preliminary Conclusions about Economic Development between 1926 and 1941", *Economic History Review* (2nd ser.) 39, 2 (1986), 282–83; Tauger, "The 1932 Harvest and the Famine of 1933", Slavic Review, vol. 50 no. 1, Spring 1991, 60–79, and *Natural Disasters and Human Action in the Soviet Famine of 1931–1933*, Pittsburgh: Carl Beck Papers in Soviet and East European Studies, University of Pittsburgh, 2001.

45 On these data, see Tauger, *Statistical Falsification in the Soviet Union*, Seattle: Donald Treadgold Papers in Russian, East European, and Central Asian Studies, University of Washington, 2001.

in 1937, probably because the 1936 drought destroyed whole fields of crops, making harvesting impossible and preventing peasants from earning more labordays, while in 1937 they had more work than ever before because of the favorable conditions.[46]

Given that natural disasters precipitated these crises, this clear evidence that peasants were able to respond to these crises and overcome them, despite the terrible effects of these disasters especially in 1932–1933, must owe something to the structure of the collective farm system. Of course, the chaos and disorganisation of the early years of the system contributed to the crisis of 1931–1933, but the evidence of the harvests and other considerations show that environmental factors were more important in that crisis and in others as well.[47] The collective farm system, by virtue of its structure, contributed to the recovery because it allowed aid that the Soviet regime provided to be allocated to groups of peasants, whole villages and districts, in a manner that on balance helped peasants to work more effectively and productively. This aid involved machinery and equipment, seed and other supplies, food relief, and especially managerial aid. All of these aspects are documented to varying degrees in the archival sources that have been published recently, even though the aim of those publications has been more to describe the suffering of the peasants during the famine and the difficulties of the system than the overcoming of the crisis.[48]

The aspect of this aid that most clearly demonstrates the modernizing effect of collectivisation is managerial aid, which came to the villages in 1933 in the form of the MTS and sovkhoz political departments, *politotdely*, small groups of personnel including workers and OGPU agents attached to the Machine Tractor Stations and the sovkhozy. Some of the politotdel activities were punitive, like removing allegedly incompetent personnel from farm and MTS administrations, and (in the case of the OGPU agents) keeping records of suspicious activities.[49] Most of their activities, however, concerned actual farm work: assisting farms administrations to motivate peasants during the famine in 1933 to sow, harrow, weed, harvest, and perform other necessary tasks, to encourage effective work and censure bad work, to assist farms in accounting and record-keeping, and other such jobs. Evidence of this can be found in the final report by the politotdel chief of the Central Blackearth oblast' for 1933.[50] This report documents the tragic conditions in the villages

46 V. B. Tsyganov, *Formirovanie administrativno-komandnoi sistemy upravleniia kolkhozami Urala (1933-iiun' 1941)*, Sverdlovsk: Urals University Press, 1991, 90.
47 See Tauger, *Natural Disaster*; Tsyganov also argued that natural disasters were the prime determinant of kolkhoz labor productivity; *Formirovanie*, 68, 69, 77.
48 See for example the document collection *Golod 1932–1933 rokiv na Ukraini: ochima istorikiv, movoiu dokumentiv*, Kiev: Vid. Politichnoi literatury Ukrainy, 1990, especially the documents from number 159 on.
49 I. E. Zelenin, "Politotdely MTS (1933–1934 gg.)", *Istoricheskie zapiski*, Vol. 76, 1965.
50 RGASPI f. 112, o. 26, d. 21, ll. 231–254. This report is discussed in more detail in Tauger, "Adaptation to Collectivisation".

in early 1933; the Central Blackearth oblast' was a major famine region in 1933. It also, however, documents significant improvements in work and in output during 1933, including earlier and enlarged sowings, much more extensive weeding, and earlier and more complete harvesting. The report documents numerous difficulties in this work, including not only deaths from starvation but also peasant resistance such as refusals to work, thefts of food from the kolkhozy, and organisation of conspiratorial groups. It also documents that most peasants came to work much earlier in 1933 than in 1932, and that in every farm many peasants won awards for conscientious work. The report also documents that allocations of new equipment during the year also contributed to the improved work. The fact that the 1933 harvest was so much larger than those of 1931–1932 means that the politotdely around the country similarly helped farms work better.

This case, and the crisis it exemplifies, relates to the modernisation issue because it demonstrates that the collective farm system served as the basis for the recovery of the farm system, and of the whole USSR, from terrible crises due first of all to natural disasters. To draw a loose analogy, the politotdely functioned as a kind of intensive, intrusive, and admittedly punitive, extension service in these years. The fact that the Soviet farming system became more accessible to governmental influence, in this context, cannot be seen purely as a negative feature, and that greater governmental involvement is also a basic characteristic of a modern farming system. Perhaps another way to view the politotdely from a modernising interpretation is to see them as analogous to government regulators, such as the agencies who investigate livestock breeding farms to evaluate their disposal of animal wastes and who often impose punitive sanctions when farms are found to be polluting land and streams beyond legal limits. The politotdely and their efforts represented an extension of government control, but also a greater incorporation of the farms into the Soviet system, but they also represented a modernising program that increased food production and overcame a catastrophic famine.

After Stalin

Between 1940 and 1980, average Soviet grain yields doubled. There were many problems: bad decisions, and possibly good decisions badly executed, like Khrushchev's corn campaigns, the MTS amalgamation with kolkhozy, the Virgin Lands campaign. But there were also improvements, massive investments in mechanisation, supplies, infrastructure, and education, higher procurement prices, pensions for farm personnel, and extension of passports.

By the end of Brezhnev's regime, however, Soviet agriculture had numerous problems. Nove outlined these problems under the following categories: large investments with little or no increased output, declining labor discipline due to declining incentives, increasing costs and prices, planning problems as a result of the expansion of the governmental bureaucracy, failings in infrastructure and in land reform, and declining production in the private plots.[51] All of these were serious problems (and there were others), and both the Gorbachev and post-Soviet regimes have undertaken a variety of measures to alleviate them.

Nonetheless, these problems showed a fundamentally modern agricultural system: a complex system that involved extensive use of machinery, chemicals, and other industrial inputs, operated on a large scale, produced a variety of products under extremely varied conditions, involved many skilled workers and scientists in planning and production (despite the influence of T. D. Lysenko, a charlatan Soviet pseudo-biologist who gained substantial control over Soviet genetics research from 1948 to 1965), and produced large amounts of food and other products, even if many observers thought that the system should have been able to produce more. Because of the system's dependence on products from the industrial sectors, planning that involved industry as well as agriculture, and limitations on investments, in part Soviet agriculture suffered from the overall decline of the Soviet economy in the 1970s and 1980s. At that time, the Soviet Union had engaged in détente with the U.S. and Europe, had significantly increased its trade with the outside world, and was still engaged in a significant arms race and in international confrontations with the U.S. on several continents.

In this context, World Systems theorists make an interesting comparative point. Frank argued that the USSR and Eastern Europe experienced the world recession of the 1970s–1980s almost as much as the West, but that the USSR could not obtain the kind of loan support that the U.S. did during these years, when the U.S. debt ballooned. The U.S. effort to overwhelm the USSR militarily with the Strategic Defense Initiative and other massive expenditures also drove both the USSR and the U.S. into debt, but the U.S. had much easier access to external loans and internal revenue resources than the USSR. The U.S. received a huge influx of money that helped the country to get through the crisis; the USSR did not and declined to collapse.[52]

This analysis would imply that the problems Nove identified in agriculture resulted in part from problems outside of agriculture, problems which other countries faced but were in a better position to solve, again because of circumstances external to agriculture. A more specific comparison can suggest a different way of looking at the crisis Nove described, a comparison with the U.S. farm debt crisis of the 1970s–1980s. At the beginning of the 1970s, a boom period, USDA officials, extension agents, and other advisors in and out of government encouraged U.S. farmers to expand their production; the "Food for Peace" Act under President Eisenhower (The Agricultural Trade Development and Assistance Act of 1954, P. L. 480) in particular promised continued U.S. governmental demand for farm surpluses. By the late 1970s, the whole situation changed, among other factors, because of the oil

51   Alec Nove, *Soviet Agriculture: The Brezhnev Legacy and Gorbachev's Cure*, RAND/ UCLA Center for the Study of Soviet International Behavior, January 1988.
52   Andre Gunder Frank, "Economic ironies in Europe: a world economic interpretation of East-West European politics", *International Social Science Journal*, UNESCO, vol. XLIV, no. 1, 1992, 46ff.

crisis, which brought drastically increased input prices for farmers, without a commensurate increase in farm gate prices for their crops and livestock. As a result, many thousands of farms ended up in debt, indirectly for doing what the U.S. government had advised them to do, and many thousands of these farmers ended up losing their farms, their livelihood, their careers.[53] This crisis created significant animosity, on the part of farmers, against the U.S. government, banks and loan officers.

In the U.S. case, the farmers overextended themselves, albeit on government advice; they took out loans, purchased machinery, rented land, grew more crops, and then faced the unanticipated drop in prices and increase in costs. In the USSR, it was the government that overextended itself with its investments in agriculture, which included substantial purchases of machinery, only to find itself running out of resources to cover the additional costs it had taken on. The underlying causes in both cases were external to agriculture.

In this context, it is important to consider the view that Soviet agriculture had an additional function that U.S. agriculture did not have. As Shaffer argued, the Soviet collective farms were not only production units, but also served as a type of rural welfare system that supported people, especially pensioners, outside of the cities.[54] Consequently, certain measures of its efficiency, especially when compared to U.S. farms, may not always represent its work fairly because they do not include this "social security" function.

Conclusions

Whether an agricultural system is modern or not, if it operates for an extended period people adapt to it and often adapt or change the system to make it suit their needs. Such a system can have weakness, flaws, etc., but if it survives it has a basic level of functioning and a certain potential. Any government that sees problems with such a system and seeks to change it to eliminate those problems has to be cautious about that functional basis of the system. Changes should find a way to take advantage of the system's potential without undermining the basic functioning that the system has.

In introducing the collective farm system, many Soviet personnel initially thought that they could eliminate the basics of the old system, but others tried to retain some of those basic elements, and they were right in doing so because some of those elements had considerable potential. One of those elements was the private sector, which represented a continuation of pre-collectivisation farming, and was to a degree neglected by Soviet modernisation efforts. Another however was the potential of peasant labor in the kolkhoz, which demonstrated its capabilities in the survival of the system, the good harvests that were produced, and the long-term successful introduction of

53   Robert Emmet Long, ed., *The Farm Crisis*, New York: Wilson, 1987.
54   Harry G. Shaffer, ed., *Soviet agriculture : an assessment of its contributions to economic development*, New York: Praeger, 1977.

mechanisation and other technical improvements. Just as the private plot had and has a potential for increased production, so the large-scale farm also had and has the potential for increased production because it allows modern methods of farming and allows peasants with the right attitude to produce a large crop in a mechanised, efficient manner. The Soviets created a farm system that was modern in principle, even if it was often not operated in an efficient and modern manner.

SARI AUTIO-SARASMO

Soviet Economic Modernisation and Transferring Technologies from the West

Introduction

This article investigates Soviet economic modernisation from the 1920s to the 1980s and the aspirations of the Soviet leadership to modernise the Soviet economy. The main focus of this chapter is economic modernisation[1] based on transferred technology from the West and imitative development in the Soviet Union.[2] In technology transfer, the focus is on the role of Co-Com's high technology embargo and the resultant scientific-technological cooperation that took place as an outcome of this policy.

The period of Soviet modernisation began in 1928 when Stalin launched his industrialisation programme. During the years from 1928 to 1984 a number of different modernisation processes took place.[3] Soviet modernisation priorities based on technology transfer were complicated in the 1950s by the West's imposition of a high technology embargo against the Soviet bloc. The main aim of the CoCom embargo was to retard Soviet technical progress in key strategic areas of technology,[4] and, as result of the embargo, technology transfer became part of the East-West rivalry. What was the role of transferred technology in the Soviet modernisation process and how was

1   The Soviet military complex was a highly prioritized sector and one of the main absorbers of western technology. Thus it was also the most modern branch of industry but as a secret and highly restricted branch it is not treated in this study. P. Hanson, *The Rise and Fall of the Soviet Economy. An Economic History of the USSR from 1945.* London: Longman 2003, 31; See also I. Dezhina and L. Graham, 'Russian Basic Science After Ten Years of Transition and Foreign Support'. *Working Papers number 24, February 2002, Russian and Eurasian Program.* Washington D. C: Carnegie Endowment 2002, 6.
2   See e.g. J. Berliner, *Soviet Industry from Stalin to Gorbachev: Essays on Management and Innovation.* Aldershot: Edward Elgar 1985, 160–181. In this paper imitative development is defined as diffusion of innovations based on absorbing the knowhow brought by transferred technology.
3   P. Gregory and R. Stuart, *Soviet and Post-Soviet Economic Structure and Performance.* Fifth Edition. New York: HarperCollins 1994, 233; Hanson, *The Rise and Fall of the Soviet Economy*, 22.
4   Hanson (1981), 223. Iceland was not a member of CoCom. In addition to NATO countries, Japan was a member.

technology transferred? What were the main tasks of transferring Western technology from the perspective of Soviet 'modernisation' and how was the policy conducted? How did the Cold War and the CoCom technology embargo affect these aims? What was the role of Soviet scientific-technical cooperation in technology transfer, taking Finland as a case study?

After the Second World War the world had changed and technological progress had taken a great leap forward. This also changed the modernisation aspirations of the Soviet leadership. In the 1950s, the Soviet leadership realized that technological progress had become a more important source of growth in the United States and Western Europe than the increases in labour and capital inputs, which had formed the basis of the Soviet Union's growth strategy since the beginning of Stalin's industrialisation process. This required the Soviet leadership to understand the social and economic forces that promoted technological progress.[5] Transferring foreign technology became one of the strategies for promoting technological progress and economic modernisation in the Soviet Union. Soviet 'modernisation' based on technological progress can be seen as an instrumental or technological rationality, because it emphasises the role of technology and economic growth in the modernisation process.[6]

Modernisation based on technology transfer was not specific to the Soviet Union. Since Peter the Great, the Russians had adopted western ideas and technology and shaped those ideas into Russian ones.[7] Western technology was transferred to Russia under the Tsars and the tradition continued after the October revolution. Western technology, being a product of the capitalist world, was defined inevitable for the industrialisation of the young Soviet state by Lenin. Despite its undisputed benefits, there was a cautious attitude towards the adoption of western technology: the main concern was to avoid a dependence on western technology. In the 1970s, however, it was argued that importing Western technology did not have any 'harmful socio-economic consequences', and western scientific discoveries and technological innovations were explained as 'a valuable means of serving the socialist ends',[8] rather than as a threat to the Soviet system. The main argument was that for the Soviet Union it was a reasonable policy to utilize western technology for its own benefit.

---

5   Berliner, *Soviet Industry from Stalin to Gorbachev,* 249. According to Berliner technological progress was a source of growth of output: France 79 per cent, Italy 78 per cent and Norway 77 per cent; See also G. Holliday, *Technology Transfer to the USSR 1928–1937 and 1966–1975: The Role of Western Technology in Soviet Economic Development.* Boulder and Oxford: Westview Press 1979, 59 and E. Hoffman and R. Laird, *"The Scientific-Technological Revolution" and Soviet Foreign Policy.* New York: Pergamon Press 1982, 93.
6   Holliday, *Technology Transfer to the USSR 1928–1937 and 1966–1975,* 12–13.
7   Gregory and Stuart, *Soviet and Post-Soviet Economic Structure and Performance,* 15.
8   Hoffman-Laird, *"The Scientific-Technological Revolution" and Soviet Foreign Policy,* 13.

Transferring technology has always been a normal part of commercial life and an important source of economic growth throughout the world.[9] Technology transfer is usually divided into two: commercial and non-commercial transfer.[10] In the Soviet Union the acquisition of machinery and knowhow were the most important activities. Technology was transferred to the Soviet Union for direct use or as a basis of designs for domestic production.[11] The latter was the starting point for the imitative development and the diffusion of innovations that eventually would have launched domestic innovation processes. According to Hietala (1992), reserves of know-how, and the adoption and diffusion of innovations can grow in two ways: an accumulation of experience and learning from the inside (learning by doing), and an active acquisition of knowledge and know-how (exploitation and imitation of the experiences of the others). In this process there are two kinds of actors: the pioneer, from whom others learn, and the imitator, acting on the strength of know-how brought from the outside.[12] By launching a modernisation process based on technological progress, the main aim was to 'overtake and surpass' the West. In the interwar period the ultimate goal of the Soviet leadership was to overcome Russia's economic backwardness and to catch up with the West in order to protect the country from foreign invasion and to advance its geopolitical interests.[13] After the Second World War, the aim of the Soviet

9   Hanson, *The Rise and Fall of the Soviet Economy*, 123.
10 Commercial transfer includes turnkey factories, licencing, joint ventures, technical exchanges, training in high-technology areas, sales of processing equipment, provision of engineering documentation and technical data, consulting; proposals and sale of products that embody technology. Non-commercial transfer includes visits in both directions of students, scientists, and businessmen or managers; the use of unclassified published technical data and patents, reverse engineering of single machines or components; and clandestine activities, i.e. the deduction of the techniques of manufacture from examination of the product itself. *Technology and East-West trade*, 100.
11 Hanson, *Trade and technology in Soviet-Western Relations*. London: Macmillan 1981, 13–14; In this sense the transfer of technology is the process whereby a technique is substantially moved from one set of users to another or the process by which innovations made in one country are subsequently brought into use in another country. E. Nironen, 'Transfer of Technology between Finland and the Soviet Union' in Möttölä, Bykov and Korolev (eds.) *Finnish-Soviet Economic Relations*. London: Macmillan Press 1983, 161; For a more detailed explanation see E. Nironen, *Teknologian siirto Suomen ja Neuvostoliiton välillä. SEV-kaupan tutkimusprojekti.* Tutkimusraportti 22. Lappeenrannan teknillinen korkeakoulu, tuotantotalouden osasto. Lappeenranta 1980, 5–10.
12 M. Hietala, *Innovaatioiden ja kansainvälistymisen vuosikymmenet. Tietoa, taitoa, asiantuntemusta. Helsinki eurooppalaisessa kehityksessä 1875–1917.* Historiallinen arkisto 99:1. Helsinki 1992, 265. Innovation is generally understood as an idea, concept, process or product which can be applied in practice and which contains something new; Gomulka defines 'innovation' as the first application by a firm or enterprise of an 'invention', S. Gomulka, *Growth, Innovation and Reform in Eastern Europe*. Brighton: Harvester Press 1986. See also Holliday, *Technology Transfer to the USSR 1928–1937 and 1966–1975*, 20.
13 Shlapentokh, *A Normal Totalitarian Society,* New York: M. E. Sharpe 2001, 17–18.

leadership was to transform the economy from an imitator to a pioneer in order to strengthen not only the status of the Soviet Union as a superpower in world politics but also its economic and ideological role as a leader of the the Eastern bloc.

Soviet technological development, as well as the role of western technology within it, has been of great interest to researchers. During the 1960s, research concentrated on Soviet technological development mainly because of the remarkable achievements of the Soviet space program. During the 1980s, when the decline of the Soviet economy was in evidence, there emerged another wave of research on the Soviet Union's technological development.[14] The results of earlier research, then based on contemporary subjects, can now be assessed in a new light and with a historical perspective. Twenty years have passed and it is now time to investigate Soviet economic modernisation from a 21st century perspective. This analysis is based on asking 'new' questions of 'old' research. Newly available materials enable a comparison to be made with contemporary research from the 1960s and 1980s.[15]

Copying and duplication

When the Bolsheviks took over Russia in 1917 they were committed to the creation of a modern, industrialized state and were enthusiastic about science and technology.[16] They wanted to make a clear distinction between the reactionary and traditional Russian empire and the progressive and modern Socialist State. In this sense the Russian revolution was, as Fitzpatrick points out, a means of escaping backwardness.[17] However, revolution did not solve the problem. On the contrary, overcoming backwardness was a determining factor in the policy making of the Soviet leadership throughout the history of the Soviet Union.[18] Backwardness also had its advantages: Russia was able to skip over some early stages of industrialisation, borrow advanced western technology and move quickly forward.[19] As a U.S. report on East-West trade (1979) stated, the Soviet practice was to wait for major innovations to be proven viable in the Western markets before attempting to incorporate them into its own production.[20]

During the New Economic Policy (NEP) in the 1920s Lenin raised the necessity of foreign expertise. The slogan: 'Learn, learn, learn!' developed

---

14 Mainly at CREES, Birmingham (Amann, Cooper, Hanson).
15 This article is a part of author's larger project "Finnish-Soviet scientific-technical cooperation and the modernisation of the Soviet economy 1955–1991".
16 L. Graham, *Science in Russia and the Soviet Union*, 173.
17 S. Fitzpatrick, *The Russian Revolution.* 2nd edition. New York: Oxford University Press 1994, 9.
18 See e.g. Shlapentokh, *A Normal Totalitarian Society,* 17–18.
19 Fitzpatrick, *The Russian Revolution*,19; See also Gregory and Stuart, *Soviet and Post-Soviet Economic Structure and Performance*, 8.
20 *Technology and East-West trade*, 242.

a new meaning – to adopt and absorb foreign know-how.[21] The main idea was that by borrowing the latest capitalist technology (being inevitable and necessary) Soviet industrial managers and technicians would learn from the capitalists. Lenin aknowledged the dangers of allowing the capitalists to operate in Russia but believed that their influence could be contained.[22] It was believed that understanding western technology was the only way to develop Soviet innovations and to create the technological basis for economic development. Soviet economic modernisation was founded on the basis of utilizing foreign expertise until the economically developed Soviet Union and domestic innovations would eventually outperform the West.[23]

Since the beginning of Stalin's industrialisation process in 1928, the strategy of economic growth in the Soviet Union was the maximum rate of mobilization of labour and capital into industrial production. The main instrument in the realisation of economic growth was centralized economic planning, which enabled the Soviet leadership to generate very high rates of investment in certain areas, and most of all, to manage the transfer of millions of workers from agriculture to industry. The slogan: 'Technology decides everything!' set the aim of the industrialisation programme. Heavy industry was prioritized in order to produce machinery for all other branches of economy. The use of technology, such as tractors and advanced tools, was strongly propagated.[24] It was believed that 'mechanisation', i.e. the use of machines and minimal use of manual work, would lead to direct economic development because fewer people could work more with the help of technology. The creation of the technological base became the main target of 'mechanisation'. For Stalin, industrialisation was equal to modernisation and the creation of a 'technological base' was the primary way to achieve this. The main aim was to increase labour productivity. In the case of the timber industry, for example, transferring technology was a means to develop the Soviet economy. By raising the efficiency of forest work, it was possible to produce more timber for export and to earn foreign currency to buy machines from abroad for the further development of heavy industry.[25] The lack of domestic technology production forced Stalin to import technology to the Soviet Union, mainly machinery from the West, in order to develop heavy industry. Technological dependence on the West became an important

21 R. W. Davies, *The Soviet Economy in Turmoil. The Industrialisation of the Soviet Union 3*. Houndsmills Macmillan Press 1989, 35; Andrle, *Workers in Stalin's Russia*, 83.
22 Holliday, *Technology transfer to the USSR 1928–1937 and 1966–1975*, 74.
23 Gomulka, *Growth, Innovation and Reform in Eastern Europe*, 42. See also *Technology and East-West trade*, 206.
24 V. Andrle, *Workers in Stalin's Russia. Industrialisation and Social Change in a Planned Economy*. Sussex New York: Harvester Wheatsheaf: St. Martin's Press 1988, 13, 32; S. Autio, *Suunnitelmatalous Neuvosto-Karjalassa 1928–1941. Paikallistason rooli Neuvostoliiton teollistamisessa*. Bibliotheca historica 71. Helsinki: SKS 2002, 105.
25 Autio, *Suunnitelmatalous Neuvosto-Karjalassa*, 91–92, 188–195, 256.

question and caused concern in the Soviet Union.[26] One way to control the dependence was to create domestic research and development (R&D) and domestic technology production based on transferred technologies.

During the 1930s, research and development (R&D) concentrated on 'replication, modification and scaling up of existing Western models'.[27] Another channel to strengthen domestic R &D based on foreign technology and know-how was opened through the concession policy and foreign specialists who came to the Soviet Union from the 1920s to the 1940s.[28] In the period from 1929 to 1945, about 175 technical assistance agreements were arranged between the Soviet Union and western companies; the latter included the most well-known and largest firms in the world.[29] Later the concession system was replaced by the licence system, which enabled Soviet enterprises to produce certain western products.[30]

A good example of commercial transfer was the Gor'kii automobile plant, which was built in the late 1920s and early 1930s on the direct model of the Ford Motor Company River-Rouge plant in Detroit. With the assistance of Ford engineers, the plant was customised to meet Soviet conditions. It was considered to be the most modern complete auto plant in the world in its time.[31] However, it also became an example of Soviet inability to improve, or even maintain, transferred technology. In the 1970s, Ford engineers found that some of the original equipment of the 1930s was still being used as late as the 1970s, and that the basic systems of the plant and its management principles were those of the River Rouge plant in the thirties.[32] A similar example was provided by the Finnish paper and pulp mills in the Karelian isthmus, which were annexed and incorporated into the Soviet timber industrial complex after the Second World War.[33] After some fifty years of economic utilization of those mills no major improvements had been carried out by Soviet authorities.

26 Gregory and Stuart, *Soviet and Post-Soviet Economic Structure and Performance*, 30; See also Hanson, *The Rise and Fall of the Soviet Economy*, 62.
27 G. Ofer, *Soviet Economic Growth: 1928–1985*. RAND/UCLA Center for the Study of Soviet International Behaviour, May 1988, 67.
28 A. Sutton, *Western Technology and Soviet Economic Development 1945 to 1965*. Third volume. Stanford Ca: Hoover Institution Press 1973, 11; There were approximately 9 200 foreign specialists in the Soviet Union during the first five year-plan (FYP) in 1928–1932. R. W. Davies, *Soviet Economic Development from Lenin to Khrushchev*. London: Cambridge University Press 1998, 493.
29 Graham, *Science in Russia and the Soviet Union*, 255. Other included Ford, Krupp, Siemens, Standard Oil, Caterpillar Tractor, Metropolitan-Vickers.
30 Hoffman-Laird, *"The Scientific-Technological Revolution" and Soviet Foreign Policy*, 90–91. During the 1970s and 1980s the trade of technological licences increased and it was seen as an important stimulus to technical planning within the socialist economy.
31 Berliner, *Soviet industry from Stalin to Gorbachev,* 172; Graham, *Science in Russia and the Soviet Union*, 255.
32 Graham, *Science in Russia and the Soviet Union*, 256.
33 For more on the incorporation of timber industry, see Autio, *Suunnitelmatalous Neuvosto-Karjalassa*, 170–172.

Technological progress changes Soviet modernisation aspirations

The founding of technological progress as a main booster of intensive economic growth in the West in the early 1950s changed the aspirations of economic modernisation of the Soviet leadership. Specific scientific and technical breaktroughs, such as automation, became important for the Soviet Union.[34] During the last years of Stalin, the attitude towards the Western scientific ideas was very complex. During the project to 'overtake and surpass' the West, Soviet scientists were encouraged to copy Western innovations, but at the same time to treat Western scholarship as 'idealistic and reactionary'. However, the fear that Western reports gave false information that was intended to mislead Soviet scientists[35] disappeared under the leadership of Khrushchev. Official political pronouncements began increasingly to stress the importance of technological progress in the management and the planning of the economy.[36] The Soviet leadership adopted a new term 'scientific-technical revolution' with the primary aim to facilitate Soviet-West trade by making it ideologically free.[37] An important part of the new ideology was the speed of technological progress and the role of scientific research in that process.[38]

The need to incorporate the latest technical ideas, and to study foreign achievements, was stressed repeatedly.[39] A fear of widening the technological gap between the Soviet Union and the West emerged. At the 22nd (1966) and 24th (1971) party congresses the themes of technological progress and acquisition of western technology were further developed. The role of technical change in economic growth required an acceleration of technical progress and technological change with East-West trade. Thus, the expansion of East-West technological exchange was defined as an essential manouevre in the strategy to modernize the Soviet economy in the 1970s. Imported technology from the West was seen as a stimulus to domestic innovation. It was also evident that the enhancement of the innovative qualities of the domestic economy was highly correlated to the expansion of trade possibilities, especially in the fields of advanced technology.[40] In his report to the 25th Party Congress in 1975, Brezhnev stated that the primary task remained the speeding up of scientific and technological progress.[41]

34 Hoffman-Laird, *"The Scientific-Technological Revolution" and Soviet Foreign Policy*, 7–8.
35 S. Gerovitch, *From Cyberspeak to Newspeak. A History of Soviet Cybernetics.* Cambridge: The MIT Press 2001, 15–16.
36 Berliner, *Soviet Industry from Stalin to Gorbachev,* 250.
37 Hanson, *Trade and technology in Soviet-Western Relations,* 87.
38 Nironen, *Teknologian siirto Suomen ja Neuvostoliiton välillä,* 65.
39 Nove, *An Economic History of the USSR,* 350.
40 Hoffman-Laird, *"The Scientific-Technological Revolution" and Soviet Foreign Policy,* 89.
41 Holliday, *Technology transfer to the USSR 1928–1937 and 1966–1975,* 61; See also L. Brezhnev, *Puheita: Helsingin ETY-kokouksesta Urho Kekkosen vierailuun Moskovassa.* Helsinki: Otava 1977, 75–76. Cohen points out that Brezhnev's policies were designed to avoid structural reform at home. S. Cohen, *Rethinking the Soviet Experience. Politics and History since 1917.* Oxford: Oxford University Press 1986, 139.

110

Speeding up technological progress was promoted by systematic transfers that ensured the fastest and most productive utilization of foreign technology purchases. Soviet buyers changed their preferences and priorities: for know-how rather than products, and for technological complexes rather than single items or processes.[42] A new policy was adopted immediately: entire plants constituted nearly one third of Soviet imports in the 1960s and 1970s.[43] The giant car factory project at Togliatti in Samara region was built with the primary assistance of the Italian firm Fiat. A cooperation agreement between Fiat and the Soviet State Committee for Science and Technology (GKNT) was signed in 1965 and production began in the early 1970s. A similar project was the Kama Truck Plant, which was commenced during the ninth five year-plan (1971–1975).[44] Priority to transfer know-how was assured by training programs for Soviet specialists in the West.[45] Ultimately 2500 Western technicians assisted equipment installation, training and startup, and 2 500 Soviet technicians were trained in Italy. According to a US report, despite the training programmes, technology employed at the Togliatti plant was not significantly improved upon by Soviet engineers.[46] The outcome seemed to be the same as in the 1930s and the 1940s. No process of remarkable assimilation of foreign know-how or actions of reverse engineering took place.

A significant bureaucratic structure was established for the support of technology transfer. In 1955 the State Committee for the Introduction of New Technology into the National Economy (Gostehnika) was established. In 1961 it was transformed into the State Committee of the Soviet Union Council of Ministers for the Coordination of Scientific Research Work (GKKNIR). With the re-emergence of the centralized ministerial system for directing the economy in 1965, a new research coordinating committee, the State Committee for Science and Technology (GKNT) emerged and it remained in existence until the end of the Soviet Union in 1991.[47] GKNT was a chief advisor to the central government on national technological policy. It created strategies for the acquisition of western technology and integration of domestic R&D capabilities. It often participated in negotiating the acquisition of sophisticated technology from the West. The Soviet Union had a massive programme of translation and dissemination of foreign scientific and technical literature.[48] In practice, detailed technical and operational data was obtained

42 *Technology and East-West trade*, 218.
43 Davies, *Soviet Economic Development from Lenin to Khrushchev*, 72. According to Davies this played a significant role in the restoration and modernisation of Soviet industry; Hanson, *The Rise and Fall of the Soviet Economy*, 30.
44 Holliday, *Technology Transfer to the USSR 1928–1937 and 1966–1975,* 114–115; Hanson, *The Rise and Fall of the Soviet Economy*, 117, 122.
45 Hanson, *Trade and technology in Soviet-Western Relations*, 108–109.
46 *Technology and East-West trade*, 231.
47 Graham, *Science in Russia and the Soviet Union,* 141, 181; See also Nove, *An Economic History of the USSR,* 350.
48 The All-Union Insitute for Scientific-Technical Information, VINITI (*Vsesojuznyi institut nauchnoi tehnicheskoi informacii*) collected and produced summaries from 22 000 scientific journals and publication series, about 8 000 books from 130 countries in

before purchasing agreements were made. The party and its bureaucracy excercised ultimate control over technology acquisition through its absolute control of personnel in state structures as it did over all sectors of society. Government organisations, mainly ministries and agencies, implemented the decisions.[49] Decisions concerning the purchase of foreign technology took place in the system of central economic planning. The State Planning Commission (Gosplan) was the unifying organisation of scientific-technical planning on the macro level.[50]

In order to keep up with the technological progress and to extract the best benefit of the transferred technology, an extraordinary emphasis was given to technical education, research and development and industrial technological innovation. Allocations to research and development (R&D) activities were generous. The R&D sector expanded at so high a rate that the number of Soviet scientists and engineers in the late 1970s was nearly 60 percent greater than in the USA.[51] In the seventies and eighties a great variety of 'associations', 'technological centers' and 'complexes' were formed.[52] According to Hanson (2003), in the Soviet Union technical innovation came in three types: by the centrally planned investment projects; the narrowly focused attention of the leadership on some particular issues; and by the competitive pressure of the arms race.[53] The expansion of Soviet R&D slowed down substantially during the 1980s. New scientific institutions were created but the outcome was poor.[54]

There were remarkable scientific and technological breakthroughs in the 1950s and 1960s, mainly as the outcome of the mission-oriented projects, and with the help of relatively quick changes in the allocation system of resources allowed by the planning system and centralized control.[55] Soviet astronomy began a period of considerable expansion in the late 1950s. At the same time,

70 different languages. J. Seppänen, *Tieteellis-tekninen informaatio Neuvostoliitossa.* Suomen ja Neuvostoliiton tieteellis-teknisen yhteistoimintakomitean julkaisusarja 2. Helsinki 1978.

49 *Technology and East-West trade*, 214–215, 217.

50 Nironen, *Teknologian siirto Suomen ja Neuvostoliiton välillä*, 75.

51 Gomulka, *Growth, Innovation and Reform in Eastern Europe*, 43; Ofer, *Soviet Economic Growth: 1928–1985*, 61; See also Gregory and Stuart, *Soviet and Post-Soviet Economic Structure and Performance*, 270–271. Governmental and social support for the research was generous but the problem was the disadvantage because of the distortion of priorities. The military complex received about 75 percent of all resources. Dezhina and Graham, 'Russian Basic Science After Ten Years of Transition and Foreign Support', 6.

52 Graham, *Science in Russia and the Soviet Union* 174–175, 185, 188. Scientific research insitutes were established during the 1920s.

53 Hanson, *The Rise and Fall of the Soviet Economy*, 21.

54 Gomulka, *Growth, Innovation and Reform in Eastern Europe*, 53; R. Amann, 'Technical Progress and Soviet Economic Development: Setting the Scenes' in *Technical Progress and Soviet Economic Development*. Oxford: Basil Blackwell 1986, 19; Holliday, *Technology transfer to the USSR 1928–1937 and 1966–1975*, 88.

55 Graham, *Science in Russia and the Soviet Union*, 180; See also Ofer, *Soviet Economic Growth: 1928–1985*, 62.

the Soviet computer designer S. A. Lebedev produced the 'MESM', the first electronic, stored-program, digital computer in continental Europe.[56] These projects were a part of the Soviet success story, behind which lay not only significant investement in R&D but also the utilisation of western know-how. The history of rockets in Russia dates back to the seventeenth and eighteenth centuries, but the major assistance for technical applications of the Soviet space program in the 1960s came from Germany after the Second World War.[57] In the West, computer technology developed quickly from the 1960s to the 1980s and became one of the indicators of technological progress. A comparison between the United States and the Soviet Union is very telling: it was estimated that the Soviet Union lagged years behind the United States in computer technology.[58] As a result of the problems of keeping up with the speed of Western developments, the level of Soviet microelectronic technology was achieved by the acquisition of western processor technology, legally or illegally.[59] In the Soviet Union computer technology was part of the clandestine military-technological complex, and this strongly affected the development of Soviet computer technology.

Technology embargo, CoCom

At the time when Khrushchev promoted the need for a more active technology import policy and Brezhnev debated the relationship between foreign trade and technological progress,[60] the Cold War set the parameters of Soviet modernisation plans. Before the Second World War, the Soviet Union was the only socialist state and it was surrounded by 'hostile' capitalist countries. After the war, the Soviet Union was surrounded by newly developed people's democracies, and in order to create an economic area inside the Soviet bloc the Council of Mutual Economic Assistance (CMEA) was established. Eco-

56 Graham, *Science in Russia and the Soviet Union,* 173, 222–223, 256. MESM was developed totally independent of western efforts; See also Gerovitch, *From Cyberspeak to Newspeak.*
57 Sutton, 270–273. During and after the war, among others two testing sites, technology and some 6000 technicians were transferred to the Soviet Union.
58 Gregory and Stuart, *Soviet and Post-Soviet Economic Structure and Performance,* 250; P. Snell, 'Soviet Microprocessors and Microcomputers' in *Technical Progress and Soviet Economic Development.* Oxford: Basil Blackwell 1986, 58. According to Snell, in general, the Soviet Union introduced microprosessors some two or four years behind the West which also made the direct quantification of Soviet production of microprosessors almost impossible; The Soviet Union organised a cooperative effort with Bulgaria, East Germany, Hungary, Poland, and Czechoslovakia all of which had computer industries. The Ryad computers began appearing in late 1972 and they were functional duplications of a IBM computer model. *Technology and East-West trade,* 233.
59 The organized stealing of technological secrets was already in evidence by 1929. KGB stolen technological data contributed as much to the country's technological progress as did Soviet scientists. Shlapentokh, *A Normal Totalitarian Society,* 93.
60 Holliday, *Technology transfer to the USSR 1928–1937 and 1966–1975,* 78–79.

nomic performance within the CMEA was based on the division of labour; the aims of economic cooperation were based on modernisation priorities set by the Soviet leadership. At the same time that Khrushchev started to open Soviet society to CMEA partners, he was also able to seek connections to capitalist countries.[61] This process was continued and even intensified by the policy of the Soviet leadership during the 1970s.

The import of advanced technology was important for the Soviet Union, but bi-polarization and the Cold War after the Second World War obstructed this aim. A multilateral export and control mechanism coordinating committee, CoCom, was established in 1949, in which the U.S. took a leading role. The western strategic embargo was operated by the NATO countries and the main aim was to retard Soviet technical progress in the key strategic areas of technology.[62] The system forged a restrictive policy intended to place an embargo on exports, including technology, that might contribute to military and civilian economic performance. In addition, tariffs were set high, trade and technology transfer facilities and mechanisms were restricted, and credits were discouraged.[63] An embargo was also directed against the Warsaw pact countries in order to prevent the trade of weapons or dual use technologies that might enhance Warsaw pact capabilities.[64] After some easing up during the 1950s and 1960s, CoCom restrictions were imposed in the early 1980s after the Soviet Union's involvement in the Afghanistan war. Especially in the 1980s, CoCom became part of the United States foreign policy, which was not regarded positively among European CoCom partners.[65] In the 1980s, when the United States strenghened CoCom restrictions, Soviet authorities condemned the American policy, which they claimed undermined détente.[66] From the Soviet point of view, the CoCom embargo and other export restrictions were artificial barriers against the Soviet Union, and the situation in Afghanistan was only a pretext for imperialistic circles in the United States to impede the relationship between the Soviet Union and the West.[67]

61   Hanson, *The Rise and Fall of the Soviet Economy*, 60.
62   Hanson, *Trade and technology in Soviet-Western Relations*, 223. Iceland was not a member of CoCom; Japan and Australia were members.
63   G. Bertsch, 'Technology Transfers and Technology Controls: a Synthesis of the Western-Soviet Relationship' in: *Technical Progress and Soviet Economic Development*. Oxford: Basil Blackwell 1986, 127–128; See also Nironen, *Neuvostoliitto läntisen teknologian tuojana*, 50–53. About the different approach to the CoCom see I. Jackson, *The Economic Cold War. America, Britain and East-West Trade, 1948–1963*. New York: Palgrave 2001.
64   Hanson, *The Rise and Fall of the Soviet Economy*, 161. As Hanson points out the Volga Automobile plant was reviewed to see if the Italian made machine-tools could be diverted to making tanks.
65   E. Nironen, 'Lännen embargopolitiikka murrosvaiheessa'. *Ulkopolitiikka* 3/1990, 46.
66   The policy of détente or 'peaceful coexistence' had became a central part of theory and practice of the Soviet foreign policy, especially from the point of view of foreign trade. Hoffman-Laird, *"The Scientific-Technological Revolution" and Soviet Foreign Policy*, 3; See also Hanson, *The Rise and Fall of the Soviet Economy*, 123.
67   M. Maksimova, 'Economic Relations between the Socialist and the Capitalist Countries: Results, Problems, Prospects' in Möttölä, Bykov and Korolev (eds.)

There were three CoCom lists organised according to the technical specifications and applications of the items contained on them and different level of restrictions.[68] Because no CoCom decision was legally binding on a member nation, all of its decisions had to be unanimous. In spite of its leading role in the embargo, the United States had only a limited ability to persuade its allies to strengthen CoCom.[69] The Soviet Union was an eligible trade partner; in the Soviet Union markets were large and it had a high credit ratio.[70] As early as the 1950s, Great Britian and France were reluctant to support the embargo of products which could become the subject of commercial trade with the Soviet bloc and especially if these products had a commercial value to the exporters.[71] Even in the United States there were discussions about increasing trade between the US and the Soviet Union without increasing trade in high technology. In the 1970s, American authorities were concerned that other CoCom nations were evading or ignoring CoCom restrictions. France, West Germany and Great Britain all had an export-oriented economy, which affected their attitudes towards trading with the Soviet Union. West Germany and Japan considered 'high technology' sales desirable elements of their normal foreign trade. In the late 1970s, West Germany was the leading capitalist trading partner of the USSR, Bulgaria, Poland and Hungary, and West Germany was the largest single Western supplier of advanced technology to the Soviet Union. Private agreements between German firms, including Siemens, and GKNT also became increasingly common.[72] West Germany's extensive trade with the Soviet Union gave rise to tensions with the United States and increased the level of criticism towards the CoCom embargo in West Germany.[73] CoCom was unable to impose a tight and unified embargo.

Western countries outside CoCom were Sweden, Switzerland, Austria, Iceland and Finland. Of these, Switzerland and Sweden were recognized as major alternative sources of some products and technologies on the CoCom lists. In addition to Switzerland and Sweden, Austria was also seen as a possible trader to the Soviet Union.[74] Finland was not assigned a high status as

---

Finnish-Soviet Economic Relations. Houndmills: Macmillan Press 1983, 25. Professor Maksimova was a head of the department of External Economic Problems of Capitalism (IMEMO).

68 CoCom lists were: 1) a munitions list contained military items, 2) an atomic energy list, 3) industrial, commercial list. On the industrial list there were products that 'lthough nominally civilian had military potential' Restriction levels were: a total embargo, the quantitatively controlled items and the exchange of information and surveillance list.

69 *Technology and East-West trade*, 155–156, 160, 14; See also Nironen, 'Lännen embargopolitiikka murrosvaiheessa', 44.

70 Hanson, *Trade and technology in Soviet-Western Relations*, 123.

71 Jackson, *The Economic Cold War*, 173, 178.

72 *Technology and East-West trade*, 12, 27, 164, 185, 180–181, 189, 224. In 1977, 34 percent of Soviet imports of high technology came from the West Germany, as did 29 percent of manufactured goods. Siemens had cooperation with GKNT and about 6 percent of Siemens' computer export went to the Soviet Union in the late 1970s.

73 Nironen, 'Lännen embargopolitiikka murrosvaiheessa', 46.

74 *Technology and East-West trade*, 153, 182.

a possible trade partner with the Soviet Union, which was quite surprising.[75] The extent of Finnish trade with Soviet Union was almost as large as West Germany's, and Finland, in 1950, was the first market economy to conclude a five year trade agreement with the Soviet Union. In 1955, Finland was the first nation to enter into an agreement on scientific and technical cooperation and, in 1977, the first to sign a long-term programme for economic, commercial, industrial and scientific and technical cooperation.[76] Because of the special arrangements, the Soviet Union was the main trade partner of Finland from 1975, and Finland was one of the main three trade partners of the Soviet Union from 1966.[77] Finland also had close cooperation with the CMEA countries. In 1973, an agreement on trade, economic and scientific cooperation between the Soviet Union, other CMEA countries and Finland was signed. The CMEA-Finnish multilateral agreement also strenghened mutual economic relations by including the exchange of licences and know-how.[78]

Finnish-Soviet trade was bilateral, and trade was handled through a clearing system, which meant that imports from the Soviet Union were not paid in a convertible currency but in Finnish exports.[79] The exhange was balanced on the level of total trade, and agreements on accounting principles as well as framework agreements were made for five-year periods. Finland imported raw materials and energy, which were not available domestically and were vital to the economy. Finland paid for these imports with exports of research-intensive and highly-processed products.[80]

Scientific-technical cooperation

One of the outcomes of the disunited embargo policy during the Cold War was that the Soviet Union started to seek alternative ways to transfer technology

75 In the 1950s the technological level in Finland was not high but by the late 1970s when this report on East-West trade was written the situation was totally different.

76 P. Rantanen, 'The Development of the System of Bilateral Agreements between Finland and the Soviet Union' in Möttölä, Bykov and Korolev (eds.) *Finnish-Soviet Economic Relations*. London: Macmillan Press 1983, 43–44, 52.

77 The other two were Great Britain and the Federal Republic of Germany (and Japan). *Finnish-Soviet economic relations*, Supplement B, 310; See also Sutton, *Western Technology and Soviet Economic Development 1945 to 1965*, 41–42.

78 I. Korollev, 'The mechanisms of the Multilateral Economic Cooperation between CMEA and Finland' in Möttölä, Bykov and Korolev (eds.) *Finnish-Soviet Economic Relations*. London: Macmillan Press 1983, 79–80.

79 P. Parkkinen, 'The Impact of the Trade with the Soviet Union on Finnish Economy' in Möttölä, Bykov and Korolev (eds.) *Finnish-Soviet Economic Relations*. London: Macmillan Press 1983, 192.

80 Parkkinen, 'The Impact of the Trade with the Soviet Union on Finnish Economy', 195; N. Smelyakov, 'Industrial Cooperation and Joint Production in Soviet-Finnish Economic Ties' in Möttölä, Bykov and Korolev (eds.) *Finnish-Soviet Economic Relations*. London: Macmillan Press 1983, 101, 106; Sutton, *Western Technology and Soviet Economic Development 1945 to 1965*, 78–79. About transferring marine technology from Finland to the Soviet Union see e.g. Sutton, 293–294.

from the West. A good example of the new type of technology transfer was scientific-technical cooperation (*nauchno tehnicheskoe sotrudnichestvo*). Through non-commercial scientific-technical cooperation the Soviet Union had an official and approved channel to transfer know-how and expertise from the West. The Soviet Union promoted cooperation with Western countries, and from the mid-1950s it had numerous inter-governmental agreements on scientific and technical cooperation with western governments.[81] The number of industrial cooperation agreements of the CMEA member states and those of western countries increased from almost zero to more than 2000 by the end of the 1970s.[82]

One of the main scientific-technical cooperation partners of the Soviet Union was neighbouring Finland. The international Soviet-Finnish agreement on scientific-technical cooperation was signed in 1955,[83] being the first treaty between any two states with different economic systems to agree upon a scientific-technical cooperation.[84] Soviet-Finnish technical cooperation was a natural continuation of Finnish-Soviet economic relations. History and geopolitical proximity are the reasons usually mentioned for the Finnish special role in Soviet-West trade. During the Cold War 'trade war', Finland remained excluded from the 'trade war' of the Cold War years and became, despite its small size, an 'East-West trading giant'. In some years Finland accounted for as much as one third of the Soviet Union's trade with the West.[85]

The Finnish partners in the Soviet-Finnish commission of scientific and technological cooperation were the Finnish Ministry of Foreign Affairs and the Academy of Finland. In the Soviet Union the partners were GKNT and the USSR Academy of Sciences. In addition to these official organizations, universities, research institutes, different sectors of public administration and economic organizations and enterprises also took part in this cooperation.[86] Direct contacts between the Finnish partner with GKNT, and the important

---

81 Bertsch, 'Technology Transfers and Technology Controls', 117, 120; Soviet government began to conclude various kinds of industrial co-operation agreements with western firms. Holliday, *Technology transfer to the USSR 1928–1937 and 1966–1975*, 47.
82 Maksimova, 'Economic Relations between the Socialist and the Capitalist Countries', 23. Maksimova mentions as cooperation partners among others West Germany, France, Italy, Japan, England, Austria and Finland.
83 Sopimus tieteellis-teknillisestä yhteistoiminnasta Suomen tasavallan ja SNTL:n välillä, 16.8. 1955. (http://www.finlex.fi/linkit/sops/19550030_2)
84 A. Romanov, 'Suomen ja Neuvostoliiton välisen tieteellis-teknisen yhteistyön tuloksia' in Möttölä, Bykov and Korolev (eds.) *Finnish-Soviet Economic Relations*. London: Macmillan Press 1983, 8. The cooperation was based on the treaty of friendship, cooperation and mutual assistance signed in 1948 between Finland and the Soviet Union.
85 V. Reinikainen and U. Kivikari, 'On the Theory of East-West Economic Relations' in Möttölä, Bykov and Korolev (eds.) *Finnish-Soviet Economic Relations*. London: Macmillan Press 1983, 8–9; Finland did not, in principle, favour any market area in the exchange of technological knowledge but the exchange was guided primarily by economic interests. Nironen (1983), 168.
86 *Suomen ja Neuvostoliiton välisen tiedeyhteistyön kanavat*, 1–2.

role of the GKNT in creating strategies for technology acquisition, gave weight to Finnish-Soviet cooperation in the field of technology transfer.

The long-term programme of Finnish-Soviet scientific-technical cooperation, as its key objective for cooperation, aimed 'to faster exploit the achievements of science and technology and new methods of production'.[87] Initially, visits were restricted mainly to factories and production units[88] but soon visits were expanding to research institutes and high technology enterprises as well.[89] The main areas of interest during these visits included process control, computer engineering and dynamic models and control systems of electrical machines.[90] Finnish partners travelled mainly to the institutes of the USSR Academy of Sciences in Moscow, Akademgorod, Kiev and Tallinn.[91] These activities were purely non-commercial transfer, although the topics investigated were in the field of high technology.

When examining this process at the level of an individual case study, Finnish-Soviet scientific-technical cooperation can be divided into two: scientific cooperation as non-commercial transfer; and technical cooperation as mostly commercial transfer. In scientific cooperation, the partners were mainly academic institutes and individual scientists, whereas technical cooperation was based on trade between Finnish enterprises and Soviet partners. For the Finnish enterprises, cooperation was extremely beneficial. In the Soviet Union markets were large, it was possible to make long-term deals and the Soviet Union's predictability was high.[92] Soviet trade was thus highly competitive among Finnish enterprises and participation in all kind of activities which helped to build a share in Soviet trade were actively sought.[93] A good example of an enterprise that was closely linked to Soviet-Finnish trade and scientific-technical cooperation was Nokia, which is now one of the leading mobile phone enterprises in the world. Nokia has a long

87 M. Kaje and O. Niitamo, 'Scientific and Technical Cooperation between a Small Capitalist Country and Big Socialist Country' in Möttölä, Bykov and Korolev (eds.) *Finnish-Soviet Economic Relations*. London: Macmillan Press 1983, 143–144; The Soviet Union was eager to make long-term trade and cooperation agreements with Finland because agreements allowed longe-term and in-depth projects. See e.g. Komissarov (1985), 95–96.

88 Tieteellis-teknistä yhteistoimintaa varten Suomen tasavallan ja Sosialististen Neuvostotasavaltain liiton välille asetetun suomalais-neuvostoliittolaisen komitean pöytäkirja 17.–25.2. 1956 Moskovassa pidetystä istunnosta (jäljennös). Commission of the Finnish-Soviet scientific-technical cooperation (STC), Archive of Finnish foreign ministry (MFA).

89 Antti Niemi's letter (Helsinki University of Technology) to Finnish-Soviet ST-commission 30.10.1970 (in Finnish). Arrived letters STC, MFA.

90 A superficial overview of the study made during three months stay in Finland by Leo Motus, Institute of cybernetics, Tallinn, USSR. July 1975. Travelogues, STC, MFA.

91 Yrjö Seppälä's travelogue to the Soviet Union 14.7.1978; Markku Nurminen's travelogue to Soviet Union 26.11.–18.12.1978. Travelogues, STC, MFA.

92 M. Häikiö, *Sturm und Drang. Suurkaupoilla eurooppalaiseksi elektroniikkyritykseksi 1983–1991. Nokia Oyj:n historia* [History of Nokia], osa 2. Helsinki: Edita 2001, 49, 55.

93 Häikiö, *Sturm und Drang,* 121.

history and from the early 20th century it has been one of the most important conglomerates in Finland. Nokia's trade with the Soviet Union through the scientific-technical commission began in 1957, and from 1969 Nokia's cooperation with Soviet partners through GKNT continued uninterrupted.[94] Especially in the 1980s, Nokia had direct trade relations with the Soviet Union within the limits of the established trade regulations between Finland and the Soviet Union. Nokia's trade strategy, based on personal relations between the partners, showed a profit – the Soviet Union became one of the most important business partners of Nokia. By the mid-1980s, Nokia had a broad trade cooperation with Soviet partners in cable technology, robotics, communication, automation and computer technology.[95]

According to Häikiö (2001) trade with the Soviet Union was, from the point of view of foreign policy, a sensitive area, especially in the early 1980s when the embargo was tightened and Nokia was very dependent on increased Soviet trade. At the same time, Nokia was dependent on American components and was forced to take into account the restrictions set by the high technology embargo.[96] When analysing trade in the long-term perspective, it is evident that Nokia was able both to continue and even strengthen its cooperation with the Soviet Union in spite of the tightening of the CoCom embargo. In this sense Nokia seemed to be in the same position as other Finnish enterprises which did not suffer from CoCom restrictions.[97]

In the context of the CoCom embargo, Finnish-Soviet scientific-technical cooperation presents an interesting example. Cooperation was so closely linked to trade that an exact distinction between non-commercial and commercial exchange was impossible to make. From the period of information exchange in mid-1950s, cooperation had by the mid 1960s already achieved a level of strong development and had became more spesific and target-oriented because of the joint plans and research projects between Finland and the Soviet Union.[98] Trade under the system of scientific-technical cooperation developed along the same lines. In this context, the main question is why Soviet-Finnish scientific-technical cooperation, in the grey area between non-commercial and commercial transfer, did *not* cause concern in the West, despite the fact that trade included items which would be defined as high technology? Evidence that Finnish trade, and especially scientific-technical

---

94 Häikiö, *Sturm und Drang,* 49.
95 Häikiö, *Sturm und Drang* , 52–57, 251, 254; Jackson, *The Economic Cold War,* 179. Communication lines were part of British interest as well when the British government tried to relax the control of telecommunication.
96 Häikiö, *Sturm und Drang*, 125–127.
97 Only in the late 1980s and early 1990s the CIA demanded the production and export of high-technology products like Rauma-Repola's submarines to the Soviet Union/ Russia be stopped. Yle TV news Tue 21.10.2003, Interview of Tauno Matomäki, former president and CEO, Rauma-Repola; Aamulehti (AL) 22.10.2003; Helsingin Sanomat (HS) 22.10.2003; (AL) 23.10.2003.
98 P. Jauho, 'Tieteellis-teknistä yhteistoimintaa Suomen ja Neuvostoliiton välillä kolmekymmentä vuotta' in *Suomen ja Neuvostoliiton välinen tieteellis-tekninen yhteistoiminta 30 vuotta.* Helsinki 1985, 4.

cooperation, would have been a way to bypass the embargo does not exist. Still, it is rather surprising that no action was taken as a result of the Co-Com embargo. One explanation is that Finnish cooperation and trade with the Soviet Union was considered so harmless that no pressure was needed. If West Germany was exporting computer technology to the Soviet Union, then, in this context, Finnish trade must have seemed rather harmless. One explanation, although very difficult to prove, is that by allowing Finland to export high technology to the Soviet Union, the United States was able to keep track of what was going on in terms of technological development in the Soviet Union. It was propable that Soviet Union transferred in technology that could not have been produced in the Soviet Union.

The undeniable fact is that the benefits of Soviet-Finnish scientific-technical cooperation were mutual: Finland benefited from the large resources of the Soviet Union and the Soviet Union benefited from cooperation with their research-orientated Finnish partners.[99] Cooperation was extremely beneficial, especially for Finnish enterprises. For the Soviet Union, scientific-technical cooperation, and especially trade, was very valuable and beneficial. Trade was handled through a clearing system, which released Soviet hard currency trade to other directions, mainly with West Germany. The analysis of micro and intermediate level case studies highlights a wide range of different practices that do not fit the former picture of Cold War trade.

Conclusion

What was the impact of transferred technology on the Soviet modernisation process? Efficiency and an intensive growth of the economy became the main targets that lasted until the end of the Soviet Union.[100] The task of technology transfer was to transform the Soviet economy from an 'imitator' to a 'pioneer' by learning from the experiences of others. Absorbing technology led, as would be expected, to a flow of domestic innovations and technological progress through which the Soviet Union would have excelled over the West. The main problem in achieving this aim was that the Soviet leadership believed that the central control and planning system allowed for new product invention and innovation more or less automatically.[101] The only structural provision that needed to be made was the establishment of the centralized

---

99 As the former deputy head of the department of Western trade in the Ministry of Foreign Trade of the USSR Iurii Piskulov claimed that Soviet demand created Finnish supply, i.e. the demands of the Soviet partners helped Finnish enterprises to create new technologies. Piskulov's statement at the seminar "Economic cold war. New evidence and new perspectives" 14.9.2003 in Helsinki, Finland.

100 See e.g. Gregory and Stuart, *Soviet and Post-Soviet Economic Structure and Performance*, 237–238.

101 Support for this presumption was provided by e.g. the Dasgupta-Stiglitz model which theoretized that the innovation rate would be highest in a socially managed, competition-free economy. Gomulka, *Growth, Innovation and Reform in Eastern Europe*, 54–55. This argument was being openly questioned by the 1980s.

research and development institutes. Output was limited only by scientific and engineering capabilities and the volume of available resources. Planning policy determined how much and where the resources were to be allocated and how the allocations were controlled.[102] By the late 1970s, the Soviet Union possessed the largest research establishment in the world, but, as Graham points out, it received an inadequate return on this enormous investment.[103]

In spite of the obvious advantages of the planning system in resource allocation and mission-oriented projects, the main problem was that innovation and plan fulfilment were almost always in conflict. A major innovation often required several years before it began to operate successfully. The planning horizon in the Soviet Union was short, and did not support several years' experimentations. Any new technology also required considerable new resources and new suppliers, which in the Soviet Union was a considerable problem because of the lack of horizontal connections between industries. All branches of industry needed to compete for the same materials, which resulted in departmental barriers being set up. The prices of new products were often set at a level that provided a lower rate of profit and counted for less towards plan fulfilment than did the older, standard products. Hence, if plan fulfilment was threatened, the tendency was to shift away from new products toward the safe, old ones.[104] Paradoxically, it was this same centralized control that enabled mission-oriented projects, such as the Soviet space programme, to introduce innovation in many other fields.[105] It was not enough to create innovations; the main target, of course, was the transformation of these innovations into competitive products. There was a great gap between scientific and engineering capability and Soviet capacity to transform scientific breakthroughs into economically competitive innovations.[106]

As all analysts emphasise, it is very difficult to evaluate the impact of Western technology on the Soviet economy. According to a 1979 US report on East-West trade, one of the fundamental goals of Soviet import policy in general was to improve the technological base of production with the help of foreign technology while at the same time carefully avoiding dependence on those imports. Relations with Western firms supplying technology were designed to be short-lived, with the aim of minimizing Soviet dependence on them. This aim also guided the country's overall import and export policy. In this sense, according to US authorities, it was quite understandable that

102 Berliner, *Soviet Industry from Stalin to Gorbachev,* 225; Hoffman-Laird, 82. Scientific research work was connected to the planning system in the thirties and forties. Graham, *Science in Russia and the Soviet Union,* 181; See also Nove, *An Economic History of the USSR, 1917–1991,* 350 and Nironen, *Teknologian siirto Suomen ja Neuvostoliiton välillä,* 90.

103 Graham, *Science in Russia and the Soviet Union,* 185–186.

104 Hoffman-Laird, *"The Scientific-Technological Revolution" and Soviet Foreign Policy,* 98; Berliner, *Soviet Industry from Stalin to Gorbachev,* 203; Amann, 'Technical Progress and Soviet Economic Development', 16; Nironen, *Neuvostoliitto läntisen teknologian tuojana,* 23.

105 Graham, *Science in Russia and the Soviet Union,* 201.

106 Berliner, *Soviet Industry from Stalin to Gorbachev,* 218.

technology transfer was looked upon during the late Soviet period as a way to overcome domestic economic shortcomings. The US report shows that the technology gap between the USSR and the West did not diminish substantially between the mid-1950s and the mid-1970s, and neither did the application or diffusion of advanced technology.[107] According to Hanson (2003), despite the major investment in R&D in the 1960s, the gap between Soviet and American technological levels was already widening.[108]

According to contemporary US estimates, Western technology imports into the Soviet Union had relatively little impact on overall growth. Imported technology subsitituted for the development of domestic capabilities and thereby actually impeded the ongoing domestic innovation necessary to close the technology gap.[109] According to Gregory and Stuart (1994), the technological achievements of the Soviet Union were modest but uneven, and the major problem in the Soviet system was that of implementation.[110] At the 27th party conference in 1986, Ryzhkov, the Chairman of the Council of Ministers, was rather sceptical about the role of foreign technology as the basis of domestic innovation and he emphasised instead the need for investment in domestic R&D.[111] The attitude of the Soviet leadership towards technology transfer had changed. According to Finnish contemporary analysts, in 1986 the main problem facing the Soviet Union was its economic system – not its inability to launch domestic technological progress.[112]

According to Berliner (1985), it is to be doubted that the import of foreign technology proved satisfactory as an approach to the adoption of a new growth strategy.[113] According to Holliday (1979), the import of western mass-production techniques played an important role during the early stages of Soviet rapid industrialisation. In the 1960s and 1970s, western technology was important in the modernisation of many Soviet industries. At a macrolevel, however, western technology played a relatively small role in Soviet economic growth.[114] A similar conclusion can be drawn from the analysis presented by Hanson (2003). He estimates that the direct and indirect contributions of strategic western technology (machinery and equipment) to Soviet growth were 'modest, but not negligible'. Hanson points out that western technology helped economic growth. Khrushchev especially managed to reduce the level of distrust towards western technology and created new possibilities

---

107 *Technology and East-West trade*, 208, 217, 219.
108 Hanson, *The Rise and Fall of the Soviet Economy*, 62.
109 *Technology and East-West trade*, 7.
110 Gregory and Stuart, *Soviet and Post-Soviet Economic Structure and Performance*, 250.
111 A. Ryzhkov, *Neuvostoliiton taloudellisen ja sosiaalisen kehityksen perussuunnat vuosina 1986–1990 ja vuoteen 2000*. APN Helsinki 1986, 34.
112 P. Sutela, 'Uuden tekniikan haaste neuvostotaloudelle'. *Ulkopolitiikka* 4/1986; E. Nironen, 'Teknologisen kehityksen nopeuttaminen SEV-maissa'. *Ulkopolitiikka* 4/1986.
113 Berliner, *Soviet Industry from Stalin to Gorbachev*, 251–252.
114 Holliday, *Technology Transfer to the USSR 1928–1937 and 1966–1975*, 172.

for the transfer of western technology. Yet, western technology could not prevent the gap widening between Soviet and western prosperity and the reason was that the Soviet system impeded the assimilation and diffusion of imported technology.[115]

What was the role of the CoCom technology embargo in the process of Soviet modernisation? In the final analysis it proved to be rather inefficient. The embargo did not prevent technological progress in the Soviet Union. The main problems for the Soviet Union in the imitation process lay in its own economic system. The Soviet Union was not able to take full advantage of transferred technology to boost its economy, as much as this was desired by the Soviet leadership. The impact of Western technology was modest for Soviet economic growth. It was put to direct use, but from the point of view of imitative development, i.e. the diffusion of innovations and transformation from a follower to a pioneer, the outcome of the policy was very poor. In many cases the Soviet Union was not even able to maintain its transferred technology, much less to advance it. The Soviet system, and its centralised economic planning system with in-built priorities, blocked the potential for technology transfer to serve as a boost for the domestic innovation process. The inability to maintain and advance transferred technology provides just one example of the broader problems facing the Soviet economic system.

---

115 See Hanson, *The Rise and Fall of the Soviet Economy*, 63, 159. The chemical industry was a one of the major users of western technology during the 1960s.

PHILIP HANSON

Changing the Rules of the Economic Game in Post-Soviet Russia

M any Russian leaders have wanted Russia to be rich. That means – whether they thought of it in this way or not – that they wanted Russia's output of goods and services per head of population to be on a par with those of Western Europe and North America. It hasn't happened yet. In fact, Russian per capita output in 1998 was about the same proportion of the US level as in 1913: between a fifth and a quarter.[1]

That does not mean that Russia is an especially hopeless case. As Egor Gaidar has observed, if Russian per capita output was about the world average in 1820, 1913 and 2001, that suggests that Russia has about world-average economic adapatability.[2] But it does provide a warning: that catching-up is not easy. And so far as the economy is concerned, it is hard to see what meaning to give to 'modernisation' – the theme of this book – if it does not mean catching-up.

After the financial crisis of 1998 the Russian economy has been growing at about 6.6% a year on average. Per capita output has been growing slightly faster, since population has been falling. However, officially-recorded output fell by more than 40% between 1989 and 1998; and the sustainability of recent growth is an open question. Those who are sceptical about it point to weaknesses in Russia's economic institutions, and contend that they are deep-seated. This, the argument goes, will inhibit Russian catching-up.

It has become fashionable in the past five years for economists to say that success both in post-communist economic transformation and (for any country) in achieving sustained, rapid growth depends on having economic institutions that work well: on having what might be called the right rules of the economic game. The problems of 'institutional quality' and institutional change are certainly much discussed in debates about Russia's current economic progress.

1   See Philip Hanson, *The Rise and Fall of the Soviet Economy*, London: Longman, 2003, 244.
2   In a talk given in Moscow on 26 February 2003, 'Sovremennyi ekonomicheskii rost i strategicheskie perspektivy ekonomicheskogo razvitiya Rossii.' I am grateful to Vladimir Mau for the text.

Previously the emphasis had been on policies: pursue the right policies of liberalisation, stabilisation and privatisation, and all will be well, wherever you are. The appropriate institutions either must be created by legislation or will develop from below in response to new policies from above. For example, legislate for privatisation, and a secondary market in shares – a stockmarket – will be developed by private initiative, because the incentives to do so will be there. The development of economic institutions was not treated as a substantial problem, distinct from policy-making.

In this chapter I shall review some of the broader issues involved in looking at Russia's current efforts at modernising as a matter of institutional change: what are economic institutions? Are there such things as 'good institutions' that are identifiable and that can be shown to assist, or even to be necessary for, rapid, long-run growth? I shall then review changes in the Russian economy since the fall of communism, asking: if there is such a thing as a set of good economic institutions, has Russia been moving towards it, and what have been the things that either block or assist such institutional improvement? I pay particular attention to the 'Yukos affair', which began in 2003, as an event that, I believe, illustrates some of the biggest impediments to modernisation in Russia.

Economic institutions

Economists currently use the term 'economic institutions' to mean a very broad set of social arrangements, including laws, formal organisations, informal organisations such as networks and commonly-understood standard practices, that regulate economic behaviour, and that can vary from country to country.

Paul Hare defines economic institutions as social arrangements that regulate economic behaviour in ways that may not coincide with short-run individual preferences; that are based on shared expectations derived from custom, trust and law, and that are best understood if economic activity is seen as a repeated game; good (my interpretation – PH) institutions entail anonymity: the rules of the game should be the same for everyone.[3]

The body of bankruptcy law, for example, is part of a country's economic institutions. But so is the basis of trust on which transactions are made: in some countries it may be the norm to trust only members of one's own family; in another country trust may be extended at least to people one has known since childhood; or trust may be based largely on written contracts enforceable in law courts; or in some countries one might do business only with people one's gunmen can reliably find and credibly threaten.

An economic system, such as Soviet-style central planning or market capitalism, is a set of formal institutions that determine a great deal about the

---

3   Paul G. Hare, 'Institutional Change and Economic Performance in the Transition Economies', UN ECE, *Economic Survey of Europe*, 2001, no. 2, 77–94.

way in which an economy operates. Economic systems are best thought of as family groupings within which there can be significant national differences, such as those between Anglo-American shareholder capitalism and German or Japanese 'welfare' capitalism.[4] Informal institutions alone can make for large differences in the character of an economy – and even between the way the economy and government work in one region of a country and the way they work in another region.[5]

In the 1960s and 1970s most economists would, I think, have doubted whether we could identify one set of economic institutions that was demonstrably better than any other for a country's economic performance. At that time there were quite a number of arrangements that seemed to work reasonably well. Two groups of people maintained that only one set of arrangements could really work well in the long run. Ardent free marketeers contended that only a capitalist, free-market economy with a minimal state could deliver the goods. Serious socialists claimed that only social ownership and planning could deliver the goods. True, they differed somewhat about what the goods were, but there was a fair amount of overlap. Most economists fudged around somewhere in the middle, being polite to both sets of zealots, in a rather Church-of-England way.

It now looks to many, perhaps most, in the profession as though the free marketeers were right. Certainly, anyone who had the chastening experience of teaching Comparative Economic Systems during the 1980s found it harder and harder to remain agnostic or ecumenical. This course, American in origin, provided in its undergraduate versions a Cook's tour of the developed world, comparing national economic institutions and performance. The textbooks of the 1960s and 1970s cheerfully treated free-market capitalism as some sort of norm, and even more cheerfully assumed that students understood it. They described interesting alternatives to it. Typical coverage included French indicative planning, the Japanese employment system, Soviet-type central planning, Yugoslav worker-management and the Hungarian New Economic Mechanism – usually held to approximate some sort of market socialism.[6] Some of the earlier US textbooks had chapters on the British socialist economy.

One by one, these alternatives collapsed. French indicative planning was fading as early as the 1960s. The Soviet economy, and others like it, ground to a halt in the 1980s; central planning was abandoned in Europe, massively diluted in China and Vietnam, and survived only in countries that did nothing for its reputation: Cuba and North Korea. Yugoslavia disintegrated and its successor-states ditched worker-management. By the mid-1980s Hungarians'

4   For an account of this difference, its origins and its prospects, see Ronald Dore, *Stock Market Capitalism: Welfare Capitalism. Japan and Germany versus the Anglo-Saxons*, Oxford: OUP, 2000.

5   On northern and southern Italy, see Robert Putnam, *Making Democracy Work*, Princeton, NJ: Princeton UP, 1994.

6   See, for a good example, E. Neuberger and Duffy, *Comparative Economic Systems. A Decision-making Approach*, Boston: Allyn & Bacon, 1976.

dissatisfaction with their attempt at market socialism had been convincingly explained by Janos Kornai, Marton Tardos and others. The Japanese permanent employment system, somewhat frayed, is still in place, but the Japanese economy has been almost stationary since 1990.

Good institutions, it seemed, or, rather, the least bad ones so far discovered, were those of the developed West. Inquests apart, there were only two interesting questions left in comparative economic systems[7]: Could the strange, mixed economic system in China produce rapid growth for much longer? And was the continental European style of capitalism, with its lesser role for stock markets and its heavier regulation of labour markets, capable of thriving in the longer term alongside the finance-driven US and British economies?[8]

In considering Russia's current difficulties in modernisation, we are touching on a separate question. It is one that belongs in a different field of research: the economics and sociology of development. The question is: why is it so hard for many countries to acquire 'good economic institutions'? Developing the 'right' formal institutions is not enough; the working of these formal institutions can be subverted by informal institutions – or perhaps one should say, by a culture in which trust is severely limited and the rule of law is resisted, not implemented. Is that the case for Russia, and does this make economic catching-up in the long run improbable?

Economic growth and the rules of the game

The current orthodoxy says that institutions are important for a country's economic progress; that we know broadly what good economic institutions are, and that countries cannot readily change the quality of their institutions. Casual inspection of the economic history of the twentieth century suggests this is credible. Econometric analysis of patterns of long-run (20+ years) growth in large numbers of countries has provided some supporting evidence.

Good institutions are, according to the prevailing view, clear and well-enforced property rights, transparent and liquid capital markets, labour markets that are not much restricted by job-security legislation, product markets that are competitive or at least contestable,[9] and state institutions (government departments, the central bank, the law courts) that are honest and impartial.

---

7   In comparisons between national economic arrangements, that is. The properties of models of different systems are of interest to some, and the working at micro-level of kibbutzim, worker-managed firms and other non-standard businesses.

8   France and Germany lag some way behind the US in output per head of population, but not in productivity more narrowly defined as output per hour worked. Those who work in the US work more hours per year; and the US, with its much lighter regulation of hiring and firing, has a far smaller proportion of the work force unemployed.

9   A contestable market is one in which there may be only one or a very few competitors at present, but in which suppliers know that new competitors can easily enter if there are high profits available; there needs also to be free market exit, so that uncompetitive firms do not hang around, perhaps supported by subsidies, using resources inefficiently.

A number of quantitative studies seem to show that the quality of economic institutions matters for economic growth. Rates of per capita GDP growth over 20 or more years are compiled for a large number of countries. The factors that have been found to work well statistically in accounting for the cross-country differences in growth rates include: the initial starting level (the further a country is in year 1 behind the leading country, usually taken to be the US, the faster, other things equal, its subsequent growth is likely to be); the rate of population change; average years of schooling initially in the workforce (the more, the better for subsequent growth, other things equal); the share of investment in GDP over the period (the higher, the better for growth, other things equal); the initial level of development of the banking system (again, the higher, the better). Recent work by Crafts and Kaiser uses the World Bank 'rule of law' measure as a proxy for good governance in the sense described in the previous paragraph, and concludes that institutional quality in this sense works well to improve the statistical 'explanation'.[10]

For data from 88 countries in 1960–95 they estimate the following ordinary-least-squares regression:

$$\text{Percap } g = -0.854 - 0.493 \, (y/y_{us}) + 0.090 \text{ popn} + 2.357 \text{ sec} + 10.765 \, (I/Y) + 1.061 \text{ RL}$$

Where g is average growth rate for each country over the period, y is per capita GDP in 1960, and the subscript US denotes the USA, popn is the average rate of population growth, sec is secondary education enrolment rate in 1960, I is average fixed investment over the period and Y average total GDP over the period, and RL is the World Bank 'rule of law' measure for each country. The coefficients measuring the influence of each independent (right-hand-side) variable are all statistically significant at the standard 5% level except for population growth, and adding RL improves, in a statistical sense, the overall power of the explanation.

In other words, statistical analyses such as this support the idea that countries in which formal institutions operate by due process, impartially and without 'capture' of the state by particular interests have in recent times experienced faster long-run growth, when other factors are adjusted for, than countries where the rule of law is absent or very patchy.

That does not mean that countries with corruptible courts or with arbitrary and extensive government intervention, or both, cannot become prosperous. The late twentieth-century development of Italy, Japan and South Korea suggests they can. Nor, after Enron, is it wise to equate good rules of the game with Anglo-American practice. But it does mean that clear and enforceable property rights help. And this is the point on which many doubts about the latest Russian attempt at modernisation are focussed.

This understanding of the sources of long-term growth does not rule out

10   Nicholas Crafts and Kai Kaiser, 'Long Term Growth Prospects in Transition Economies: A Reappraisal', *Structural Change and Economic Dynamics*, Vol. 15/1 March 2004, 101–118.

significant improvements in economic performance over the medium term in the absence of a general improvement in institutions. A study of 'growth accelerations' between 1957 and 1992 found that quite small changes in the business environment could trigger such improvements.[11] All cases in which a nation's annual economic growth rate increased by at least two percentage points, and this improvement was sustained over eight years, were included. It turned out that such accelerations were often triggered by fairly small changes: a rise in the price of a key export or quite limited liberalisation; the full set of standard reforms as prescribed by the International Monetary Fund was not a pre-requisite. On the other hand, it did appear that more thorough-going changes were necessary for sustained, long-term acceleration. This finding may be relevant to post-1998 Russia.

The question of Russian institutions and rules of the game

The rule-of-law measure used in the Crafts-Kaiser study makes Russia's prospects seem dim. This measure for post-communist countries around 2000 was 0.706 for Hungary, 0.538 for Poland, 0.507 for Estonia and for Russia, -0.722. Moreover, it is Crafts' judgement, from the study of long-run growth in many countries, that institutional quality has in the past been very slow to change in any one country: Argentina does not easily become Chile. By extension, Russia would not easily become Estonia. If Russian society has deeply-ingrained patterns of 'anti-modern' behaviour in which informal rules predominate over formal rules, and patron-client and other networks matter more than formal institutions (courts, government agencies, etc), it is hard to see how property rights can be made clear and be reliably enforced, how 'state capture' by private interests can be avoided, and the resulting limitations on economic growth can be escaped.

There is a great deal of evidence that Russian society in recent years has had weak economic institutions: private interests have captured parts of the state; most recently, an interventionist state has captured private assets; the courts have not been independent; banks have done little to channel funds from savings to investment; crime and private protection arrangements play a large part in the economy; government, particularly regional government, has intervened pervasively in the economy, impeding the working of competition.[12]

11 R. Hausmann, L. Pritchett and D. Rodrik, 'Growth Accelerations' National Bureau of Economic Research working paper 10566, June 2004.

12 See, for example, Richard E. Ericson, 'The Russian Economy: Market in Form but "Feudal" in Content?' in Michael Cuddy and Ruvin Gekker (eds), *Institutional Change in Transition Economies*, Burlington, VY: Ashgate, 2002, 3–35; Alena Ledeneva, *Unwritten Rules. How Russia Really Works*, London: Centre for European Reform, 2001; Richard Rose, 'Getting things done in an anti-modern society: social capital networks in Russia', University of Strathclyde, *Studies in Social Policy*, 304 (1998);

But are there signs of improvement over time in post-communist Russia's economic institutions? If there is any change, what propels it, and what are the prospects over the next decade? The next section is an attempt to answer the first of these questions. The final, concluding section contains tentative answers to the second.

The pace and nature of institutional reform in Russia

In his and the following section I shall argue that post-communist Russia's economic institutions have indeed taken new, capitalist shapes, and in many respects the quality of those institutions has improved. But identifiable gains in economic organisation, such as the shift away from barter or the improvement of corporate governance or the simplification of the tax system, have tended to be the result (not always the intended result) of policy actions; have often been followed by the emergence of new institutional problems; and may not have been accompanied by any improvement of institutions at a deeper level, where widely-held attitudes and expectations still limit the rule of law.

The first thing to say is that Russia's institutions and rules of the economic game have changed massively since about 1990. When, in 1989–90, the Communist Party of the Soviet Union lost control over social activity, the institutions of a centrally-planned economy ceased to function in ways that had been generally accepted before. The state planning committee, state-owned enterprises, collective farms, branch ministries, foreign trade organisations ceased to operate together as parts of a system. It was no longer clear who had rights to determine how particular assets (natural resources and man-made capital) would be used, who had rights to revenue from those assets, and who had the right to dispose of them. Those with control at operational level (factory directors, for example) often did their best to grab those rights and make fortunes from them; they no longer feared control from above. What has been called a 'systemic vacuum' came into being.

Part of the subsequent development of a different economic system has come from consciously-devised policies, with both intended and unintended consequences for economic institutions. Part might best be described as having evolved from below. The box below lists some fundamental changes that are easily taken for granted. The comparison is with 1987 as perhaps the last ordinary Soviet year.

Philip Hanson, 'Long Run Barriers to Growth in Russia', *Economy and Society*, 31: 1 (2002), 62–84. For a Russian exposition of the institutional reforms needed, see Evgenii Yasin (ed), *Bremya gosudarstva i ekonomicheskaya politika: liberal'naya al'ternativa*, Moscow: Fond "Liberal'naya missiya", 2003. Much of that diagnosis and prescription is summarised, though with some interesting additions, in three articles by Yasin under the heading 'Chto delat'?' in *Vedomosti*, 23 and 30 July and 6 August 2003.

Figure 8. Some organisational changes in the USSR/Russia, 1987–2003

	USSR 1987	Russia 2003
Who decides what is produced?	Political leaders + central planners.	Producers + consumers.
Who sets prices?	Central planners & black market.	The market, but state controls on housing, energy.
Who determines capital investment?	Central planners.	Mostly private firms.
Who allocates producer goods? ply cttee.	Mostly the market.	State material-technical sup-
Who sets exchange rates?	Government & black market.	Market, central-bank steering
How does a production unit survive?	Govt. support if wanted.	Some sectors sink-or-swim; Some still protected.
What is the typical production unit?	State enterprise.	Private firm (many forms).
What do banks do?	Monobank monitors plan fulfilment.	'Standard' central bank; other banks semi-'normal'; thin on fin. intermediation.
What are the functions of money?	Unit of account only.	All 'normal' functions: unit of account, means of exchange, standard of deferred payment, store of value.

The changes shown Figure 8 are not merely a default outcome that has sprung automatically into operation when communist power was switched off. In Belarus, Uzbekistan or Turkmenistan an equivalent list would show far more centralised arrangements in the third column, even though formal central planning has ended. In other words, the changes in Russia are the result only in part of a simple relapse to default arrangements – what people would be likely to do when central control was removed. They are also in part the result of government-planned and legislated reforms and policies: the January 1992 de-control of most prices; the mid-1992 floating of the (legal) exchange rate; the privatisation programme launched in late 1992; reforms of the banking system; restrictive fiscal and monetary policies (applied only waveringly and slowly, it is true) that made the rouble an acceptable currency with, latterly, a degree of exchange-rate and purchasing-power stability.

It would therefore be odd to argue that Russian society since communism has shown little ability to adapt its economic institutions. The question is whether its particular institutional mutations have been helpful or unhelpful to future prosperity. So far, policies and institutional changes have evidently been less successful than in the eight ex-communist countries now joining the European Union. Crafts and Kaiser speculate that the incentive of EU membership has been important. It has required the adoption and implementation of the *acquis communautaire* (which is all about institutions) and thus played a part in the very rapid change of institutions in those eight countries. That incentive has been lacking in countries that are not EU candidates. This may well be the case (whatever one thinks of the *acquis* and its suitability for Russia[13]), but other circumstances almost certainly play a role, too: initial economic conditions and longer-term cultural inheritance, in particular.

The point is that institutional change has, by definition, been very large in all ex-communist countries. Institutional change in Russia has been broadly typical of all 29 ex-communist countries, as measured by the European Bank for Reconstruction and Development's (EBRD's) transition index: less 'good' than most of central Europe and the Baltic states, but more characteristic of the whole class of ex-communist nations than these star pupils have been.[14]

Does Russia's track record since 1991 suggest that successful modernisation and catching-up might, at last, be on the cards? It is useful to look back over this short period – a mere thirteen years at the time of writing – and take stock. In this stock-taking I shall use some Western assessments and prescriptions that seemed at the time to be authoritative, to provide benchmarks. One conclusion that comes out of it is that specific institutional weaknesses that have seemed important at particular times have either been remedied or have mutated into apparently distinct institutional problems. The other main conclusion is that specific institutional problems – but not perhaps the social causes that lie beneath them – can be circumvented by changes in policy.

'The transformation of the Soviet economy is bound to be extraordinarily complex and will take many years to complete.' Thus spoke the combined voices of the IMF, World Bank, OECD and EBRD in 1990.[15] They then made recommendations under three headings: macroeconomic policies, systemic policies and sectoral issues. There were recommendations for institutional change throughout.

Recommendations for systemic policies centred on the de-control of prices and (in due course) the privatisation of most of the economy. There were calls for specific institutions to be created, e.g., for the supervision and regulation of banking and for accounting, auditing and statistical reporting systems appropriate to a market economy. Of more general interest is the following: 'Market-based systems are strongly dependent upon an adequate civil

---

13 Vladimir Mau and Vladimir Novikov have argued that for Russia in the near term only 5½ of 29 chapters of the *acquis* would be desirable, and that several of the undesirable ones, such as the social chapter, would impede competition. See their 'Otnosheniya Rossii i ES: prostranstvo vybora ili vybor prostranstva?' *Voprosy ekonomiki*, 2002: 6, 133–45.

14 For details see Hanson, *op. cit.* in note 12.

15 IMF, IBRD, OECD and EBRD, *The Economy of the USSR. A study undertaken in response to a request by the Houston Summit. Summary and Recommendations*, Washington, DC, Paris and London: IMF, IBRD, OECD and EBRD, 1990 (December), at p. 16. Notwithstanding the references to Soviet reform in the title of the report and elsewhere, the authors showed an awareness that the USSR was becoming radically decentralised, if not broken up.

law foundation, i.e., clearly defined property rights, the ability to exchange property through enforceable contracts and a system for enforcement of those rights.' (p. 35) This was followed by recommendations about legislation.

One particular paragraph about law-enforcement institutions identifies an institutional problem that is still acute fourteen years later. At the time of writing, the Russian state's attack on the leading Russian oil company, Yukos, has weakened business confidence, reduced investment in the oil industry and slowed the growth of investment in total. Much of this attack was conducted by the Procuracy (Prosecutor's office), apparently at the behest of the presidential administration and with no obstacle raised by the courts to a use of the legal system that was at best highly selective.

The Soviet Procuracy, another unique institution with responsibility for the general supervision of legality, as well as investigation and prosecution, currently has nearly unlimited rights to review business records and other information and to conduct "fishing expeditions" for legal violations. The most effective means for limitation of the Procuracy's role in private business affairs would be to amend the statute governing its activity to eliminate or restrict powers of general supervision over private activities. (*ibid.*)

The great bulk of the early policy advice has been followed in Russia, pushed through by an elite of young free-market reformers.[16] Sometimes they were assisted by pressure from outside in the form of IMF conditionality and sometimes they were not.[17]

If the results were disappointing for at least seven years (1992–1999), it was always possible to argue that reforms were damagingly incomplete or inconsistent. Privatisation was pushed through rapidly but large enterprises mostly passed initially to insider control by managers and workers; in the absence of a liquid and transparent stock-market, there was no market for corporate control, so there was no threat of takeover to force these insiders to use efficiently the assets they controlled. Bureaucratic impediments to the establishment of new firms also limited competition. Large firms were allowed to survive by running up debts to one another and to the tax authorities that remained unpaid, and by resorting to barter settlement (in which the values assigned to the items bartered were inflated). Meanwhile macro-economic stabilisation was very slow in coming; when monetary emission and inflation slowed in 1995, and budgetary discipline was still lacking; this smoke-and-mirrors stabilisation collapsed with the financial crisis of August 1998.

At the same time, the state failed to provide an arena in which the more efficient and competitive firms would do well and less efficient firms would lose ground. It was commonplace for large and medium-sized businesses to deploy the state, via more or less corrupt personal connections, to undermine

16 Plus Evgenii Yasin, who drafted early reform programmes, was for a time Economy Minister and is currently pressing for more consistently liberal policies (see note 12 above); he is of their parents' generation.

17 Because the timing of IMF loans was often bad (missing a domestic political window for reform, for example) or the conditions were not enforced (as when loans seemed designed more to support Yeltsin's re-election in 1996 than to reinforce good policies).

competitors. A 1999 study by the McKinsey Global Institute, covering the competitive process in ten industries, brought this out very sharply: competition was not being allowed to operate freely.[18]

OECD surveys of the Russian economy in 1995, 1997, 2000, 2002 and 2004 provided some of the best-informed and sharpest analysis of the economy's problems.[19] The evolution of their references to institutional issues is indicative of changing perceptions in the western 'expert' community more widely. It also illustrates the slippery nature of the whole notion of institutional change and of institutional obstacles to improved economic performance. Here is a very brief and rapid overview of the evolving institutional concerns expressed in the surveys. I shall say rather little about the 2004 survey because it was written before the full dimensions of the Yukos affair had become apparent, and focuses mainly on other things.

The 1995 *Survey* noted (p. iii) that '...the legal and institutional basis of a civil society has yet to be fully established.' In the conclusions to that report, it is noted that particular corporate interests have been able to capture parts of government (p. 136); that extensive crime and corruption reflect 'inadequacies of government and the court system' (p. 137); that an 'institutional infrastructure' of share registers and share-transaction recording is needed to make capital markets work (p. 140); and that government agencies discriminate against new firms (p. 142).

The 1997 *Survey* focussed on macro-economic stabilisation, commercial banking development and corporate governance, and ended with a section on 'Institutional development, competition and future prospects' that dwelt especially on the then-marked tendency to form financial-industrial groups – in part to capitalise on particular informal links with federal and sub-national government. The report's authors referred (p. 144) to '...the implied absence of a level playing field for the fostering of market competition, based upon rule of law, which [the absence of a level playing-field – PH] can perpetuate inefficiencies, promote wasteful rent-seeking activities and corruption, and compromise the ability of the economy to adapt quickly to changing market conditions.'

The 2000 *Survey* included special studies of the phenomenon of non-monetary settlements[20] and of fiscal federalism (budgetary relations between the federal government and sub-national governments). The former problem was already dwindling after the huge rouble devaluation of 1998 (see below).

The 2002 *Survey* was the first to appear when Russian economic recovery was clearly well under way. It focussed on small firms, on gas and electricity

---

18 McKinsey Global Institute, *Unlocking Economic Growth in Russia*, published on www.McKinsey.com in 1999.

19 OECD, *OECD Economic Surveys. The Russian Federation 1995*, Paris: OECD, 1995, and so on (year of publication and year in title always the same).

20 The use of barter, money surrogates like bills of exchange (*vekzels*) and simple non-payment in dealings between firms, between firms and utilities like gas and electricity supply, and between firms and the tax authorities.

reform and again on fiscal federalism. One conclusion was that recovery was fragile; to make it sustainable, there was a need for 'key structural reforms' to address 'a number of institutional weaknesses'. 'A still very difficult environment for business and investment finds reflection in large net capital outflows from the country, rather low domestic investment outside...oil and gas, and relatively few small private businesses.' (p. 10)

These structural reforms included reforms of taxation, bankruptcy law and regulation of small firms (essentially, reducing the bureaucratic hurdles entrenched in law to the establishment and development of small firms), and a breaking-up of the gas and electricity monopolies in order to introduce competition wherever possible, e.g., in electricity generation. (pp. 13–24).

The authors of the 2002 *Survey* noted considerable improvements (in addition to the fundamental fact that output was going up, not down): the reduction of non-monetary settlements, the evidence that entrenched insider control of firms was weakening and it was becoming possible for potentially more efficient owners and managers to wrest control of assets from less competent incumbents. They also noted that the government had a reform programme that was broadly convincing, and some of which was already being implemented.

This picture is markedly different from earlier assessments. It illustrates a general point: that for much of the preceding decade economists had been identifying apparently crucial impediments to Russian growth that either were overcome or changed shape dramatically. One remarkable feature of economic change in post-communist Russia is that it has been so turbulent and so rapid that it is apt to throw up what look like critical problems in year n but which have almost disappeared from the agenda by year n + 2. Often it takes longer to analyse them properly than it does for them to fall off the radar screen.

One example is the problem of non-monetary settlements. It loomed large in the Russian economy in 1995–98. The drastic devaluation of the rouble in summer 1998 abruptly reduced the problem to manageable proportions by reviving a large population of moribund manufacturing enterprises that could now compete as suppliers of import substitutes, and thereby had their liquidity restored. Yet analyses of the problem continued to appear, and improve, for several years.[21] It receded in importance because of an act of policy.[22]

A second example is the regional segmentation of the Russian economy into something akin to feudal baronies, which prevailed in the 1990s.[23] Two developments greatly reduced this problem: President Putin's re-imposition from 2000 of a 'power vertical' intended to diminish the discretionary power

21 C. Gaddy and B. W. Ickes, 'Russia's Virtual Economy', *Foreign Affairs*, 77: 5 (September/October 1998); *idem*, 'An Evolutionary Analysis of Russia's Virtual Economy', in M. Cuddy and R. Gekker (eds), *Institutional Change in Transition Economies, op. cit.,* 2002, 72–100.

22 The act of policy was one forced upon the government, not the result of well-planned choice.

23 See Ericson, 'The Russian Economy...' 2002.

of regional leaders; and the spread across Russia of Moscow-based business groups, breaking up former cosy alliances between regional political bosses and regionally dominant firms.

None of this tells us that Russia's problems in developing the institutions of an efficient market economy are illusory; rather, it suggests that policy and institutions interact, there had been real progress, and the nature of the institutional blockages was apt to alter. Any one particular blockage was apt to be dissolved or circumvented by acts of policy. But the existence of institutional blockages of some sort seemed to be entrenched.

By the time of the 2004 OECD *Survey*, the Russian state had adopted a more interventionist stance in the natural resource sector. The OECD *Survey* authors reviewed the state of play in the gas and electricity industries, in pension reform, in judicial reform, and in banking. In most of these domains, institutional reform was shown to be slow. The Yukos case was not treated at length, but the *Survey* pointed out (pp. 42–4) that there were new concerns about property rights, and that private oil companies had made a large, direct contribution to recent growth, while state-controlled companies like Gazprom and state-owned oil companies had not. The Yukos case and its implications for Russian modernisation will be discussed later.

Has there been an improvement over time, then, of Russian economic institutions? The changes illustrated in Figure 8 are far from comprehensive, but they are enough to show that basic capitalist, market institutions have been put in place. But what can be said about changes over time in the quality, as distinct from the type, of economic institutions? What seem at first like intractable institutional problems have surfaced, and then been resolved by policy actions. But they can be succeeded by other institutional problems that are in some ways their successors. For instance, the problem that Evgenii Yasin identifies in the survival of a large 'non-market sector' of gas, electricity, railways, housing and housing services[24] is the descendant of the non-monetary-settlement problem. So what can we say about any overall improvement in institutional quality?

Here I think it makes sense to concentrate on the period from 1999 when the economy has at long last started growing and – effectively from the start of 2000 – a new President and partly-new leadership team have been in place.

This entails looking at both legislation and the putting of that legislation into practice.

If the legislation proves to be purely decorative, it changes nothing. Getting round the rules is an ancient Russian tradition, and communism honed rule-bending skills. As a western commercial lawyer remarked to me in the 1980s, 'Russians are both lawless and highly legalistic.' An illustration of this side of Russian economic culture is the popular expectation about the de-bureaucratisation laws of 2001–03: 'The good news is that the authorities will be allowed to inspect a firm only twice a year. The bad news is that each inspection will last six months.' In other words: we expect the authorities

24 Yasin, *Bremya...*, 2003.

to bend any new rules; alternatively expressed, we expect the authorities to operate by informal, not formal, rules.

The subjects, as well as the authorities, bend the rules. In the 1990s taxes were massively avoided and evaded. Yet a staple selling item in street markets of the time was guidebooks to the latest tax legislation. It was not that Russians were not paying attention to the tax laws; they just weren't paying taxes.

The observations of Putin-era reforms that follow are only a sketch. After this quick sketch of reforms and their implementation, I shall look separately at the Yukos affair and what it says about modernisation.

So far as reform legislation under Putin is concerned, it has been extensive, and there is more to come. Here is a brief list of the main pieces of legislation: a new land code in 2002, allowing the development of a market in farm land; a revised law of bankruptcy in late 2001, re-balancing the responsibilities of debtors and creditors when cases of insolvency come to court; a series of de-bureaucratisation laws, starting in 2001, formally limiting the number of inspection visits to firms that could be made in a year by many state agencies (though not the police), simplifying business registration requirements and cutting the number of business activities requiring licences and the number of products requiring certification; a new customs code, coming into effect at the start of 2004, that limits the powers of the Customs authorities to dream up their own regulations and detain goods entirely at their own discretion; tax reforms in 2001–03 that have removed some exemptions, abolished some taxes and lowered the rates of others; the breaking-up and (in principle) introduction of competition into electricity supply (2003); reform of the public service to revise its structure, responsibilities and recruitment (for more detail, see Stefanie Harter's contribution to this volume); judicial reforms strengthening in some respects the tenure of judges; banking reform (partly already legislated) raising capital-adequacy, accounting and financial-reporting requirements for banks (if they are to receive banking licences)[25].

Of those Putin reforms that have been legislated so far, only the electricity reform has been subjected to much criticism by economic liberals; its final form has been a compromise that might turn out to be insufficient to generate effective competition in electricity generation and (parts of) distribution. There is nothing especially Russian, however, about problematic privatisations and de-regulations of electricity markets – as US citizens have found. On the other hand, the Putin leadership hs made it clear that state control of the gas industry (through Gazprom) and of oil and gas pipelines (through Transneft', Transnefteprodukt and, again, Gazprom) is to be preserved and strengthened. It is also increasing, not decreasing, state control of the oil industry (see below). This amounts to deliberately maintaining Yasin's

25 For more detail see Anders Åslund, 'Russia's Economic Transformation under Putin', *Eurasian Geography and Economics*, XXXXV: 6 (September 2004), 397–421; on the electricity reform, see a particularly thoughtful political-economy assessment by Leon Aron, 'Privatizing Russia's Electricity', American Enterprise Institute *Russia Outlook*, Summer 2003 (www.aei.org).

'non-market sector', with its damaging consequences for competition and for prices that stimulate efficiency.

What of implementation?

Russia's tax reforms are widely agreed to be a success. They have not so far demonstrated the existence of the legendary Laffer Curve – a Californian fiscal dream in which a lowering of tax rates (e.g. of marginal income tax rates) has such favourable incentive effects, through reducing the pay-offs for tax avoidance and tax evasion and increasing the return to productive effort at the margin, that more is produced and the total tax take is increased. But they have not produced a slump in tax revenues, which have held up reasonably well. The 13% flat tax on personal incomes has reduced incentives for personal tax evasion and avoidance. Together with the reduction in payroll tax (for health care and state pensions), it has apparently decreased the use of elaborate schemes by employers to understate their wage bills – for example, by remunerating employees with insurance-based annuities rather than overt salaries.

One set of reforms that is being subjected to systematic monitoring of its effects is the de-bureaucratisation legislation. This group of measures (see above) was greeted with weary scepticism in the Russian press, on the grounds that it was daft to expect bureaucrats to de-bureaucratise themselves: they would either ignore or circumvent measures designed to reduce their capacity to extort bribes from firms. Six-monthly surveys of 2,000 small firms are being conducted by the Center for Economic and Financial Research (Cefir), a Russian think-tank, with financial support from the World Bank. From the second round of this survey, it is clear there have in fact been improvements on the ground, as reported by the firms themselves – the usual victims of bureaucratic rent-seeking. Over six months the number of visits by government control bodies was down by 26% and the number of licences required was down by 42% – and inspections and licensing were the two components of the de-bureaucratisation legislation that were in place by the time of the second survey. Some further, though smaller, improvement was found in the third survey.[26]

Banking reform has been slow and Russian banks still do rather little financial intermediation. Nonetheless, reasonable measures of the effectiveness of the financial services sector show improvement over time, at least into summer 2004: increasing monetisation (rouble broad money supply as a proportion of GDP), the growth of bank credit to private non-bank firms and households, and a growing share of bank credit in the finance of fixed investment. All these measures are low by Central European and Western standards, but at least up to the bank crisis of May-July 2004 they were improving.

26 www.cefir.ru.

So far as change from below is concerned, there is widespread agreement that the business environment has lately been improving in Russia, not only because of the upturn in economic activity and the legislating of reforms, but also because companies have improved their accounting (many of them moving to GAAP accounting from the traditional Russian system), made more information about themselves and their finances publicly available and improved their treatment of minority shareholders.[27]

In short, there is evidence of recent institutional improvement, not just change, in Russia. Certainly corporate governance, the financial sector, taxation and the regulation of small firms have all shown measurable improvement. And these changes have been happening alongside economic growth that cannot simply be dismissed as entirely the product of a low exchange rate, high oil prices and prudent fiscal policies. A cheap currency and dear oil have helped, but are not the whole story. Growth in 2001–04 has been driven by domestic demand, with both household consumption and domestic fixed investment growing rapidly. One indicator of business confidence, the net balance-of-payments flow of private-sector capital, had been substantial and negative for many years; the net outflow fell markedly in 2003, rose again in 2004 when confidence was rocked by the state's attack on Yukos, and finally went (marginally) positive as inward foreign direct investment rose sharply and gross capital flight, though still high, levelled off.[28]

The Yukos affair

In the midst of this new era of Putinesque political stability, economic growth and economic reform, the Russian state, or more precisely the Putin leadership, showed that this was still Russia, and things were not quite as good as they seemed. The state in July 2003 launched an attack on the leading oil firm, Yukos. By December 2004 the company's market capitalisation had been reduced from $30 billon to $2 billion, its main production subsidiary was being sold off, and Yukos looked unlikely to survive unless as a small shadow of its former self. By summer 2005 the main production asset was back in state hands and the man who had built up Yukos was in a prison camp.

Yukos was a born-again, good-corporate-governance company run by a man, Mikhail Khodorkovskii, who seemed to see himself, before his arrest and imprisonment, as a home-grown George Soros, supporting charities, think-tanks and liberal parties. His action in cleaning up Yukos' corporate act gave rise to the term *yukosizatsiya*, denoting the bringing in of international

---

27 One quantification of this is by the Economist Intelligence Unit, *World Investment Prospects. Comparing Business Environments Across the Globe*, London: EIU, 2001, and subsequent updates. Continued improvement in the corporate transparency of 60 leading Russian companies has been found by the rating agency Standard & Poor's: average scores of 100, against average UK/US levels of about 70: 2002: 34; 2003: 40: 2004: 46, *Finansovye Izvestiya*, 13 October 2004.

28 For details see the Central Bank of Russia website, www.cbr.ru (under 'statistika').

standards of accounting and reporting to facilitate the raising of funds on western markets and perhaps, in due course, sale of the company to a foreign concern. The charges, including embezzlement, fraud and tax evasion, brought against the company and against Khodorkovskii and several close associates, could probably be replicated against all other leading Russian companies with their roots in 1990s privatisations.

The point, for the purposes of this chapter, is not why the attack on Yukos was launched, or what the rights and wrongs of the specific cases are. The worry is that this is a classic example of *ad hoc*, particularistic political intervention in business. The views of lawyers on the whole affair are, predictably, less than uniform. One view is that the fraud, embezzlement and tax evasion charges brought against Khodorkovskii and his associate Platon Lebedev and the tax debts claimed against the company have some foundation in Russian law (though this is not to judge the evidence for the charges) but that the freezing of Yukos assets was excessive and looked designed to cripple the company, and the prolonged pre-trial detentions were also excessive; another expert view is that due process has been derisively abandoned; another is that the principle of equality before the law has been breached by the singling out of Yukos and its core stakeholders.[29]

To give a sense of the style in which the affair has been conducted, it is worth mentioning the contribution at a very early stage of Aleksandr Voloshin, at that time the head of the Presidential Administration, on 30 July 2003. This was soon after the arrest of Yukos core shareholder Platon Lebedev but three months before the arrest of Mikhail Khodorkovskii and before the presentation of bills for back tax (totalling $28 bn. at the time of writing) against the company.

Voloshin summoned representatives of the Western business press (only; no Russian media) to a briefing at which he requested anonymity. He featured in their reports as a 'senior Russian official'; the Russian press identified him the next day. The idea was to calm the fears of Western investors – the new 'useful idiots', a Russo-sceptic might say. He said the whole affair was not authorised by Putin, that the president disapproved of it, realising it was bad for Russia's image; Putin had sent corresponding 'signals' to the Procuracy but could not intervene directly for fear of seeming to interfere with

29 These views come from, respectively, Peter Claterman, 'Summary and Analysis of Report on Criminal Case # 18/41-03', *Johnson's Russia List* (*JRL*), 10 December 2003 (JRL 7462) and 'Summary and Analysis of the "Statement on the Form of the Indictment Presented to Platon Lebedev"', *JRL* 16 April 2004 (JRL 8170); Chatham House Roundtable on 'Using Tax Administration to Advance Russian Statist Goals: The Impact on Economic and Democratic Reforms', 17 November 2004; and press release of the Parliamentary Association of the Council of Europe (PACE), Strasbourg, of 18 November 2004. The last of these records the adoption by the PACE Committee on Legal Affairs and Human Rights of a report on the Yukos affair by a former German Justice Minister. The Committee noted serious departures from due process and described the affair as 'a coordinated attack by the state' to weaken an outspoken political opponent, intimidate others and regain [state] control of strategic economic assets.

the judicial process. (What wavelength was he signalling on, commented *Vedomosti,* that the procuracy didn't respond?)

Voloshin said, 'It's a typical Russian story, competitors [of Yukos] brought information to the procuracy.'[30] In other words: You understand, this is Russia, so businesses can routinely get public prosecutors to do down rivals.

Unfortunately for the longer –term development of Russia, this sort of informal deal has nothing to do with the rule of law. Unfortunately for Voloshin, Putin never called the Procuracy off; Voloshin was removed from his post; and at successive stages of the affair the action against Yukos continued to escalate.

The affair showed that informal rules still prevail. In October 2003, the Russian Union of Industrialists and Entrepreneurs (RUIE) proposed two pieces of legislation: a law that would reduce the period of the statute of limitations for fraud and embezzlement, and a law that would establish what constituted unacceptable forms of lobbying. These would have clarified the rules of the game between the state and big business. The Presidential Administration did not respond. All the signs are that Putin and his immediate team are choosing to operate by informal rules, keeping all major business actors in a 'state of suspended punishment' and keeping themselves free of any constraint by the judicial system.

Russian society received the message in the traditional manner. Of the 27 board members of the RUIE, heading an organisation full of people against whom charges similar to those against Khoodorkovskii could be raised, only six spoke out in public against the arrest of Khodorkovskii.[31]

It might be said that all of this has much in common with the entangling of law and politics in Berlusconi's Italy; certainly, it has striking parallels in a recent series of arrests of the super-rich in China.[32]

Meanwhile some of the changes in economic performance suggest that real damage has been done – though the evidence is so far only circumstantial and fragmentary.

30   *Vedomosti*, 31 July 2003.
31   *Vedomosti*, 31 December 2003.
32   On the Chinese arrests, see *Economist*, 16 August 2003. On Berlusconi's Italy, including the reported disappearance by 2002 of public criticism of Berlusconi on mainstream TV, see Tobias Jones, *The Dark Heart of Italy*, London: Faber and Faber, 2003.

Table 2. Some indications of falling business confidence in Russia in 2004

	2000	2001	2002	2003	2004 Jan-Sept
Net flow of private capital into (+)or out of (-) Russian assets(balance of payments, $ bn)	-24.8	-15.0	-8.1	-2.3	-10.9

	2000	2001	2002	2003	2004 projected
% year-on-year growth of fixed investment	18.1	10.2	3.0	12.9	10.5

	2003	2004
Level of fixed investment in the oil industry in Jan-June (index)	100	85

Sources: www.cbr.ru/statistics/credit_statistics/print.asp?file=capital/htm (Central Bank of Russia website, accessed 26 November 2004); Troika Dialog, *Russia Economic Monthly*, December 2004, p.2; last row derived from the above and the Economic Expert Group, www.eeg.ru?OBZOR/4.html, accessed 26 November 2004.

Interpretation and conclusions

One strand of the conventional wisdom is that Russian society, because of its history, is riddled with attitudes, and expectations about the behaviour of individuals and the state, that are profoundly antithetical to economic modernisation. Trust may be extended to small groups of known individuals, but it is not extended to formal institutions. Due process is not expected; cheating is. This handicaps the functioning of institutions such as law courts that are vital to the good functioning of a private-enterprise, market economy. International comparative surveys of attitudes have tended to support this view.[33] The Yukos affair is a sign that this underlying problem has not gone away.

Yet there is evidence recently, not only of strong economic growth, but also of improvements in specific economic institutions. That does not necessarily destroy the doomed-perpetual-laggard view of Russia. Spurts of rapid economic growth have occurred before. This one is so far quite brief. Institutional improvements are from low levels and leave Russia still far from the leading countries in a whole array of economic organisational arrangements and practices.

The optimistic interpretation of recent institutional improvements is as follows. Russia, like other ex-communist countries, faced a process of institutional change that has no historical precedent. Lessons about the diffi-

33   See the material quoted in Hanson, 'Long-term barriers...', cited in note 12.

culty of improving a nation's 'institutional quality', derived from previous history, might not apply in this special situation. At the same time, both the degree of distortion in Russia's initial economic conditions around 1990 and any cultural legacy from Soviet and Tsarist times were less favourable than the initial conditions and cultural inheritance of, say, the Czech Republic, Hungary or Estonia. Therefore its adjustment was always likely to be slower and more difficult than theirs. But institutional change in all of them has no historical precedent.

All the ex-communist countries may perhaps face another particular circumstance that makes their economic modernisation just a little less problematic than it has been in earlier periods for other relatively backward countries. The steep reductions in transport, travel and communication costs that characterise the post-World War Two pattern of world growth – foreign investment growing faster than trade which in turn grows faster than output, creating the phenomena sometimes known as globalisation – have strengthened the influence of rich-country examples on poor-country social arrangements. This influence may often be for the worse, not the better, but it may be helpful for countries that have the educational and skill levels to benefit. Thus Russian companies have found financial transparency and all the apparatus of so-called 'corporate governance' valuable to acquire when they wanted to attract foreign direct investment or, as most of the leading Russian companies have been doing in the past three years, raising loans and issuing bonds on Western financial markets.

At the same time, the world of national economies is more clubbable than it was when Japan, for example, abandoned isolation in 1868, joining the world economy on very idiosyncratic terms. The developed world is full of rich-country clubs that it would be desirable to join but which impose all sorts of institutional requirements for admission. It would be useful to be inside rather than outside that selectively-protectionist club, the European Union, but that is not an option for Russia. To become 'normal', it is desirable at any rate to join the World Trade Organisation (WTO), and the exercise of negotiating WTO accession has put pressure on Russia to reform its damaging Customs system and to reduce the implicit subsidies to manufacturers contained in its artificially low domestic energy prices.[34]

With this background of potentially helpful circumstances, the recent growth of the Russian economy may itself be a source of institutional improvement. The hypothesis is as follows. Rising domestic output, prompted at first by the 1998 rouble devaluation and the 1999 rise in oil prices, raised confidence on the part of Russian businesspeople in the future of the Russian economy. Suddenly, and without precedent in the post-communist transformation, in Russian experience, domestic output went up – not just of oil, gas and metals, but also of products for the domestic market. Recent experience influences expectations, and Russian businesspeople began to get used to the

---

34 This links up with Yasin's reform agenda. By no means all the demands on Russia by existing WTO members are constructive (for Russia, that is). EU demands for a low ceiling on Russian farm subsidies is a joke in particularly poor taste.

idea that economic activity could rise, and perhaps even go on rising. The developments in confidence are charted by Sergei Tsukhlo's monthly surveys of business confidence among large and medium-sized firms.[35]

This has meant that the attractions of investing in Russia, as opposed to storing wealth somewhere safe (offshore) increased. That in turn would foster a demand for improved institutions: for banks that could be relied upon, for taxes that were predictable and in general for relationships, especially with the state, that did not carry the cost of 'suspended punishment' associated with adhering to informal rules and breaking formal rules.[36] If there is therefore a demand for Russia's notorious informal rules to converge with the formal rules, then the supply of better formal rules (via reforms, e.g., of taxes) meets a constituency – part, at least of the business community – that wants to enjoy the benefits of due process after all.

It is characteristic of those with wealth to wish to protect their property rights, and it may be difficult to do so without inadvertently protecting, through the state, the property rights of others. Once, as Sergei Stepashin observed in 2001, there is nothing left in Russia to steal [from the state], the rule of law may even have started to be popular.

Meanwhile, the Yukos case serves as a grim reminder that actions by the leadership can undermine any such process of improvement. Once more we see a state that is grandiose and arbitrary in its dealings with its subjects. Or will this reversion to old-style ways of running the national economy prove to be merely a brief interruption of a process that has strong support from both domestic interests and external stimuli, and that will therefore resume?

35 See www.iet.ru. The Moscow Narodny Bank monthly Purchasing Manager Index series, separately for manufacturing and services, tells broadly the same story.

36 This notion comes from Ledeneva, *op. cit.* in note 12. If, for example, you, as a company director, cut a deal with your local tax office that both you and they know to be at variance with the letter of the law but which both parties regard as being 'just' (*spravedlivyi*) though not lawful (*zakonnyi*), you remain at risk of somebody – probably a business rival – getting information about your tax affairs and using it, through a link with some higher authority, against you. See Eva Busse, *The Formal and Informal Workings of Russian Taxation*, Cambridge University PhD dissertation, 2001.

MELANIE ILIČ

The Impact of Modernisation on Soviet Women

This chapter examines the impact of 'modernisation' on women, the family and gender relations in the Soviet Union during the twentieth century.[1] The twentieth century is commonly regarded as a period of unprecedented progress in terms of the advance of women's rights and sexual equality – this was, indeed, a 'Century of Women'[2] – at least in the industrialised, developed and western world. In the course of the analysis of Soviet women and modernisation a number of important questions arise: what was the broader context and what was the content of modernisation for women in the Soviet Union? To what extent was the process of modernisation state-governed? How was modernisation championed and received by women? What were the limitations and the costs of modernisation for women, for the family and for relations between the sexes? These are questions that could be asked of any country undergoing a period of modernisation, but of particular interest here is the specific role played by the Soviet regime in the modernisation of women, the family and gender relations during the twentieth century.

It is worth remembering also that, although the term modernisation is often used by historians and social commentators to explain the processes of change and reform experienced by many countries in the late modern period as well as in the contemporary world, the idea of modernisation has a long history. One of the essential components of modernisation, at least insofar as women are concerned, can be identified as an advocacy of greater equality in relations between the sexes. Modernisation also presupposes a shift to a more democratic, less hierarchical family structure, which has been reflected increasingly in the industrialised world in the replacement of multi-generational households with the nuclear family. This study identifies modernisation, in part, with conscious and active programmes of reform that include as a deliberated necessity advances in the political, economic and social participation of women.

1   I am grateful to Lynne Attwood for her comments on an early version of this chapter.
2   I have taken this phrase from S. Rowbotham, *A Century of Women: a History of Women in Britain and the United States.* London: Penguin, 1999.

The processes of modernisation have impacted on women's lives at a number of levels.[3] At the core of active reform programmes – often spearheaded by women – has been the improvement of women's legal status, especially that of wives, and the extension of constitutional guarantees to women. Women have been granted access to education, and to the formal institutional frameworks that oversee the production and transfer of knowledge.[4] They have gained access to the public realm – including the male-dominated and highly masculinised worlds of politics and paid employment – through the extension to women of the rights to vote and to work outside the home. 'Modern' understandings of the importance of sanitation, public health and nutrition also had significant consequences for women and the family. They impacted enormously on the welfare and well-being of everyone in the western world during the twentieth century, and this was not least reflected in the sharp decline registered in the levels of infant and maternal mortality. Advances in modern medicine also offered women much greater control over their reproductive capacities, as well as offering a degree of bodily integrity and sexual freedom. The twentieth century phase of the modernisation process, therefore, can be characterised by the progressive breakdown of the barriers to women's inclusion in the public sphere, the 'modernisation of motherhood' and the sexual revolution.

These aspects of twentieth century modernisation had their roots in earlier historical periods. 'Modernisation' is a term that has been applied to pre-revolutionary Russia much in the same way that it has been applied to the histories of many other countries. Tsarist Russia had a succession of rulers with ambitions to open up the Russian empire to the outside world, and to 'catch up with', emulate and even supersede their more advanced neighbours in the west. Although these ambitions were mostly based on military pretensions, their programmes for reform invariably included the introduction of policies that impacted both directly and indirectly on the status and role of women.[5] It is evident, therefore, that despite the fact that the twentieth century saw

3   For a useful introduction to comparative studies of women in late modern Europe, see M. J. Hutton, *Russian and West European Women, 1860–1939: Dreams, Struggles and Nightmares*. Oxford: Rowman and Littlefield 2001.

4   In 'pre-modern' societies women's educational role was largely confined to the domestic realm in the nurturing and upbringing of children, and in safeguarding family morality.

5   The great periods of reform and 'modernisation' in tsarist Russia are mostly and commonly associated with the reigns of Peter the Great (1682–1725), Catherine the Great (1762–1796) and Alexander II (1855–1881). There is not room to detail the changes that impacted on women here. For systematic overviews, see N. L. Pushkareva, *Women in Russian History: From the Tenth to the Twentieth Century*. New York: M. E. Sharpe 1997; and B. A. Engel, *Women in Russia, 1700–2000*. Cambridge: Cambridge University Press 2004. See also E. Levin, *Sex and Society in the World of the Orthodox Slavs, 900–1700*. Ithaca: Cornell University Press 1989; and B. E. Clements, B. A. Engel and C. D. Worobec (eds), *Russia's Women: Accommodation, Resistance, Transformation*. Berkeley, CA: University of California Press 1991. For documents on women in pre-revolutionary Russia, see R. Bisha, et al. (eds), *Russian Women, 1698–1917: Experience and Expression*. Bloomington, IN: Indiana University Press 2002.

unprecedented changes for women, the 'modernisation' of women in Russia was not specific to the twentieth century, and neither should it be regarded as a particular achievement of the Soviet period (1917–1991), despite the regime's radical proclamations.

One of the fundamental beliefs of the Bolshevik founders of the Soviet Union was that the exploitative economic relationships evident under capitalism, and the social inequalities these generated, would be eradicated with the introduction of socialism in Russia. Far reaching changes were introduced to the running of the economy by the Soviet authorities during the twentieth century, but the social relationships arising from these initiatives, especially between the sexes, were less radically altered. The attention given to the 'woman question' throughout the lifetime of the Soviet Union – from Lenin to Gorbachev – was sporadic and often instrumental. The high points for the discussion of women's issues were: firstly, the immediate post-revolutionary period through to the late 1920s; secondly, the period of Khrushchev's term of office (1956–64); and, finally, the period of *glasnost'* and *perestroika* under Gorbachev, most effectively from 1987 to the collapse of the Soviet Union in 1991. In addition, the policies and reform programmes followed by Stalin (1928–53) and Brezhnev (1964–82) also had important repercussions for the 'modernisation' of Soviet women, the family and gender relations.

On paper the Soviet regime's achievements in the promotion of women's rights looks very impressive, as will be illustrated, and many policy initiatives were introduced decades in advance of their western equivalents. Yet, in essence, the impact of these policy decisions and outcomes was often limited because successive Soviet leaders lacked not only the financial resources to pay for some of the more women-friendly initiatives proposed by their supporters, but also the political will to implement them in full. They also proved ignorant of the need to break down the institutional frameworks and, moreover, the cultural practices that allowed sexual inequality and structured disadvantage to persist after the revolution. The remainder of this chapter examines in more detail a number of case studies that reveal the gap between official policy and Soviet reality on women's rights and sexual equality.

Politics and the Public Sphere

This section examines: the early Bolshevik efforts to 'politicise' Soviet women in the aftermath of the revolution; the election of women to public office in the Soviet Union; and the impact of Gorbachev's *perestroika* on women in public life.

Female enfranchisement was a common feature of many of the advanced countries of Europe and the western world during the first decades of the twentieth century, and in itself is considered an important measure of the achievement of modernisation. In Russia, as was the case elsewhere, women's rights to vote and to participate in the processes of politics and government were the focus of decades of active campaigning that involved the formation of a whole array of women's organisations and parties, and the discussion of a broad agenda for reform, such as that put forward at the First All-Russian Congress of Women in St Petersburg in 1908.[6] There is no evidence to suggest that any of the Russian tsars or their leading advisors had demonstrated a keen interest in, or support for, the idea of women's political rights, let alone the issue of female enfranchisement. It was left to the Provisional Government to grant to all women over twenty years of age (alongside previously un-enfranchised men) the right to vote in July 1917, predating the Bolshevik takeover of power by several months.

In contrast to the western democracies, where the enfranchisement of women was often seen as an end in itself, female enfranchisement in Russia and then the October revolution of 1917 marked the beginnings of active campaigns on the part of the new Bolshevik leadership to politicise women and draw them in to public life. The Soviet Constitution of 1918 endorsed the principle of equality between the sexes, and this was subsequently reiterated in the Constitutions of 1936 and 1977.[7] The First All-Russian Congress of Women Workers and Peasants, convened in Moscow in November 1918, attracted well over one thousand delegates. Soon after, a women's department, the *Zhenotdel*, was established within the Communist Party to oversee the promotion of women's rights. What happened to the *Zhenotdel*, and indeed the very question of women's liberation in the Soviet Union, clearly illustrates the tension between the priorities given by the Soviet leadership to the broader goals of the revolution and what was often regarded as the more peripheral issue of women's emancipation.

The *Zhenotdel* has a well-documented history.[8] It offers a stark example of some of the contradictions of the Soviet 'modernisation project', not least in so far as women were concerned. The *Zhenotdel* as an institution was not the brainchild of the male-dominated Bolshevik leadership or rank-and-file, but can be seen as an almost reluctant concession to some of the Bolshevik party's most vociferous and passionate female supporters. Work in the *Zhenotdel* was never highly regarded amongst the Bolshevik party hierarchy; its

6   For more information on the women's suffrage movement in Russia, and other feminist campaigns, see L. H. Edmondson, *Feminism in Russia, 1900–1917*. London: Heinemann 1984. See also R. Stites, *The Women's Liberation Movement in Russia: Feminism, Nihilism and Bolshevism, 1860–1930*. Princeton, NJ: Princeton University Press 1978.

7   1918 RSFSR Constitution, Article 22: guaranteed 'the equality of rights of all citizens'; 1936 'Stalin' Constitution, Article 122: 'Women in the USSR are accorded equal rights with men in all spheres of economic, government, cultural, political and other public activity'. See *Women and Communism: Selections from the Writings of Marx-Engels-Lenin-Stalin*. London: Lawrence and Wishart 1950, 49; 1977 'Brezhnev' Constitution, Article 35: 'Women and men have equal rights in the USSR'. See *Soviet Legislation on Women's Rights: Collection of Normative Acts*. Moscow: Progress Publishers 1978, 28. Discussions about constitutional reform under Gorbachev included the questioning of the necessity to include an article on the equality of women and men.

8   For introductions to the work of the *Zhenotdel*, see Stites, *Women's Liberation Movement*, 329–345, and B. E. Clements, *Daughters of Revolution: a History of Women in the USSR*. Illinois: Harlan Davidson 1994, 52–65.

offices were regularly understaffed and its campaigns were poorly funded. By the time of the 1927 Congress of Women Workers and Peasants[9] – convened to mark the tenth anniversary of the October revolution – the *Zhenotdel* had virtually ceased to have any political clout whatsoever. In 1930, the *Zhenotdel* was formally disbanded and the 'woman question' was declared resolved in the Soviet Union.[10]

The *Zhenotdel* had faced a difficult task in the 1920s, and was partially successful in its aims. During the first decade of Soviet power, women became more active in public life, particularly in decision-making and policy formation in the rural and municipal soviets, attending the delegates' assemblies and sitting on factory committees and school boards as just a few examples. Nevertheless, its work was severely hampered by a deep-seated antipathy to the very idea of women's involvement in the public sphere, even sometimes amongst the party faithful, especially when this came at the expense of men's domestic comfort and convenience or if it threatened to undermine their public authority. Likewise, even women's education and literacy campaigns could be met with apathy and inertia. The *Zhenotdel's* failure to recognise the social and cultural challenges it was up against was most dramatically illustrated by the disastrous outcomes for many Moslem women of the unveiling campaigns in Soviet Central Asia.[11]

In measuring the level of women's political inclusion in the Soviet Union, we need to look beyond the legal entitlements and constitutional guarantees. After the demise of the *Zhenotdel,* from the early 1930s further organisational structures were put in place to encourage women's public participation, but these were often short-lived.[12] Furthermore, these bodies were now engaged in mobilising women to take part in state initiated economic production campaigns and to endorse the Communist Party programme rather than trying

9   For impressions and speeches at the 1927 Congress, see G. Alexander and F. Nurina (comps), *Women in the Soviet Union.* London: Modern Books, 1929.

10 On the work of the *Zhenotdel* in the late 1920s and its eventual closure, see C. Scheide, '"Born in October": the Life and Thought of Aleksandra Vasil'evna Artyukhina, 1889–1969', in M. Ilič (ed.), *Women in the Stalin Era.* Basingstoke: Palgrave 2001, 9–28.

11 The classic study of women in Soviet Central Asia is G. Massell, *The Surrogate Proletariat: Moslem Women and Revolutionary Strategies in Soviet Central Asia.* Princeton, NJ: Princeton University Press 1974. Bolshevik campaigns on the 'woman question' in Central Asia have been the subject of intensive research in recent years. See, for example: D. Northrup, *Veiled Empire: Gender and Power in Stalinist Central Asia.* Ithaca: Cornell University Press 2003; S. Keller, 'Trapped Between State and Society: Women's Liberation and Islam in Soviet Uzbekistan, 1926–41', *Journal of Women's History*, 10, 1 (1998), 20–44; A. L. Edgar, 'Emancipation of the Unveiled: Turkmen Women under Soviet Rule, 1924–1929', *Russian Review*, 62 (2003), 132–149. For the situation of Central Asian women in the late and post-Soviet periods, see S. Akiner, 'Between Tradition and Modernity: the Dilemma Facing Contemporary Central Asian Women', in M. Buckley (ed.), *Post-Soviet Women: From the Baltic to Central Asia.* Cambridge: Cambridge University Press 1997, 261–304.

12 The literature on these institutions is scanty, but for some introductory detail see M. Buckley, *Women and Ideology in the Soviet Union.* Hemel Hempstead: Harvester Wheatsheaf 1989, 124–127.

to promote women's issues *per se*. The rates of women's election to public office and Communist Party membership, although significantly above the levels of women's political participation in the west, remained far short of women's proportional representation in the Soviet population as a whole.

The women's organisations of the 1920s and 1930s were undoubtedly successful in bringing about an increase in the proportional representation of women on the local soviets. Rates of political inclusion were higher on urban soviets than in rural areas, where prejudice against women's office holding remained strong. By the 1950s and 1960s, women constituted around 40 per cent of deputies on the local soviets and around one third of deputies at Union and Republican level.[13] Women made up less than 10 per cent of party membership at the time of the revolution, but this proportion rose steadily thereafter. From a level of around 15 per cent in the late 1930s, women's membership of the Communist Party hovered around 20 per cent for much of the immediate post-war period, and had risen to nearer 25 per cent by the late 1970s.[14]

It is clear from the following data that in the Soviet Union, as was the case elsewhere in the world, the higher the level of office and the more prestigious the post, the less likely there was to be a female incumbent. Women remained only a small proportion – well under five per cent – of those elected to the Communist Party Central Committee for most of the Soviet period.[15] The first female member of the Politburo, Ekaterina Furtseva, was not elected until 1957, a full forty years after the revolution, and she held office for only three years. By this time Khrushchev had revived the 'woman question' and was actively promoting the formation of women's councils (*zhensovety*) throughout the Soviet Union. The future for women in public office, though, was bleak. As Buckley has indicated, 'No woman sat on the Politburo during the whole 18 years of Brezhnev's leadership'.[16] At the 19th party conference in June 1988 Gorbachev pointed out that 'women are not duly represented in governing bodies'.[17] In the late Soviet period, two further women became members of the Politburo: Aleksandra Biryukova joined in a non-voting capacity on 1988, but resigned in 1990; Galina Sememova became a member in 1990.[18]

Some of the other women who rose to prominence in Soviet government and the Communist Party made their names outside the sphere of politics. For example, Pasha Angelina, the tractor-driving heroine of the 1930s, became a

13 *Women and Children in the USSR*. Moscow: Foreign Languages Publishing House 1963, 109–110; *Women in the USSR: Brief Statistics*. Moscow: Foreign Languages Publishing House 1960, 67–68.
14 See G. W, Lapidus, *Women in Soviet Society: Equality, Development, and Social Change*. Berkeley, CA: University of California Press 1978, 210.
15 Lapidus, *Women in Soviet Society*, 219.
16 Buckley, *Women and Ideology*, 178.
17 See R. Sakwa, *Gorbachev and His Reforms, 1985–1990*. London: Philip Allan 1990, 153, citing *Pravda,* 29 June 1988.
18 See M. Buckley, 'Political Reform', in M. Buckley (ed.), *Perestroika and Soviet Women*. Cambridge: Cambridge University Press 1992, 60.

representative on the USSR Supreme Soviet. Nina Popova, the first chair of the Committee of Soviet Women from 1958, had worked previously in the trade unions. Valentina Tereshkova, the first woman into space, sat on the Central Committee. In 1968 Tereshkova was appointed head of the Soviet Women's Committee, a post she held until 1986.[19] Celebrity, as much as ability, seems to have been one of the factors influencing women's participation in public office.

In assessing the achievements of the Soviet regime in the politicisation and 'modernisation' of women, we need to proceed with caution. In part, the relatively high level of female participation in public office in the Soviet Union in comparison with the western democracies was the result of the operation of strict quota systems that ensured the election of all under-represented groups – ethnic minorities, workers and peasants, as well as women – to positions of responsibility and power. Once elected, women's domestic and family responsibilities meant that, inevitably, there was a higher rate of turnover amongst female representatives as wives and mothers had less time to dedicate to their public roles. In office, women mostly held the least prestigious posts, and dominated those dealing exclusively with women's issues. Soviet state-sponsored women's organisations often had a largely ceremonial and functional role and offered little scope for the transmission of women's concerns articulated at grassroots level to the higher, decision-making bodies.[20] After Gorbachev effectively abolished quotas in the electoral reform of December 1988, the numbers of women elected to public office fell dramatically.[21] Furthermore, once competitive elections were introduced, women proved less willing to put themselves forward for selection, they were less likely to be chosen as candidates and, as we have seen, were less likely to be elected to office.

With Gorbachev pushing an agenda of radical economic reform and the decline in female representation in public office, it was clear that less attention would be paid to women's issues in the formal political arena. Under Gorbachev, it could be argued, political and economic 'modernisation' came at the expense, amongst other costs, of women's public voice. Nevertheless, left to their own devices women made a formidable impact in the area of informal politics. The Committee of Soldiers' Mothers, for example, became an important pressure group, calling for an end to the brutal practices revealed as part of Soviet military training and for better social security provision for war veterans who had fought in Afghanistan. Women even came to form their own political parties (which failed to gain substantive electoral success). By the end of the Soviet period, a number of independent

19 For more on Tereshkova, see S. Bridger, 'The Cold War and the Cosmos: Valentina Tereshkova and the First Women's Space Flight', in M. Ilič, S. E. Reid and L. Attwood, *Women in the Khrushchev Era.* Basingstoke: Palgrave 2004, 222–237.

20 On the weaknesses of the *zhensovety* and the Soviet Women's Committee by the late Soviet period, see G. Browning, 'The *zhensovety* revisited', in Buckley, *Perestroika*, 97–117.

21 For more detail, see Buckley, 'Political Reform', 55–58.

women's organisations had developed an orientation and outlook that was more distinctly feminist, in both Russian and western terms, and a Centre for Gender Studies had been established in Moscow under the auspices of the Academy of Sciences.[22]

The Economy and Production

This section examines: the mass recruitment of Soviet women to paid employment and the consequences of this for women's domestic roles; the persistence of sex stratification in the Soviet labour force; and the consequences of economic restructuring for women's employment in the late Soviet period.

One of the important markers of economic modernisation is taken to be the shift from agriculturally based production to industrial manufacture and output. In this sense, 'modernisation' is closely tied to the industrialisation process. In 'modern' industrial economies, production takes place outside the home and is assisted by the use of machines. Another marker of modernisation has been the recognition and implementation of women's right to work. The demand for women's right to work requires some qualification. In reality, women had always worked and formed a vital part of the domestic economy and household survival. This was as much the case for pre-revolutionary Russia, where peasant women played a vital role in the rural household economy and urban women were beginning to take up jobs in the factories and mills, as anywhere else in the world. By the mid-nineteenth century, women's right to work had come to mean women's right to *go out* to work and to earn an independent wage or salary. By the beginning of the twentieth century, many women, by dint of poverty and destitution, were already forced to do this anyway. Most others continued to be employed for the benefit of their household and in the domestic sphere for no direct payment whatsoever. As was the case in many industrialising economies, women in Russia had constituted a significant proportion of the industrial labour force long before the Bolshevik revolution, and many others worked as unpaid labourers in the agriculture sector.

In the western economies, the separation of home and work resulted in the emergence of the (middle-class) ideal of a non-working wife. A man's wife and his children would be supported through his ability to earn a 'family wage'. This ideal presumed the economic dependence of a woman on her husband (father, brother or other male provider). The persistence of such an ideal also meant that when the opportunities for earning a living were restricted – in times of economic recession and unemployment, for example – then men should have first access to available jobs. The understanding that men would have priority in employment was also seen in the years following the first and second world wars, when the domestic ideal was heavily promoted. In this respect, women have been identified as a 'reserve army of labour'

---

22   See O. Lipovskaya, 'New Women's Organisations', in Buckley, *Perestroika*, 72–81.

to be called upon when necessary. Economic circumstances determined the level of acceptance of the very idea of female employment as well as women's position in the labour market. It should be pointed out also that in industrialising economies men have been more closely associated with the technologies of modernisation, most evidently in the operation of machinery. The privileges that professional, experienced and skilled male workers in particular had built up in the workplace were often closely protected by practices of outright exclusion, the trade unions and even by law. The pattern of economic modernisation in the Soviet Union both challenged and reinforced the western model in terms of its impact on the working lives of women.

One of the undoubted achievements of the Soviet Union in relation to women's rights and 'modernisation' was the high level of female participation in the paid labour force. According to Leninist thinking, the key to women's emancipation lay in their participation in paid employment. This would free them from economic dependence on men and allow them a degree of personal autonomy. Lenin argued also that women should be spared the drudgery of housework and that the tasks that fell to women in the domestic sphere should be socialised.[23] In fact, paid employment was considered not only a woman's right in the Soviet Union, but also a duty, and those who consciously avoided work without due reason could be fined and imprisoned.

Women's paid employment was not only an ideological concern, but also an economic necessity by the time of Stalin's forced industrialisation drive in the 1930s, when full employment and labour shortages propelled the Soviet authorities in to seeking new sources of labour from sectors of the 'non-working' population, including urban housewives and school leavers.[24] By the outbreak of war in the Soviet Union in 1941, women constituted approximately 40 per cent of all industrial workers, and many women were employed in the heavy industrial sectors of the economy traditionally dominated by men. From a wartime peak of 55 per cent, the proportion of women employed in the national economy fell after the war, but continued at a level of near 50 per cent until Gorbachev introduced his market reforms in the late 1980s.[25] For much of the history of the Soviet Union, the vast majority of working-age women were engaged in paid employment.

The mass recruitment of women to paid employment in the Soviet Union had obvious benefits for the economy, but it also had serious repercussion for women's lives in the domestic sphere. The planned services and in-

23 See Lenin's Speech at the Non-Party Conference of Women Workers' in 1919, and Lenin, 'A Great Beginning', in *Women and Communism*, 50–57. For more background on women in the pre-revolutionary Russian and early Soviet economies, see also M. Ilič, *Women Workers in the Soviet Interwar Economy: From 'Protection' to 'Equality'*. Basingstoke: Macmillan 1999, passim.

24 For more detail, see W. Z. Goldman, *Women at the Gates: Gender and Industry in Stalin's Russia*. Cambridge: Cambridge University Press 2002.

25 A useful guide to women's employment in the Soviet Union is provided by the series of statistical handbooks entitled *Zhenshchina v SSSR*, published annually. Employment data were also collated in the various Soviet population and occupational censuses.

frastructures to ease women's accommodation in to the labour force were slow to materialise. The network of state funded nurseries and crèches to facilitate the employment of mothers, especially those with young children, was slow to develop, and the provision of funding for the socialisation of household tasks was simply not considered a priority, at least in the period before Khrushchev took office. Many Soviet women themselves questioned the benefit, quality and utility of communal nurseries, dining rooms and laundries, preferring instead to rely on traditional family networks for child-care and to cook and clean clothes at home. Time budget surveys regularly revealed that, in comparison with men, although women spent slightly less time in paid employment, they spent many more hours on household tasks. Women also enjoyed less leisure time and fewer hours of sleep than men. The obligation to work, combined with the fact that women had almost total responsibility for household management formed the basis of Soviet women's 'double burden', graphically illustrated in Natalya Baranskaya's novella *A Week Like Any Other*.[26]

A closer examination of stratification in the Soviet labour force also provides evidence of the limits of Soviet economic modernisation for women. In some ways the experience of economic modernisation for Soviet women was similar to that of women elsewhere. It is worth remembering also that the patterns of stratification found in women's industrial, professional and service sector employment were further reflected in the collectivised agricultural economy, where millions of women worked for little monetary reward. Outside of agriculture, women were mostly employed in the light industrial and service sectors, in lower skilled and poorly paid jobs. Women were widely employed in unskilled, auxiliary occupations and had restricted access to jobs requiring the use of complex machinery. They were prohibited by law from employment in many of the occupations that attracted higher wages. The provision of the Soviet Labour Code of 'equal pay for equal work' was not guaranteed in practice, and women continued to earn significantly less on average than men. Women trained in vast numbers for professional occupations, such as medicine and engineering, but when these became heavily feminised they no longer carried the same status as they did in the west.

The on-going commitment of the Soviet regime to female employment, and indeed the very idea of women's right to work, was put to the test when the introduction of market reforms under Gorbachev in the late 1980s threatened the Soviet economy with unemployment for the first time since the 1920s. As part of his reform agenda during *perestroika*, Gorbachev professed a desire to return Soviet women to their 'purely womanly mission'.[27] The practical outcomes of economic restructuring were growing instability in the labour market and widespread female underemployment and unemployment. Pro-

---

26 First published as 'Nedeliya kak nedeliya' in the literary journal *Novyi mir* in 1969, and in English by Virago in 1989.

27 M. Gorbachev, *Perestroika: New Thinking for Our Country and the World*. London: Collins 1987, 117.

tective labour laws, the enforcement of which was so often neglected in the past, were now rigorously upheld so that women working in the proscribed occupations now had to relinquish jobs to men. One of the paradoxes of *perestroika* was that women could now be freed from an intolerable double burden by returning them to the home.[28]

Women, Reproduction and the Domestic Sphere

This section provides: an overview of Soviet policy on marriage, motherhood and the family; the consequences of these policies for women's everyday lives; and the impact of market relations on women and the family during the period of *perestroika*.

One of the common features of modernising societies in the late modern period has been the weakening of the structures of the extended household and the bonds of the patriarchal family. Married women have been provided with greater entitlements within marriage – to the guardianship of their children and to the ownership of property, for example – and have been granted the possibility of legally dissolving their marital ties. Motherhood has also undergone a radical transformation, and women have, with medical advances, been provided with greater opportunities to control their own fertility, both through the use of contraception and via access to abortion. Divorce and legal separation, remaining unmarried, single parenthood and childlessness all, to a large extent, lost their negative stigma during the twentieth century, especially in the years after the end of the second world war. Nevertheless, women's commitment to the institutions of marriage and motherhood remained strong in the twentieth century, with the majority of women opting to marry and to have children, and this was no less the case in the Soviet Union than anywhere else in the developed world. Moreover, traditional understandings of women's role and responsibilities in the domestic sphere also remained entrenched.

As part of the challenge to the traditional authority of the Orthodox Church in Russia and progressive secularisation after the October revolution, the Bolsheviks introduced a series of decrees that provided a new legal framework for the institution of marriage. From 1918, weddings were conducted by civil, rather than religious, authorities; openly accessible and simplified procedures for divorce were introduced, the illegitimate status of children born out of wedlock was undermined, and 'common law' marriages were effectively recognised. In addition to the provisions of the Family Code, the 1918 Labour Code introduced relatively generous provision for paid maternity leave and welfare benefits. The Labour Code also included the opportunity for working mothers to take nursing breaks to feed their babies and to work at a place near their home. The right to work of pregnant women and new mothers was protected. In 1920 the Soviet Union became the first country in

---

28   See J. Shapiro, 'The Industrial Labour Force', in Buckley, *Perestroika*, 14–38.

the world to legalise abortion. This, however, was a rather reluctant concession to women (in the absence, it should be noted, of reliable contraception), introduced with the intention of improving women's health and protecting them from the dangers of illegal operations rather than offering a genuine 'right to choose'.

Despite these radical proclamations, the weakening of marital ties, the availability of abortion on demand and the privileges accorded to pregnant women and new mothers in the workplace did not always work in women's favour. The simplification and easy affordability of the new marriage and divorce procedures induced a rather relaxed attitude towards marriage and parental responsibilities amongst some men. By the mid-1920s women were complaining that they were too readily abandoned once they became pregnant, and they had no means of raising a family on their own. Revisions to the Family Code in 1926 tightened up divorce procedures (doing away with the so-called system of 'postcard divorce') and introduced stricter provisions for the payment of child support and alimony.[29] In the 1920s also, when unemployment was high and there was a ready supply of labour, employers proved reluctant to uphold the employment rights of pregnant women and new mothers.[30] Women's economic vulnerability and consequent sexual exploitation were reflected in the official concern about the continuing prevalence of prostitution in the Soviet Union after the revolution.[31]

The social problems arising from unstable domestic relationships and growing demographic pressures propelled Stalin to introduce sharp reversals in family policy in the mid-1930s. The procedures for obtaining a divorce became more complex and more expensive in 1935, and abortion was re-criminalised in the following year, after much debate in the press.[32] In the late 1930s and again in 1944 honorific titles and medals, as well as financial inducements, were awarded to mothers of large families in an attempt to boost the birth rate. The institution of the family, identified as a bourgeois concept in some Marxist and early Bolshevik thinking, now became the mainstay of Soviet society. Juvenile delinquency, deviancy and crime were increasingly blamed on absent fathers and particularly on inadequate mothering. The legal provisions of the mid-1930s were not overturned until after Stalin's death in 1953. Under Khrushchev, more social support was provided

---

29 For women's advocacy of changes in the Family Code, see W. Z. Goldman, *Women, the State and Revolution: Soviet Family Policy and Social Life, 1917–1936.* Cambridge: Cambridge University Press 1993.

30 For the introduction of these provisions and the failure to uphold them, see Ilič, *Women Workers*, ch. 5.

31 E. Waters, 'Victim or Villain: Prostitution in Post-Revolutionary Russia', in L. Edmondson (ed.), *Women and Society in Russia and the Soviet Union.* Cambridge: Cambridge University Press 1992, 160–177.

32 J. Evans, 'The CPSU and the "Woman Question": the Case of the 1936 Decree "In Defence of Mother and Child"', *Journal of Contemporary History*, 16 (1981), 757–775. For documents on the legal provisions and debates, see also R. Schlesinger, *The Family in the USSR. (Changing Attitudes in Soviet Russia).* London: Routledge and Kegan Paul 1949.

to help parents meet their family and civic responsibilities, and court action was taken against those who did not.[33]

In addition to marriage, motherhood also came under scrutiny in the Soviet Union. In the aftermath of the revolution, the Bolshevik authorities attempted to counter the population losses of the war and civil war years by promoting motherhood through the replacement of traditional patterns of childbirth and child rearing with modern, medical practices. A recently published ethnographic study has revealed the varieties of practice in mothering in Russia and the Soviet Union across different regions and generations, and has highlighted the persistence of superstition and folkloric beliefs, some of which were demonstrably harmful to babies, well in to the twentieth century.[34] As an earlier study had already pointed out, Enlightenment thinking on modern mothering was late to enter Russia, but even so it predated the October revolution by many decades.[35]

Soviet attempts to 'modernise' motherhood consisted almost exclusively of a medical model of childbirth and the teaching of mother craft along the lines of a scientific method, in much the same way as 'modern' motherhood was promoted in the west. The traditional village midwife was presented as an ignorant and potentially harmful interference in much of the early Soviet visual culture and literature on motherhood. Births came to be increasingly attended by doctors and medically trained midwives, and to take place in hospitals and sanitaria. The shared intimacy of the maternity wards provided an opportunity for women to talk about private aspects of their lives more openly with other women.[36]

The public discussion of private realities was brought into sharp relief by Gorbachev's advocacy of *glasnost'* (openness) as an integral part of his own modernising agenda in the late 1980s. The relaxation of censorship and state control over the media resulted in seemingly endless broadcasts and publications that revealed the delicate condition of the Soviet social fabric. With the economic downturn precipitated by *perestroika*, Soviet women's precarious social status and growing economic vulnerability was again reflected, as it had been in the 1920s, in official concern over such issues as domestic disharmony and family instability, and in the increasing sexual exploitation and abuse of women.[37] By the late 1980s divorce was

33 See D. Field, 'Mothers and Fathers and the Problem of Selfishness in the Khrushchev Period', in Ilič, Reid and Attwood, *Women in the Khrushchev Era*, 96–113.

34 D. L. Ransel, *Village Mothers: Three Generations of Change in Russia and Tataria.* Bloomington, IN: Indiana University Press 2000.

35 E. Waters, 'The Modernisation of Russian Motherhood, 1917–1937', *Soviet Studies*, 44, 1 (1992), 123–135.

36 For a fictionalised account, see J. Voznesenskaya, *The Women's Decameron.* London: Quartet books 1986.

37 See, for example, E. Waters, 'Restructuring the "Woman Question": *Perestroika* and Prostitution', *Feminist Review*, 33 (1989), 3–19; R. Shreeves, 'Sexual Revolution or "Sexploitation"?: the Pornography and Erotica Debate in the Soviet Union', in S. Rai, H. Pilkington and A. Phizacklea (eds), *Women in the Face of Change: the Soviet Union, Eastern Europe and China.* London: Routledge 1992, 130–146.

commonplace and was often initiated by disgruntled wives. Many women, living in constrained financial circumstances and in confined domestic accommodation, especially in the major urban centres, were opting to have only one child. They endured repeated abortions in an attempt to limit the size of their families. Reports investigating the impact of the cutbacks in public funding in the areas of health and welfare revealed the unsanitary and sometimes dangerous conditions in which these abortions were performed. The proposed return of women to the domestic sphere coincided with some unpleasant revelations about its limitations and realities.

'Modernisation' in Question

In this section we return to the questions set out in the introduction. The 'modernisation' of Soviet women took place in a country where the specific conditions of socialism were supposed to eradicate social inequalities. The Soviet example illustrates clearly what we could identify as the 'persistence of patriarchy' under socialism, not only in the domestic sphere, but also in the relationship between state and society.[38] The Soviet modernisation project drew women in to the public realm, in politics and employment, but left in place structural frameworks and cultural practices that allowed inequalities between the sexes to continue. Women's almost exclusive responsibility for childcare, household management and domestic servicing remained unchallenged, as did their secondary status in public decision-making and the paid labour force. The process of modernisation was state governed and law driven in the Soviet Union. Women's rights to vote and to participate in policy formation, to work outside the home and to 'choose' in the areas of motherhood and sexuality were enshrined in law, but were also much constrained in their implementation.

There was little evidence of an open and independent women's movement in the Soviet Union for much of its history. The periods of the most vociferous and public championing of women's issues were the 1920s and late 1980s, both periods in which the modernising agenda was dominated by economic concerns. At other times, women's voices were confined to the underground, *samizdat* press, and some of the advocates of women's rights were expelled from the Soviet Union.[39] The concessions offered to women to enable them more easily to fulfil their public duties were not always gratefully received. Public services were so often inadequately funded and sometimes of such poor quality that they offered little in the way of relief to women's domestic burdens. The outcome for women was a daily double shift of paid employment

---

38 See the arguments advanced in S. Ashwin (ed.), *Gender, State and Society in Soviet and Post-Soviet Russia.* London: Routledge 2000.
39 See, for example, *Woman and Russia: First Feminist Samizdat.* London: Sheba Feminist Publishers 1980; T. Mamonova (ed.), *Women and Russia: Feminist Writings from the Soviet Union.* Oxford: Blackwell 1984; and T. Mamonova, *Russian Women's Studies: Essays on Sexism in Soviet Culture.* Oxford: Pergamon Press 1989.

and unpaid domestic labour. Gorbachev's modernising agenda only served to marginalise women and debates about women's issues in the public sphere, to place many women in financially precarious and vulnerable positions and to expose them to economic and sexual exploitation. Paradoxically, this final assault on women's rights in the Soviet Union paved the way for an active and vocal women's movement in Russia after 1991.

RICHARD SAKWA

The Modernisation of Leadership:
From Gorbachev to Putin

The presidency is the most powerful and at the same time the most controversial political institution in contemporary Russia. The presidency
emerged under Mikhail Gorbachev in the final days of the Soviet Union to
counteract the residual powers of the declining Communist Party of the Soviet Union (CPSU), and as an institution it was then forged in Russia in the
heat of conflict between Boris Yeltsin and the legislature in the early 1990s.
The constitution adopted on 12 December 1993 established the presidency
as the core of executive authority, and these powers were then put to use by
Russia's first president, Yeltsin, and his successor, Vladimir Putin. What
has been dubbed a 'hegemonic presidency' affects all aspects of Russian
political life and under Putin became the heart of what many see as a system
of 'managed democracy'. The presidency became hegemonic in the sense
that it is the core of the institutional arrangements of Russian governance
and seeks to subordinate all these institutions to its leadership. It is equally
hegemonic in that it seeks to dominate, if not control, political processes
and outcomes as well. It is for this reason that the presidency is not only
institutionally powerful but also politically controversial. It is also for this
reason that questions can be raised about the degree to which contemporary
Russian leadership has been modernised.

The modernisation of leadership: a conceptual framework

The concept of modernisation is by definition relative: an earlier type of social organisation characterised by one set of features gives way to another in
which a different set of characteristics predominate. In our case traditional
patrimonial-type leadership should give way to a functionally differentiated,
accountable and delineated system of rule for leadership to be called modern. Leadership of course does not operate in a vacuum, and the nature of
state development and the principles on which the social order is based will
affect the shape of leadership. Although this chapter will adopt a Weberian
approach to leadership (Weber's analysis, although incomplete and fragmented, still retains a powerful explanatory methodology rooted in a dynamic
of contrasting traditional and modern approaches to leadership), in certain

160

respects the onset of what is sometimes characterised as post-modernism also heralds the challenge of post-Weberian approaches. Post-structural or discourse analysis approaches to leadership have much to offer, but we will no more than allude to these. The key point is that the modernisation project itself has dissolved into a welter of competing legitimating terrains, and where leadership is concerned traditional hierarchical and party-based systems have fragmented into a number of neo-traditional charismatic orders. It could be argued that Russia has leapt straight from pre-modern into post-modern modes of leadership.

We will offer four basic characteristics that define a modernised leadership. For clarity of exposition these will take the form of binary pairs, with the first element reflecting a dysfunctional factor (from the perspective of effective state-building), while the second is supportive of modern forms of constitutionalism. The first focuses on the tension between neo-patrimonialism and liberalism. According to Weber the boundaries of patrimonial are typically unclear, with the powers exercised by leaders and officials considered personal and derived from the relationship to the office-holder rather than a clearly demarcated and institutionalised office.[1] Although highly bureaucratised, the state does not function as a clearly delineated bureaucracy. To compensate, there is an expansive dynamic to the powers of office holders as they try to reduce risk by extending their authority. This process is characteristic not only of the state but also of all other social organisations; and in our case the legislature but it is equally applicable to ministries and enterprises.[2] In his study of China Walder argued that authority patterns in enterprises were 'neo-traditional', with the authority of the director reinforced by the party-state to reproduce in new forms traditional authority patterns of personal loyalty and discretionary powers of leaders.[3] A liberal order corresponds to Weber's rational administrative system governed by genuine constitutionalism, the separation of powers and the rule of law.[4]

The second feature is the contrast between emergency and 'normal' (non-emergency) forms of rule. Much of Russian history is characterised by this tension. In his *Discourses* Machiavelli makes the following crucial observation.

---

1   H. H. Gerth and C. Wright Mills (eds), *From Max Weber: Essays in Sociology* (New York, Oxford University Press, 1946), 244, 297–8.

2   Hans Van Zon, 'Neo-Patrimonialism as an Impediment to Economic Development: The Case of Ukraine', *Journal of Communist Studies and Transition Politics*, Vol. 17, No. 3, September 2001, 73–74.

3   Andrew Walder, *Communist Neo-Traditionalism: Work and Authority in Chinese Industry* (Berkeley, University of California Press, 1986).

4   See András Sajó, *Limiting Government: An Introduction to Constitutionalism* (Budapest, Central European University Press, 1999). For a classic presentation of the issues, see M. J. C. Vile, *Constitutionalism and the Separation of Powers* (Oxford, Oxford University Press, 1967; second edition, Indianapolis, Libery Fund, 1998). See also Levent Gönenc, *Prospects for Constitutionalism in Postcommunist Countries* (The Hague, Kluwer, 2001).

> In a well-ordered republic it should never be necessary to resort to extra-constitutional measures; for although they may for the time be beneficial, yet the precedent is pernicious, for if the practice is once established of disregarding the laws for good objects, they will in a little while be disregarded under the pretext for evil purposes. Thus no republic will ever be perfect is she has not by law provided for everything, having a remedy for emergency, and fixed rules for applying it.[5]

Politics under Yeltsin remained embroiled in what might be called a permanent state of insurgency (axiological politics), sometimes known as the politics of transition. Yeltsin's rule was less anti-constitutional rather than, to use Machiavelli's phrase, 'extra-constitutional'. No settled legal order emerged where the executive itself became subordinate to law. The issue was explored in revolutionary England by John Selden, where he distinguished, as Richard Tuck puts it, 'between the arena of law and that of necessity'.[6] Selden insisted that the plea of necessity 'could never be used *within* the legal order',[7] and its use is an implicit admission that the civil order has broken down, or, in Russia's case, has not yet been constituted. As with the Bolsheviks earlier, a displacement of sovereignty took place; the regime eschewed responsibility to the actual people existing at that time, and instead a mythical people of the future was invoked that would emerge as a result of the 'transition' policies of the regime. Just as communism was built on the bones of the contemporary generation so, too, Yeltsin's regime took on neo-Bolshevik features insofar as it appeared willing to sacrifice the needs of this generation for the good of the next.

The third feature is the tension between stability and order.[8] This was a feature of Brezhnev's rule that in the end gave way to stagnation. Stability is the short-term attempt to achieve political and social stabilisation without having resolved the underlying problems and contradictions besetting society. Thus Brezhnev refused to take the hard choices that could have threatened the regime's precarious political stability, and thus his stability gave way to stagnation. Order in this context is something that arises when society, economy and political system are in some sort of balance.[9] An ordered soci-

---

5   Niccolo Machiavelli, *Discourses on the First Ten Books of Titus Livius*, in Max Lerner (ed.), *The Prince and the Discourses*, translated by Christian E. Detmold, (New York, Modern Library, 1950), 203.

6   Richard Tuck, 'Grotius and Selden', in J. H. Burns (ed.), *The Cambridge History of Political Thought, 1450–1700* (Cambridge, Cambridge University Press, 1991), 529.

7   Tuck, 'Grotius and Selden', 528.

8   I first discussed this distinction in 'The Soviet State, Civil Society and Moscow Politics: Stability and Order in Early NEP, 1921–24', in Julian Cooper, Maureen Perrie and E. A. Rees (eds), *Soviet History 1917–1945: Essays in Honour of R. W. Davies* (London, Macmillan, 1995), 42–77.

9   For the theory of congruence and its application to Russia, see Harry Eckstein, Frederic J. Fleron Jr., Erik P. Hoffmann, and William M. Reissinger, *Can Democracy Take Root in Post-Soviet Russia? Explorations in State-Society Relations* (Lanham, MD, Rowman & Littlefield Publishers, Inc., 1998).

ety operates according to spontaneous processes, whereas in a system based on the politics of stability administrative measures tend to predominate. In an ordered society there are clear rules of the game backed by the rule of law, secure property rights and governmental accountability. In a stability regime the bureaucrat exercises arbitrary authority and the government acts in a neo-patrimonial manner. While Russia had the full panoply of democratic institutions by the end of the 1990s, something was clearly missing. Shevtsova identified it as the absence 'of a mechanism for elaborating and implementing socially effective decisions. [The power system] cannot develop independently and depends entirely on manual control'.[10] The new order was not working automatically but depended on individual management, something that continued into the Putin years. The shift from stability to order is the politics of normalisation. As Gleb Pavlovsky argued, the main source of conflict in the Russian political elite is 'resistance to normalisation'.[11] As far as he was concerned, Russia faced a choice between the rule of the new security establishment or 'the financial rule of the seven boyars'.

The fourth is the contrast between the informal relations of power established within the framework of regime politics, on the one hand, and the institutionalised politics characteristic of a genuinely constitutional state.

Leadership under Gorbachev

A presidential system emerged in the last Soviet years to compensate for the decline of the CPSU and the weakness of parliament.[12] Despite the resurrection of the revolutionary slogan 'all power to the soviets', the revived legislatures failed to live up to expectations. The constitutional amendments of 1 December 1988 made the USSR Congress of People's Deputies (CPD) the highest power in the land, and following the elections of March 1989 Gorbachev was elected chair of the new body. The basis of his rule began to shift from the CPSU to the new legislature. On the very day that the Communist Party officially lost its monopoly on power, 14 March 1990, the powers of the Soviet presidency were strengthened. An executive presidency independent of the legislature was established, and Gorbachev was elected to this post in an uncontested ballot by the CPD on 15 March 1990. His refusal to face national elections undermined the legitimacy not only of the post but marked the point where his credibility as a democratic reformer was fatally damaged.

Presidential powers were increased during the course of the year, and at the Fourth USSR CPD in December 1990 the shift was completed by the transformation of the old Council of Ministers into a more limited 'cabi-

10 Liliya Shevtsova, 'Beg na meste', *Izvestiya*, 12 February 1998, 4.
11 *Izvestiya*, 9 September 2003.
12 See Stephen White, 'The Presidency and Political Leadership', in Peter Lentini (ed.), *Elections and Political Order in Russia* (Budapest, Central European University Press, 1995), 202–25.

net', with the prime minister and ministers nominated by the president and accountable to him. At the same time, the purge and reorganisation of the Politburo in July 1990 conclusively marginalised it as a policy-making body and ended its ability to assert collective accountability on Gorbachev. As Breslauer puts it, Without seats for leaders of the state, military, or police bureaucracies, the Politburo ceased to be an oligarchy of elites that could pretend to dictate policy in all sectors or that could attempt to subject Gorbachev to the discipline of the collective leadership'.[13]

The powers of the prime minister remained limited and the executive powers that were more properly the prerogative of the government were devolved to the Supreme Soviet's Presidium. While the powers of the presidency were greatly increased, the powers of the Soviet legislature were not correspondingly diminished. A new type of dual power emerged that was inherently unstable but manageable as long as the chairmanship of parliament was in safe hands. The chair of the Soviet Congress, Anatolii Luk'yanov, however, betrayed Gorbachev in the attempted coup of 18–21 August 1991, and later, after much the same system was reproduced in Russia, the struggle between the presidency and parliament dominated the first phase of Russia's independent statehood. In a country where the party system was rudimentary and the pluralistic representation of social interests barely formed, the struggle between the presidency and parliament at this time reflected not so much a contest between two distinct but equally valid principles of legitimate authority as a battle for hegemonic dominance over Russian politics, and with it the power to distribute resources and manage political processes.

Yeltsin's leadership

By the end of his leadership Gorbachev had effectively repudiated the CPSU as an instrument of leadership and sought to root his power in a presidential system. His leadership however was never rooted in the legitimacy based on the ballot box and remained characterised by the politics of the emergency. Thus, as always with Gorbachev, his leadership mixed both modern and traditional elements. Yeltsin's leadership in formal terms was far more unequivocally modern; but this was vitiated by the development of a state and social system that reproduced in new forms of traditionalism.

The rise of Yeltsinite presidentialism

The Russian CPD was elected in March 1990, and at its first convocation in May-June all factions united in favour of a strong leadership. With Yeltsin's election to chair the Supreme Soviet in a hard-fought contest in May a signif-

13   George W. Breslauer, *Gorbachev and Yeltsin as Leaders* (Cambridge, Cambridge University Press, 2002), 89.

icant step was taken towards the development of the presidential system. In 1990 the Russian parliament passed some 150 acts affecting virtually every aspect of Russian life. Even so, Yeltsin insisted that the crisis of executive power remained acute.[14] Yeltsin's conservative opponents began to have second thoughts over the merits of a presidential system. They were outmanoeuvred, however, by the opportunity offered by Gorbachev's referendum of 17 March 1991 on the 'renewed Union'. In Russia a second question was added to the ballot asking the people to endorse the creation of a directly elected presidency. Russians voted by the same margin for the union and a directly elected president of Russia.[15] If during the communist era the 'leading and guiding' role of the Party was legitimated by its claims to be leading the country in building communism, now the presidency's leading role was legitimated by the need for strong leadership in the 'reforms' required to build capitalism.[16] It is this common *purposive* nature of power, which by definition displaces sovereignty away from the people as they actually exist at any given time towards the sovereignty of over-riding ideal, that prompted Reddaway and Glinski to dub Yeltsin's regime 'market Bolshevism'.[17]

It would be a long struggle, however, before Yeltsin could dominate the political system. When Yeltsin became chair of the Russian Supreme Soviet in May 1990 he gained executive authority but his powers were firmly subordinated to the legislature. The strengthening of parliament, designed initially to compensate for the declining power of the CPSU and to ensure the continuation of 'reform', was stymied by the emergence of a presidential system rooted in the newly 'empowered' legislatures but which gradually increased its powers at the expense of the legislature that had given it birth. From a functional perspective, the Party-state was replaced by a presidential-state. The Congress, headed at the time by Ruslan Khasbulatov, sought to challenge this to create a parliamentary state. Khasbulatov's ambitions were no less hegemonic than Yeltsin's, and the restoration of Soviet-type parliamentarianism under his leadership would have been as much of a challenge to the liberal separation of powers as the triumph of Yeltsin's presidentialism appeared to be. Parliamentary hegemonism came into conflict with presidential hegemonism. The state as an independent arena for the impartial operation of the rule of law in both versions remained under-developed.

At the Third (Emergency) Congress from 28 March 1991 Yeltsin, in one of those reversals of fortune that mark his career, turned the tables on those who had sought to curb his powers and emerged with a mandate for a strengthened presidency. The Afghan war veteran and noted patriot, Alexander Rutskoi, defected from \the orthodox party line and formed his own

14 *Moscow News*, No. 25 (23 June 1991), 1.
15 A total of 73.6% of the vote was cast for the Union, and 69% for the presidency in Russia.
16 See Breslauer, *Gorbachev and Yeltsin as Leaders*, 145–6 and *passim*.
17 Peter Reddaway and Dmitri Glinski, *The Tragedy of Russia's Reforms: Market Bolshevism against Democracy* (Washington, DC, The United States Institute of Peace Press, 2001).

'Communists for Democracy' faction. The balance shifted in Yeltsin's favour. Not only were the proposed constitutional changes affecting the powers of the presidency accepted and arrangements made for elections on 12 June, but the Congress on its last day, 5 April, accepted Yeltsin's surprise demand for immediate powers to issue presidential decrees within the framework of existing legislation to hasten economic and political reform in Russia. The necessary amendments were made to the constitution at the Fourth CPD on 22 May.[18] The extensive powers of an executive presidency were enshrined in law, but so too were a number of potential conflicts.

The session adopted a law on the election of the president, and after an intense two-week campaign the first direct elections for Russia's presidency were held on 12 June 1991. Yeltsin's decisive victory, polling 57 per cent of the vote and thus winning outright in the first round,[19] endowed his presidency with a popular legitimacy that Gorbachev's had lacked and helped him withstand the August coup. Instead of the largely ceremonial presidency, as in Czechoslovakia (and later in the Czech Republic) and Hungary, Russia found itself with an executive presidency on the American model. Victory gave Yeltsin freedom of manoeuvre in relations with parliament and allowed him to confront the CPSU. But, as with the Soviet parliament earlier, while the authority of the presidency had increased, the powers of parliament had not correspondingly diminished. From this it is clear that the strong presidential powers enshrined in the 1993 constitution had their roots in the way that the presidency as an institution emerged in the final Soviet years, and did not simply represent the victory in October 1993 of the presidency over Khasbulatov's parliament.

Even before the coup Yeltsin had prepared a series of decrees strengthening presidential power, and these were swiftly implemented in the following months. He was granted yet more powers by the reconvened Fifth CPD (28 October – 2 November 1991), including the right to reorganise the government, but now attempts were made to define the legal relationship between the president and the Supreme Soviet to avoid presidential power turning into dictatorship. On 2 November 1991 the Congress gave him the power for one year to appoint ministers and pass economic decrees without reference to parliament.[20] On 6 November Yeltsin assumed the post of prime minister, in addition to his other responsibilities, and placed himself at the head of a 'cabinet of reforms', with the RSFSR Council of Ministers now officially called the Russian government.

While defending strong executive authority, Yeltsin's entourage recognised the need for some separation of powers to avoid a return to a new form of despotism, which would once again exclude Russia, as they put it,

18 Law on the Presidency, *Vedemosti S"ezda narodnykh deputatov RSFSR i verkhovnogo Soveta RSFSR*, No. 17 (1991), 512.
19 For details of the vote, including regional analysis, see D. Yurev, *Prezidentskie vybory* (Moscow, 1991).
20 *Rossiiskaya gazeta*, 31 October and 1 November 1991; *Izvestiya*, 2 and 4 November 1991.

from 'civilised society'.[21] The idea of 'delegated legislation', in which a government is allowed to rule for a time through decrees with the force of law, is used by democratic states in times of emergency, and the idea was taken up in an analogous way by Guillermo O'Donnell in his notion of delegative democracy.[22] In periods of delegated legislation, however, the legislature usually establishes limits to the emergency powers, overseen by a constitutional court, and a set period that can only be renewed with the assent of parliament. In Russia no such stable system emerged. The expanding powers of the presidency were at first delegated by parliament but thereafter were converted into a self-sustaining presidential system. The appeal to the logic of the struggle against communism, already seen in 1990–91 in the form of 'wars of the laws' and declarations of sovereignty, perpetuated the legacy of administrative arbitrariness. The executive was able to free itself from effective popular oversight and accountability while becoming parasitic on the state and inhibiting the institutionalisation of the latter.

When in opposition Yeltsin had assaulted the old system with a hybrid programme encompassing a populist critique of the privileges of the power elite, an appeal to social justice, economic reform, the restoration of Russian statehood, and the radicalisation of democratic change. Once in power, however, he tempered these demands. No longer the challenger but the incumbent, Yeltsin soon came to rely on the instruments of the state rather than the mass politics of the street, though on occasion he was not averse to using the crowd. Yeltsin soon freed himself from the popular movement (above all Democratic Russia) that had brought him to power while at the same time ensuring that the presidential regime remained relatively unconstrained by the legal-normative principles represented by a constitutional state. While this meant that Yeltsin remained a free agent politically, it also suggested a failure to ensure an adequate institutional framework or political constituency to support the presidency. Yeltsin went on to build the presidency on the basis of his personal authority, to the detriment of institutions and mass political structures. Just as Gorbachev had freed himself from the discipline of collective leadership by establishing the presidency so, too, for Yeltsin the presidency served as an instrument to free himself from the constituency that had propelled him to power.[23] However, as Gorbachev had discovered earlier, strengthened presidential power was no guarantee of legitimacy or effective government.

The constitutional powers of the presidency

These fears appeared to be justified by the strengthening of presidential powers following October 1993. In the wake of the defeat of Khasbulatov and

---

21 *Demokraticheskaya gazeta*, 12 (15) (12–19 September 1991), 3.

22 Guillermo O'Donnell, 'Delegative Democracy', *Journal of Democracy*, Vol. 5, No. 1 (January 1994), 55–69.

23 Breslauer, *Gorbachev and Yeltsin as Leaders*, 89 and *passim*.

his fellow insurgents on 3–4 October 1993, Yeltsin placed a presidentialist version of the constitution before the people on 12 December, supported by 58.4 per cent of the vote on a 54.6 per cent turnout.[24] There remain some questions about the legitimacy of the vote, coming in the wake of the violent conflict amid accusations of vote rigging. The head of the Duma's state construction committee, Luk'yanov (who had now reinvented himself as a democratic politician), for example, noted that only 23 per cent of the electorate supported the new document.[25]

The most controversial aspects of the 1993 constitution concern the provisions dealing with the presidency. As we know, the adoption of the new constitution, to replace the much-amended 'Brezhnev' constitution of 1977 and its Russian variant of 1978, took place in the heat of bitter conflicts over the most appropriate institutional arrangements for the newly independent Russia.[26] The framers of the constitution sought to avoid the instability and conflicts that had wracked late Soviet and early Russian politics by creating a firm source of executive authority; but at the same time they were keen to ensure that the new political system repudiated Russian imperial and Soviet authoritarian to create a liberal and democratic system. In the event, they were perhaps more successful in enshrining the principles of liberalism than they were in ensuring the balanced democratic separation of powers. Nevertheless, for the first time in Russian history a constitution made a serious attempt to define, and thus to limit, state power. The problem, however, was not that the constitution lacks the idea of the separation of powers, but that this separation is allegedly fundamentally unbalanced. As Robert Sharlet puts it, The Russian Constitution of 1993 created a strong executive presidency to which the government is subordinated within an imbalanced separation of powers arrangement. This constitutional model has been a major source of Russia's chronic crises'.[27] The precise responsibilities of executive power outlined in Arts. 110–117 of the constitution were excessively wide and diffuse.[28]

Russia's semi-presidential constitution, modelled on French lines, approximates the 'presidential-parliamentary' type of mixed system that Matthew Shugart and John Carey consider the most unstable.[29] They distinguish

24 Richard Sakwa, *Russian Politics and Society*, Third Edition (London and New York, Routledge, 2002), 61.

25 'Kontrol'naya dlya demokratii', *Nezavisimaya gazeta*, 2 March 2000, 3. In fact, just over 30 per cent of the electorate voted for the constitution. The point here was to show the persistent questioning of the legitimacy of the basic law, and thus the insistence by people like Luk'yanov on the need to amend it.

26 These are discussed in my 'The Struggle for the Constitution in Russia and the Triumph of Ethical Individualism', *Studies in East European Thought*, Vol. 48, Nos. 2–4 (September 1996), 115–57.

27 Robert Sharlet, 'Russian Constitutional Change: Proposed Power-Sharing Models', in Roger Clark, Ferdinand Feldbrugge and Stanislaw Pomorski (eds), *International and National Law in Russia and Eastern Europe* (Amsterdam, Kluwer Law International, 2001), 361.

28 This is argued by K. S. Bel'skii, 'O funktsiyakh ispolnitel'noi vlasti', *Gosudarstvo i pravo*, No. 3, 1997, 14–21.

29 Matthew Soberg Shugart and John M. Carey, *Presidents and Assemblies:*

between semi-presidential systems that oscillate between presidential and parliamentary predominance, as in the French Fifth Republic, which they call 'premier-presidential', and systems that give the president greater powers to form and dismiss governments independently of parliament, which they call 'presidential parliamentary'.[30] The former are considered more likely to create a stable democratic system since there is greater accountability to parliament, whereas in a presidential-parliamentary system the government is torn between accountability to both the president and parliament. While the French system's ability to flip between a presidential and parliamentary mode creates a 'safety valve' which ensures that political tensions between president and parliament do not evolve into a constitutional conflict,[31] Russia's 'presidential parliamentary' system engendered endemic conflicts under Yeltsin, and under Putin it seemed that the only way to resolve them was by ensuring a compliant legislature.

The powers of the presidency are based on a combination of appointment powers and policy prerogatives. The 1993 constitution grants the presidency extensive powers in naming governments, introducing legislation and making policy. The president is the head of state and the 'guarantor' of the constitution (Art. 80), elected for a four-year term with a maximum of two terms but without an age limit (Art. 81). The president nominates the prime minister and can chair cabinet meetings, proposes to the State Duma the director of the Central Bank, nominates to the Federation Council members of the Constitutional, Supreme and Supreme Arbitration Courts, and also nominates the Procurator-General. The president is also head of the Security Council, confirms Russia's military doctrine, appoints the commander-in-chief of the Armed Forces, and 'exercises leadership of the foreign policy of the Russian Federation' (Art. 86). The president is granted the right to introduce a state of emergency and suspend civil freedoms until new federal laws are adopted. The president reports annually to a joint meeting of the two houses of the Federal Assembly on the government's domestic and foreign policy. The president has the right to issue binding decrees (*ukazy*), which do not have to be approved by parliament, that have the power of law; they must not, however, contradict the constitution; and they are superseded by legislative acts. Impeachment is extremely difficult, requiring a ruling on a demand by a Duma commission (set up with at least 150 votes) by both the Supreme and Constitutional Courts, to be confirmed by two-thirds of both the State Duma and the Federation Council, and can be initiated only in the event of 'treason or commission of some other grave crime' (Art. 93.1).

The Russian system meets the criteria established by Elgie, who defines a semi-presidential system as one in which there is a popularly elected fixed

Constitutional Design and Electoral Dynamics (Cambridge, Cambridge University Press, 1992).

30 Shugart and Carey, *Presidents and Assemblies*, 23–27.

31 Ezra N. Suleiman, Presidential and Political Stability in France', in Juan J. Linz and Arturo Valenzuela (eds), *The Failure of Presidential Democracy: Comparative Perspectives* (Baltimore, Johns Hopkins University Press, 1994), 137–62.

term president working with a prime minister and cabinet responsible to parliament.[32] The level of governmental accountability to parliament, however, is contentious since the government is appointed by the president and responsible to him or her. The government is chaired by a prime minister, but at the same time a large block of 'power' ministries come under the direct responsibility of the presidency. Like the Tsar according to the 1906 constitution, who reserved to himself responsibility for foreign policy, control of the armed forces and the executive, the 1993 constitution (Art. 80) grants the president control over four key areas: security, defence, home and foreign affairs. Russia's presidency in effect acts as a duplicate government, with the functions of ministries often shadowed by agencies under the presidency. The prime minister exerts only partial control over his or her own ministers, and is deprived of control over the so-called 'power ministries' responsible for domestic security. The president plays an active role in the policy process, initiating and vetoing legislation. Yeltsin used his decree powers with great gusto, issuing over 1500 policy-relevant *ukazy* during his terms in office.[33] Thus the nature of prime ministerial and cabinet responsibility to the Duma is episodic and unclear in the constitutional order that emerged in late 1993. The Duma has the choice of rejecting the president's nomination to the premiership and can adopt no-confidence motions in the cabinet, but other than that the lines of accountability between government and parliament are relatively weak. The government is subordinated to the president and, formally, does not have to represent the majority party or coalition in parliament.

Under Yeltsin the state lost both administrative capacity and steering capability. In conditions of institutional decay many of the normal functions of the state deteriorated. Russia became at best a weak democratic regime, where social interests gained direct access to the state. The exploitation of connections with government officials proved to be one of the most lucrative economic resources, allowing insider deals in the privatisation process, in gaining export licences and in carving out spheres of risk-free enrichment through the use of state funds designated for wages, social needs and welfare payments. The country's leadership was weak and devoted itself largely to personal enrichment, while the elite grouping around Yeltsin by the end focused on saving itself.

Executive authority became more independent of the legislature, though it remained constrained by law and regulated by parliament within the framework of 'delegated legislation'. Remington stresses that the 1993 constitutional settlement, while indeed granting the presidency considerable powers as part of the 'adaptive evolution' of the system in response to the chronic political crisis of 1990–93, nevertheless provided significant 'compensatory side payments' to other actors to ensure their participation in the new

---

32 Robert Elgie (ed.), *Semi-presidentialism in Europe* (Oxford, Oxford University Press, 1999).

33 John P. Willerton Jr, 'The Presidency: From Yeltsin to Putin', in Stephen White, Alex Pravda and Zvi Gitelman (eds), *Developments in Russian Politics*, 5th edn (Basingstoke, Palgrave, 2001), 29.

constitutional order. Paradoxically, according to Remington, the Russian parliament emerged as a more effective and representative body than earlier legislatures.[34] Many questions remained, however, including the limits to presidential power. Would a strong executive encourage the development of democracy in society, or would it act as a substitute for popular democratic organisation? Would not the 'strong hand' inevitably take on aspects of the Bolshevism that it sought to extirpate, and perpetuate rather than overcome traditions of authoritarianism and arbitrariness? While the 1993 constitution embodies the principles of liberalism, it is predicated on the assumption that the strong president will also be a liberal. In the event of this not being the case, the authoritative (if not authoritarian) elements in the constitution could come into contradiction with its liberal provisions. Is this what has happened?

Leadership under Putin: state and regime

François Mitterand referred to the post of president, as created by Charles De Gaulle in 1958, as a 'permanent coup d'etat', and shortly before his death he warned that French political institutions 'were dangerous before me and could become so after me'.[35] Many felt that this warning was no less appropriate for Russia. The presidency there overshadows all other political institutions, to the degree that Klyamkin and Shevtsova call it an 'elected monarchy'.[36] The paradox under Yeltsin, however, was the emergence of a strong presidency in a weak state, something that created a whole range of power asymmetries and distortions. This was not a problem unique to Russia. As Stephen Holmes has argued, the 'universal problem of post-communism is the crisis of governability produced by the diminution of state capacity after the collapse of communism'.[37] The creation of the presidency had been intended to compensate for the weakening power of the Communist Party, and now it filled the vacuum created by the ebbing of state authority and the weakness of civic initiative.

The potential and formal powers of the state, however debilitated under Yeltsin, remained enormous, and under Putin the reconstitution of the state became the central theme of his programme. This was recognised by no less a figure than the oligarch Boris Berezovsky. Speaking on 23 February 2000 in his constituency (he had been elected a Duma deputy on 19 December

34 Thomas F. Remington, *The Russian Parliament: Institutional Evolution in a Transitional Regime* (New Haven, CT, Yale University Press, 2001).
35 Thomas M. Nichols, *The Russian Presidency: Society and Politics in the Second Russian Republic* (Basingstoke, Macmillan, 2000), 2.
36 Igor Klyamkin and Liliya Shevtsova, *This Omnipotent and Impotent Government: The Evolution of the Political System in Post-Communist Russia* (Washington, DC, Carnegie Endowment for International Peace, 1999).
37 Stephen Holmes, 'Cultural Legacies or State Collapse? Probing the Post-Communist Dilemma', in M. Mandelbaum (ed.), *Post-Communism: Four Views* (New York, Council for Foreign Relations, 1996), 50.

1999), Berezovsky said that 'For the first time in 15 years, power in Russia is being consolidated'. He noted that 'a new stage of creating a strong state has begun. Russia will have neither a strong army nor a strong society without consolidating power'.[38] At that time he rejected claims that totalitarianism was being revived,[39] although later (after Putin had targeted him as one of the most dangerous oligarchs who had abused access to the corridors of power) he was to argue precisely the opposite. Nevertheless, there cannot but be profound ambiguities between liberalism and state strengthening.[40]

In the Russian context state reconstitution would appear to enjoy advantages not available to countries still in the throes of the early stages of development.[41] The Russian state has not collapsed, and in certain areas retains the ability to mobilise resources to pursue policies, if not effectively, then at least vigorously. Russia has enormous reserves of intellectual potential, a trained administrative elite and the basic infrastructure of a modern state. Russia suffered not so much from a crisis of the state as a crisis of governance. Clearly, they cannot be separated, yet they are analytically distinct; the remedy for one problem is not the same as that for the other. Improvement of governance requires political institutionalisation, that is, the process whereby organisations, procedures and norms not only acquire legitimacy and stability but are conducted within the framework of law and in the spirit of state service. The response to a crisis of the state, by contrast, can take numerous forms, not all of them compatible with constitutionalism and the rule of law. In the transition from communism many had called for a 'firm hand', even of the Pinochet type where in Chile political liberty was traded in exchange for economic growth. Others have stressed the Bonapartist features of Putin's rule, a system defined in Marxist terms as 'an authoritarian government that temporarily gains relative independence and reigns above the classes of society, mediating between them'.[42] Medushevsky, for example, has developed this model, with the appointment of the *polpredy* (the presidential representatives at the head of the seven new Federal Districts) acting as the functional equivalents of the Napoleonic prefects.[43] For Lukin, the key point was to end 'the excesses of the "democratic revolution" while preserving its major achievements'.[44] Putin certainly scraped off the revolutionary froth and tried to restore order, strengthen the consti-

38 *Newsline*, 25 February 2000.
39 *Nezavisimaya gazeta*, 24 February 2000.
40 Explored, for example, by Lilia Shevtsova, 'Power and Leadership in Putin's Russia', in Andrew Kuchins (ed.), *Russia after the Fall* (Washington, D.C., Carnegie Endowment for International Peace, 2002).
41 For a comparative study, see Mark R. Beissinger and Crawford Young (eds), *Beyond State Crisis? Post-Colonial Africa and Post-Soviet Eurasia in Comparative Perspective* (Washington D.C., Woodrow Wilson Center Press, 2002).
42 The definition is from Alexander Lukin, 'Putin's Regime: Restoration or Revolution?', *Problems of Post-Communism*, Vol. 48, No. 4, July/August 2000, 47.
43 Andrei Medushevskii, 'Bonapartistskaya model' vlasti dlya Rossii?', *Konstitutsionnoe pravo: vostochnoevropeiskoe obozrenie*, No. 4 (33) / No. 1 (34), 2001, 28.
44 Lukin, 'Putin's Regime', 47.

tutional state and improve the quality of governance, but these ambitious 'post-revolutionary' tasks were entwined with the problem of the nature of the power system. While some have stressed the establishment of a system of 'managed democracy',[45] this chapter argues that Putin's project was far more complex and ambivalent.

Regime politics

The constitutional order enshrined in the December 1993 constitution, as we have seen, is focused on the presidency. When the president is weak, so is governance. The effectiveness of the state is dependent on the strength of the presidency in general and on the character of the incumbent in particular. It is this entwining of institutional and personal factors in a weak constitutional order and under-developed civil society that gives rise to what we call regime politics. A regime here is defined as the network of governing institutions that is broader than the government and reflects formal and informal ways of governing and is usually accompanied by a particular ideology. The regime in Russia is focused on the presidency but is broader than the post of president itself. As suggested above, the power system focused on the regime could theoretically dispense with the presidency and instead could base itself on a parliamentary system, as had earlier occurred in Italy and Japan. In a parliamentary regime system the power elite is less threatened by the emergence of an independent president appealing to the constitutional powers of the state to curb the political pretensions and social power of the regime bloc. A presidential regime system, however, allows greater room for manoeuvre for the chief executive. The presidency under Putin sought to free itself from societal pressures (above all in the form of oligarchs, regional barons and parliamentary faction leaders) by appealing to the normative framework of the constitution.

At the heart of the regime system that emerged under Yeltsin was the oligarchy and its allies, which represented a fusion of financial and industrial capital with direct access to government. The traditional distinction between the market and the state was eroded, and lobbying interests enjoyed an extraordinarily close relationship with government. Russian politics became characterised by the salience not so much of the formal institutional structures of government and management but by informal relationships. Above all, given the weakness of the state, the emergence of what might be termed quasi-state actors became particularly important. For example, the banks (including the Central Bank), and the large energy companies (above all Gazprom and Unified Energy Systems – UES), acted as substitute sinews of the state, providing financial resources not available through general taxation, and serving as indirect enforcers of federal policy, while at the same

---

45 A. Verkhovskii, E. Mikhailovskaya and V. Pribylovskii, *Rossiya Putina: pristrastnyi vzglyad* (Moscow, Tsentr 'Panorama', 2003).

time ensuring that federal policy was not hostile to their interests. A type of 'state' bourgeoisie emerged, dependent on access to the state, rather than a more independent entrepreneurial bourgeoisie.

The Russian presidency began to take on the features of the Tsarist or Soviet systems, with weak prime ministers, a minimal separation of powers and with politics concentrated on the person of the leader, like a monarch in their court or the Politburo and its Central Committee apparatus. Once again an unwieldy concentration of power took place, marked by corruption and inefficiency. The Yeltsin presidency became enmeshed in a variety of informal power cliques, including the so-called 'oligarchs' who benefited from the disbursement of state property at knock-down prices, a group that in part over-lapped with the 'family', the colloquial term for the combination of favoured oligarchs, insider politicians, political advisors, and some of Yeltsin's blood relatives. The group included Yeltsin's daughter Tatyana Dyachenko, Sibneft Oil Company executive Roman Abramovich, arch-oligarch Boris Berezovsky, presidential chief of staff Valentin Yumashev and his successor Alexander Voloshin. In ideological terms there was little to distinguish between the groups; their struggle was largely one for state resources and reflected the consolidation of a power system (a regime) operating between the constitutional state and popular representation.

Personalised leadership inhibited the development of institutions. The political regime was focused on Yeltsin and the family and operated largely independently from the formal rules of the political system, whose main structural features were outlined in the constitution. Behind the formal façade of democratic politics conducted at the level of the state, the regime considered itself largely free from genuine democratic accountability and popular oversight. These features, as Hahn stresses, were accentuated by the high degree of institutional and personal continuity between the Soviet and 'democratic' political systems.[46] While a party-state ruled up to 1991, the emergence of a presidential-state by the mid-1990s had given way to a regime-state that perpetuated in new forms much of the arbitrariness of the old system. Both the regime and the constitutional state succumbed to clientelist pressures exerted by powerful interests in society, some of whom (above all the so-called oligarchs) had been spawned by the regime itself.[47] These constituted a fluid ruling group.

The regime system can be seen as a dynamic set of relationships that include the president, the various factions in the presidential administration, the government (the prime minister and the various ministries), and the informal links with various powerful oligarchs, regional bosses and other favoured insiders.[48] We have suggested above that Yeltsin's old guard represents one

46 Gordon M. Hahn, *Russia's Revolution from Above, 1985–2000: Reform, Transition, and Revolution in the Fall of the Soviet Communist Regime* (New Brunswick, NJ, Transaction Publishers, 2002).
47 For details, see A. A. Mukhin and P. A. Kozlov, *"Semeinye" tainy ili neofitial'nyi lobbizm v Rossii* (Moscow, Centre for Political Information, 2003).
48 Sakwa, *Russian Politics and Society*, Third Edition, 454–8; see also 'The Regime

of the factions in the regime; another is the *Pitery* brought in by Putin to establish a power base of his own.[49] Our model of Putin's presidency suggests
a tension between the presidency and the regime, in which the former sought
to gain greater autonomy from the latter by relying on a revived constitutional
state and a reinvigorated civil society and popular support.

The regime in Russia, where legitimacy ultimately derived from the ballot box, was caught between the legal order represented by the state (the
formal constitutional institutions of administration and the rule of law), and
the system of representative institutions (above all political parties) and accountability (primarily parliament). The regime acts as if it stands outside
the political and normative principles that it had formally sworn to uphold,
but at the same time is constrained by those principles. It is as much concerned with its own perpetuation as the rational administration of the country.
Similar regimes relatively independent of the constitutional constraints of
the rule of law and of popular accountability had emerged in post-war Italy
and Japan, and in general appear to be a growing phenomenon in post-cold
war political systems.

Regime politics in post-communist Russia, therefore, is not like traditional authoritarianism, and the regime could not insulate itself from aspects of
modern liberal democratic politics such as media criticism, parliamentary
discussion and, above all, from the electoral cycle. The regime looked in
two directions at once: forwards towards democracy, international integration and a less bureaucratised and genuinely market economy; while at the
same time it inherited, and indeed perpetuated and reinforced, many features
of the past – bureaucratic arbitrariness in politics and the economy, a con-
temptuous attitude to the citizenry, knee-jerk anti-Westernism, pervasive
patron-client relations, Byzantine court politics and widespread corruption.
If under Yeltsin this took patriarchal forms,[50] under Putin it was rather more
patrimonial. Regime politics is parasitic on liberalism while undermining the
genuine pluralism and individual responsibility and accountability that lie
at the heart of liberal politics. It perpetuates a type of neo-patrimonialism in
which the regime claims an exclusionary and priority relationship over the
political nation and over the country's resources.

Modernising the leadership system

The leadership of the hegemonic presidency, however, was challenged by
various projects to establish parliamentary hegemony. In structural terms the
'hegemonic presidency' is embedded in a social context that is fragmented

System in Russia', *Contemporary Politics*, Vol. 3, No. 1, 1997, 7–25.
49 A. A. Mukhin, *Piterskoe okruzhenie prezidenta* (Moscow, Centre for Political
Information, 2003).
50 Breslauer describes patriarchalism as 'a form of personalism that treats the political
community as a household within which the leader is the *pater familias*', *Gorbachev
and Yeltsin as Leaders*, 176.

and part of a dynamic and fluid power and elite system (the regime). The attempt under Putin to 'reconstitute' the state sought to root presidential power in the normative power of the constitution, and thus represented a bid to shift the basis of presidential hegemony away from dependence on oligarchical or other forces. There was an attempt to move away from 'manual control' of political processes to allow a more self-regulating (autopoeic) system to emerge. In this context, arguments in favour of diluting the powers of the presidency or establishing greater parliamentary control over the government are not clear cut.

The strong executive and strong state

The dissolution of the Communist Party and the disintegration of the USSR created a power vacuum that was filled by a hegemonic presidency. A presidential system emerged in the last Soviet years to compensate for the decline of the Communist Party, and later the presidential option looked increasingly attractive to overcome the crisis of reform in Russia. Under Yeltsin executive authority became relatively independent from the legislature, a trend given normative form by the 1993 constitution. Many functions of the old legislature, including some of its committees and commissions, were incorporated into the presidential system, providing yet more impetus to the inflation of the presidential apparatus. By the same token, some of the conflicts that had formerly taken place between the two institutions were now played out within the presidential system itself. No autonomy was granted to any particular leader or to the institution that they represented. The institutional aspects of this have been dubbed the politics of 'institutional redundancy' by Huskey.[51] The Russian presidency began to take on the features of the Tsarist or Soviet systems, with weak prime ministers responsible mainly for economic affairs, a minimal separation of powers and with politics concentrated on the leader. Under Yeltsin an unwieldy concentration of power was achieved, marked by corruption, clientelism and inefficiency.

As Samuel Huntington noted, political order in changing societies sometimes requires the hard hand of the military or some other force that is not itself subordinate to democratic politics.[52] Putin on a number of occasions explicitly sought to distance himself from this sort of tutelary politics. For example, in his question and answer session with the Russian people on 19 December 2002, in response to a query about how the excesses of the media could be curbed, he insisted that 'it is impossible to resolve this problem, *to resolve it effectively that is* [italics added], simply with some kind of tough administrative measures'. This was linked in his view to the fact that the old Soviet-style politics that treated the whole population as infants was no longer viable since society had matured: '...our whole society is becoming

---

51 Eugene Huskey, *Presidential Power in Russia* (Armonk, NY, M. E. Sharpe, 1999).
52 Samuel P. Huntington, *Political Order in Changing Societies*, (New Haven, CT, Yale University Press, 1968).

more adult'.[53] Rather than seeing politics as a cultural struggle to impose a single truth, Putin appeared to accept a more pluralistic vision of societal diversity. It proved difficult, however, to give adequate political form and expression to this diversity.[54]

Putin's attempts to reconstitute the state as an independent political force began to threaten the privileges of the regime, and it was perhaps this more than anything else that explains the renewed interest in establishing a more parliamentary form of government (see below). An autonomous presidency whose legitimacy was grounded in the legal-constitutional order represented by the constitutional state appeared far too dangerous for the regime. Parliamentary government appeared far more controllable and amenable to the instruments of power capable of being exerted by the rising capitalist class. However, as always with Putin his approach was contradictory. He both challenged the regime, and the neo-patrimonialism that it represented, in the name of the liberal constitutional state, but at the same time hesitated to repudiate entirely the apparent stability and security offered by regime politics.

From the very first days of his presidency Putin drew on constitutional resources to re-affirm the prerogatives of the state *vis-à-vis* segmented regional regimes. The struggle for the universal application of the rule of law, however, threatened to intensify at the federal level the lawlessness that characterised so much of regional government. Yeltsin's personalised regime represented a threat to the state, but its very diffuseness and encouragement of asymmetrical federalism allowed a profusion of media, regional and other freedoms to survive. Putin's new statism carried both a positive and a negative charge: the strengthening of the rule of law was clearly long-overdue; but enhancing the powers of the regime and the presidency was not the same as strengthening the constitutional rule of law. The weakening of the federal pillar of the separation of powers was not likely to enhance the defence of freedom as a whole. The key test would be whether the revived presidency would itself become subordinate to the new emphasis on 'the dictatorship of law', and thus encourage the development of a genuine ordered rule of law state, or whether it would attempt to stand aloof from the process and thus once again perpetuate the traditions of the 'revolution from above', if

---

53 V. V. Putin, *Razgovor s Rossiei: Stenogramma "Pryamoi linii s Prezidentom Rossiiskoi Federatsii V. V. Putinym',* 19 December 2002 (Moscow, Olma-Politizdat, 2003), 14.

54 Russia is not the only country where democratic consolidation has lacked depth. András Bozóki notes how the coalition government of Victor Orban between 1998 and 2002 saw electoral victory as an opportunity to achieve a fundamental cultural change. The programme of 'more than government change' saw one vision of Hungary being imposed on the rest. Bozóki notes that this sort of *Kulturkampf* politics has emerged in a mature democracy such as Italy, 'where the former power of multiple parties has disappeared and the only frontline of political struggle lies between pro-Berlusconi and anti-Berlusconi people'. András Bozóki, 'Hungary's Social-Democratic Turn', *East European Constitutional Review*, Vol. 11, No. 3, Summer 2002, 80–86, at 85.

only to put an end to the revolution, and thus perpetuate typical patterns of stability politics.

The selective approach to the abuses of the Yeltsin era, the attack on segmented regionalism that threatened to undermine the development of federalism, and the apparent lack of understanding of the values of media freedom and human rights, suggested that Putin's reforms could become a general assault on the principles of federalism and democratic freedom. The dependence of the presidential regime on 'power structures', as part of an unstable alliance of the presidency, certain oligarchs and the power ministries suggested that rather than *reconstituting* the state, that is, drawing on the normative resources of the constitution to establish the impartial rule of law, a less benign form of statism could emerge. We call this the *reconcentration* of the state in which the rhetoric of the defence of constitutional norms and the uniform application of law throughout the country threatens the development of a genuine federal separation of powers, media and informational freedoms, and establishes a new type of hegemonic party system in which patronage and preference is disbursed by a neo-nomenklatura class of state officials. There were many indications that United Russia sought to become the core of a new patronage system of the type that in July 2000 was voted out of office in Mexico after 71 years.

While the presidency under Putin sought to carve out greater room for manoeuvre, Putin was hesitant to subordinate the regime entirely to the imperatives of the constitutional order or to the vagaries of the popular representative system (elections). Yeltsin earlier had feared that the untrammelled exercise of democracy could lead to the wrong result, the election of a communist government that would undo the work of building market democracy, threaten Russia's neighbours in pursuit of the dream of the reunification of the USSR, and antagonise the country's Western partners. It was for this reason that factions in the regime had called for the 1996 presidential elections to be cancelled. The dilemma was not an unreal one, and reflected the regime's view that the Russian people had not yet quite matured enough to be trusted with democracy. Like the Turkish military and the army in some Latin American countries, the regime considered itself the guardian of the nation's true ideals. This was the tutelary ideology explicitly espoused by some of the regime's policy intellectuals such as Gleb Pavlovsky and Sergei Markov, and it was not entirely devoid of rationality. A neo-traditional type of paternalism replaced the purposiveness that had characterised the Bolshevik and early Yeltsin years. However, we know that whenever the military acts against democracy as the 'saviour of the nation' the results are usually the opposite of those intended, and the regime's mimicry of the military stymied the development of a political order robust enough to defend itself against the enemies of democracy.

Modernisation of administration

According to Rose, 'Organizational failure in Russia reflects the combination of too many regulations and too little adherence to bureaucratic norms'.[55] One of the challenges facing Putin was to improve the efficacy of the presidential administration itself. A decree on the reform of the organs of state power in 2003–04 sought to implement the proposals of German Gref, at the head of the Ministry for Economic Development and Trade. He noted the need to 'develop the system of self-regulated organisation in the economy' by reducing the state's interference in private business by ending excessive state regulation and limiting the duplication of powers by federal bodies of the executive power.[56] The basic idea of the reform was to prevent the state and its agencies (for example, the Central Bank) being both referees and players. State bodies were to be divided into three categories depending on their function: law setting, supervisory and service providers. There was to be a shift from Soviet-style 'sectors' to spheres, from a ministry of railways for example to a ministry of transport. The whole system, moreover, was to be simplified and the duplication of functions both within the government and between the government and the presidential system to be reduced.[57] Leaving aside organisational changes, the key to the effective rebuilding of the state, as Hanson notes, is whether Putin could 'recruit reliable officials who genuinely feel that it is their duty, and not only in their interest, to act in accordance with official institutional norms'.[58] The key to that was to establish a robust structure of disincentives against corruption while ensuring a viable financial and moral incentive structure for officialdom to serve the people rather than itself. As Hanson notes, a strong autocracy is one in which 'state functionaries consistently enforce the will of the ruling elite rather than use their power to build local personal fiefdoms'.[59]

Modernisation of the constitutional order

The 1993 constitution stabilised the Russian political system, but debates over the need for normative modernisation, by which we mean the development of a political order subordinated to the rule of law and constrained by effective constitutionalism, are certainly far from over. According to McFaul, the crisis of 1993 was provoked by the sheer scale of fundamental decisions that had to be taken in a context of political polarisation and economic crisis.

---

55 Richard Rose, 'Living in an Antimodern Society', *East European Constitutional Review*, Winter/Spring 1999, 74.
56 *Russian Mirror*, No. 40, 6 August 2003, 6. At this time Kasyanov's government appointed the respected deputy prime minister Boris Alyoshin to take control of the commission for state reform.
57 *Rossiiskaya gazeta*, 27 December 2002.
58 Stephen E. Hanson, 'Can Putin Rebuild the Russian State', *Security Dialogue*, Vol. 32, No. 2, 2001, 263.
59 Hanson, 'Can Putin Rebuild the Russian State', 264.

The stability since 1993 according to him is largely due to the narrowed policy agenda and greater clarity over the balance of power.[60] However, some issues remain contentious, and no sooner was the constitution adopted in 1993 than the debate over the need to amend it began. The main criticism of the 1993 constitution is its lack of balance in the horizontal separation of powers between branches of national government (leaving aside the no less contentious vertical separation of powers in the federal system). However, the question of 'balance' is far more than a technical one, since balance is something derived from the alignment of social and political forces and in new states these forces are far from stable. Although Vitalii Tretyakov, at the time editor of *Nezavisimaya gazeta*, may have condemned the new constitution as being 'a constitution for presidents in general and for President Yeltsin in particular',[61] it is not clear how it could have been otherwise at that time.

To avoid the endless constitutional changes made between 1988 and 1993, the new document is far more rigid and relatively impermeable to amendment. The new constitution is thus torn between a commitment to liberalism while at the same time seeks to provide a normative framework for the principles of order, a factor that to a degree vitiates some of its democratic features. In a country torn by political conflict and threatened by strong centrifugal forces, the framers of the document sought to avoid in Russia the 'constitutional logic' that arguably had been responsible for the disintegration of Yugoslavia (and possibly the USSR and Czechoslovakia).[62] The problem however is to ensure that democratic executive power is not used corruptly or despotically: under Yeltsin there was tendency towards the former, under Putin many feared the latter.

As we know from Soviet experience, the mere existence of a constitution does not guarantee the triumph of constitutionalism – with the latter defined as the definition of the role of political institutions, the imposition of constraints on the use of political power and with the life of the community governed in letter and spirit by the rule of law.[63] Abstract constitutionalism is always vitiated by the political context in which it has to operate. As suggested above, in Russia the principle of 'order' was introduced into the 1993 basic law to counteract political chaos and national disintegration. At the same time, this passive element of a strong executive presidency was accompanied by a more active characteristic, the perceived need for *purposive* government to lead the country out of Soviet failure. It was also to provide direction in a dangerous international context to allow Russia to become that 'normal great power' so beloved of liberals, nationalists and communists alike.

Alleged imbalances in executive power and lack of accountability repeat-

60 Michael McFaul, *Russia's Unfinished Revolution: Political Change from Gorbachev to Putin* (Ithaca and London, Cornell University Press, 2001).
61 *Nezavisimaya gazeta*, 9 November 1993, 1.
62 Robert Hayden, *Blueprints for a House Divided: The Constitutional Logic of the Yugoslav Conflicts* (Ann Arbor, University of Michigan Press, 1999).
63 For a recent discussion, see András Sajó, *Limiting Government: An Introduction to Constitutionalism* (Budapest, Central European University Press, 1999).

edly provoked debates on 'rebalancing' the constitution, intended above all to achieve effective constitutionalism.[64] From at least the time of Yevgeny Primakov's premiership there have been calls for constitutional reforms that would shift power away from the presidency towards a more parliamentary form of rule.[65] In June 2000 Primakov himself, by then head of the Fatherland-All Russia faction in the Duma, proposed giving the Duma greater power over the Federation Council.[66]

Putin was a constitutional conservative, fearing that the process of constitutional amendment could spark of a chain reaction with the potential not only to destroy the relative political peace inaugurated by the 1993 constitutional settlement but also to threaten the unity of the country and even to provoke civil war. He was supported by one of the authors of the constitution, Sergei Shakhrai, who warned that 'unsealing' the constitution would unleash a power struggle between the presidency, cabinet and parliament, while arguing that substantial political reforms could take place without revising the constitution, and he used the example of the creation of the seven Federal Districts as an example of para-constitutional change.[67] Mikhail Krasnov, who had also contributed to drafting the constitution, warned that 'The ideology of constitutional amendment based on the principle of 'take away and give me" opens the door to the destabilisation of the state'.[68] Instead, his proposals for the INDEM foundation suggested a balanced review of the constitution while retaining its fundamental features including a strong role for the presidency. As Nataliya Varlamova notes, constitutional modernisation can be seen as 'a play on words, a game of reforms or playing with fire'.[69] As Medushevskii notes, constitutional reform could be seen as part of a struggle for power.[70] Constitutional conservatives cite the example of the United States where in the course of 215 years and 42 presidents there have only been 26 amendments to its constitution, whereas in the USSR almost every leader had their own constitution.

Putin insisted that it was preferable to work within the framework of the existing constitutional order rather than opening up the whole institutional framework of governance to debate once again. In his 'Russia at the Turn of the Millennium' document he argued 'Amending the constitution does not seem to be an urgent, priority task. We have a good constitution. Its

64 Described by Sharlet, 'Russian Constitutional Change', op cit, 361–72.
65 The debates and issues raised at this time are analysed by Robert Sharlet, 'Russian Constitutional Change: An Opportunity Missed', *Demokratizatsiya: The Journal of Post-Soviet Democratization*, Vol. 7, No. 3, Summer 1999, 437–47.
66 The Jamestown Foundation, *Monitor*, 9 June 2000.
67 *Argumenty i fakty*, No. 50, 11 December 2002.
68 Mikhail Krasnov, 'Konstitutsiya Rossii: zapovednaya territoriya ili sreda obitaniya?', *Konstitutsionnoe pravo: vostochnoevropoeiskoe obozrenie*, No. 4 (29), 1999, 138.
69 Nataliya Varlamova, 'Konstitutsionnaya modernisatsiya: igra v terminy, igra v reformy ili igra s ognem?', *Konstitutsionnoe pravo: vostochnoevropoeiskoe obozrenie*, No. 2 (31), 2000, 122–5.
70 Andrei Medushevskii, 'Konstitutsionnyi perevorot ili konstitutsionnaya reforma: popravki k Konstitutsii 1993 goda kak instrument bor'by za vlast'', *Konstitutsionnoe pravo: vostochnoevropoeiskoe obozrenie*, No. 3 (28), 1999, 154–67.

provisions for individual rights and freedoms are regarded as the best constitutional instruments of its kind in the world'.[71] As he argued on the seventh
anniversary of the document's adoption:

> Russia's new character is to a large extent determined by our state's
> constitution. Our constitution has been criticised, criticised sharply, even
> before its adoption, and throughout the following years there have been
> demands for its restructuring, review and reform, on the grounds that
> it was based on immediate political advantage and therefore it had no
> legitimacy or future. But time has made things clear. Our constitution
> reflects not only the spirit of our much-longed for changes but became
> the firm basis for the country's stable development. We have spent a few
> years trying to master this important democratic instrument. Let us learn
> how to use it effectively'[72]

Russia's constitutional order was modified under Putin, but through legislation and presidential decrees rather than through a process of constitutional
amendment. However, towards the end of his first term in office he appeared
to be willing to discuss constitutional changes that would shift power away
from the presidency. In his state-of-the-nation speech in May 2003 he noted: 'I believe it possible, taking into account the results of the forthcoming
election to the State Duma, to form a professional and efficient government
based on the parliamentary majority'.[73] Shortly afterwards, in his press conference of 20 June, Putin stressed that no changes would take place before the
next elections.[74] As the expert on French constitutionalism, Yurii Rubinskii,
noted in this context, it is possible to have one constitution but a number of
political regimes based on it. As in Russia, he notes that both when the right
or the left were in power in France, 'the "party of power" became closely
entwined with the state apparatus'.[75] Gaullism remained in the Bonapartist
tradition, and as in Russia this entails a failure effectively to separate the
political regime (the government and its social supports) from the impartial
constitutional order represented in theory by the state.

Modernisation of governance

A number of influential business interests and the parties that they spon-
sored spoke in favour of a parliamentary republic, with the cabinet formed

71 Putin, *First Person*, 215–16.
72 'Putin predupredil "politicheskikh tenevikov"', *Nezavisimaya gazeta*, 14 December
    2000, 3.
73 http://www.president.kremlin.ru/text/appears/2003/05/44623.shtml; BBC Monitoring,
    16 May 2003; in *Johnson's Russia List* (henceforth *JRL*) 7186/1.
74 Press_office@prpress.gov.ru; *JRL*, 7233, 21 June 2003.
75 Yurii Rubinskii, 'Gollistskaya Rossiya: vlast' bez rotatsii', *Nezavisimaya gazeta*, 8
    July 2003, 11.

on the basis of a parliamentary majority.[76] Those in favour of the so-called 'project of the parliamentary majority' were allegedly the representatives of the Yeltsin elite: Voloshin and his deputy Vladislav Surkov, backed by the oligarch Mikhail Khodorkovsky, who may well have had ambitions to take on the premiership himself.[77] There is of course the possibility that after the end of the two terms as president allowed by the constitution, Putin could himself seek to use the enhanced powers of the premiership to continue his leadership. A powerful group around Putin, bringing together *siloviki* and liberals, feared that the passage of a constitutional amendment allowing a party or coalition of parties to form the government and nominate the prime minister would deliver the country into the hands of the oligarchs.[78] It was this that provoked the attack on Khodorkovsky and his Yukos oil company over the summer of 2003. Attention was deflected from constitutional amendment to the threat of a revision of the economic settlement of the 1990s.

This is not the place to enter into details of the Byzantine manoeuvrings that have attended this discussion.[79] What the debate over a shift from a presidential to a parliamentary republic suggests is not an attempt to undermine hegemonic power as such in favour of a more liberal and pluralistic political process, but a struggle between rival hegemonic forces. In that context, a hegemonic presidency may be a lesser evil than the hegemonic powers of oligarchical capitalism. A shift to a government based on a parliamentary majority may well signal the transition from a hegemonic regime system based on the presidency to one based on parliament, and thus undo the settlement imposed after October 1993. A state-centred hegemonic regime would give way to a societally-based one. Both types reflect the under-development of a robust pluralism that would underpin any genuinely liberal politics.

Conclusion

In the twilight years of Soviet power the presidency emerged as an institution that could act as the functional substitute for the waning powers of the Communist Party. In the early years of independent Russia the absence of adequately structured political forces in society, above all political parties, allowed a struggle for two contrasting hegemonic forces to emerge: represented by the presidency and parliament. In 1993 this struggle took on ever more entrenched forms and culminated in the violent resolution of September-October. Out of this conflict a constitutional settlement emerged that codified the powers of a hegemonic presidency. The presidency became the core of a shifting structure of power that we call a regime system, in which the formal provisions of the constitution are adhered to but the spirit of constitutionalism

76 *Versiya*, No. 21, 9–15 June 2003.
77 Pavel Ivanov, 'Putin's Sad Anniversary', *Asia Times*, 16 May 2003; *JRL*, 7184/7.
78 *Versiya*, No. 21, 9–15 June 2003.
79 For an indicative analysis, see Vladimir Pribylovsky, 'Oligarchs, True and False', *Russia and Eurasia Review*, 10 June 2003.

is undermined by the ability of the regime to remove itself from popular and representative accountability. Instead of a party-state, a regime-state emerged. Regime politics in the late Yeltsin years allowed social forces direct access to the resources of the state, but the presidency remained implicitly the gate-keeper. Under Putin the reassertion of state authority represented the robust reassertion of these gate-keeping functions. Statist regime politics ensured that the constitution became the fundamental regulation mechanism of the Putinist regime. Oligarchical interests were tempered by control exerted by the bureaucracy and state officialdom. Dissatisfaction with this state of affairs encouraged attempts to modify the constitution to create a parliamentary-based hegemonic regime system. Statist regime politics would give way to societal regime politics.

On coming to power Putin declared that his main task was, in the words of one commentator, 'to transform Russia from a "manually controlled" country into a fine-tuned mechanism functioning regardless one person's will'.[80] The shift, however, from patrimonialism to liberalism, from stability or order, would prove more complex and contradictory than he imagined. The central tension of Putin's leadership is that his struggle for liberal constitutionalism is conducted in traditional neo-patrimonial ways, a contradiction that has been both a source of his power and a clear weakness in that it has imbued all that he does with an inner tension. Putin's reforms have the potential to transform Russia's political space, but for that regime management of political processes would have to give way to the autonomy of a genuinely competitive political market place. It was not clear that Putin was quite ready for that – or indeed whether the country was. A competitive party system began to emerge, but parties are still not adequately embedded in the country's social structure, they do not effectively represent social interests, they are not yet genuinely national in scope, they do not legitimise power and they did not directly form governments.

Only when the regime is brought under the control of law and the constitution and within the ambit of political accountability can Russia be considered to have achieved democratic consolidation. This would be a revolution every bit as significant as the fall of communism itself in 1991, and was the main challenge facing Putin's presidency. It is this process that we call the reconstitution of the state, literally rendering the political process and regime actors subordinate to the legal constitutional system and responsive to the needs of citizens. What Max Weber had called sham constitutionalism would to give way to real constitutionalism where political institutions are subordinated to the rule of law and where human and civil rights are defensible by law. Genuine liberalism would replace the neo-patrimonial struggle for hegemony, order would replace stability, and the emergency would give way to the normal.

80 Marina Volkova, *Rossiiskaya gazeta*, 26 March 2003.

II
Case Studies

TOMI HUTTUNEN

Montage Culture: the Semiotics of Post-Revolutionary Russian Culture

The [1]October Revolution of 1917 served as a perfect catalyst for the exceptional burst of simultaneous but heterogeneous formations – different art forms, cultural languages and texts – striving for a similar structural code. Common to these initially diverse languages is the principle of Modernist montage, a seemingly obvious alternation (in terms of post-revolutionary Russia) between deconstruction and reconstruction, separation and reassembling, fragmentation and reintegration, dissolving and recomposing, and differentiation and reunification. The inevitably complex relationship between the two cultures – the old and the new – is manifested in different sign systems of the culture.

The question of montage culture means both the examination of the code itself and the montage principle discernible in various Modernist and Avant-garde art forms and artistic texts. I will apply a semiotic understanding of culture[1] to a whole that consists of different art forms (including literature, cinema, theatre, painting and photography) and different kinds of texts (novels, poems, films, plays and photographs). Montage is a gratifying subject for a semiotic approach, in that montage as a phenomenon of 1920s culture influenced the understanding of Russian semiotics in different ways. The famous theses of the Tartu-Moscow School introduce the principle of montage culture as an example of a uniform cultural mechanism, which opposed the tendency towards diversity.[2] It is in no way an exaggeration to see the film theoretician Sergei Eisenstein as being one of the most influent early Soviet pre-semioticians, a predecessor of such theoreticians as Vyacheslav Ivanov, Yurii Lotman and Alexander Zholkovskii.

---

1   The approach used here presupposes the application of cultural semiotics, where culture is understood as a hierarchical sign system comprised of many subsystems, i.e. cultural languages. Culture, then, is a sign system consisting of sign systems, or, as in Yurii Lotman's later post-Structuralist theory, a *semiosphere of semiospheres* (Yu. M. Lotman, *Universe of the Mind: a semiotic theory of culture*. London: I. B. Tauris 1990, 123–130; Yu. M. Lotman, *Izbrannye stat'i*. II. Tallinn: Aleksandra, 1992, 11–24).
2   V. V. Ivanov, Yu. M. Lotman, A. M. Pyatigorskii, V. N. Toporov, B. A. Uspenskii, *Theses on the Semiotic Study of Cultures* (= Tartu Semiotics Library 1). University of Tartu, 1998, 32.

Understood as an intersemiotic cultural principle, montage can be approached as a kind of paradox, a reconstructive or revitalizing strategy of Modernism for creating a new mythology, art language or culture in general. The tendency towards uniformity apparent in post-revolutionary Russian culture is also an inevitable context for the emergence and the accelerated formation of one of the main cultural languages of the 20th century, the language of cinema. Naturally, it is important to note that cinema itself can be regarded as a synthetic language, and the Russian intellectual cinema of the post-revolutionary period was treated as a kind of universal means to avoid the differentiation of languages.[3] Hyperbolizing the idea of conflict in their art, and concretizing it, for example, in the collision between the shot and the counter-shot, the theoreticians of early Soviet cinema (practicing their own theory as film directors) were able to create the unique Soviet Russian grammar for this modern new medium.[4]

The concept of montage is a broad one and can mean a great deal in the context of post-revolutionary Russian culture. I will try to identify the means of survival of post-revolutionary Russian culture, which proclaimed itself as new, while keeping in mind that nothing in any particular culture can be entirely new, that the new is always bound up with the old and is dependent on tradition. With culture, things exist in a continuum that produces new meanings; they do not exist in a vacuum. This condition at least partially explains the constant interaction between *de*construction and *re*construction, which must be remembered whenever montage is examined. Montage theory developed in post-revolutionary Russia specifically in the hands of film theoreticians, but a corresponding phenomenon became simultaneously predominant in other arts, including literature, theatre, photography and painting. Thus there is good reason to speak of a cultural montage principle, which can be seen not only in the different arts but also more broadly in cultural life.[5]

3   Yu. Tsivyan, *Istoricheskaya retseptsiya kino: kinematograf v Rossii 1896–1930.* Riga: Sinatne, 1991, 324–327.

4   Ibid., 324. Naturally, Russian cinema had its own style even before the revolutionary years. Yet montage is indeed the dominating element for Russian theoreticians in their search for cinematic *grammar*.

5   The concept of montage had already appeared in the middle of the 19th century, and was principally connected to the combination of photography and the traditional visual arts, e.g. paintings to which photographic components have been attached. Consequently the crucial starting points for montage are the intermediation of arts and dissimilar origination of components. The trick films made at the turn of the century (Méliès) are classics of montage art, but in the art of photography the concept of photomontage came into use only after the First World War, when the Berlin Dadaists were seeking a name for their new technique of embedding photographs in their art. They wanted to combine ideas of art and engineering in their works which they began to call 'photomontages'. (See e.g. D. Ades, *Photomontage.* London: Thames & Hudson, 1996 and B. H. D. Buchloch, 'From Faktura to Factography', In: *October*, 30, 1984, 96–97.) The Berlin Dadaists claimed to have invented the principle, although Gustav Klutsis, a Suprematist disciple of Kazimir Malevich, made his first photomontage in 1918, and Malevich had experimented with Suprematist

The starting point in Russian montage theory proved to be Lev Kuleshov's famous experiments with re-editing. Kuleshov made what he considered to be a startling observation: that juxtaposing two pictures produces a kind of third one, which is not connected to either of the others. This was called the *Kuleshov effect*.[6] This crucial Soviet Russian Avant-garde principle of juxta-position[7] and the new meaning it produced are at the core of montage theory. Different schools of montage theory immediately sprang up within film the-ory. Eisenstein represented the idea of the conflicting montage, as opposed to Kuleshov, who emphasized the syntactic nature of montage. Kuleshov's student, Vsevolod Pudovkin, also underlined the principle of juxtaposition but concentrated on montage's narrative nature and on significant details. Dziga Vertov, meanwhile, emphasized montage as a rhetorical device in representing the new Soviet reality. To generalize, we can name these four schools of thought as Eisenstein's conflictual montage, Kuleshov's syntac-tic montage, Pudovkin's narrative and metonymical montage, and Vertov's rhetorical montage.[8] Common to these classics of Russian film theory is that they all raise the question of the film viewer's active participation – as the 'reader' – in the creative process.

Eisenstein and the new reader

Montage should be understood in the context of Russian Modernism in general. As a reaction to the Russian realistic tradition, Modernism at the

montage already in the middle of the 1910s. In the 1920s the montage theoreticians already related the montage principle with different arts, thus creating a basis for a more universal understanding of the principle – within this discourse, montage is closely related with the general questions of selection, juxtaposition, combination and re-combination in culture. (See e.g. B. V. Raushenbakh (ed.), *Montazh: literatura, iskusstvo, teatr, kino.* Moskva: Nauka 1988; M. Tupitsyn, *Gustav Klutsis and Valentina Kulagina: Photography and montage after constructivism.* Göttingen: Steidl, 2004, 15–16; M. Teitelbaum (ed.), *Montage and Modern Life 1919–1942.* Cambridge, Massachusetts and London: MIT Press, 1992; J. Dunne & P. Quigley (ed.), *The Montage Principle: Eisenstein in new cultural and critical contexts.* Amsterdam: Rodopi, 2004.)

6   See L. Kuleshov, *Sobranie sochinenii.* Moskva: Iskusstvo 1988, 49. Kuleshov juxtaposed the same picture of the actor Mozzhukhin's face with pictures of a soup bowl, a woman in a coffin, and a child playing. Depending on the juxtaposition, viewers saw the face expressing the emotions of hunger, sorrow, and tenderness, respectively.

7   Lotman, *Izbrannye stat'i*, II, 174.

8   On different montage theories and practices in early Soviet film see Yu. M. Lotman, *Semiotika kino i problemy kinoestetiki.* Tallinn: Eesti Raamat, 1973; Yu. Lotman & Yu. Tsivyan, *Dialog s ekranom.* Tallinn: Aleksandra, 1994; M. Tupitsyn, 'From the Politics of Montage to the Montage of Politics. Soviet Practice 1919 Through 1937'. In: M. Teitelbaum (ed.), *Montage and Modern Life 1919–1942*, 82–127; I. Karelina, *Den ryska montagefilmen.* Lund: Studentlitteratur, 2006.

beginning of the 20th century underlines such ideas as the complexity of reality and the correspondence of realities, the need for the reader's participation and, as a result of this, the artistic text as a process. In order to speak of Modernist montage with respect to a text, it must, first of all, be fragmentary.[9] In a fragmentary montage text, the elements as such carry signifying potential, and they acquire their final meaning in parallel with corresponding elements, through juxtaposition. The bestowal of the general meaning of the text occurs in the reader's mind, in reconstructing the connections between the elements of the text. To put it briefly, the Modernist montage text is an apparently fragmentary text that consists of heterogeneous elements. The reader is supposed to bring such a text together into a unified whole in relation to its general meaning. Fragmentariness, heterogeneity and process would therefore be the basic conditions defining a montage text.

The earliest aims of Sergei Eisenstein's immense oeuvre were fairly straightforward and closely related to agitation and propaganda, due to his agitprop work in the Proletkult theatre of Moscow. In his early theory he concentrated on making the most powerful impression possible on the recipient with the help of different emotional, psychological and intellectual stimuli, or *attractions*. According to him, an attraction is "any aggressive moment in theatre (...) that subjects the audience to emotional or psychological influence, verified by experience and mathematically calculated to produce specific emotional shocks in the spectator (...) These shocks provide the only opportunity in perceiving the ideological aspect of what is being shown, the final ideological conclusion."[10]

The active and co-operative role of the reader is a crucial question for both Modernism and Avant-garde in general, and Russian montage culture in particular. The various Russian montage theories are based on the notion of alternating (author's) deconstruction and (reader's) reconstruction. A kind of synthesis of these ideas is found in Eisenstein's article "Montage 1938", in which he defends his early theses against critics and presents the communication model of the artistic text, where the reader is described as a reconstructive actor, the co-author of the text, in fact. According to Eisenstein, the author has an *idea* or an *image* (*obraz*), which he divides into fragments, i.e. descriptions (*izobrazhenie*). With the help of these fragments the reader

---

9   See Lotman, *Izbrannye stat'i*, II, 169. Fragmentariness here should be understood in the same way as discreteness, i.e. the elements' clear distinctiveness. For us to be able to speak of a montage text, the significant units of the text must be easily distinguished from one another, and seemingly unconnected, to make possible the perception of the mutual relationship between them – this forming the basis of the montage effect. In relation to cinematic theory, the idea of such interrupted (non-continuous) texts is a typically Russian phenomenon. In fact, Russian montage is often defined as *visible*, as opposed to *invisible* Western montage.

10   S. M. Eizenshtein, 'Montazh attraktsionov'. *Lef*, 3, 1923, 70–1. Cited in R. Taylor & I. Christie (eds.), *The Film Factory: Russian and Soviet cinema in documents 1896–1939*. London & New York: Routledge, 1988, 87.

reconstructs the same idea the author had in mind. The emergence of this image is the aim of the text as a dialogue.[11]

According to this theory, a work of art is always a process between the author and the reader. The signification itself has to be understood as a process, since the meaning in montage is never given, but becomes or emerges (*stanovlenie*) in the reader's mind through the juxtaposition of the elements presented fragmentarily in the text. The text therefore contains seemingly fragmentary corresponding relationships, which are supposed to be synthesized into the general meaning of the work, the image. In this process the author is also able to direct the reader emotionally, intellectually, and ideologically, with the result that after experiencing the work of art the reader is no longer the same as he or she was before, having drawn certain conclusions, directed by the author.

Eisenstein combines two theoretical lines crucial to, and typical of, the montage culture of the 1920s. Originating in both pre-revolutionary Russian Modernism and the culture of post-revolutionary Avant-garde, these are as follows: the new means of reading the artistic works, and the power of montage as a tool for agitation. The first, in itself, is a purely Modernist idea dealing with the active role of the reader in the production of art. This is a necessary condition for the post-revolutionary new culture and new way of thinking, and for understanding the new reader. It is precisely the continuous juxtapositions, the intratextual and often also intertextual correspondences that force the reader to actively participate in the reconstructive process, in the formation of the general meaning of the text. The second principle is founded on the first. Here, the active role of the reader makes it possible for the author to attempt to shock the reader and thereby direct him or her ideologically, via intellectual-emotional stimuli, so that he or she will form certain ideological conclusions influenced by the author's intention. In this sense, Eisenstein treats the viewer of his films (more generally, the viewer of montage texts) as material to be moulded in a certain way.

It is tempting to reconsider Eisenstein's theory while trying to separate different readers in his concept of reception, or more generally, to reconstruct different phases in the evolution of the implicit reader in montage culture, on the basis of his theory: the Modernist/Symbolist reader, the reconstructive reader and the utopian reader. Such categories are, naturally, broad and artificial, but some preliminary remarks are nevertheless worth making.

The reader postulated by the complexity of the Modernist text is an active participant, willing to understand and capable of understanding the Modernist aesthetics. In Russian context, the Symbolist reader is educated by the elitist, or even esoteric, cultural codes of Russian Symbolism, the culture of the late 19th and early 20th centuries. One must remember that Symbolism was not in any way a reader-oriented movement, but rather concentrated on the creator (*teurg*), that is, on the image of the author, reminiscent of Romanti-

11   S. M. Eizenshtein, *Izbrannye proizvedeniya*. T.2. Moskva: Nauka, 1964, 163.

cism's image of the creative genius. The Symbolist text postulates an erudite reader, capable of combining different complex polygenetic sources, along with pan-aestheticism, mysticism, philosophical allusions and other references to different cultural contexts and traditions.[12] The perfect, final reader of the Symbolist text is a completely dedicated participant, even a carrier of a mystical experience similar to that of the author-Symbolist.

Montage culture means a major change in relation to the implicit reader. The reconstructive reader is, on the one hand, a necessary condition for early Soviet ideology concerning the collectivisation of the art language and the superiority of cinema among the arts.[13] The reconstructive subject is a mass reader, who participates in the creative process the way the author wants him or her to, the one who does the final work and without whom it is hard to speak of the completed work, the product, in the Russian sense of the word (*proizvedenie*). In theatre, the change from observer-spectator to active participant of the play was especially abrupt, and, in a way, montage theatre serves as a laboratory for the emergence of the cinematic reader.[14]

The emphasis on the factographic representation of the new reality challenges the reader into a transformation. Ultimately, the utopian reader is the actual new reader, the reader of the future. This type does not yet exist, but still the texts contain material for them, since the text is supposed to be effective enough to direct the readers in a certain direction. As we can see, there are two somewhat contradictory aspects crucial to the interpretation of Eisenstein's understanding of the reader: the artistic and the social.[15] Socially, his reader could be placed into two roles: the mass reader (an inevitable role for the reader of the 1920s texts) and the new reader (the reader of the future). Artistically, the profile of the reader is quite different, since such a reader should be educated by the Symbolists, i.e. by art that is not for the masses, but rather for a select audience.

In early Soviet film, montage begins to mean, on the one hand, the purely technical editing of a film and its assembly from separate elements, whether explicitly related to each other or not. On the other, it simultaneously refers to Modernism, to a new kind of reception of the works, in which film as a new art form can show other arts the way. Naturally, a reader who is educated in Symbolist esoterica and who actively participates in the reconstruction of the artistic text, as if he or she were part of a collective work of art, is much easier to direct than a passive reader, who simply receives a part from an already constructed and given whole.

12 On the pan-aestheticism of Russian Symbolism, see Z. G. Mints, *Aleksandr Blok i russkie pisateli*. Sankt-Peterburg: Iskusstvo SPb, 2000, 456–536.
13 See Taylor & Christie, *The Film Factory*, 56–57.
14 O. L. Bulgakova, 'Montazh v teatral'noi laboratorii 1920-h godov', In: B. V. Raushenbakh (ed.), *Montazh*, 99–100.
15 Tsivyan, *Istoricheskaya retseptsiya kino*, 338.

Montage and the new reality

Agitation and propaganda are by no means exclusive to film, even though this new art form was seen from the very beginning as a tool of a powerful propaganda machine. The contradiction typical of Modernist montage culture is quite apparent in the art of the 1920s. In the visual arts, Russian montage is best crystallized in the work of Gustav Klutsis, Alexander Rodchenko and El (Lazar) Lissitzky. Klutsis himself considered his own *Dynamic City* (1919) to be the first Russian photographic montage, and the basis for calling the work a montage is its construction from different components. *Dynamic City* is still a fairly pure representation of the abstract Avant-garde: it can be looked at from any direction, there being no fixed viewing angle. Nevertheless, this is Klutsis' manifesto against abstract art and for utilitarian application of abstraction. Montage in Klutsis' work is represented as heterogeneity of the material: photographic (iconic) elements, such as photographed skyscrapers, mixed into an abstract composition, reminiscent of Malevich's Suprematism. The author is thus not only the painter, but also the organizer of the ready-made material.

In *Dynamic City* a photograph is, according to Klutsis, applied as a material of surfacial structure (*faktura*) and used to create a contrast with the painted elements. The work "exemplifies that an abstract construction in itself acquires the specificity of a construction site by means of montaged photographs of workers and buildings."[16] During the 1920s Klutsis kept making photomontages in which he showed his use of montage as a political rather than formal means, although elements of abstract art can still be seen in them. One of the famous reflections of the Bolsheviks' historical optimism was his photomontage *Old world and world being built* (1920) with an admirable Lenin's image in front, schematic symbols (chains, church, alcohol) representing the past and Suprematist city representing the future. Klutsis wanted to make a clean break with the abstract Avant-garde. Nevertheless, its influence remains visible until his later, purely political propaganda posters. For Klutsis photomontage was a way of influencing the masses. He declared in 1931 that the real militant and political photomontage was born in the Soviet Union as a reaction to late non-objective art.[17] His shift from abstractionist to political activist is clearer than Rodchenko's or El Lissitzky's.

Alexander Rodchenko participated actively in the operations of the Futurist magazine *Lef*, founded in 1923; for example, he prepared the magazine's cover from the very beginning and took care of its layout. *Lef* declared that photomontage was a means similar to Modernist montage in general. The question of the impact on the reader appeared together with the idea of documentary representation, and this meant the superiority of the new vehicle

16   M. Tupitsyn, *Gustav Klutsis and Valentina Kulagina*, 18.
17   See D. Ades, *Photomontage*, 63–64.

Illustration 1. Gustav Klutsis, Dynamic City (Dinamicheskii gorod), 1919. Cut-and-pasted photographs, paper, aluminium foil, gouache, and pencil on paper. Source: Tupitsyn, M. Gustav Klutsis and Valentina Kulagina: Photography and Montage After Constructivism. Göttingen: Steidl. 2004.

in comparison with traditional graphic representations.[18] Photomontage was defined as an agitation tool for the urban mass reader, as it appeared in cinema also. At the same time, another significant shift took place: the separation between art and life that had been apparent in the literature and art of the 1910s, with their search for facture (*faktura*) instead of fact (*fakt*), was replaced by utilitarianism in the 1920s, and the new culture of *factography*, in which the principle of montage played an important role.[19]

18   *Lef*, 4, 1924, 41–44.
19   See Buchloch, 'From Faktura to Faktography', 95–99.

In the first issue of *Lef* magazine, the Futurists stressed the necessity of describing Soviet reality. Osip Brik proclaimed that a poet should not create his own topics, but should instead take them from the surrounding reality and thus impersonally fulfil his socialist duty.[20] Film director Dziga Vertov, who followed a radical documentarist line, also actively pondered the relationships between the description of the new reality, authentic material, and montage. In his film *The Man and the Movie Camera* (1929), Vertov wrote his grammar of film purely by cinematic means. Without a screenplay or on-screen texts, and with only the help of alternating pictures (montage), Vertov's film portrays a weekday in the land of the Soviets, and as such, is already a noteworthy documentation of Russian life at the end of the 1920s. Nevertheless, *The Man and the Movie Camera* is at the same time a theoretical treatise on the language of film, a manifesto of the independence of the cinematic language.[21] In fact, it is a fantastic example of how montage as an artistic vehicle in an artistic text can serve as a means to reveal the grammar of the language (art form) in question. Vertov's montage text manages to reveal the very essence of the cinematic language.

However, montage cannot mean pure documentation, since it is a rhetorical device. For instance in Dziga Vertov's documentaries, tinged with rhythmical editing, montage provides a means of creating the perfect reality for the author. Naturally, this turns out to be an illusion or an imitation of reality – the forming, through choice and arrangement, of an image of reality in a way different from that which Vertov himself proclaims in his writings. One example could be Kuleshov's famous experiments with what he called the "created person": in his montage experiments of 1921 he constructed, or rather, let the viewers reconstruct, an image of a woman from close-ups of different parts of women's bodies.[22] Montage serves as a device to make a fictional person out of the elements of reality. But for Vertov, this is a way of creating the "perfect person", because the *cine-eye* (*kinoglaz*) is superior to the human eye, or the *cine-truth* (*kino-pravda*) supersedes the seen truth, and because montage means organizing the material of the seen world, in its new and perfect order.

The criticism of montage presented by the French director Andre Bazin reveals the artistic power of montage – its core. According to him, in the works of Russian directors the montage logic of corresponding relationships

20 O. Brik, 'T.n. formal'nyi metod'. *Lef*, 1, 1923, 214.
21 Vertov wrote in his diaries that the film is "a practical, even a theoretical performance on the screen". Cited in Yu. Tsivyan, '"Chelovek s kinoapparatom" Dzigi Vertova – k rasshifrovke montazhnogo teksta'. In: Raushenbakh (ed.), *Montazh*, 78.
22 There were, in fact, six experiments, of which one was "the arbitrary combination of the parts of different people's bodies and the creation through montage of the desired model actor", i.e. the 'created man' experiment. See M. Yampolsky, 'Kuleshov's experiments and the new anthropology of the actor'. In: A. Horton (ed.), *Inside the Film Factory: New approaches to Russian and Soviet Cinema*. London & New York: Routledge, 1991, 45.

between the descriptions is not parallel to the natural logic of the described and documented facts of history. For Bazin, the rhetorical basis of montage is somewhat false, since such documentary films create an illusion in the minds of the spectators, who think that a true document is in front of them, though in fact it is merely a series of two-minded facts that have been cemented together by the author of the text.[23] This is the case in visual rhetoric, with montage as the manipulation of reality persuading the reader that in front of him or her is an original document. With the help of montage, non-artistic material could become artistic. The organization of the material, the creation of the new meaningful whole, is decisive.

This leads us to the question of the author's role in the montage texts proclaiming the new reality. The role of the author is to arrange the material the way he or she wants to, and even the use of purely documentary material in this case leads to an artistic text (or at least one bearing the author's significant subjective commentary) and serves as a primitive version of conceptual art. Rodchenko's work against Klutsis' agitprop tendencies, for instance, can be understood from this perspective. Rodchenko was not so interested in presenting Soviet realities; a multi-level poeticism can be seen in his works as well as an arrangement of elements as the expression of the author's imagination, both of which add up to aesthetic montage. What was essential for him were surprising juxtapositions and absurd contexts for the pictorial elements. Perhaps that is why he is more easily compared with the Berlin Dadaists (such as Hannah Höch and George Grosz) than with Klutsis. Vladimir Mayakovski's poem *Pro Eto* (1923) is a clear example of how, in montage culture, different art forms work together towards a common goal, using the same formal means. Rodchenko's photomontages complement Mayakovski's poetic world in an indispensable way and open new opportunities for interpretation, which are transmittable only in another language, the language of photographic art.

Imaginist montage

The montage technique was used in both the prose and poetry of 1920s Russia, for not only did the different art forms follow a common principle to a great extent, but prose and poetry also came closer to one another. Prose began to be taken over by shortened, telegraphic forms, and the texts were more fragmentary than narrative.[24] Metaphorical prose, ornamental plotlessness and fragmentation dominated the field.

The new literature of the day was closely related to the idea of the new reality and its description in literature. 'Literature of fact' (*Literatura fakta*) was the declaration of the magazine *New Lef*, begun in 1927, that followed

---

23 See A. Bazin, *What is Cinema?* Berkeley: California University Press, 1972, 57.
24 Yu. N. Tynyanov, *Poetika. Istoriya literatury. Kino*. Moskva, 1977, 168.

the above-mentioned *Lef*, the organ of the Futurists. In the *New Lef*, Brik stated his disgust with 'generalizations and abstractions', because the details and precise descriptions of Soviet life should be given precedence.[25] The magazine also emphasized the priority of the material over the author's views, because the author should be only the discoverer of new material, not an inventive or creative person. And so factography, the use of elements of reality as a basis for art, became the best example of how art was connected to life. The focus on reality was taken to an extreme. Interestingly, however, the montage of 1920s literature appears to be a vehicle with a two-sided fix on reality: it both brings the elements of reality into literary texts and also underlines their literariness (*literaturnost*).[26]

In prose texts the use of the documentary material is often connected with the montage technique of composition, since it concerns the idea of heterogeneity in the surface structure of montage texts. In literature, a montage of fragments can be understood as one specific aspect of intertextuality. Most of the attention is on the correspondence between the basic or general space of the text and the textual joints, or 'intexts' (a text within a text). The double function of montage in relation to reality and fictionality can be approached from this aspect as follows: an original document that is joined to an artistic text, in correspondence with a fictional narrative, is transformed from an icon into an index. The document becomes an artistic sign of documentation and an imitation of the original document.[27]

The seemingly independent birth of montage literature and montage cinema was almost simultaneous. Yet the cinema's subsequent influence on literature is by no means the only explanation for literature's montage principle in 1920s Russian culture. In fact, literary montage has its obvious roots in both Realistic (Lev Tolstoi) and Symbolistic (Alexei Remizov) prose. As well, fragmentary non- or half-fictional autobiographic prose (Vasilii Rozanov) had a great influence on the telegraphic development of prose in the 1920s. Naturally, when speaking about the dominance of fragmentariness in literature one cannot forget the reminiscences of Romanticism and its significant impact on Modernism.[28] And, finally, the appearance and existence of Formalist theory (especially Tynyanov, Shklovskii and Eichenbaum) is dependent on this manifold dialogue between literature and cinema.

The Russian Imaginists (1918–1924) represent a fascinating aspect of the question of montage literature in the early 1920s, although they manifested

25 O. Brik, 'Blizhe k faktu'. *Novyi Lef*, 2, 1927, 32–34.

26 P. A. Jensen, 'Art-Artifact-Fact: the set on "reality" in the prose of the 1920's'. In: N. Å. Nilsson (ed.), *The Slavic Literatures and Modernism*. Stockholm: Almqvist & Wiksell, 1987, 117–123.

27 See Lotman, *Izbrannye stat'i*, II, 180.

28 The Romantic fragment was cultivated by post-revolutionary culture, in both poetry and prose. See M. F. Greenleaf, 'Tynjanov, Pushkin and the Fragment: through the lens of montage'. In: B. Gasparov et al. (eds.), *Cultural Mythologies of Russian Modernism: from the golden age to the silver age*. Berkeley etc.: University of California Press, 1993, 268–269.

themselves as an opposition to the utilitarianism in literature and to the cult of factography.[29] Here I shall concentrate on two authors, Vadim Shershenevich and Anatolii Mariengof.[30] The following poem, entitled "Catalogue of Images" was written in 1919 by Shershenevich.

Дома –
Из железа и бетона
Скирды.
Туман –
В стакан
Одеколона
Немного воды.
Улица аршином портного
Вперегиб, вперелом.
Издалека снова
Дьякон грозы – гром.
По ладони площади – жилки ручья.
В брюхе сфинкса из кирпича
Кокарда моих глаз,
Глаз моих ушат.
С цепи в который раз
Собака карандаша
И зубы букв со слюною чернил в ляжку бумаги.
За окном водостоков краги,
За окошком пудами злоба
И слово в губах, как свинчатка в кулак.
А семиэтажный гусар небоскреба
Шпорой подъезда звяк. [31]

---

29 The Imaginists attacked the journal *Lef* in their own journal "The Hotel for the Travelers in Beautiful": *Gostinitsa dlya puteshestvujushchikh v prekrasnom*, 1, 1922, 1–2. The journal, which held four issues, was dedicated to radical and national aestheticism.

30 In addition to Shershenevich and Mariengof, the key figures of Imaginism included Sergei Esenin, Ryurik Ivnev, Ivan Gruzinov and Matvei Roizman, and also such artists as Georgii Yakulov and Boris Erdman. (See e.g. E. M. Shneiderman (ed.), *Poety-Imazhinisty*. Sankt-Peterburg: Peterburgskii pisatel' 1997; *Russkii imazhinizm: istoriya, teoriya, praktika*. Moskva: Institut mirovoi literatury, 2005; T. Huttunen, 'Imazhinisty – poslednie dendi respubliki'. In: G. V. Obatnin & P. Pesonen (eds.), *Istoriya i povestvovanie*. Moskva: Novoe literaturnoe obozrenie, 2006, 317–354.)

31 *Houses / Of iron and concrete / Hay-stacks. / Fog – / Into a glass of eau de cologne / Some water. / The street in tailor's rule / Crooked, bent. / From far again / The storm's deacon – the roar. / Along the palm of the market – the brook veins. / In the belly of a brick sphinx / My eyes' cockade, / My eyes' tub. / Off the chains which once / The Pencil's dog. / And the letter teeth in ink slobber on the paper's thigh. / Outside the window the sewer leggings, / Outside the window pounds of hatred. / And the word in my mouth like a lead weight in my fist. / The seven-story hussar skyscraper / Spurs' clink in the stairs.*

In the above poem the attention is attracted by at least two features: the poem's format and its complete lack of verbs. The typographical arrangement of the poem is unusual: the verses are justified on the right side of the page, rather than on the left.[32] We can read the poem only by reconstructing the omitted verbs and the images hidden in between the juxtaposed words. We are reading a montage poem consisting of nouns, reminiscent of urbanism and the catalogue poetry by Walt Whitman.[33] The first lines (1–3) produce the image of houses described as hay-stacks, which leads us to an actual for the Imaginists conflict between the urban and the rural in post-revolutionary Russia. The next image of the fog (4–7) is constructed by omitting the verb describing the mixture of eau de cologne and water. Gradually we are being forwarded into an image of the lyrical subject poet looking out from his window and observing the rain (10–11; 12), and, presumably, revolutionary fighting (20) on the street. The motif of the poetic creation is juxtaposed with the lack of freedom (16–18), which is also related with the fighting. The words of the poet are treated as an important and proper image of the revolution (21). The interpretation of the text is thus dependent on the reader's reconstructive competence. Shershenevich was very active in theorizing on the poetics of the Imaginist group, one of the many post-Symbolist Avant-garde movements of the post-revolutionary period.

In their poetry and manifestos, the Imaginists proclaimed the superiority of the image. The core of poetry was, according to them, the interplay between individual images. Combining the ideas of the Italian Futurist Marinetti and the Russian Symbolist Andrei Belyi, Shershenevich forms a synthesis: "Poetry is the art of combining *autonomous words*, *word-images*. A poem is an uninterrupted series of images".[34] This declaration was an attack on the Cubo-Futurists, who had first introduced the concept of the *autonomous word* in their famous manifesto, *A Slap in the Face of Public Taste*. The Futurists are the main targets of Imaginists' loud manifestos, since they "spoke of the form, but thought only about the contents".[35] Naturally, the Imaginists turned out to be the true Formalists, who "cleared the form from the dust of the contents better than the shoe-polish man on the street".[36]

According to the Imaginists, the verb becomes unnecessary in poetry. Further, they claim that the metaphor in poetry is self-oriented, and that the metaphoric nature of the Russian language can be best expressed by using nouns. As a result they end up omitting verbs in their poetic syntax. The reading of poetry without verbs challenges the reader to participate in the

---

32 See A. Lawton, *Vadim Shershenevich: from Futurism to Imaginism*. Ann Arbor: Ardis, 1981, 36. According to Anna Lawton, it is probably meant to attract attention to the ends of the verses and to underline the orchestration of rhymes and assonances. This is easy to understand considering Shershenevich's theories of assonance.

33 About Shershenevich's interest in Whitman's poetry, see A. Mariengof, *Bessmertnaya trilogiya*. Moskva: Vagrius, 1998, 245.

34 Ibid., 33. Italics mine.

35 Cf. *Poety-Imazhinisty*, 8.

36 Ibid.

reconstructive action of combining juxtaposed elements and finding the predication (in the Eisensteinian sense: the *third* new meaning) between them.[37]
The active and expressive role of the reader is also often emphasized in the
Imaginists' theoretic writings. In their first manifesto, *Deklaratsija*, they
were expecting the *new* reader, the reader of the future:

> In our time of ice-cold homes only the heat of our works can warm the
> souls of our readers, the viewers. For them, for the receivers of our art,
> we are happy to donate the whole intuition of reception. We can appear
> even so humble that later on, when you, the still weakly talented reader,
> will grow up and become wiser, we shall even let you take part in a
> dispute with us.[38]

We can read Shershenevich's "Catalogue of Images" only by trying to make
up the predication, fitting verbs between the nouns in order to arrive at a unified, complete thought. This is the core of montage poetry: the reader should
reconstruct the causal connection between the images (as in film, between
shots; or in photography or painting, between the separate heterogeneous
elements) and should almost guess the missing verbs. Eisenstein wrote that
montage corresponds to the structure of the Chinese language, in that the
verbs in them are produced from juxtapositions: the combination of ideas
meaning water and eye produces the idea 'to cry', the combination of mouth
and bird produces 'to sing', and so on.[39] The *third* element, produced by the
juxtaposition of words, corresponds in montage poetry to the verb omitted
by the author, and is for the reader to discover.

The Imaginist catalogue of images may be regarded as a dominant
compositional device in Anatoly Mariengof's first fictional novel *Cynics*
(1928)[40], the story of two "ex-people", unemployed historian Vladimir and
his lover Olga. *Cynics* is a montage novel, and it can be treated as a collection of heterogeneous, apparently disparate and non-related fragments. It is
written as the first-person narrator Vladimir's fragmentary diary from the
years 1918–1924. Vladimir is a historian, so the diary consists of his own
numbered notes, contemporary news items and historical documents. The
narrator demonstrates the method in the entry from 1922:

37 Eisenstein himself wrote about the predication as an analogue to montage in cinema:
    Eizenshtein, *Izbrannye proizvedeniya*, 2, 429.
38 Ibid, 10.
39 See Eizenshtein, *Izbrannye proizvedeniya*, 2, 285. The idea had appeared already in
    the writings of the Imagist Ezra Pound and the Russian Imaginists in the beginning
    of the 1920s, see V. Shershenevich, *2x2=5*. Moskva: Imazhinisty, 1920, 37.
40 The novel was written in 1928, the Russian text was published the same year in
    Berlin. Mariengof was attacked after the publication by the All-Russian Union of
    Soviet Writers (VSSP), the novel was labeled an "anti-social proclamation", and it
    was not published in the Soviet Union until 1988.

1

In the autumn of 1921 my fingers began to itch once again. Tattered scraps of paper appeared on my writing desk and sharp little black points appeared on my pencils. Each morning I fully intended to buy a notebook, and each evening I fully intended to apply my mind. But then I was beset by laziness, and I am not by habit so gauche as to resist the advances of such a charming creature.

The soft sheets of paper containing my 'drafts' were impaled on the spike in the 'thinker's cell', the hard sheets were preserved. I am grateful to Olga for her squeamishness.

Since I always forget to write the day of the week and the date, I am obliged to present them in chronological disorder.[41]

The "chronological disorder" described by the narrator is the core of the montage technique used by Mariengof in his first fictional novel. As any element in a montage text (and in an Imaginist poetic catalogue), the novel's fragments, when viewed in isolation, may be defined as relatively autonomous and polyvalent, carrying semantic potential. This potential can be actualized only in juxtaposition with other elements. In the actual text, which according to Eisensteinian interpretation is a result of communication between the author's fragmentation and the reader's (re)integration, these elements often turn out to be multifunctional, and capable of generating new meanings on different levels of the text. In Shershenevich's Imaginist jargon, these elements are characterized as "pregnant word-images", meaning nouns bearing in themselves the potential image.[42] Only in Mariengof's prose are these "word-images" translated into "chapter-shots", or seemingly disparate fragments. Their actual meaning depends on discrete juxtapositions or non-discrete combinations with other fragments. The reconstruction of the correspondences is done, naturally, by the active co-author of the text, the *new* reader, who uses the lens of montage in his or her *pince-nez*. The next dramatic passage, where the heroine Olga tells Vladimir that she has been unfaithful to him (with his brother, the Bolshevik Sergey) is illuminative as a montage of heterogeneous fragments:

45

One o'clock in the morning. Olga is sitting at the table, reading the interminable minutes of even more interminable meetings.

The Revolution has already created grandiose departments with mighty bureaucratic bosses.

I think about immortality.

One of Balzac's characters once threw a coin into the air and shouted: " 'Heads' for God".

"Don't look!" his friend advised him, catching the coin in mid-air. "Chance is a great joker".

---

41   A. Mariengof, *Cynics*, In: *Glas. New Russian Writing*, 1, 1991, 68.
42   Shershenevich, *2x2=5*, 39.

How stupid it all is. How many more centuries must drag past before we can stop playing "heads or tails" when we think of immortality?
Olga hid her papers away in her briefcase and went over to the stove. The gleaming coffee-pot was frothing over.
"Would you like some coffee?"
"Yes, please, I would."
She poured out two cups.
Fruit-drops of various colours lay on a porcelain parrot. Olga selected a sour green one.
"Oh yes, Vladimir..."
She placed the sweet in her mouth.
"...I almost forgot to tell you..."
The wind slammed the small window shut.
"...I was unfaithful to you today."
The snow outside the window went on falling and the fire in the stove went on cracking its nuts. Olga leapt up from her chair.
"What's wrong, Vladimir?"
A tiny golden coal tumbled out of the stove.
Somehow I was quite unable to swallow. My throat had become a narrow bent straw.
"Nothing."
I took out a cigarette. I tried to light it, but the first three matches broke, and the head of the fourth went flying off. The coal that had tumbled out of the stove had burnt through the parquet.
"Olga, could I ask you one trifling favour?"
"Certainly."
She deftly picked up the coal.
"Would you mind taking a bath, please?"
Olga smiled.
"Certainly..."
My fifth match lit.
Outside the window the snow still went on falling and the stove went on cracking its wooden nuts.

46
Concerning the Moscow fire of 1445 the chronicler wrote:
"...the entire city was burnt, so that not a single tree was left, and the churches of stone did fall asunder and the walls of the city did fall asunder".[43]

The juxtaposed fragments contain several curiosities of montage technique. The narration in the 45th fragment is based on the succession of laconic dialogue and short descriptions, reminiscent of film narration in early cinema. This alteration creates a certain rhythm and makes it possible to find the culmination points having special tension. The first such moment is the close-up description: "She placed the sweet in her mouth."

43   Mariengof, *Cynics*, 33–35.

The dominant metaphor in the passage is, of course, the fire. It functions first to direct the changing viewpoints and is transformed into a reflection of Vladimir's emotions. His reaction is not given or described; the reader must instead reconstruct it from the detailed descriptions of the stove, matches and coal, as if something was 'burning' in his heart. The iconic signs lose their iconicity and attain symbolic value with the help of repetition. Such detailed analysis could be continued, however the main purpose of the metaphor is revealed in the next fragment, which is a non-fictional document about one of the Moscow fires. After the 44th fragment is juxtaposed by the reader with the 45th, none of the colliding fragments remain as they were. They have lost their 'iconicity' as well, and only the result of their combination is left, the metaphorical synthesis about Vladimir's *true* way of experiencing Olga's unfaithfulness.

Mariengof had already underlined the active role of the reader in his article 'Buyan-Ostrov' (1920), where he claimed that the main goal of a poet is to create maximum inner tension in the reader's mind. In an Imaginist text this is best achieved by a constant collisional juxtaposition of 'pure' and 'impure'. The author chooses the most shocking juxtapositions for metaphors in order to force the reader to participate in a reconstructive process of generating synthetic meanings. This Imaginist principle is clearly seen in the metaphors used in *Cynics*. In the mind of the narrator, nothing pure is expressed without its constant juxtaposition with something impure: love, for instance, is juxtaposed with constipation and enemas, flowers with severed heads, sentimental episodes with detailed descriptions of hygienic problems, and so on.

In his longer Imaginist poems, for instance, in *Magdalina* (1920), Mariengof uses complex heteroaccentual rhyming, with the rhyming pair being separated by an irregular number of lines. For the reader this presents the intriguing challenge of reconstructing the causality of the text. The heteroaccentual rhyme is one of the main features of Mariengof's poetics, rather than just a random experiment. From the point of view of textual orchestration the focus here is on the memory of the text and the long-distance connection between textual segments.

The narrative nature of the relatively autonomous fragments and descriptive passages in *Cynics* is related to the poetics of transition described above. The repetition of certain motif-like descriptions or metaphors creates several intextual narratives within the novel. The most evident examples are the descriptions of the characters. In fact, all characters are described analogically in terms of the montage principle in cinematography. This is achieved with the help of associative details, while the formation of the character, which appears to be a narrative text within a text, is left to the reader. Every character is given a dominant detail, upon which his or her image is based, and which conveys the narrator's attitude towards the character: Bolshevik Sergey's (repulsive) face, *nepman* Dokuchaev's (aggressive) hands, heroine Olga's eyes, comrade Mamashev's rapturous saliva, etc. The following descriptions of Vladimir's maid Marfusha are typical of Mariengof's montage technique:

Marfusha is standing barefoot on the windowsill wiping down the panes with a soapy sponge. Her naked, smooth, pink, warm, heavy calves are trembling. As though the woman has two hearts beating passionately in her legs.[44]

I hear the slapping of soft bare feet along the corridor.[45]

(...) there is the sound of bare feet along the corridor on the other side of the wall.[46]

The Imaginist thematics of love and revolution play an important role in *Cynics*. In fact, Mariengof was obsessively keen on juxtaposing love and revolution in his early poems, where these two elements are connected almost without exception with the help of intertextual references to the Bible. The dominant motif is 'decapitation' (especially John the Baptist's execution), which functions as a semiotic border between intimate love passages and descriptions of the massacres of the October Revolution. The role of the Bible in this thematic triangle seems to underline Mariengof's ambivalent attitude towards the revolution. The juxtaposition of love and revolution thus becomes the main theme in *Cynics* as well. The role of several biblical allusions (related through cut-off heads) is again to reveal their interconnection. On one hand, they express the history of decapitation in Russian culture (according to the narrator of the novel), and the October Revolution appears to be just another replary of this history. On the other, they are used in romantic passages, where the narrator describes his love for the heroine.

The factographics of the novel (i.e. Mariengof's use of documentary material) present another aspect of the montage principle evident in *Cynics*. In 1928, the year *Cynics* was written, Mariengof took part in an attempt to organize a new literary association called *Literatura i byt*, focussing on the use of authentic documentary work as the main material for literary texts. The association was never given an official status. Its programme, however, is very close to the ideas discussed by *Lef*, whose notions about factographics it embraced. When approached from the point of view of factographics, the surficial structure (*faktura*) of *Cynics* becomes more understandable. Recognizing this post-Futurist effort is essential when trying to reconstruct the role of Imaginism in Mariengof's work at the end of the 1920s. The novel *Cynics* appears to be in a paradoxical position between Imaginism and post-Imaginism. On one hand, it is almost unique example of Imaginist prose in Russian literature, but on the other, it can be interpreted as a kind of fictional epilogue in the history of Russian Imaginism. After *Cynics*, Mariengof did not continue writing Imaginist prose, with the exception of the novel *The Shaved Man* (1930) containing certain Imaginist features. He became more interested in the factographic and historical aspects of literature and turned to autobiographical prose, memoirs and diaries.

44 Ibid., 27.
45 Ibid., 50.
46 Ibid., 61.

It is obvious that the dominant idea of the post-revolutionary period – the question of cultural conflict and constant juxtaposition – is typical of Russian Imaginism and of Mariengof, as it is of most post-Symbolist literary movements in Soviet Russia in the 1920s. In fact, the Imaginists as a group could be characterized from this point of view more generally. They manifested themselves as individualists, in a society where the newly born Soviet people were living under collectivism. They declared all of the preceding movements unworthy and meaningless, even the Futurists, to whom their poetry owed a great deal. These 'dandies of the Republic' represent an illuminative example of montage culture in the post-revolutionary period, even though the word "montage" was never mentioned in their theoretical writings.

CHRISTOPHER WILLIAMS

The Modernisation of Russian Health Care: Challenges, Policy, Constraints

Introduction

This chapter discusses the alternative Russian approaches to the modernisation of welfare focusing in particular upon the period from the War Communism to late Stalinism. It examines key indicators of modernisation in relation to health care, such as free health care to all, free access for all, and the role played by the state, and considers what impact the Stalinist emphasis on industry and agriculture to the detriment of social welfare, had on welfare provision and policy. The study makes use of key public health journals, statistical handbooks and new material from the declassified Narkomzdrav (Ministry of Public Health) archives in order to assess the main challenges to modernisation (trends in morbidity, mortality, health service development, the socio-economic and political context and its impact on health policy and decision-making, and above all on relations between the medical profession and the state) and the degree of success or failure in Russian modernisation of welfare strategies after October 1917. The process of modernisation of Russian welfare was very much the product of the economic and political circumstances and debates that took place after the 1917 October revolution. Russian leaders had a reasonably clear conception of what modernisation of welfare meant. It referred to the need to eradicate the tsarist legacy and the desire to move towards a welfare system along socialist lines. Although the Bolsheviks were keen to transform the old backward tsarist system of welfare provision into a truly modern welfare state that would be the envy of the world, the reality of Russian rule – revolution in a backward country faced initially with civil war and famine then with large scale social, economic and political transformation followed again by war and famine – made this modernisation task extremely difficult from the outset. As a result the modernisation of Russian welfare did not proceed smoothly and debates occurred here, as elsewhere, about what were the most appropriate methods for bringing about change and also about the speed of change. Over time, as we shall see, the objectives of welfare modernisation changed from simply eradication (of tsarist legacy) to the desire to create a Russian welfare state that was far superior to its Western counterpart. Moreover as Stalinism developed apace the goal was to use welfare as a tool to ensure that the Soviet Union was able to catch up and overtake the West in economic and technological terms. However as this chapter demonstrates the failure to prioritise welfare and thereby ensure that it kept pace with modernisation drives elsewhere, especially in the economy, had adverse knock on effects which put severe constraints on the success of the modernisation of Russian welfare under Stalin. In the long-term, as the last part of this chapter suggests, Russian welfare never truly recovered from its Stalinist legacy, despite Gorbachev's last minute attempts to address this issue.

The challenges

In spite of advances made in the great cities, the rural population of Russia lived and died practically without medical care.[1]

The tsarist government left Soviet power a terrible heritage of unsanitary conditions. The exceptionally bad material conditions of the working masses of town and country, the police oppression which stifled all public activity, the merciless exploitation of the workers and poorer peasants, the low cultural level of the population and the consequent low sanitary culture, all combined to create a favourable soil for epidemic diseases among the population.[2]

These two opening verdicts from C. A. E. Winslow, Professor of the Yale Medical School and American Red Cross Mission member, and Nikolai Semashko, Soviet Russia's First Health Minister, show the extent of the difficulty facing the Bolsheviks when they took power in October 1917. From the outset, Russian leaders and Marxist theoreticians saw pre-1917 welfare provision as backward and exploitative. Thus Maistrakh noted 'tsarist health care lacks uniformity of plan or method of operation'[3] and Lisitsyn commented that before 1917

A vast part of Russian had no provisions for medical aid the result of which was a distressing sick rate and mortality from communicable disease as well as generally very low health standards.[4]

In the case of industrial workers this meant

unbearable working conditions in plants and factories, frequent mutilations, (a) short life span, weak health and poor physical development.[5]

---

1 N. A. Semashko, *Health protection in the USSR*, London, Gollancz 1934, 11.
2 C. E. A. Winslow, 'Public health administration in Russia' in *Public Health Reports* 28 Dec. 1917, US Public Health Service, Washington Government Printing House, 1918, 3.
3 K. V. Maistrakh, *Organizatsiya zdravookhraneniya*, 4th ed., Moscow, 1956, 8.
4 Iu. Lisitsyn, *Health protection in the USSR*, Moscow: Progress publishers 1972, 19.
5 Ibid, 21.

The reasons why this occurred, according to Russian Marxists, were firstly, a lack of a centralised medical service because each tsarist Ministry had its own medical division which competed with various religious, philanthropic and public organisations; secondly, the fact that health and welfare provision was unevenly distributed, and finally, welfare was provided by dedicated zemstvo and other staff but they were over-stretched and poorly funded. As a consequence, Russia's pre-revolutionary health and welfare system lacked the infrastructure and resources to combat epidemics, famine, a high death and infant mortality rate, and it was not in a position to reverse the falling birth rate[6].

Lenin's modernisation of welfare strategy

It is against this background that Lenin embarked upon his modernisation of Russian welfare policy. In Semashko's words, this was to be based on

a radical revolution in order to bring about order out of the chaos.[7]

and involved a reorganisation

of the entire public health system both in the principles on which it was based, in its organisation and its practical aspects, along entirely new lines.[8]

The new Leninist principles of health and welfare included:

1. state responsibility for public health
2. the development of public health within the framework of a single plan
3. centralisation of health care
4. provision of free and comprehensive medical aid
5. an emphasis on preventive medicine and
6. unity of theory and practice

Difficulties in putting this strategy into practice stemmed largely from a mixture of internal difficulties and external pressures, as we shall now see.

State responsibility for health and welfare was to be exercised using two guiding principles: *nationalisation*, whereby private ownership was abolished and state control implemented, and *municipalisation*, which meant increased local government control over health and welfare. Both were inter-connected and involved turning private health establishments into publicly owned ones

6   N. A. Semashko, *Des'yat let Oktiabria i sovetskaya meditsina*, Moscow: Izd. NKZdrava RSFSR, 1927, 3.
7   Semashko, *Health protection,* 11.
8   Ibid, 15.

that were run at a local level. But even here conflicts broke out. Schaeffer Conroy argues that in relation to pharmacies this led to conflicts between staff and the new management of the muncipalised pharmacies over how these new establishments would be run and also over pay and work hours. Furthermore there were also shortages of staff in some areas such as Petrograd, which further hampered things. In the end, calls were made in the case of pharmacies for a transfer of ownership not from private to local but to central authorities.[9]

Recently declassified Russian Ministry of Public Health archive material suggests that an inexperienced Russian government and public health officials got lost in the minutiae and found it extremely hard to prioritise things.[10] As a consequence policy and decision-making was rather ad hoc and reactive in character. However, such a response cannot simply be attributed to inexperience. The Bolsheviks were also in the midst of civil war, widespread epidemics and famine in the period 1918–20.[11] At the same time, there were significant shortages of staff (some of whom had emigrated[12]) and some sections of the medical profession were hostile to the new socialist regime.[13] This made implementation of the first aspect of Lenin's modernisation of welfare policy problematic.

It was extremely difficult to put into place a single health and welfare plan under the conditions prevailing during War Communism. Although the creation of Narkomdrav (Ministry of Public Health) in June 1918 was geared towards facilitating greater direction, co-ordination and monitoring of health and welfare activity by the state, shortages of food, fuel, poor quality housing, sanitation and unclean water, all hampered Narkomzdrav's work and pulled staff and policy in different directions. Furthermore, the tendency to prioritise the Red Army, which was natural under civil war conditions, meant that health and welfare of the urban and rural population as a whole was neglected. This situation also resulted in urgently needed reforms, such as a modification of the medical curriculum, being put on the back burner.[14]

But these problems were nothing compared to the need to rely on tsarist trained staff in order to push modernisation through. As Lisitsyn notes, the problem was that

9 M. Scaeffer Conroy, *In health and in sickness: Pharmacy, pharmacists and the pharmaceutical industry in late Imperial, early Soviet Russia*, New York: Columbia University Press 1994, 398–399.

10 See Council of Medical Boards minutes in Gostudarstevennyi Arkhiv Rossisskoi Federatsii (GARF) f. A-482, op. 4, d. 31.

11 C. Williams, 'The 1921 Russian famine: Centre and periphery responses', *Revolutionary Russia* 6 (1), December 1993, 277–314.

12 See C. Williams, 'War, medicine and revolution: Petrograd doctors, 1917–20', *Revolutionary Russia* 4 (2), Dec. 1991, 259–288.

13 GARF f. A-482, op. 2, d. 231.

14 GARF f. A-482, op. 1, d. 505, l. 58.

not all doctors sided conclusively with Soviet power. Some of them failed to grasp the aims of the revolution…. and opposed the undertakings of the young Soviet state.[15]

For a long time Russian scholars, such as Barsukov and Zhuk, and some Western experts, such as Field, have argued that the bitter and irreconcilable differences between the medical profession (especially the Pirigov Society) and the Bolsheviks hampered the success of Lenin's welfare modernisation.[16] Very few, with the notable exception of Peter Krug, argued that this view had been exaggerated.[17] We now know, thanks to the opening up of the archives, that Krug was correct. One Narkomzdrav review of 1921 shows, for instance, that most of those involved with Lenin's modernisation of welfare policy had in fact been born in the late 19th century (in the 1880s–90s) and so had qualified as medical personnel just before the first world war. When the author examined a random sample of around 100 medical staff from this 1921 Narkomzdrav survey of various medical staff ranging from feldshers (nurses) through to doctors and other specialists (psychiatrists, surgeons etc.), he discovered that 90 percent of those working for the Russian state had been very experienced, long standing medical practitioners, in some instances with up to 37 years service.[18] Hence, most medical staff were ex-tsarist professionals and prepared to put differences of political outlook behind them in order to combat epidemics, fight disease and to create a new socialist welfare state.

It seems, therefore, that Lenin had correctly judged the mood of the medical profession when he pointed out at the 7th Congress of Soviets that

> Of course there are still doctors who regard the working-class government with prejudice and distrust and prefer to receive fees from the rich rather than throw themselves into the hard struggle against typhus, but they are in the minority, their numbers are growing less and less. The majority are of the kind who are willing to struggle to solve the fundamental problem of the salvation of our culture, and these doctors are devoting themselves to the hard and difficult task with as much self-sacrifice as a military specialist. They are prepared to give their strength to the promotion of the common cause.[19]

---

15 Lisitsyn, *Health protection*, 24.

16 M. I. Barsukov and A. Zhuk, *Za sotsialisticheskuyu rekonstruktsiyu zdravookhraneniya*, Moscow, 1932, 13–14; M. I. Barsukov, *Velikaya oktiabr'skaya sotsialiticheskaya revoliutsiya i organizatsiya sovetskogo zdravookhraneniya (oktiabr' 1917g – iiul 1918g)*, Moscow, 1951, 86–88 and M. G. Field, *Soviet socialised medicine: An introduction*, New York: Free Press, 1967, 28, 55, 58.

17 P. Krug, 'Russian public physicians and revolution: The Pirigov Society, 1917–20', PhD in History, University of Wisconsin-Madison 1979, 311.

18 'Spiski meditsinskogo personela NKZa RSFSR po sostoyannego na dekabr' 1921 goda' in GARF f. A-482, op. 2, d. 231 list 2 ob-3 ob.

19 Cited in Semashko, *Health protection*, 39–40.

Nevertheless the second and third features of Lenin's modernisation of welfare strategy, the development of a single plan and centralisation of health and welfare, were difficult to implement. Thus one Narkomzdrav document explained how

> Medical work during the civil war was the product of two contradictory forces, namely the favourable social conditions, unlimited scope for curative measures and the enthusiasm of the toiling masses, on the one hand, and difficult economic conditions, blockade and civil war on the other.[20]

The fourth modernisation principle – open and free access to health care – was geared towards making access to health care based not on class or ability to pay but on need. For a whole range of reasons from War Communism, throughout NEP and into the Stalinist era, this principle was never strictly adhered to. "Class" was an important determinant of access, but fees of one sort or another always applied.

The notion of 'preventive medicine' (the fifth aspect of Lenin's welfare modernisation strategy) occupied a central place at the start with Semashko remarking that 'Prophylactic measures are the basis of the entire health service.'[21] In line with this philosophy, a comprehensive series of measures were gradually introduced to prevent the spread of disease. As Semashko explained in 1927

> preventive medicine involves not simply the treatment of disease, but more important it involves rendering the population healthy by eradicating the causes of disease at source.[22]

For Russian medical experts and Marxists – poor housing, sanitation, environmental pollution, diet and difficult working conditions (poor ventilation, light and the absence of safety measures) – all caused ill-health. Unfortunately a mix of circumstances and contradictory policies ensured that these factors adversely impacted upon health conditions in the period under discussion.

The unity of theory and practice was the final important principle in Lenin's modernisation of welfare policy. This strategy refers to the notion that research findings must be applied to clinical settings. In Lenin's time this meant immunization and inoculation and later, on top of this, this strategy led to dispansarisation, an emphasis on industrial and rural health care (the so-called face to industry and face to the countryside policies) and finally to cost cutting (or the 'regime of the economy') during NEP.

This analysis illustrates that a combination of internal and external pressures made Lenin's desire to

20 *Narkomzdrav, Otchet Narkomzdrav k 8-mu S"ezdu Sovetov*, Moscow, 1920, 6–7.
21 Semashko, *Health protection*, 22.
22 Cited in I. G. Kochergin, 'Osnovye voprosy teorii sovetskoi meditsiny i zdravookhraneniia v trudakh N. A. Semashko', *Sovetskoe zdravookhranenie* 1965, no.5, 27.

> make an historically unprecedented leap from backwardness and poor
> health to a social system of health protection which would ensure a rapid
> improvement of all indices of social health.[23]

proved very difficult from the start. Thus during War Communism, despite the
rhetoric, fees for health and welfare existed and rationing of welfare services
prevailed. As a consequence by early NEP, delegates at the 3rd All-Russian
Congress of Public health departments, held between 27 October –1 November
1921 criticised the use of fees, unequal access to health care and blamed
this on the priority given to health care for the insured to the detriment of
other sections of society.[24] Furthermore, although the emphasis on preventive medicine was retained during NEP, financial constraints, following the
transition from central to local funding after 1922, hindered health service
development, recovery from revolution and civil war and above all the successful implementation of Lenin's welfare modernisation plans. Moreover
the principles on which this policy was based were gradually eroded as NEP
progressed. From the mid-1920s onwards, therefore, "illness" and "entitlement" to health and welfare benefits both began to be defined in ideological
terms, so that coverage was limited to those able to work; whilst others la-
belled as "scroungers" were excluded. But it was not just politics that got in
the way. Economic factors (in particular fiscal constraints) led to a shortage
of personnel, medicines, equipment, which coupled with housing and food
problems, created enormous difficulties.[25] In this context, it is worth noting
that the 'regime of the economy' in public health was partly responsible for
this situation as it was designed to make savings, reduce inefficiency and
waste and rationalise the use of health and welfare resources. On top of these
problems, welfare modernisation was hampered by the gradual clamp-down
on bourgeois medical practitioners who had now served their purpose. They
had helped the Russian state build a health service and restore health conditions to normal by the mid-1920s. Finally, within the broader political context
of the industrialisation debate of the 1920s, late NEP saw a new emphasis
on 'improving health in order to increase labour productivity'[26], a principle
that would later become a vital part of Stalin's revolution from above and
his welfare modernisation policy as we shall now see.

Stalin's modernisation of welfare strategy

Stalin's welfare modernisation in some respects marked a continuation with
Lenin's strategy whilst in others it constituted a fundamental break with the
past. The abandonment of NEP, the introduction of central planning and the

23 Lisitsyn, *Health protection*, 27.
24 Ye. D. Gribanov, *Vserossisskie s"ezdy zdravotdelov i ikh znachenie dlia praktiki
    sovetskogo zdravookhraneniia*, Moscow 1966, 73–74.
25 Semashko, *Health protection*, 46.
26 Ibid, 61.

pursuit of rapid industrialisation and forced collectivisation all had an adverse effect upon health service development and health conditions generally.[27] Housing provision and food supplies could simply not keep pace with the mass influx of peasants from the countryside, who arrived in search of work in the towns despite Donskoi's claim that

> the tempo of public health development must be in line with the rate of (Soviet) economic and cultural development.[28]

This principle adhered to the shifting emphasis placed upon the health of workers and peasants during Stalin's socialist reconstruction phase. Stalin's welfare modernisation strategy therefore sought to

> improve the level of medical provision for the insured, that is the industrial proletariat, factory workers and those in key industries.[29]

and also to

> devote its fullest attention to medical care for the socialised sector of the economy, namely agricultural workers in sovkhozy and kolkhozy.[30]

The overall aim of the welfare modernisation policy, which was to be implemented via a series of five year plans (hereafter FYP), was to improve health conditions, increase the food supply, raise labour productivity, stress health and welfare in industrial centres, cut the level of industrial accidents, increase health awareness (sanitary culture) and maintain a unified dispansary system.[31] During the first FYP, a total of 480 million roubles was spent on public health[32], thereafter Stalin planned to invest a massive 4 milliard roubles on health by 1937.[33] The main source of this expenditure would be bank loans, special means, local and then finally state funds.[34]

However the reality was very different. Thus one 1933 planning document, looking back on the results of the first five-year plan for health, 1928–32, notes in relation to medical care in Leningrad, a city crammed full of the industrial proletariat, factory workers and lots of key industries, that

27 For more see C. Williams, 'The Revolution from above in Soviet medicine, Leningrad 1928–32', *Journal of Urban History* Volume 20 (4), August 1994, 512–540.
28 M. Donskoi, 'Ocherednye zadachi planirovaniia zdravookhraneniia', *Voprosy zdravookhraneniia* 1928, No. 1, 11.
29 V. I. Smirnov, 'Osnovy 5-letnogo perspektivnogo plana zdravookhraneniia Leningradskoi oblasti', *Zdravookhranenie* 1929, No. 1, 3.
30 Ibid, 4.
31 'Finansovyi plan organov zdravookhraneniia na 2-e piatiletie 1933–37gg, t. 1 in GARF f. A-482, op. 26, d. 22, l. 12.
32 'Finansovyi plan' in GARF f. A-482, op. 26, d. 26, l. 8.
33 'Finansovyi plan' in GARF f. A-482, op. 26, d. 26, l. 14.
34 'Finansovyi plan' in GARF f. A-482, op. 26, d. 26, l. 25.

staff were in short supply, hospitals were closed, provisions were highly unsatisfactory, new construction was not forthcoming and capital investment was virtually non-existent.[35]

The primary reason for the gap between welfare policy and the reality was a failure to actually prioritise health and welfare, coupled with rampant inflation, and a cut in real terms in health and welfare spending. The latter meant that hospital repairs were not carried out, building programmes abandoned and crucial medical staff not hired. All in all, this resulted in the health service not be able to cope with the problems generated by Stalin's industrialisation and collectivisation policies. Furthermore, planning simply set unrealistic health and welfare targets, such as 1 doctor per 25,000 population; 1 bed per 4,000 insured and 1 bed per 8,000 uninsured in addition to 1 doctor per industrial district and 1 medical laboratory per 50,000–120,000 population.[36] Although minimal health plan indicators might have been achievable, Stalin's welfare modernisation strategy expected the earth and set its health and welfare targets far too high.[37] Such failures and cutbacks came at a time when many cities, Leningrad included, were trying to combat a new wave of health challenges (such as a rapid rise in infectious diseases such as typhus and typhoid, scarlet fever, whopping cough, dysentery and malaria[38]). This was clear evidence that there were many contradictions in Stalin's welfare modernisation strategy which was not geared towards addressing challenges such as changes in health conditions or in the population's changing welfare needs due to the revolution from above.

Although Russian Health Ministry officials, such as T. S. A. Nechokova, were right to talk in terms of the tremendous leap that Russia had made from being an agrarian, backward uncultured nation in 1917 to a highly developed modern industrial state by 1937, pointing in particular to the role played by the health service in dramatically improving health conditions (morbidity and mortality) and in developing a welfare state rather than a ad hoc set of welfare organisations[39], no one in the health and welfare sphere were resting on their laurels. This is illustrated by the targets for health and welfare incorporated into the second (1933–37) and third (1938–42) FYPs, both of which envisaged major quantitative improvements in the number of medical personnel, houses, hospital beds etc, all of which was to be financed

---

35 *Raionnoe planirovanie: Materialy*, Leningradskia oblastnaia planirovania komissia, Leningrad, 1933, p. 33. Closures were not restricted to just the first FYP. In Leningrad's case included medical facilities at the Baltinskii and March factories as well as out-patient facilities at Vyborg district factories occurred in 1933 (GARF f. A-482, op. 15, d. 388, l. 39, 43).

36 'General'nyi plan po zdravookhraneniiu RSFSR na desiatiletie 1926-36gg' in GARF f. A-482, op. 26, d. 2, l. 1-1 ob, l. 2.

37 For example, the target for sanitary doctors was 1,031 in the minimum variant but 2042 in the maximum variant whilst that for a tuberculosis bed was 7,134 (minimal) and 15,472 (maximal) and so forth (GARF f. A-482, op. 26, d. 2, l. 5, 11). GARF f. A-482, op. 10, d. 2448, l. 1, 1 ob, 4, 4 ob., 10, 10 ob., 13, 13 ob., 16, 16 ob.

38 GARF f. A-482, op. 24, d. 964, l. 1, 3–4.

39 GARF f. A-482, op. 24, d. 964, l. 3–6, 14.

via extensive capital investment. Such an approach from 1933 onwards was aimed at eradicating infectious disease epidemics, improving the quality of water supplies, tightening up on food and labour hygiene, combating so-called "social diseases" (tuberculosis, alcoholism and venereal disease) and cutting down on high infant mortality rate and abortion levels. To do this necessitated training more medical cadres, building more hospitals and halls of residence to house them, as well as building more houses and schools for their families. Finally, from 1933–42, the Russian state embarked upon large-scale inoculation and vaccination programmes and banned abortion.[40]

However, as with the first FYP, things do not quite go to plan during the 2nd and 3rd FYPs because medical staff were often having to go without pay, despite being overworked, which affected their morale.[41] Whilst most 'remained friendly and helpful', others didn't. Hence hospital patients complained about nurses who sat and read books rather than assist the sick; of catering staff who let the food 'go cold' meaning it was 'worse than in our stoloviya'[42] and of poorly trained staff, who had probably qualified during the acceleration of medical education training from 1928–32, and hence were slow to take patient's temperatures and often contradicted one another on diagnosing patients illnesses. This made treatment difficult.[43] Not surprisingly patients formed a "poor impression" of some staff and in other cases misdiagnosis resulted in death, as one daughter found when she arrived in Moscow from Smolensk by train after her mother had died. She almost blamed herself because she lived so far away and was not able to offer her mother the daily care and attention she deserved.[44] To try and remedy these problems, average medical wages were to be increased by around 5 percent from 1938 onwards[45] and more medical staff (including feldshers, midwives, dental doctors, pharmacists and nurses) trained.[46]

Although in quantitative terms Stalin's welfare modernisation was deemed an official "success", it was a clear "failure" by qualitative measures. In this context, mixed results occurred in relation to the 3rd FYP. Thus the infant mortality rate in Russia declined 3-fold in towns and 2-fold in the countryside during the 3rd FYP (1938–42) but the death rate from tuberculosis rose by around 25 percent.[47] Such problems are hardly surprising because the 3rd FYP for health was drawn up against the backdrop of the purges, Russia's

40 GARF f. A-482, op. 24, d. 949, 1.19.
41 GARF f. A-482, op. 24, d. 266, 1. 20, 20 ob.
42 GARF f. A-482, op. 24, d. 266, 1. 25–26.
43 'Plan 3-i piatiletka po zdravookhraneniiu 1938–42gg. T. 1' in GARF f. A-482, op. 26, d. 36, 1. 82.
44 GARF f. A-482, op. 26, d. 39, 1. 21.
45 GARF f. A-482, op. 24, d. 266, 1. 28, 30.
46 'Plan 3-i piatiletka' in GARF f. A-482, op. 26, d. 36, list 6-7. 'Ob'yasnitel'naya zapiska k planu zdravookhraneniya na 3-go piatiletku i materialy k planu' in GARF f. A-482, op. 24, d. 1113, 1. 56.
47 On this see J. Barber and A. R. Dzeniskevich (ed.), *Zhizn' i smert' v blokirovannom Leningrade: Istoriko-meditsinskii aspekt*, St. Petersburg, Dmitrii Bulganin, 2001 and A. R. Dzeniskevich, *Na grani zhizn' i smerti*, St. Petersburg, Nektor, 2002.

involvement in the Spanish civil war, the signing of the Nazi-Soviet Pact and during the run up to and eventually the outbreak of the Second World War. Resources were urgently needed in heavy industry and defence, which resulted in widespread shortages of medical staff, equipment, beds, new hospitals and leaders to manage these and other pressing problems.[48] World War Two then exacerbated things further, with Leningrad facing a life and death situation through the siege.[49] Despite this, Vinogradov is correct to remark that the Russian welfare state "withstood these trials honorably".[50]

After the war, although the 'material and technical base of public health and medical science' in the USSR was extensively developed, changing health conditions once again, such as the 1947 famine[51], coupled with the outbreak of the Cold War, meant that welfare modernisation was made a low priority. Health and welfare generally was therefore unable to modernise during late Stalinism in an effective and efficient way because Stalin's priorities lay elsewhere and his resources were spread too thinly.

Eradicating the Stalinist legacy

We saw above that the main characteristic of both Lenin and Stalin's welfare modernisation policies, though to varying degrees, was the key role played by the state in determining social need and in establishing the means (i.e. bureaucratic mechanisms) to implement policy decisions. This monopoly role was particularly evident in the Stalinist period (1928–53) when the primacy of heavy industry and defence were emphasised to the detriment of consumer industry and social services. As a result, the latter developed in an ad hoc, fragmented and often unplanned way and although quantitative achievements were impressive, quality was sacrificed. Chronic shortages, low pay and a rapid deterioration in the level of health care offered and in the health status of the Russian population were common. This was the case for several reasons: alarming levels of pollution; poor working and living conditions; inadequate diet (due to food production and distribution difficulties); excessive use of tobacco and alcohol and low levels of personal hygiene.

Whilst official rhetoric about welfare modernisation talked in terms of health and welfare 'improving with each phase of the development of the (Soviet) socialist state'[52], Stalinist neglect of health and welfare did not end

---

48 N. Vinogradov, *Health protection in the Soviet Union*, Foreign Languages Publishing house, Moscow, 1956, 23

49 On this see V. F. Zima, 'Zasukha, golod, 1946–47', *Istoriya SSSR* 1991, No.4, 3–19; V. P. Popov, 'Golod I gosudarstvennia politika (1946–47gg.)', *Otchestvennaya istoriya*, 1992, No. 6, 36–60; I. V. Volkov, 'The drought and famine of 1946–47', *Russian Studies in History* 1992, 31 (2), 31–60 and V. F. Zima, 'Golod v Rossii 1946–1947 godov', *Otchestvennaya istoriya*, 1993, No. 1, 35–52.

50 Lisitsyn, *Health protection*, 23.

51 J. C. Dutton, 'Causes of Soviet adult mortality increases', *Soviet Studies* 33 (4), October 1981, 548–559.

52 Thus the number of doctors increased three-fold from 14.2 per 10,000 in 1950 to

with his death. From the mid-1960s to the mid-1980s, people in Russia worked longer hours, suffered from increased journey time due to the deterioration of public transport, and had to spend more time queuing to secure basic necessities. This situation was in turn reflected in a number of adverse trends: declining life expectancy; increased mortality for all age groups, but especially males (as a result of cardiovascular diseases, accidents and poisoning, cancer); a rise in the number of working days lost etc.[53]

The Russian welfare state from Khrushchev to Gorbachev which was charged with combating this deterioration in health conditions continued to face many problems: chronic under-funding and under-investment; deterioration of plant, especially hospitals; inadequate facilities; widespread shortages of medical services, drugs and equipment; overcrowding; high turnover of staff (who were poorly paid; forced to take on extra jobs; tired and demoralised) and so forth. As a consequence, doctor-patient relationships became difficult, but patients had little opportunity to choose their doctor. Queuing meant that visits to a Russian GP were very time consuming. Undoubtedly without the use of *blat* (influence) to get on the books of another doctor or the substantial black market in pharmaceuticals, the health of Russian citizens would have deteriorated further. Major inequalities existed because resources were allocated not on the basis of need but according to the economic and political priorities of the Russian state. Thus if one region was more important than another, it received and was able to provide better quality medical care.

Thus although after Stalin, there were steady increases of inputs and health service outputs, the issue of poor quality and significant inequalities in the distribution of welfare resources remained.[54] It was difficult to attract good quality staff because the average wage in the health sector only increased from 48.6 roubles in 1950 to 134.9 roubles a month by 1986. Despite this 3-fold increase, medical workers' wages declined from 75.7 percent of the national average in 1950 to 69 percent by 1986. This situation had a number of adverse effects: firstly, low wages reduced the quality of entrants to medical and nursing schools; secondly, there were high levels of turnover, especially among middle-ranking personnel; and finally, as wages were not linked to performance, there were few incentives for higher productivity etc. The declining state budget allocations to health care also made it extremely difficult for *Minzdrav* and its Republican counterparts to keep hospitals and

---

42.0 per 10,000 by 1985 and a similar rate of growth occurred among paramedical personnel. The number of hospital beds doubled while the number of hospitals rose by just over 5,000 or 144 hospitals a year. All this was achieved on a declining proportion of the state budget allocated to health which fell by 50 percent between 1950 and 1985 from 10.5 percent to only 4.6 percent of overall budget expenditure. By 1985, the Soviet medical system employed about 7 million people or 6 percent of the total labour force (C. Williams, 'Health care in transition', in C. Williams, V. Chuprov and V. Staroverov (ed.), *Russian Society in transition*, Dartmouth, 1996, 186).

53   Ibid, 187.
54   Ibid.

other medical establishments in good condition and for the health sector to purchase essential pharmaceutical goods and medical equipment.[55] Such a situation had a detrimental impact on health conditions. Although Russia initially showed a great improvement in the two decades after the second world war (hence life expectancy at birth rose from 47 years in 1938–39 to 70 years in 1965–66) which stemmed from improvements in the fields of housing, diet and income distribution, over the next two decades this trend was reversed – the death rate increased from 7.1 in 1964–65 to 9.4 per 1,000 in 1975–76 and similar increases also took place in the infant mortality rate. These trends were partly offset by a rise in the birth rate from 17.4 in 1970 to 19.8 per 1,000 population in 1983. However, in overall terms, life expectancy at birth fell from 62 years for males and 73 years for females by 1982. As a consequence, the party and state authorities became increasingly critical of the health sector in the early-mid 1980s.[56] All the time however, senior party-state officials had access to *elite* welfare facilities in the form of the 4th Administration; as did senior staff employed in the Ministries of Foreign Trade, Finance, Defence, State Security, Internal Affairs, the military in all its forms and the railroads, waterways and civil aviation.[57]

As I have shown elsewhere[58], Gorbachev set about embarking upon his major health and welfare reform during perestroika, which emphasised among other things, an anti-alcohol campaign; improving the quality of medical care and increasing the effectiveness of public health policies by sacking inefficient managers and heads; increasing pay; improving the supply and distribution of medicines and medical equipment by accelerating the level of technological progress; placing greater emphasis on biomedical R & D and finally, reforming the nature of medical foreign trade by putting it on a market footing. This increased the level of medical inputs, finance and output of the medical system, led to a modest growth in the facilities, personnel and outputs of the medical supply system but it was still the case that Russia's domestic medical industries were unable to meet demand for pharmaceuticals, vitamins and medical equipment, meaning that deficits had to be met using imports, 90 percent of which came from the socialist countries.[59]

Thus despite gallant attempts to modernise welfare by eradicating shortages of medical equipment, reducing the levels of queuing etc., the Russian welfare system was unable to prevent a deterioration in health conditions during perestroika. As a result in the period 1985–91, life expectancy at birth remained stagnant while the death rate continued to be high due to shortages of food; increased consumption of tobacco and alcohol; a reduction in housing construction; a deterioration in sanitary conditions, especially in public

55   Ibid.
56   Ibid, 185.
57   Ibid, 188.
58   Ibid, 189.
59   C. M. Davies, 'The health sector in the Soviet and Russian economies: From reform to fragmentation to transition', in *The former Soviet Union in Transition*, Vol. 2, JEC, US Congress, Washington, 1993a, 855–858.

establishments; pollution; a rise in the number of infectious and degenerative diseases; an intensification of the problems associated with capital stock, labour and supplies in the health sector (for example, according to a 1990 survey, 9 percent of hospitals were said to be in a dangerous condition; 14 percent needed major reconstruction; 15 percent had no water supply; 49 percent no hot water and 24 percent no sewer system)[60] and the fragmentation of the health sector. All this occurred against the backdrop of demands for devolution of power and the crumbling of the USSR.

All in all, by the end of the Gorbachev era, the Russian economy, and the health sector within it, were facing enormous difficulties. On the health front: the birth rate in 1990 stood at 13.4 per 1,000 while the death rate totalled 11.2 per 1,000. The age-standardised death rate was 12.0 per 1,000; the infant mortality rate stood at 17.4 per 1,000 births and life expectancy was 69.3 years on average (but 63.8 for men and 74.4 for women), a slight decline since 1986. The level of abortions had reached 4 million by 1990 (195 per 1,000 births) and maternal mortality was high (54 per 100,000 live births). Furthermore, mortality from diseases of the circulatory system, especially heart disease, from malignant neoplasms (cancer of the trachea, bronchus and lung), from suicide and self-infected injuries and from road traffic accidents, all increased between 1986–90. Only diseases of the respiratory system and of infectious and parasitic origins were showing systematic declines.[61] Gorbachev's radical welfare modernisation policy was meant to eradicate the Stalinist legacy and give welfare a higher priority. Although it resolved some of the old problems, this strategy also created new sets of problems which are still being worked through today.

Implications for our understanding of modernisation

This chapter shows that there are several distinctive features that mark out Russian modernisation: firstly, what can be referred to as primarily, though not exclusively, economic modernisation which involved reducing the gap between levels of output between the USSR and leading Western powers, so bridging the gap preoccupied successive Russian regimes from Lenin onwards; secondly, modernisation also emphasised the need to achieve military parity or superiority, which stemmed from Russia's invasion complex, both real and imagined. In line with the previous two points, modernisation

60 On the reasons for this trend see C. M. Davis, 'The health sector in the Soviet and Russian economies: From reform to fragmentation to transition', in: US Congress, JEC, *The former Soviet Union in Transition* Vol. 2, Washington D.C. 1993a, 862; C. Davis, "Health crisis: The former Soviet Union", *RFE/RL Research Report* Vol. 2, No. 40, 8 October 1993b, 35–43.

61 J. Dunlop et al. 'Profiles of the newly independent states: economic, social and demographic conditions', in: R. F. Kaufman and J. P. Hardt (ed.), *The former Soviet Union in Transition*, M. E. Sharpe: New York, 1993, 1021–1187 and M. Ryan, *Contemporary Soviet society: A handbook,* Edward Elgar: Aldershot, 1990, 37, 50.

therefore included finding ways of making Russia more productive in general, the debate was how? It was not just a question of economic modernisation but also social modernisation (changing social structure, position of women, meeting the welfare needs of society etc) and political modernisation (leadership, building democracy, institutional reform etc). This chapter shows that modernisation was a constant feature of Russian policy but achieved in a variety of ways and by a variety of means. The process of the modernisation of Russian health care meant change and reform but Russian health care, except in quantitative terms, never really caught up with the West. It is also evident that socio-economic, political and other factors had an impact on choice and decisions at crucial turning points in the historical development of the Soviet Union (with the focus here on the Lenin, Stalin and Gorbachev eras, and the degree of continuity and change between them). It needs to be borne in mind that Russian modernisation took place in a backward country, constituted an unprecedented leap forward, was designed to build and consolidate socialism and geared towards overtaking the capitalist countries; but these objectives took place amidst revolution, civil war, famine, disorder, terror, purges and from the late 1960s in an era of stagnation. It is clear that medical professionals of all varieties were both shaped by and helped shape health care trends and policy. This book in general raises the question: how prepared were specific sectors for modernisation? Some were better prepared than others and some received greater priority. The consequence in the case of health care was that we had distorted and incomplete modernisation. This also occurred in part because the process of Russian modernisation was ad hoc and often responding to a crisis – rising morbidity and mortality etc. This chapter also demonstrates that the modernisation process in relation to health care was largely state-led (a revolution from above) rather than driven from below (a revolution from below). However, in relation to the late Soviet period, International actors and agencies also started to determine Russia's modernisation policy. So the outcomes were a mix of changing internal dynamics and a changing external context. What are the implications of this analysis for our understanding of the inter-relationship between economic, social and political modernisation? Can each take place independently? Does failure in one area derail modernisation and have knock on effects elsewhere? This chapter suggests that the failure to adequately modernise Russian health care was the product of the state's neglect of this sector and of the uneven, complex and contradictory nature of the modernisation process itself. It was uneven because of the clampdown on innovation, repression, inefficiency, lack of incentives etc. But significant barriers to modernisation also existed, such as the poor quality of leaders of the health care system who often resisted the process of change. This partly occurred because Russian modernisation was far too ambitious and involved risk and with risk came consequences. Even though the failure to prioritise health care was endemic to many planned economies of the former communist bloc, most of the problems highlighted here are the product of the particular priorities of successive Russian leaders.

JEREMY SMITH

Khrushchev and the Path to Modernisation through Education

The eternal problem of maintaining an economically less advanced country as a great military power faced Khrushchev in 1955–64 as it had faced Ivan the Terrible, Peter the Great, Nicholas II and Stalin over four centuries.[1]

Much of Russian history consists, indeed, of attempts to overcome the country's relative economic and social backwardness and compete militarily with the western great powers – at different times Britain, Sweden, France, Germany, Austro-Hungary and the United States. The imperative to 'catch up with' the West informed the driving policies of rulers from Peter the Great through Alexander II and Stalin. But at times simply catching up was not enough. Several examples could be cited where modernisation in Russia has reflected an aspiration not only to make up a gap, but to surpass the world, an aspiration that was achieved in a number of cultural, political, military and economic spheres at different times. No Russian leader has been any more committed to the cause of modernisation than Nikita Khrushchev. The aim of the seven-year plan of 1959–65 was not only to catch up with, but to surpass the United States, not merely in terms of military hardware and industrial output, but also in standards of living, technological research and the cultural level of the population. Khrushchev's ambition was matched by his willingness to experiment and innovate, as reflected in his series of 'hare-brained schemes', however ill advised they were in both conception and execution.

It is no coincidence that the control figures for the seven-year plan were announced on 12th November 1958 simultaneously with Khrushchev's 'Theses of the Central Committee of the CPSU and Council of Ministers of the USSR on Strengthening the Relationship of the School with Life and on the Further Development of the System of Public Education in the Country'.[2] The

1   R. W. Davies, *Soviet Economic Development from Lenin to Khrushchev* Cambridge: Cambridge University Press, 1998, 71.
2   The full text of the theses was widely published in the Soviet press, including *Pravda*, 16th November 1958. The bulk of the text dealing with schools is available in *Narodnoe obrazovanie v SSSR. Sbornik dokumentov 1917–1973 gg.* Moscow:

JEREMY SMITH

centrepiece of the reform was a move to a 'polytechnical' system of education whereby pupils would engage in various forms of labour and gain practical experience of productive work in conjunction with their studies, particularly in the later years. Complete secondary education was to be genuinely universal (as already decreed in 1956), and in order to accommodate work experience and the demands of modern education, the basic period of secondary education was to be extended from 10 years (seven in the first stage and three in the second stage) to 11 years (eight in the first stage and three in the second stage). The reform also introduced a universal curriculum to be applied throughout the USSR, and which put more emphasis than before on mathematics and science, at the expense of humanities. Modern teaching methods, based partly on earlier Soviet pedagogical science, and partly on Western educational theory, were to replace the Stalinist approach, increasingly seen in many quarters as old-fashioned and stultifying. The overall aim was to produce a system which would prepare all pupils to play a full part in production, to create rounded socialist personalities, and to overcome the division between mental and manual labour which Marx had identified as one of the most undesirable features of capitalism.

The educational reform of 1958/59 combined two of Khrushchev's major obsessions: education and technology. According to a recent biography Khrushchev, who had only received four years of formal schooling himself, held an ambivalent attitude to education: 'He valued it highly and consistently sought both to further his own education and to widen access to education for Soviet people. At the same time, he constantly emphasised the importance of practical experience and the limitations of formal or "theoretical" study in preparing people for "real life"....Knowledge was a tool with which he wished to *do* things, not a good to be pursued for its own sake'.[3] This lifelong view of education made him one of the most ardent supporters of the proposal to reintroduce polytechnical education, approved by the Nineteenth Congress of the CPSU in 1952, before Stalin's death, and informed his later reforms.

At the same time Khrushchev, like many communists of his generation, was devoted to the rapid development of new technologies. His son and biographer Sergei Khrushchev testifies at length to this obsession. Khrushchev's favourite viewing in 1957 was a documentary on 'Science and Technology', while he never wavered from the firm belief that the development of missile technology was the key to military parity or superiority.[4] Soviet progress in nuclear weapons and the space programme, culminating in the launch

Pedagogika, 1974, pp.48–53. Two English translations of the full text are available: *Soviet Education* (hereafter *SE*), vol.I, no.4, February 1959, 3–14; George S. Counts, *Khrushchev and the Central Committee Speak on Education*, Pittsburgh: University of Pittsburgh Press, 1959, 31–66. Counts' translation is used here. The theses are referred to hereafter as TCC.

3   William J. Thompson, *Khrushchev: A Political Life*, Basingstoke: Macmillan, 1995, 14–15.
4   Sergei N. Khrushchev, *Nikita Khrushchev and the Creation of a* Superpower, Philadelphia: Pennsylvania University Press, 2000, 214–217.

222

of Sputnik in 1957, gave the impression that the Soviet Union had, indeed, surpassed the United States in technological advance. Khrushchev himself remembered 'For some time the United States lagged behind us. We were exploring space with our Sputniks. People all over the world recognised our success. Most admired us; the Americans were jealous'.[5] Superiority in missile technology was, however, most likely illusory, while in any case advances in the military and space sectors were exceptional, and served to disguise an alarming and growing gap in other key technology areas. Of particular interest is Ron Amann's study of the Soviet chemical industry, which reveals that the output of the Soviet chemical industry in 1950 came to only one sixth of the US total.[6] The importance of the chemical industry was highlighted at the XX Congress of the CPSU in 1956, and capital investment was to be increased by 2.3 times in the sixth five-year plan of 1956–60. But this was a modest increase compared to the '"grandiose programme" for the development of the chemical industry...[which] formed the centrepiece of the new seven-year plan (1959–65)'[7] announced in November 1958. Total output of synthetic fibres was to increase by 12–13 times, and of plastics by over seven times. Investment was to be increased by 27% (compared to 9.6% for the whole economy) in each of the seven years of the plan. The emphasis was on the increased output of fertilisers, plastics, and synthetic fibres, in all of which the Soviet Union lagged well behind western countries. Growth in these areas would not only benefit the high-technology defence and space sectors, but would also increase availability of foodstuffs and synthetic consumer products to the obvious advantage of living standards for the population as a whole.[8]

The priority given to the chemical sector was part of a broader drive to replace the extensive economic growth of the Stalin period with intensive growth based on technological innovation, heralded by Bulganin in a speech to the CC of the CPSU in July 1955 and resulting in the creation of the State Committee on New Technique (Gostekhnika) in May of the same year.[9] The drive for a technologically advanced economy required not only a revision of investment priorities, it entailed the creation of a cadre of specialists to produce and develop the technologies and an educated and trained workforce capable of implementing them to full effect.

Before turning to the relationship between Khrushchev's education reform and modernisation, it is necessary to deal briefly with two widely held interpretations of the reform. The first may well go a long way to explaining the short-term thinking behind it, but lacks any documentary support on which

5   *Khrushchev Remembers: The Last Testament*, Boston: Little, Brown and co., 1974, transl. by Strobe Talbott, 54.
6   Ronald Amann, 'The Soviet Chemicalisation Drive and the Problem of Innovation', in Ronald Amann and Julian Cooper (eds), *Industrial Innovation in the Soviet Union*, New Haven: Yale University Press, 1982, 145.
7   Amann, 'The Soviet Chemicalisation Drive', 147.
8   Amann, 'The Soviet Chemicalisation Drive', 146–54.
9   Alec Nove, *An Economic History of the USSR*, Harmondsworth: Pelican Books, 1976, 341.

to base further discussion, and is in any case not connected to the theme of modernisation. The second is, at best, highly contentious.

The first explanation of the reform is connected to the Soviet Union's unusual short-term demographic situation. The extremely low birth rate of the war and immediate post-war years meant that there were far fewer 12–18 year olds than would normally be the case. This meant there would be a shortage of new entrants into the workforce over the coming years. Given that the most radical aspect of the reform was the introduction of young people into the workforce on a part-time basis, particularly in the final three years of secondary education, this is an attractive interpretation of the reform. Indeed, one of the major failings of the reform was held to be the way in which factories and farms used pupils as a source of cheap labour without providing them with the training that was supposed to satisfy the demands of polytechnical education. Incidentally, it has also been argued that this demographic gap also provided an ideal opportunity for school reform. Any major reform of education is bound to cause a short-term disruption as teachers adjust to the new methods, new teachers are trained, buildings are constructed or adapted, especially when, as in this case, the overall length of education is increased. But as a counter-balance to these effects, the relatively small numbers of students would reduce the additional short-term burdens on teachers and provide a breathing space for the development of infrastructure. Even where disruption was unavoidable, at least fewer pupils would suffer than in other years. The only concession in Khrushchev's theses to the possible disruptive effects of the reform concerned the regular supply of entrants to institutes of Higher Education: 'In the elaboration of the plans for the reorganisation of the secondary school the question of providing higher institutions of learning with a sufficient number of graduates from secondary schools should be borne in mind. The national economy cannot permit any interruption in the reinforcement of trained personnel with young and highly qualified specialists. For this reason each Union republic, in case of necessity, should preserve during the transition period (apparently, four or five years) a certain number of secondary schools now in operation'.[10] The otherwise apparent haste with which the reform was to be implemented supports the hypothesis that it represented a short-term fix to the demographic problem created by the war, nor does the absence of any public statements in support of the hypothesis render it unlikely to be true. While we can, therefore, accept that this may have been a factor that would certainly have influenced the timing, we shall see that it does not address adequately other aspects of the reform and in any case, lacking documentary evidence, it will have to remain no more than a hypothesis.

The second theory concerning the reform is also closely connected to the timing of its introduction. It states that it was introduced on the crest of a wave for the Soviet education system, that it was designed to consolidate and move forward the relative advantage of that system over those of

10 TCC article 25 in Counts, *Khrushchev*, 49.

western powers, particularly the US, the ultimate proof of which was to be seen in the scientific advances which had culminated in the launch of Sputnik in 1957. This was indeed the tone of the opening lines of the preamble to Khrushchev's theses: 'The Soviet country is living through a period of extraordinary growth. The economy of the state is developing at a tempestuous rate. Science and culture are flourishing as never before.'[11] Further on, technological achievements are explicitly linked to the school system: 'The Soviet school has prepared millions of educated, cultured citizens, active participants in socialist construction. It has reared remarkable contingents of outstanding scientists, engineers, and builders whose researches and creative work are embodied in such historic scientific and technological triumphs as the artificial earth satellites, atomic electric power stations, atomic icebreakers, and swift jet passenger planes. But the Soviet people cannot rest on their laurels.'[12] The link between educational success and Sputnik was explicit: 'The Soviet Union has advanced to one of the first places in the world with respect to the development of science and technology….When the first Soviet artificial earth satellite burst into the expanses of the cosmos, many sober and thoughtful people in the capitalist world acknowledged that the broad development and the high level of secondary and higher education in the USSR were among the primary causes responsible for the brilliant victory of Soviet science and technology. The American press wrote in alarm that the Soviet secondary school devotes much more time and attention to the study of mathematics, physics, chemistry, and biology than the American'.[13] Such gloating at the expense of the US was commonplace at the time. An article by I. M. Lavrukhin in *Sovetskaia Pedagogika* in October 1958 was one of several to gleefully recount the current failings of the US system and again linked Sputnik to the successes of the Soviet school: 'Then, however, 1957 came, the year of the fortieth anniversary of the Great October Socialist Revolution. After the Soviet artificial earth satellite rose headlong into the cosmos, the myth created by the reactionary press, concerning the prosperity of the American economy and the weakness of Soviet scientific and technical thinking, was finally dispelled.'[14]

More tellingly, the panic created by Sputnik seems to have led to the same conclusions being drawn in the US. Lavrukhin quotes US Senator Henry Jackson: 'if Sputnik were the sole isolated proof of Soviet achievements in the field of technology, it would not arouse too much anxiety. However, the launching of Sputnik is not an isolated event. It is one of the component elements of a clearly distinguishable occurrence, the continuously growing Soviet successes in the scientific, technical and military fields'. Donald K. David, then Chairman of the Board of Trustees of the US Committee on Economic Development, linked these advances to the Soviet social system,

11 TCC article 1 in Counts, *Khrushchev*, 31.
12 TCC article 2 in Counts, *Khrushchev*, 32.
13 TCC article 8 in Counts, *Khrushchev*, 37.
14 I. M. Lavrukhin, 'On the crisis in US education', *SE*, vol.I, no.2, December 1958, 49.

including education: 'Behind Sputnik we see a rocket, and behind the rocket we see advanced science and technology. But behind them something bigger is concealed. This is a social system, a system of human institutions, which in the present instance has made the right decision about what goals it is necessary to establish and has motivated and organised the conditions for achieving them.'[15] American educationalist George S. Counts warned that 'More than any other in history the Soviet state has endeavoured to marshal all the forces of organized education....to achieve its purposes and advance toward its distant apocalyptic goal of Communism. And here, apart from the dictatorship itself, is the key to the undertaking of the swift growth of this mighty colossus. The Central Committee regards education with a degree of seriousness far surpassing anything known in the history of our country'.[16] Economic historians, including R. W. Davies in this volume, have extolled the high level of scientific knowledge and expertise produced through the Stalinist education system. Writing in 1969, Alec Nove extolled the advance of education at all levels as 'among the most creditable achievements of the entire Soviet period' and compared it favourably to the systems of Britain and the United States.[17] The notion that Stalin's education system was largely responsible for Sputnik continues to be influential in academic discourse today.[18]

The superiority of the education system took a prominent place in Soviet propaganda both at home and abroad, apparently to great effect. An official Soviet report on a European conference on education held in Paris in 1958 boasted the leading role played by Soviet delegates and claimed that 'many delegates from England, Belgium, India and Brazil, demonstrated a great interest in the Soviet system of education and in Soviet culture and science in general.'[19] If these boasts and fears are to be believed, then Khrushchev's reform can only be viewed as modernising in the sense of innovation which went beyond anything that had already been achieved elsewhere.

However, there is much to suggest that these impressions were an illusion. Counts himself demonstrated convincingly that Sputnik could not be put down to the superior education system, not least because any scientist involved in the space programme or other scientific advances, including the three joint winners of the Nobel Prize for Physics in 1957, would have received all their schooling either before the revolution or under the very different school system of the 1920s.[20] As already noted, all the boastful words about Sputnik concealed a distinct unease about the widening technology

15 Ibid.
16 Counts, *Khrushchev*, 1–2.
17 Nove, *An Economic History*, 350.
18 e.g. James Pitt and Margarita Pavlova, 'Pedagogy in Transition: from Labour Training to Humanistic Technology Education in Russia', in Stephen Webber and Ilkka Liikanen (eds), *Education and Civic Culture in Post-Communist Countries*, Basingstoke: Palgrave, 2001, 231–32.
19 *SE*, vol.I, no.1, November 1958, 86. Original in *Sovetskaia Pedagogika*, September 1958.
20 Counts, *Khrushchev*, 15.

gap between the USSR and the US in a number of other fields. And there is plenty of evidence to suggest that, far from riding the crest of a wave, the Soviet education system was clearly failing by 1958. Numerous studies point to the inadequate educational methods such as rote-learning, the imposition of an inflexible curriculum, schools geared towards university entry which was available only to a few number of pupils, and the disappearance of psychology from education under Stalin, all of which led to falling standards and rising delinquency.[21] Several Western scholars of the Stalinist education system have been far less sanguine than economic historians in their assessments: 'Stalinism stifled scholarship, scientific research, and cultural creativity'.[22] Writing from Israel in 1988, former school teacher, headmistress and school inspector from the Kharkov district Dora Shturman testified to a system which, on the eve of Khrushchev's reforms, was characterised by poorly trained teachers, an incoherent curriculum, outdated teaching techniques, an ever burdensome bureaucracy, *protsentomaniia* (the pressure to award higher grades), and inadequate resources for a comprehensive system.[23]

But we do not need to turn to distant memoirs or academic studies to see that Khrushchev's reform was addressing the needs of an apparently failing system. The lively and widespread press and public discussion that followed publication of Khrushchev's theses revealed numerous and often bitter complaints against the current state of education on the part of parents and teachers alike.[24] However upbeat the tone of the actual theses, Khrushchev himself admitted in the pages of *Sovetskaia Pedagogica* 'In the talks which I have had occasion to hold....a serious dissatisfaction with the present state of affairs in secondary and higher education has come to light'.[25] The resolution of the Supreme Soviet of the USSR on 24th December 1958 admitted '....our general-educational middle special and high schools fail to meet the demands of communist construction, they display serious deficiencies.'[26] This fell well short of reflecting many of the criticisms of the existing system, as well of the proposed changes, which were aired at the Supreme Soviet itself.

21 Bereday et al., *The Changing Soviet School*, pp.69–74; John Dunstan, *Paths to Excellence and the Soviet* School, Windsor: NFER, 1978, 24–27.

22 George Z. F. Bereday, William W. Brickman and Gerald H. Read (eds), *The Changing Soviet School*, London: Constable and Company, 1960, 78.

23 Dora Shturman, *The Soviet Secondary School*, London: Routledge, 1988, translated by Philippa Shimrat, 95–108

24 My review of the public discussion is mostly limited to the pages of the Russian-language newspaper of the Communist Party of Estonia, *Sovetskaia Estonia*, but it can be assumed that this was not altogether untypical of comments elsewhere. Jeremy Smith, 'Popular Opinion under Khrushchev: A Case Study of Estonian Reactions to Khrushchev's School Reform, 1958–59' in Timo Vihavainen (ed.), *The Soviet Union – a Popular State? Studies on Popular Opinion in the USSR*, St. Petersburg: Evropeiskii dom, 2003, 318–337.

25 N. S. Khrushchev, 'Regarding the strengthening of ties between school and life and the further development of the public education system', *SE* vol.I, no.2, December 1958, p.3. Original in *Sovetskaia Pedagogika* for October 1958.

26 *Narodnoe obrazovanie v SSSR. Sbornik dokumentov 1917–1973 gg.*, Moscow: Pedagogika, 1974, 54–55.

An apparent contradiction appears to exist between assessments of an education system which produced some of the foremost scientists in the world, and views of it as being based on outdated methods, under-resourced, bureaucratic, and generally stultifying. One explanation for this contradiction can be found in the most recent western study of teaching in the 1930s which, among other findings, highlights the massive unevenness across the USSR in standards and methods of education, which depended on local policies, levels of investment in schools, and the quality and commitment of teachers.[27] But more generally, it would seem to be the case that the school policy of Stalin and Zhdanov aimed specifically at producing a relatively small number of high grade recruits to higher education who would go on to rise to the elite of the scientific and academic establishments. For the rest, while standards of literacy among school leavers were high by international standards, a system which focussed on the elite could easily lead to feelings of neglect. In any case, this did not suit the requirements of Khrushchev and his colleagues for a highly educated workforce which could both produce and effectively employ the latest technologies throughout the economy, as well as become self-fulfilled socialist citizens. The system itself was therefore in need of modernisation, as it no longer met the demands of the modern economy or Khrushchev's vision of modern Mankind.

So it is appropriate to view Khrushchev's education reform as part of a broader attempt at modernisation. It can be seen as modernising in three senses: firstly, the system of education itself was deemed to contain backward characteristics, especially those introduced by Stalin, and was in need of modernisation along the lines suggested by either foreign models or by Marxist-Leninist theory and traditions in Russian education; secondly, we shall see how the reform was linked to efforts to modernise the economy, especially in the development and implementation of new technologies; thirdly, the reform sought to satisfy Khrushchev's vision not just of modern Man, but of the Man of the future, *Homo Sovieticus*. That there existed a link between these three modernising aspects is pointed to in the theses themselves: 'The accelerated development of mechanisation and automation, the use of chemistry in production, the wide application of electronics and computing machines, and the utmost development of electrification and other highly productive methods will alter radically the nature of work...Today workers are expected to know how to use improved machine tools and the most precise measurements which control instruments and apparatus. They must have knowledge of complex calculations and blueprints. Thus the immediate and future prospects for the technical-economic development of the Soviet Union make ever-increasing demands on all the toilers of our society. For them an all-round education becomes a vital necessity...gigantic technical progress will lighten physical labour immeasurably, and many occupations which exhaust man are disappearing and will continue to disappear in the future. But the harmonious development of man is unthinkable without physical labor

27   E. Thomas Ewing, *The Teachers of Stalinism: Policy, Practice and Power in Soviet Schools of the 1930s*, New York: Peter Lang, 2002.

which is creative and joyous…by participating in socially useful work the new generation of builders of Communist society should engage in physical labour suited to their strength and in most diverse forms.'[28] Khrushchev's vision is of a world where men and women, freed from much of the drudgery of physical labour by technological advances, will be able to develop as rounded personalities engaged in joyous work, where full education will both promote that personality and fulfil the conditions for achieving the necessary technical advancement.

In addition to the general abandonment of progressive methods in education already noted, the most obviously 'backward' steps taken by Stalin were the abolition of co-education for boys and girls in 1943 and the reintroduction of school fees in 1940. These two measures had already been abandoned in the early years of destalinisation, in July 1954 and June 1956 respectively.[29] It is therefore fair to see the later reforms as a continuation of the process of destalinisation in education. As with many elements of destalinisation, the attempt to modernise schools appealed to a model which was really a case of 'back to the future'. Destalinisation involved frequent appeals to the writings of Lenin and the supposed golden age of the 1920s, and this case was no exception. In laying the groundwork for Khrushchev's reforms, *Sovetskaia Pedagogika* devoted a large part of its April 1958 issue to articles on Lenin's contribution to the theory of education.[30] But in this particular case it was Lenin's wife, Nadezhda Krupskaia, who was portrayed, somewhat misleadingly, as the theoretical mother of the type of polytechnical education Khrushchev was determined to introduce. An editorial in *Sovetskaia Pedagogika* had already portrayed Krupskaia in these terms in February 1958.[31] The February 1959 edition of *Sovetskaia Pedagogika* was largely turned over to articles marking the 90th anniversary of Krupskaia's birth,[32] with six further articles devoted to Krupskaia over the next four issues.[33]

Krupskaia and Lenin's writings were of little direct help in designing the reform, however. While progressive Western educational theories informed some aspects of teaching, they provided little in the way of experience in vocational training. The combination of education with work appears, indeed, to derive from a particularly Russian tradition going back to Konstantine Ushinsky in the mid-nineteenth century and developing through Chernishevsky, Pisarev, and Leo Tolstoy, before it was adopted by a number of American educationalists.[34] Models were more readily available, however, from the other countries of the Communist Bloc. The GDR had introduced compulsory

28 TCC article 5 in Counts, *Khrushchev*, 35.
29 Shturman, *The Soviet Secondary School*, 63.
30 *Sovetskaia Pedagogika*, vol.XXII, no.4, April 1958.
31 'N.K.Krupskaia o trudovom vospitanii i politekhnicheskom obuchenii', *Sovetskaia Pedagogika*, vol.XXII, no.2, February 1958.
32 *SE* vol.I, no.6, April 1959.
33 *SE* vol.I, nos, 7,8,9,10, May – August 1959 (originals in *Sovetskaia Pedagogika* for March – June 1959).
34 Nicholas Hans, *The Russian Tradition in Education*, London: Routledge and Kegan Paul, 1963, 160–61.

11-year polytechnical education in 1955, which was closely studied by Soviet educationalists.[35] Bulgaria had approved 12-year polytechnical education in July 1958.[36] The most established model was Czechoslovakia, which had introduced a 13/14 year system in 1948 but moved to an 11-year (8+3) system in 1953. Addressing the Eleventh Congress of the Central Committee of the Communist Party of Czechoslovakia in 1958, First Secretary Alexander Novotny deployed arguments similar to Khrushchev's: 'The chief task of our school must become the training of thoroughly developed people, who possess the basic facts of knowledge in the field of science and technology, and at the same time are trained for skilled physical labor and conscious participation in the construction of communist society. To create such a truly socialist school means, by all possible methods, to join teaching in school increasingly more tightly with the productive labor of pupils...' Intriguingly, however, just as Khrushchev was drafting his reforms, the Central Committee of the Czechoslovak Party had decided that the 11-year system had difficulty incorporating the required vocational training, and on 1st September 1958 decided to set up 13 experimental 12-year (9+3) schools.[37]

Whatever may have been the lessons carried over from the experience of the satellite states, according to the theses it was Soviet pedagogical science which was to inform the content of the new schools: 'The science of pedagogy must play an important role in the reconstruction of the school.....An important part of the activity of scientific pedagogical institutions should be devoted to elaborating the scientific foundations of the content of school instruction (teaching plans, programs, and textbooks), to perfecting methods of teaching and Communist rearing of youth.'[38] The detailed structure, curriculum and textbooks of the secondary school was given over to the responsibility of the Academy of Pedagogic Science, which had evidently been engaged in this work well before the theses were published.[39]

Aside from the polytechnical element there is little in the way of radical innovation either in the curriculum or teaching methods, in spite of the claims to a scientific design and a willingness to distance the new school from the dated methods of the Stalin system.[40] Special schools for pupils with especial talents in the Arts were one feature of the new system. But this, as with other features of the system in practise, was very much a part of an established

35   *SE* vol.I, no.1, November 1958, 61–63. Original in *Sovetskaia Pedagogika* for September 1958.
36   *SE* vol.I, no.2, December 1958, 51–52. Original in *Sovetskaia Pedagogika* for October 1958.
37   G. A. Kasvin and A. A. Shibanov, 'The reform of the schools in the Czechoslovak Republic', in *SE* vol.I, no.4, February 1959, 65–70. Original in *Sovetskaia Pedagogika* for December 1958.
38   TCC article 24, in Counts, *Khrushchev*, 48.
39   M. A. Melnikov, 'The content of education in the eight-year school', in *SE* vol.I, no.5, March 1959, 9–14. Original in *Sovetskaia Pedagogika* for January 1959.
40   'Eliminating formalism in the make-up of lessons', *SE* vol.I, no.3, January 1959, 19–26. Original in *Sovetskaia Pedagogika* for November 1958.

Russian tradition.[41] In fact the most truly modernising aspect in reality was the general expansion of universal compulsory education across eleven grades of secondary education, which the theses exhorted republics to enforce and promised the resources to realise.[42] We will now turn to the areas of economic and social modernisation which the reform promised to facilitate.

Articles 5 and 8 of Khrushchev's theses, already referred to, explicitly linked the reform to new developments in science and technology. A shift in emphasis towards the sciences and technical subjects was a part and parcel of the reform: 'Special attention should be paid to the teaching of physics, mathematics, chemistry, drawing, and biology'.[43] This emphasis ran through into higher education: '...it is necessary to raise the theoretical level of the training of specialists in the light of the newest achievements in science... [people] should be thoroughly familiar with the appropriate fields of science and technology'.[44] Khrushchev made the link between education and technology explicit in *Sovetskaia Pedagogika*: 'particularly great is the role of education in our time when the successful development of the national economy would be impossible without the broadest utilisation of the latest achievements of science and technology.'[45]

Table 3. Total hours of study in Soviet schools by selected subject classification, comparison of old 7-year school and new 8-year school

Subject Classification	Total hours: In 8-year school	In 7-year school
The Humanities	1662	1400
Natural science-mathematics	1750	1383
The arts	245	140
Physical Culture	280	210
Labour and Practical Activities	560	210

Source: M. A. Melnikov, 'The Content of Education in the Eight-Year School', *Soviet Education* vol.I, no.5, March 1959, 12. Original in *Sovetskaia Pedagogika* for January 1959.

In the proposed curriculum for the first stage of secondary school, of the four broad subject areas which obtained extra hours, excluding labour and practical activities, science and mathematics received the biggest boost by

41 James Muckle, *A Guide to the Soviet Curriculum: What the Russian Child is Taught in School* (London: Croom Helm, 1988), pp.6–7; Hans, *The Russian Tradition*, passim.
42 TCC article 22, in Counts, *Khrushchev*, 47.
43 TCC article 18 in Counts, *Khrushchev*, 45.
44 TCC article 36 in Counts, *Khrushchev*, 55.
45 Khrushchev, 'Regarding the strengthening of ties...', 3.

far, 367 hours (see table 1). By subject area, the hours devoted to chemistry doubled in some cases, from 70 to 120–140, and mechanical drawing from 35 to 70; Physics rose from 175 to 245; Maths from 1452 to 1609.5 on average; Drawing from 207 to 242. Other growth areas were foreign languages, singing, and physical culture. The total hours devoted to Russian language and literature and the History and Constitution of the USSR barely rose at all, and fell on a yearly average. Total hours devoted to Biology and Geography actually fell.[46] This represented a clear overall shift in priorities.

But the shift was even more marked in the second stage of secondary education (grades 9 to 11) where, with the ground already prepared by mastering mathematics in the first stage, the emphasis in science was on Physics and Chemistry. Although hours varied between different types of school, the applications to which these sciences would be directed could not have been clearer. In Physics, greater stress would be laid on 'the physical basis of some of the processes of automation, the physico-mechanical processing materials, the properties of building materials; and there is provision for the students to become familiar with certain semi-conductors and electronic appliances. Also a significantly larger place will be assigned to questions of the peaceful application of atomic energy'. Students would obtain knowledge of various sources of energy used in production; the conversion, transmission and utilisation of power; the construction and operation of different types of engines and machines; the physical essentials of automation; electrical relays and magnetic starters; processing of materials; the physical basis of construction; the operation of various sorts of transportation and communication; principles of stress and structural strength in construction; and the properties of specific building materials.[47] In short, 'the connection of the study of physics with technology is necessary for purposes of polytechnical education'.[48] For Chemistry, 'In taking this course the student will become familiar with plastics, artificial and synthetic fibres and rubber, and the most typical processes of their industrial production. In the chemistry course as a whole, there will be a more effective clarification of questions related to the basic aspects of the chemical industry, and the application of chemistry to various types of production and living.'[49] The old school system was heavily criticised for ignoring the practical applications of chemistry, and although the new curriculum contained a strong theoretical element, it was carefully geared towards a full understanding of the contribution of chemistry to industrial and agricultural production in the final years of school.[50]

46   Melnikov, 'The content of education', 10.
47   A. I. Yantzov, 'The content of education in the schools for the worker and rural youth', SE vol.I, no.5, March 1959, 19. Original in Sovetskaia Pedagogika for January 1959.
48   V. F. Yuskovich, 'Content of Physics courses in first and second stage schools', SE vol.I, no.6, April 1959. Original in Sovetskaia Pedagogika for February 1959.
49   Yantzov, 'The content of education', 19.
50   L. A. Tsetkov, 'Chemistry course in the eight-year and secondary school', SE vol.I, no.8, June 1959, 8–13. Original in Sovetskaia Pedagogika for April 1959.

At a higher level, special institutes for engineering and agriculture were to undergo expansion, while the theses called for a significant increase in the output by universities of 'mathematicians, particularly in computation mathematics; biologists and first of all, biophysicists, biochemists, physiologists, and geneticists; physicists, especially in nuclear and radio physics; and chemists in the field of catalysis and high polymers.'[51] In the first few years after 1958, Research and Development in chemical engineering doubled, new institutions devoted to chemical engineering were created in Penza, Severodonetsk, Kiev, Tambov and Iaroslavl', and VUZy were expanded to produce 70,000 specialists in chemical technology between 1959 and 1965.[52]

While 'strengthening the relationship between school and life' rested mainly on sending pupils on work experience, the content of the new curriculum pointed firmly in one direction. Schools were to produce adults familiar with the science behind computers, automation, construction, energy, electronics, and the production and application of fertilisers, plastics, rubber and synthetic fibres. A number of them were to go on to specialise in the further development of these technologies. This was Khrushchev's vision of a modern curriculum for a technological age.

Krupskaia's idea of polytechnical education, following Marx, aimed at the emergence of fully rounded individuals who would find fulfillment in labor while still playing a full part in cultural life. Khrushchev's proposals, by contrast, aimed at the better preparation of Soviet citizens for productive labour, to the extent that Roy Medvedev accused him of abandoning truly polytechnical in favor of purely vocational training.[53] This is, however, to do Khrushchev something of a disservice. While the shift in favour of vocational training and the teaching of practical science was clear, the theses frequently reaffirmed the commitment to the teaching of culture, languages and humanities and the development of a communist spirit.[54] Even the teaching of science was not geared exclusively to production. A. I. Yantzov noted that doubts had been raised over the continued teaching of Darwinism and Astrology, presumably because of their lack of practical relevance, but argued that 'these subjects, useful in forming a basis for a dialectical-materialist view of the world, should be retained in the curriculum'.[55] L. A. Tsvetkov pleaded the general pedagogical value of teaching chemistry, based as it was on the observation of experiments.[56] The first four grades of school concentrated on Russian language and literature, with a small amount of maths and no science. An emphasis on moral development, 'aesthetic training',[57] special schools for artistically gifted children, and the surprising increase in hours

51 TCC article 40, in Counts, *Khrushchev*, 60–61.
52 Amann, 'The Soviet Chemicalisation Drive', 149 and footnote 128.
53 Donald Filtzer, *The Khrushchev Era: De-Stalinisation and the Limits of Reform in the USSR, 1953–1964*, Basingstoke: Macmillan, 1993, 35–6.
54 TCC article 12; article 17; article 18; article 20; article 40 in Counts, *Khrushchev*, 41, 42, 45, 46, 61.
55 Yantzov, 'The content of education', 18.
56 Tsvetkov, 'Chemistry course', 8.
57 Melnikov, 'The content of education', 9.

given over to Music testify that, while science ruled, culture and personal development were not ignored.

While not as clearly discernible as the drive to technology, there are signs in the theses that a secondary aim was the promotion of Khrushchev's vision of *homo sovieticus*, a modern humanity suited not just to the new conditions of production but to the personal fulfillment provided by a socialist society. It is easy to dismiss many of its proclamations as mere rhetoric: 'We must reconstruct public education so that Soviet secondary and higher schools may play a more active role in the entire creative activity of the Soviet people'.[58] But there are more specific pointers to the ways in which Khrushchev envisaged Soviet individuals and society developing. A good example concerns one of the most notorious and controversial provisions of the theses, article 19, which allowed for the abandonment of Lenin's principle that children should receive instruction in the mother-tongue, giving parents the right to decide the language of instruction, and thus threatening to undermine the status of the national language in the republics.[59] The clause provoked uproar in the republics and at the Supreme Soviet, and a struggle which culminated in high-level purges in the Communist Parties of Latvia and Azerbaijan.

The move was primarily political, aimed at rolling back the powers granted to the republics in return for their support in Khrushchev's struggle with the anti-Party group in 1957.[60] But a deeper motive was hinted at in the preamble to the theses: 'The Soviet Union no longer has any backward national "borders" as in the time of tsarist Russia'.[61] Given that the USSR included many times more national borders than was ever the case in the Russian Empire, presumably the emphasis here is on 'backward'. But this accords well with Khrushchev's well-known doctrine of the 'merger of nations', which replaced the earlier doctrine of the 'brotherhood of nations'. National differences were now considered backward, and would play no role in the future socialist society. The theses paid some lip service to the traditional rights of the republics with regard to education: 'The plan of changing to the new system of school education must be elaborated in each Union republic and be adapted to the characteristics of its economic and cultural development'.[62] In practise, however, the elaboration of a standard curriculum ignored any such possibility. The resultant struggle provided Khrushchev with the opportunity to remove leaders accused of nationalism, such as the Latvian Berklavs, at the same time as laying the basis for a unified, Russian-speaking Soviet people (if the worst fears of article 19's opponents had been realised).

Some special attention was devoted to the education of girls in secondary schools. 'In the preparation of girls for labour in the eight-year school the

58   TCC article 2, in Counts, *Khrushchev*, 32.
59   TCC article 19, in Counts, *Khrushchev*, 45–6.
60   Y. Bilinsky, 'The Soviet education laws of 1958–59 and Soviet nationality policy', *Soviet Studies*, vol.XIV, no.2, 1962, 138–57; Tompson, *Khrushchev*, 191–2.
61   TCC article 8, in Counts, *Khrushchev*, 36.
62   TCC article 25, in Counts, *Khrushchev*, 49.

peculiar features of women's work should be taken into consideration'.[63] 'Women's work' related to industrial production included involvement in the instruments, radio-technical, electrotechnical, textile, sewing, and knitting industries.[64] While based on the notion that women were physically unsuited to other areas of production, this was seen as a way of involving women more directly in industrial production rather than being largely confined to the service occupations and trade. Special effort, moreover, was to be devoted to the enrolment of girls in the higher school grades in the 'Eastern' republics.[65] The full and (more or less) equal involvement of women and national minorities in production, together with the general thrust of Khrushchev's polytechnical reform, were necessary for the fulfillment of his own utopian vision of a cohesive and happy communist society, which would be based on devotion to labour: 'society will be highly organised, with a degree of discipline, and that discipline will depend not on any coercive means, but on fostering a feeling of duty to fulfil one's obligations…the discipline in communist society will not be a burden for people, because every member of society will be brought up in the spirit of the necessity for everyone to participate in work'.[66]

Khrushchev's education reform has generally been regarded as a failure. Factories and farms used pupils assigned to work there as a source of cheap, unskilled, manual labour and failed to provide them with any training. The enterprises complained that to assign skilled workers to supervise children would lead to falls in productivity, while middle class parents opposed the loss of advantage their children had previously enjoyed in securing university entry, and head teachers complained that the reforms led to a lowering of academic standards.[67] Compulsory vocational training at school was eventually abandoned. In the economy, at least in the short time, the results of the drive to develop and deploy new technologies were not evident. The planned massive growth of output of the chemical industries under the seven-year plan was hit by systemic failings, lack of supplies, and a slow rate of new plant construction, but also revealed 'a clear rift between science and production'.[68] The failure of fertilisers to improve agricultural production led Khrushchev to announce an additional 5,800 million rouble investment in the project in 1963, but the problem was not solely one of investment: the lack of enthusiasm for and knowledge of how to apply fertilisers reflected poorly on the short-term effects of Khrushchev's education reform.[69] Russification of education was only partially successful in the schools of the RSFSR and the cities of the western republics, and not at all successful elsewhere, and

---

63 TCC article 12, in Counts, *Khrushchev*, 41–2.
64 TCC article 27, in Counts, *Khrushchev*, 51.
65 TCC article 25, in Counts, *Khrushchev*, 49.
66 Quoted in Tompson, *Khrushchev*, 238.
67 Filtzer, *The Khrushchev Era*, 36–7.
68 Amann, 'The Soviet Chemicalisation Drive', 151.
69 Amann, 'The Soviet Chemicalisation Drive', 152; Martin McCauley, *Khrushchev and the Development of Soviet Agriculture: the Virgin Land Programme 1953–1964*, Basingstoke: Macmillan, 1976, 130.

the events of the late 1980s demonstrate the failure of Khrushchev's ambition to eliminate national differences. While sociological studies of the 1960s and 1970s provide conflicting evidence, the late Soviet era is generally characterised by apathy and work-shyness rather than Khrushchev's vision of a citizenry devoted to labour and communism.

And yet many elements of Khrushchev's reforms informed the educational practise of the remainder of the Soviet period: universal secondary education; a nationwide curriculum with a strong science content; at least some teaching methods based on advanced pedagogical science. Literacy levels were high by international standards, and the Soviet Union continued to produce an extraordinary number of outstanding scientists. But these scientists found their efforts thwarted by the cumbersome economic system. And in this lay one of the fundamental paradoxes of Soviet modernisation: while the centrally planned economy and a coercive state may have suited the extensive industrial growth of the 1930s, it proved impossible to adapt to the demands of the age of high-technology. The combination of a highly educated workforce with an under-performing economy, limited civil society and political rights was ultimately a key factor in the collapse of the Soviet system.

KATRI PYNNÖNIEMI

In Celebration of Monumentalism: Transport Modernisation in Russia

Introduction: ritual and repetition

Soviet ideology stemmed from the idea of 'active changing of the world'[1] in terms of which space was understood as collective action rather than passive location.[2] The beginning of socialism was brought closer by a collective thrust of 'miracle-working' – heroic workers creating a shock of historical change.[3] The direction and meaning of the change was articulated in the monuments dedicated to building Socialism (in one country). The word *monument* comes from the Latin word 'monumentum', a reminder. The very act of building a monument is a public ritual that fixes the meaning of place in a collective memory. Without this 'monumental illusion before the eyes of the living, history would be a mere abstraction', writes Marc Augé.[4]

1   Russian philosopher Nicolas Berdyaev explains that in the Soviet context 'freedom' was understood as 'active changing of the world' and 'collective construction of life in the general direction of the communist party'. This type of freedom did not recognize the individual right to choose or freedom of conscience. N. Berdyajev, *The Origin of Russian Communism*. First published by Geoffrey Bles 1937. Ann Arbor: The University of Michigan Press: Ann Arbor Paperbacks, 1960, 152.
2   This goes back to Heidegger and his understanding of space as activity of being-in-the-world. M. Crang 'Time: Space' in P. Cloke and R. Johnston *Spaces of Geographical Thought*. London, Thousand Oaks, New Delhi: Sage Publications, 2005, 204.
3   The idea of heroic builder was the very locus of Soviet style aesthetics. It departs from Kant's notion of aesthetics in a sense that it is not 'disinterested interest' for which the model of aesthetics is in play, argues Mikhail Epstein, but 'disinterested labor' – 'gigantic quantities of which are expended for its own sake, indifferent to the results: All that matters is the bitter satisfaction and oblivion that labor itself provides'. See S. Buck-Morss, *Dreamworld and Catastrophe. The Passing of Mass Utopia in East and West*. Cambridge – London: the MIT Press, 2002, 111, 212, 181. See also D. R. Weiner, 'The Genealogy of the Soviet and Post-Soviet Landscape of Risk', 212; S. Kotkin, *Magnetic Mountain. Stalinism as a Civilization*. Berkeley – Los Angeles – London: University of California Press, 1995, 203.
4   D. Harvey, *The Condition of Postmodernity*. Cambridge and Oxford: Blackwell Publishing 1990, 85; M. Augé, *Non-places. Introduction to an anthropology of supermodernity*. London – NY: Verso, 1995, 59.

In this sense the practical, economic or even military function of the GOELRO plan in the early 1920s, the Great Stalin Plan for the Transformation of Nature, the Virgin Lands campaign of Khrushchev, Brezhnev's plan to re-route Siberian rivers southward, and the construction of the ill-fated Baikal-Amur railroad was secondary to their importance as 'icons of modernity'.[5] An interesting question worth posing is: how are the BAM or other Soviet era *dolgostroi* projects perceived today in the Russian discourse on the modernisation of the transport infrastructure and the communications network? In other words, how is the investment in Soviet era *dolgostroi* projects, for example a road building project between Chita and Khabarovsk or the building of the North Muisk tunnel on the BAM, to be explained now?

With Soviet ideology gone, the fervour that was characteristic of 'building' Socialism in those years is naturally lost too. The gigantic construction projects of the Soviet era played an important role in fostering the new socialist reality, rebuilding not only new industry and infrastructure but, first and foremost, a new man. Today, however, instead of building (heroic) socialists, the Russian government aims to build 'international transport corridors' that, it is hoped, are instrumental in enhancing the competitiveness of Russia in global markets and its (active) role in global politics. Thus, the previous vocabulary (including such expressions as, 'shock work', 'building socialism',) has become obsolete and is replaced with a new set of 'code words' such as 'transparency', 'market', and 'international transport corridor'. The repetition of the 'code words' on the occasion of a public ritual ('heroic worker' and 'developed socialism' at the occasion of the opening of the BAM railway in 1984 and 'great Russia' and 'globalization' in the framework of the opening of the North Muisk tunnel in December 2003) reinforces their meaning, even if only temporarily.

In this article I will discuss the meaning of Soviet transport modernisation in two senses: in terms of the *rationality* criteria of industrialization of the Soviet Union (mainly in the 1920s and 1930s), and secondly in terms of *performance of the ritual of construction*. The analysis that follows stems from the idea of the construction of monuments as a *public act* that functions as a catalyst where the new social reality is fostered and manifested. The primary challenge of cultural analysis thus becomes to define the nature of the 'logic' in accordance with which certain practices are counted as *actions*. 'The crucial thing about social practices – and a feature that differentiates them from most habits', writes Swindler, 'is that they are the infrastructure of repeated *interactional* patterns. They remain stable not only because habit ingrains standard ways of doing things, but because the need to engage on another forces people to return to common structures'.[6] Thus practices are

5   D. R. Weiner, 'The Genealogy of the Soviet and Post-Soviet Landscape of Risk'. In A. Rosenholm – S. Autio-Sarasmo, *Understanding Russian Nature: Representations, Values and Concepts.* Aleksanteri Papers 4/2005, 213.

6   A. Swindler, 'What anchors cultural practices'. In T. Schatzki, K. Knorr Cetina, E. von Savigny *The Practice Turn in Contemporary Theory.* London – NY: Routledge, 2001, 76–87.

more than just repetitions of patterns of action.[7] In this Kierkegaardian sense an act of repetition is directed towards a future rather than to the past. It is 'an attempt to receive everything back albeit in a different form'.[8] Following architect and designer Vladimir Papernyi's suggestion[9] the main question to be asked is: how are different elements borrowed from the Soviet past as well as from western practices combined? Are we witnessing something which is a recollection of the past or seeing the past repeat itself (in a new form?)

The BAM myth

> Valentin Petrovitsh, who had slept very little during the past few weeks,
> examines the track. He does not want to reveal his feelings.
> Not at this moment. But his heart sinks. The track is not yet ready.
> The railway sleepers gleam in the snow, devoid of tar.
> This is only a makeshift track. But we drive along it anyway,
> as the guests of honour arrive in our wake.[10]

Valentin Petrovitsh, a worker from the 582 brigade, had been working until six o'clock in the morning to complete a 52-kilometre stretch of the Bai-kal-Amur railway between Umbella and Davan. During a twenty-four-hour period his brigade had 'pulled out all the stops' and managed to complete the last remaining one and a half kilometres of track up to Davan, which was at that time the easternmost tip of the Baikal-Amur railway in the Buryat ASSR. The pace of construction had been dictated by the 60-year anniversary of the Young Communist Youth League, Komsomol, that would take place the very next day on 29 October, 1978. The occasion was commemorated in typical style: red flags, caviar and champagne, and a Komsomol agit-train. It had arrived from St. Petersburg with actors putting on a show for the locals as well as for the guests of honour.[11] The same ritual of 'opening' and 'completing' was repeated time and time again during the thirty years which followed. Each railway completion performance reinforced the sense of progress and

---

7   Schatzki refers here to Wittgenstein, Derrida, Foucault and Kuhn who all, in one way or another, argued that order is a matter of family resemblance rather than some action being repeated in a similar way time and time again. T. Schatzki, 'Practice mind-ed orders'. In T. Schatzki, K. Knorr Cetina, E. von Savigny *The Practice Turn in Contemporary Theory*. London – NY: Routledge 2001, 42–43.

8   M. Pound, 'Lacan, Kierkegaard, and Repetition'. In *Quadlibet Journal* Vol. 7 No. 2 April-June 2005; S. Kierkegaard, *Toisto*. Jyväskylä: Atena Kustannus Oy 2001.

9   V. Paperny, *Architecture in the age of Stalin. Culture Two*. Translated by John Hill and Roann Barris in collaboration with the author. Cambridge: Cambridge University Press. 2002, xxi. First Published as *Kultura "Dva"*. Ann Arbor: Ardis Publishers 1985.

10 Carita Backström describes how the first train arrived in Davan along the BAM railway on the occasion of the Komsomol's 60th anniversary. C. Backström, *Tulevaisuuden topparoikka. Muistiinpanoja Baikalin-Amurin ratatyömaalta*. Espoo: WSOY, 1979, 139.

11 C. Backström, *Tulevaisuuden topparoikka*, 138–139.

the *'building of socialism' as a public act*. This was an important part of the creation of a new Socialist 'form of life'.[12]

The BAM railway is a good example of the way in which Soviet ideology was represented as real. The BAM route, which traverses Eastern Siberia and the Russian Far East approximately 400 to 500 kilometres north of and parallel with the Trans-Siberian railway, was first proposed already in the 19th century. Most of the Eastern section was built during the 1930s and 1940s by prison labour. The project was abandoned after Stalin's death but the idea resurfaced again in the late 1960s when relations with China deteriorated. This time, however, the workers on the BAM were recruited from among Komsomol youth; in fact the BAM construction was the last big Komsomol project commenced.[13]

Valentin Petrovitsh and the other 'bamovets' who practised workers' heroism irrespective of Soviet ideology knew only too well that to reach Davan in accordance with the Plan it was enough to go through the ritual of 'reaching Davan' and thus, humanity's 'triumph' over nature was made explicit. The fact that the tangible achievements of the BAM were poor was irrelevant since going through the ritual itself meant that something had been accomplished.[14] Only much later was it acknowledged that the glass raised at the ceremony was half empty rather than half full. Igor Levitin in one of his first interviews as a new minister of transport, criticized the Russian practice of building large industrial towns without adequate consideration of how they would be situated in terms of local and foreign markets, or even worse, how these towns could be reached from the adjacent regions and by their local residents. The former Kremlin Chief of Staff Dmitry Medvedev openly criticized the construction of the BAM and cited it as an example of a wasteful project to be avoided in the future. 'We do not need yet another huge construction project with an unpredictable outcome, as was the case with the BAM', he remarked in April 2004.[15]

The code words used in creating the BAM myth of the 1970s and 1980s had their referent in the late 1920s and early 1930s discourse on rapid industrialization. In the Soviet press the work on the taiga was pictured as a struggle comparable to the battles of the Second World War. The words 'gigantic' and 'enormous' were used to evoke the magical character of the project. Other words used in this connection – 'quickly' (*bystro*), 'speed' (*skorost*), 'shock

---

12 See discussion on 'forms of life' in J. Margolis, *Texts without Referents. Reconciling Science and Narrative*. Oxford: Basil Blackwell, 1989, 338–349.

13 Moscow News 'BAM: project, railroad, outdated symbol'. 12 July 2004, 22:06 MSK; S. Blagov, 'BAM railway to become export route', *Eurasia Daily Monitor*, Vol.2 issue 116, June 15, 2005.

14 Ilmari Susiluoto discusses ritualisation and deritualisation of language in the Soviet Union. I. Susiluoto 'Deritualization of political language: the case of the Soviet Union'. In S. Hänninen and K. Palonen *Texts, contexts, concepts. Studies on Politics and Power in Language*. The Finnish Political Science Association. Jyväskylä: Gummerus, 1990.

15 *Nezavisimaja Gazeta* April 29, 2005. Moscow News 'BAM: project, railroad, outdated symbol'. 12 July 2004, 22:06 MSK.

tempo' (*udarnyi ritm*) and 'acceleration' (*uskorenie*) helped to create the fiction of the BAM's relentless journey towards its promised completion.[16]

Throughout the whole period of construction, perception of the BAM remained immune to the changes in society and the life of the country.[17] While 'bamovets' were in effect digging the same foundation that Andrei Platonov depicted in his novel *The Foundation Pit* (1930), the public representation of the BAM remained Socialist Realist along the lines of Kataev's novel *Time, Forward* (1932).[18] However, by the time of the Brezhnev era, the (ritualistic) use of code words had degenerated into a knee-jerk reaction that bore little resemblance to the rigid observation of language use in Stalin's Soviet Union.[19] At that time the skilful use of the right words was a sign of political awareness and it conferred magical powers on the user. An attempt to hide the gloomy details of Soviet life under 'fruits and vegetables' is one of the most tragic (and cruellest) examples of the disconnection between language (words) and reality that existed in the Soviet Union. In the 1930s, the heavy-goods trucks carrying prisoners in Moscow and elsewhere in Russia had the words 'bread', 'meat' or 'vegetables/fruits' painted on the sides. 'Fruits and Vegetables' also appear in a narrative told by famous physicist and dissident Andrei Sakharov. In order to travel to the secret town of Saratov, Sakharov had to first visit the 'Fruit and Vegetable' shop from where he would then get a *propusk*, special permission and exact coordinates of the train and compartment he should travel in.[20] These are perhaps extreme examples but nevertheless they help to illustrate how the code words were actually used and the secretive approach to space that was characteristic of the Soviet system.

But reality was not just couched in code words; the totalitarian elements of language erased the difference between idea and reality completely. The fusion of discourse and 'real' led to a paradox: a country where space was in excess, and spatial relations were secondary.[21] Space in this sense remains

16 C. Ward 'Selling the "project of the century": Perceptions of the Baikal-Amur mainline railway (BAM) in the Soviet Press 1974–1984'. In *Canadian Slavonic Papers*, March 2001, 5–8.

17 C. Ward 'Selling the "project of the century"', 10.

18 Platonov's novel shows the senselessness of self-destruction brought about by the heroic digging of the foundation for an enormous building to provide housing for the proletariat of the world. Kataev's novel *Time, Forward* tells a similar type of story set in the Magnitogorsk metallurgical plant in the Urals. Here the shock workers struggle, this time to break the 'world record' of pouring concrete in one eight-hour shift. These two novels reflect very different beliefs about Soviet heroism. While Kataev's novel was published as early as 1932, Platonov's novel remained unpublished in the Soviet Union until 1987. S. Buck-Morss, *Dreamworld and Catastrophe,* 181; S. Kotkin, *Magnetic Mountain*, 69.

19 See the discussion on the evolution of language use in connection with the notion of 'individual' and 'kollektiv' spheres of life in O. Kharkhordin, *The Collective and the Individual in Russia. A Study of Practice.* Berkeley – Los Angeles – London: University of California Press, 1999.

20 A. Solzhenitsyn, *Ensimmäinen Piiri.* Toinen nide. Helsinki: Suuri Suomalainen Kirjakerho 1973, 323; A. Appelbaum, *Gulag, A History.* London: Penguin Books, 2003, 160; A. Saharov, *Muistelmat.* Juva: WSOY 1991, 140–141.

21 S. Medvedev, 'Post-Soviet Developments: a Regional Interpretation (a

in the background. It is not just empty but it is also passive. On the surface, vertical, hierarchical and administrative relations subordinated horizontal, territorial and everyday practices and created them. The peculiarity of the Soviet absolute space lay in the fact that 'faraway was close at hand there, whereas nearby was distant. Distances in the landscape were not linked with the distances in physical space but were tied to status or position in the power structure', in the words of Russian geographer Vladimir Kaganskii. 'The whole space: place and position, relations and connections, distances, directions – are differentiated according to (specific) status. Place in the space is (the same as) status in the state'. Thus, the contours of Soviet space were those of its 'administrative market': the discourse (Logos) preceded actual physical reality and created it.[22] In the process, the connection between the 'code words' of Soviet ideology and societal life was all but severed.

Ideational, spatial and temporal contours of the Soviet space

The building of the new socialist reality required the assembling of existing infrastructures all over again. In Lenin's vision, decaying railways would be replaced by new electric transport, new roads would spread throughout the land, a new and happier Communist industrialism arising again.[23] The creation of 'the new, different thing' that Lenin anticipated was to emerge as a result of the October revolution was self-sufficient by nature: the Soviet reality was created in part by conveying that it did indeed exist. Dialectical materialism was a prism through which the Bolshevik leadership saw the 'new and different things' and in terms of which these things acquired their Soviet colour and shape. In other words, 'dialectical materialism' provided the basis of reasoning for transport policy-making in the Soviet context.

The locus of Soviet ideology, writes Berdyaev, was 'spiritualization of matter' where 'characteristics of spirit, freedom, activity, and reason are transferred to matter'. Since matter, in normal understanding, is 'formed by the jostling of atoms', it cannot be 'dialectic' because that presupposes the existence of Logos. Thus, it follows that 'dialectic materialism is compelled to believe in a Logos of matter itself, in a Meaning revealed in the development of material productive forces, that is to say, in the rationality of irrational processes'. The inherent contradiction – the union of matter and logic – transcends into a 'theological' doctrine and politics becomes a

Methodological Review)'. In Segbers, Klaus - Stephan De Spiegeleire (eds.), *Post-Soviet Puzzles. Mapping the Political Economy of the Former Soviet Union.* vol II, *Emerging Geopolitical and Territorial Units, Theories, Methods and Case Studies.* Baden-Baden: Nomos Verlagsgesellschaft, 88.

22   The main components of this 'total space' included the Soviet 'administrative-territorial division' (ATD) and the military-industrial complex (MIC). V. Kaganskii, *Kulturnii landchaft i Sovetskoe Obitaemoe Prostranstvo.* Moskva: Novoe Literaturnoe Obozrenie, 2001, 137–153, 170.

23   H. G. Wells, *Russia in the Shadows.* London: Hodder and Stoughton Limited, 1920, 135–136.

matter of orthodoxy or heresy rather than truth or error.[24] Stalin, listing the achievements of the First Five Year Plan at the Joint Plenum of the Central Committee and the Central Control Commission on January 7 1933 would conclude by saying that 'Sure are the facts'.[25] And sure they were. But, as noted by avant-garde photographer Aleksandr Rodchenko, the question was always one of 'socialist facts'[26] in accordance with which the road to the future was paved with heroic deeds.

Rational versus dynamic landscape

With Marx, Diogenes' theatrical gesture took on an entirely new meaning.[27] 'Capital', he wrote, 'is not a thing or a set of institutions; it is a process of circulation between production and realization'.[28] This in effect produces a highly dynamic landscape where infrastructures are both a means of and barrier to circulation. Here 'spatial distance reduces itself to time: the important thing is not the market's distance in space, but the speed with which it can be reached'.[29] Neither movement nor circulation have ever proved easy in Russia. Nevertheless, the modernisers of Russia have always been keen to assign a certain meaning, namely direction, to movement.

The central idea of the First Five Year Plan, and Soviet-type modernisation in general, was a rapid industrialisation of the country on the basis of large-scale heavy industry. The decision to prioritise the development of heavy industry, together with the collectivisation of agriculture was, to a large extent, a blueprint for the building of socialism in one country.[30] In turn, the GOELRO plan, the electrification of the whole country, was seen as a step towards large-scale industrialization and modernisation – the re-equipment and reorganization of industry, transport and agriculture, 'on the basis of socialism'[31]. The first priority in railway electrification was given to the lines in Southern Russia, especially the Donbas region. The electrification of lines in the centre and in the Urals was given second and third place in

24 N. Berdyaev, *The Origin of Russian Communism,* 149–151.
25 J. Stalin· 'The Results of the First Five Year Plan'. Speech delivered at the Joint Plenum of the Central Committee and the Central Control Commission of the CPSU, January 7, 1933. Published in J. V. Stalin, *Problems of Leninism*. Peking: Foreign Languages Press, 1976, 623.
26 M. Tupitsyn, *The Soviet Photograph 1924–1937*. New Haven – London: Yale University Press, 1996, 61.
27 Diogenes gesture refers here to Eleatic denial of motion and its refutation in practice by Diogenes, who simply paced back and forth. S. Kierkegaard, *Toisto*, 11.
28 Cited in D. Harvey *Spaces of Capital. Towards a Critical Geography*. Edinburgh: Edinburgh University Press, 2001, 265.
29 D. Harvey, *Spaces of Capital*, 244. Later Paul Virilio elaborated this insight into 'dromology', that is, the science (or logic) of speed. P. Virilio, *Speed and Politics. An Essay on Dromology*. NY: Semiotext(e), 1986.
30 E. H. Carr, *Socialism in One Country 1924–1926*. Harmondsworth: Penguin Books, 1970, 378.
31 J. Stalin· 'The Results of the First Five Year Plan', 578–630.

the priority list. According to Westwood, it was no earlier than the thirties that the main-line electrification actually took place.[32]

Following Marx, transport was regarded as a unitary whole within the framework of the production cycle of the economy. In typical Soviet terms:

> Transport is the common property of the people and is a constituent part of the single socialist system of economy. The systematic, proportional development of socialist economy conditions the rational development and distribution of all forms of transport over the territory of the country. The distribution of the transport in its turn fosters a systematic distribution of production all over the country... Unlike the elemental and anarchic development of the means of transportation in the capitalist countries, the railways, waterways, automobile and air transport have developed in the USSR as a single system of transportation which systematically combines all forms of transport and works in accordance with a plan established by the state.[33]

In the above extract it is assumed that in the socialist system transport is, in essence, more rational than in the capitalist system. An essential question concerns what was considered *rational* in this context. Furthermore, what were the criteria for *rational distribution* of all forms of transport? The explanation again begins with Marx, and Engels.

Marx rejected the market on the basis that it was not rationally understandable. The fluctuations of the market were not accessible to scientific understanding, and therefore the market, in accordance with the left Hegelian dialectic was irrational and ought to be rejected.[34] The dynamism of the capitalist landscape, and thus, *irrationality*, was to be replaced by what became known as centralized planning in the command economy. The emphasis on planning coincided with the decision registered by the fourteenth party conference to promote the metal industry. The planning and the development of heavy industry were two sides of the same coin. 'The development of heavy industry,' writes Carr, 'meant planning, and planning meant, first and foremost, the development of heavy industry.' Until the fourteenth party congress, held in December 1925, the controversy over planning reigned within the party but when an expansion of heavy industry was announced as a principal party objective it was clear, as shown by Carr, that the advocates of planning had won.[35]

This was particularly the case with the geographical location of productive

32 J. N. Westwood, *A History of Russian Railways*. London: G. Allen and Unwin, 1964, 224.

33 R. E. H. Mellor, 'The Soviet concept of unified transport system and the contemporary role of the railways'. In L. Symons and C. White, *Russian Transport. An Historical and Geographical Survey*. London: G. Bell and Sons Ltd, 1975, 76.

34 A. Megill, *The Burden of Reason. (Why Marx rejected Politics and the Market)*. Lanham – Boulder – NY – Oxford: Rowman and Littlefield Publishers, Inc, 2002, 164, 173.

35 E. H. Carr, *Socialism in One Country 1924–1926*, 521–541.

forces that, contrary to practices under capitalism, would not be developed *unevenly* or *irrationally*. By irrational, Soviet planners meant the concentration of industry in those regions of the country where it yielded the quickest and greatest profits.[36] Instead, the 'Great October Socialist Revolution', explains General Andrey Lagovskiy, 'which eliminated the capitalist mode of production in our country, also put an end to the irrational location of newly constructed industrial enterprises. In the process of the construction of socialism, the ugly legacy of the capitalist location of productive forces was gradually liquidated, although it has not yet been completely overcome'.[37]

Distance, however, was not counted as one of the planning criteria of the new industrial areas. In fact, 'the Soviet policy on transport and industrial infrastructure in general', writes Russian economist Goritsheva 'was based on a denial of geographical factors'[38]. The ideational basis of the concept of a 'unified transport system' was the so-called 'Engels dictum' – Engels' contention that large-scale industry should be 'freed from the restrictions of space' and be equally distributed within and across a socialist country:

> Large-scale industry…has thereby to a considerable extent freed production from the restrictions of place…society liberated from the barriers of capitalist production can go much further still… the abolition of the separation between town and country is therefore not utopian, even in so far as it presupposes the most equal distribution possible of large-scale industry over the whole country. It is true that in the huge towns civilization had bequeathed us a heritage to rid ourselves of which will take much time and trouble. But this heritage must and will be got rid of, however protracted the process may be.[39]

Formulated as a practical policy recommendation, it was asserted that 'the means of transportation on most occasions do not determine the choice of region and site for the construction of iron and steel works. On the contrary, the construction of the metallurgical works determines the organization of the corresponding system of transport connections', writes historian Rees.

The planning for the volume of traffic in railway transport was not calculated by the Ministry of Ways and Communications (NKPS) but was subordinate to the plans for the various sectors of the economy.[40] This meant, according to Westwood, that 'whatever traffic was produced the railways had to carry it and the allocation of resources to transport was limited strictly to the minimum amount necessary to enable the increments of traffic to be moved. The NKPS and the railways only planned the distribution and the

36 F. Hill – C. Gaddy, *The Siberian Curse. How Communist Planners Left Russia Out in the Cold*. Washington: Brookings Institution Press, 2003, 90.

37 Cited in F. Hill – C. Gaddy, *The Siberian Curse*, 90.

38 L. Goricheva, 'Natural conditions of development of national economies in Russia and Western Europe'. In *Mirovaja Ekonomika I Mezhdunarodnye otnoshenija* 2 2004, 58.

39 Cited in F. Hill – C. Gaddy, *The Siberian Curse*, 89.

40 E. A. Rees, *Stalinism and Soviet Rail Transport 1928–41*. London: Macmillan Press, 1995, 29; J. N. Westwood, *History of Russian Railways*, 253.

handling of the traffic'.[41] Consistent with the above-mentioned conceptualization of rationality, it was maintained that '[the] economic activity should be *evenly distributed* throughout the union so as to ensure maximum utilisation of infrastructure, natural and labour resources'. It was also emphasized that the 'choices of locations for production must be consistent with the need to strengthen defensive capacities of the USSR'.[42]

Scale and tempo of movement

The problem of the transport component, as Westwood puts it, is 'a consequence of the geographic feature of Russia, the union of an enormous territorial expanse into a single economy. Integrating distant industry into the general economy meant that both the tsarist and Soviet regimes manipulated freight rates in favour of the long-distance shipper'.[43] This contributed to the dominance of railways as a principal mode of transport in Russia. Arnuff Grubler has compared the dynamics of technological change in the US and the Soviet Union and comes to the conclusion that the two countries had an infrastructure system which was very similar structurally. Gruber argues that the main driving force in the evolution of transport infrastructure and technological development is the 'human time allocation mechanism' that is explained by 'the law of constant travel time'. Simply put, the structural change of infrastructures is linked to the technology of speed rather than the type of economic system or relative transport cost/price structure.[44]

Therefore, because the Soviet Union was '"decoupled" from the major economic expansion pulse that characterized the post World War II growth of Western market economies' the infrastructure development had a very different *growth pulse* even if its structural pattern of infrastructure development was similar to that of, for example, the US. On the temporal scale, there was a thirty-year difference compared to technological development in the US. In terms of the scale of the infrastructure network, the prioritization of rapid modernisation of heavy industry was instrumental in creating the T-shaped arterial system. The head of the T-shape was the north-south movement axis along the railways between the north-western industrial area, the Central Industrial and Central Black earth regions and the Industrial South,

41 Less than 2 per cent of the traffic was planned at the local railway level. The essential part of the plan originated at the centre. In the late 1950s the system was changed in such a way that over a third of the traffic was planned at the local level together with the railways, sovnarkhoz and other local planning organs. J. N. Westwood, *A History of Russian Railways*, 253, 255–256.

42 P. Kirkow, *Russia's Provinces. Authoritarian Transformation versus Local Autonomy?* London: Macmillan Press, 1998, 26.

43 J. N. Westwood, *Soviet Railways to Russian Railways.* NY: Palgrave, 2002, 79.

44 The major structural difference concerns canals that, in the Soviet Union, were phased out slower and much later than in the US. A. Grubler. *The Rise and Fall of Infrastructures. Dynamics of Evolution and Technological Change in* Transport. Laxenburg: Physica-Verlag Heidelberg, 1999, 196.

accompanied with strong arterial movements along the east-west axis from the Central Industrial area via the Urals to western Siberia and Baykalia. The structure of inter-regional commodity flows in the Soviet Union in the mid-1970s showed that 'about half the area of the country is not involved to any significant extent in the transport system; in fact, 55 per cent of the country lies more than 100 km from a railway line'. At the same time, the majority of the freight traffic was concentrated on just half of the route length.[45]

This reveals an inherent contradiction in the Soviet transport policy – the simultaneous striving to create a unified transport system and thereby an integrated economic area and the prioritization of the development of heavy industry. The latter policy objective dominated and thus resulted in the prioritization of certain trunk lines and the distinctive traffic pattern described above. As a result, the Soviet space was a combination of a rather well-integrated network of urbanized nodes of economic, industrial and administrative activities (cities of different rank) that were situated in an otherwise fragmented space.

The logic and pace of movement in the Soviet space had its specific codes as well. In terms of cargo transport, the rationality principle of even distribution, prioritization of heavy industry and the objective of self-sufficiency were translated into a practice known as *marchroutization*. In simple terms, it meant faster speed of delivery of certain key commodities (coal, oil, ferrous metals, ore, timber, firewood, grain, and mineral building materials), which comprised the bulk of the total railway freight traffic. The practice was first introduced in the late 1930s and continued until the late 1990s. In the new Railway Charter adopted in 1998 the 'Marchrout' was no longer compulsory.[46]

Marchroutization was a combination of several factors. The carriage of these eight types of freight was centrally planned and, when possible, reconstructed lines were used. The most advanced trains carried only one type of goods and travelled from origin to destination without delays at sorting yards or at boundaries separating the different railways. The practice was a result of the 'concentration of transport demand on a limited number of trunk lines' as well as of a 'relatively simple commodity flow of a narrow range of items in large quantities'. In the course of this practice, the real costs of long hauls were not taken into consideration and the transport of key commodities was operated on below-cost tariffs instead.[47]

World Bank experts estimate that once Russia's agricultural and industrial sectors conform more closely to those of a market-oriented economy, the

45   R. E. H. Mellor, 'The Soviet concept of unified transport system', 83–92.
46   In the late 1930s, three-quarters of railway freight traffic was found in those above-mentioned eight categories of goods. J. N. Westwood, *A History of Russian Railways*, 231; J. N. Westwood, *Soviet Railways to Russian Railways*, 98.
47   For example in the mid-1970s, 85 per cent of the goods-traffic turnover of the four main media comprised bulk goods. As mentioned already earlier, transport flows were highly concentrated, in fact 46 per cent of the route length carried 86 per cent of all freight traffic J. N. Westwood, *A History of Russian Railways,* 231, 258–259; R. E. H. Mellor, 'The Soviet concept of unified transport system', 92.

average size of consignments will decline as the diversity of freight origins and destinations increases. These changes will produce conditions that favour road rather than rail transport.[48] The change currently underway is from a rail-dominated, state-managed system towards one with an emerging road transport sector that is driven by commercial interest.[49] The scenario depicted in the World Bank Policy Note seems plausible. The 'creative destruction' of the 1990s set precedents for the emergence of a new form and direction of infrastructure development.[50]

Conclusion: a return to the BAM

The BAM 'myth' outlived the Soviet Union. This was illustrated at the opening ceremony of the North Muisk tunnel on 5 December 2003, which was every bit as grand as the performances of the Soviet era. The only difference was that the Soviet slogans were replaced with a new set of words. The former head of the JSC Russian Railways, Gennadi Fadeev, concluded his short speech at the site by addressing the builders (tonnel'shchiki) with the words: 'God will take care of you!' (Pust' berezhet Bog).[51] In a speech published later on the company's website, Fadeev talks up the BAM and dubs it 'a unique monument to contemporary art; a construction that serves the faith and truth of the Homeland (Rodina)'[52]. Another speaker at the ceremony, the President of the Republic of Buryatia, L. Pomanova, declared the North Muisk to be the very 'golden key' of the BAM. This was a recollection – a moment of reflection on the past rather than on the future.

On 24th March, 1984, the Central Committee of the Communist Party announced that the 'golden link', that is, the final section of the Baikal-Amur railway, would be commenced 'ahead of schedule' by the 67th anniversary of the 'Great October' (Velikogo Oktjabrja). This would allow the opening of the railway to regular traffic a year earlier than was originally planned.[53] The grand opening was held at Buryat's Kuanda station in October 1984, but it was not until 1989 that the first trains started to run on the BAM.[54] And

---

48 The railways are still the major mode of surface transportation as about 80 per cent of surface ton-km in Russia goes by train. The share of the railways is 86 per cent of the total volume of cargo transportation and the railways carry from 80 to 98 per cent of coal, coke, ore, ferrous metals, fertilizers and grain transportation. B. Eijbergen – L. Thompson – R. Carruthers – K. Gwilliam – R. Podolske, 'Russia: the Transport Sector'. *World Bank Policy Note,* August 2004, 14.

49 B. Eijbergen (et. all), 'Russia: the Transport Sector', 2–4.

50 A. Gruber, *The Rise and Fall of Infrastructures,* 275.

51 E. Glikman, 'Dobrovol'nye nevol'niki, ili moja stykovka s Bamom'. *Novaja Gazeta* 28 Feb 2005.

52 Words of the head of the Russian Railways, Gennadi Fadeev, at the opening of the North Muisk tunnel on 5 December 2008. 'Oktrytie Severo-Muiskogo tonnelja'. http://www.rzd.ru/documents/index.html?he_id=892. Page visited 14.2.2006.

53 *Ezhegodnik Bolshoi Sovetskoi entsiklopedii.* Moskva: Sovetskaja Entsiklopedija, 1985, 33.

54 Christopher Ward argues that in fact the commemoration of the railway's completion

when the railway finally started its operations, three out of four railcars ran empty. This was mainly because the projected boom of West Siberian oil failed to materialize and since there was nothing else for them to carry, a maximum of 5 trains out of 60 dispatched daily from Komsomol'sk rolled over the BAM.[55]

The emptiness of the railcars turned out to be a permanent phenomenon. After the Soviet Union collapsed, the scale of the 'absence' only increased. At the time of the opening of the North Muisk tunnel in 2003, the JSC Russian Railways announced that it would reorient transport of 6 millions tons of cargo from the Trans-Siberian railway to the BAM. The current amount of cargo transport on the BAM was, however, omitted in the text.[56] Thus, the BAM saw 'neither' cargo 'nor' the development of societal space. In fact, the cessation of construction gave the authorities an excuse to demolish the 27-year-old 'temporal' settlements adjacent to the North Muisk tunnel construction site. Residents of a worker settlement called 'Tonnel'nyi' went on hunger strike in the summer of 2004. They were protesting against the closing down of the construction site without providing them with adequate housing and other benefits they had earned while working on the previous century's 'largest construction site'.[57]

This was an instance of repetition when the borrowed elements (a ritual from the Soviet past and the new vocabulary of the present-day market reforms) were turned into a form where temporal 'non-place'[58] subordinated that of the permanent, lived realm. E. Glikman, a Russian journalist who visited the BAM in 2005, answers a rhetorical question: 'So, why was the BAM needed?':

> In order that thousands of men and women met, got married and raised children. That's it, and everyone benefited, to my mind. But this very thing I should not say and therefore, it would have been better if the BAM had not existed at all.[59]

While the BAM is rejected as a model of modernisation, its contradictory past continues to haunt official discourse in which the general absence of

in 1984 marked the ceasing of official interest towards its *de facto* completion. C. Ward, 'Selling the "project of the century"', 9.

55 V. Mote 'BAM, Boom, Bust: Analysis of Railways past, present and future'. *Soviet Geography* 5 (1990), 326.

56 Instead, the press release mentioned that between 1995 and 2002 the transport along the BAM and the Trans-Siberian railway grew by a total of 35 per cent (to 61.7 million tons per year). By 2010 it is estimated that the transport will grow another 30 per cent. 'Novosti kompanii'. 5 December 2003, 14:13 MKT. www.rzd.ru.

57 Moscow News 'BAM: project, railroad, outdated symbol'. 12 July 2004, 22:06 MSK; E. Glikman, 'Dobrovol'nye nevol'niki, ili moja stykovka s Bamom'. *Novaja Gazeta*, 28 February 2005.

58 M. Augé, *Non-places. Introduction to an anthropology of supermodernity*. London – NY: Verso, 1995.

59 E. Glikman, 'Dobrovol'nye nevol'niki, ili moja stykovka s Bamom'. *Novaja Gazeta* 14 March 2005.

function of the BAM goes unnoticed. A large part of the glossary of terms attesting to the fact that the BAM myth once made sense has become obsolete or transformed into kitsch. The new vocabulary of transport modernisation in turn includes such words as 'reliability', 'public-private partnership', 'market-value', 'transparency' and 'ecologically sustainable' (ekologicheski chistuyu). In general, the change is from an introvert to extrovert framework of discourse while, at the same time, ritualised use of language has retained its importance as a form of action.

However, the contemporary imitation of the Soviet-type public rituals has more to do with recollection than repetition. The way in which Soviet, Tsarist and 'Reformist' slogans, gestures and images are blended is a neither/ nor position that derives from the abolition of revolution as a way forward. The 'thaw'-like suspension, a labyrinth of checks-and-balances created in and around the Kremlin establishment is aimed at combating eternal recurrence: the inevitability that a revolution has no last 'number'.[60]

The idea of 'Moscow – port of five oceans'[61] highlights the extent of change in the framework of transport infrastructure planning in Russia. After the Soviet Union collapsed, Russia lost two of the five points on its star. The port of Odessa belongs to Ukraine and the port of Baku is in the territory of Azerbaijan. The changes in the geographical scale were accompanied by similarly drastic changes in semantic and temporal spheres as well. It is quite obvious that the contemporary discourse on transport modernisation and its key word 'international transport corridor' is devoid of the image of 'heroic worker'. Instead of building a 'sacred' space, corridors denote a sense of 'power over the space', a (geo)political order on the global scale. This has to do with the fact that the notion of transport 'corridor' is a technical, bureaucratic term which, despite requiring the existence of tangible things, cannot be reduced to the 'building' of those things. Rather, corridors are a set of (new) practices (systems of constitutive rules) and regulations that define the very intersection of the domestic/international continuum.

This opens up a new layer of discourse where the vocabulary includes, for example, the words 'samobydnost', 'mezhduranodnaja', 'zapad', and 'evraziitsvo'. These are used in articulating Russia's either/or position vis-à-vis things borrowed from Europe. The reconstruction of the border crossing points, airports and railway stations in St. Petersburg, Moscow, or Jekaterinburg and the main road and rail connections between the two major cities are visible markers of a change towards a type of a 'non-place'

60 Evgeny Zamyatin's anti-utopia *We* problematises the paradox inherent in every revolution: a belief in the durability of the order created by revolution and the very impossibility of stopping the eternal recurrence of the revolutionary movement. The book is often characterized as a precursor to George Orwell's *1984*, Aldous Huxley's *Brave New World*, and Ray Bradbury's *Fahrenheit 451*. It was written and completed in 1920 and first published in English in 1924. In Russia it was first published in 1952. E. Zamyatin, *We*. Moscow: Raduga Publishers 2000,189.

61 The image was published for example in the magazine 'USSR in Construction' 1937 (no. 9–12). See also A. Medvedev – Yu. Shaburov, *Moscow port of five oceans*. Moskva: Moskovskii Rabotsii, 1985.

described by French anthropologist Marc Áuge. Russia's current leadership welcomes this 'opening' to global 'space of flows'.[62] The adoption of a common vocabulary of 'international transport corridors' enhances changes for successful dialogue with the EU. At the same time, the sense in which the words 'international' and 'corridor' are understood in the Russian context is quite different from that of the EU. Thus, it is the silences and gaps in the discourse, together with the (ritualistic) repetition of the code words, that convey the extent of change (or that of continuation) in the way in which Russia is modernized.

---

62   This is a term used by Manuel Castells to describe interaction patterns in global scale. See M. Castells, *The Information Age. Economy, Society and Culture. Vol. 1 The Rise of the Network Society*. Oxford: Blackwell Publisher 1996.

LINDA TRAUTMAN

Modernisation of Russia's Last Frontier: The Arctic and the Northern Sea Route from the 1930s to the 1990s

The Russian people would seem to identify with the Arctic in ways that predispose them to act vigorously and to produce great effects there. The desire to master the North and appropriate its resources reaches far into Russia's past.[1]

Introduction

Modernisation of the Russian Far North presented formidable challenges over the course of the twentieth century. The vast northern landmass and seas represent Russia's last frontier. In a geographic sense the maritime areas follow the longest contiguous coastline of any state in the world, and include the Northern Sea Route (NSR) eastwards from Murmansk, through the Barents, White, Kara, Laptev, East Siberian and Chukchi Seas, and then extending south through the Bering Straits and the Sea of Okhotsk to Vladivostok. In an economic sense this frontier has provided opportunities for exploration and trade, generated by indigenous Northerners, foreign explorers and traders, and Russian entrepreneurs and scientists of Tsarist, Soviet and post-Soviet regimes. The northern landmass above the 62nd parallel offered enormous wealth: fur and timber for Imperial Russia; precious metals and ores for Soviet industrialisation; oil and gas for the Russian Federation. In a strategic sense the last frontier represented a remote northern boundary which posed formidable obstacles to any would-be aggressor. Yet, increasing threats from both east and west, particularly for Soviet regimes of the 1920s and 1930s and during the Cold War made a secure navigable route more urgent.

The Stalinist regime of the 1930s linked economic modernisation in the Far North to the region's resources and to the Northern Sea Route. Most of the development projects were consolidated under the Main Administration of the Northern Sea Route and there was an enthusiastic commitment to

---

1   F. Griffiths, 'Arctic in the Russian Identity', in L. Brigham (ed) *The Soviet Maritime Arctic*. London and Cambridge: Belhaven in association with the Scott Polar Research Institute 1991, 84–86.

252

Arctic *osvoenie*. Behind the confident boasting about socialist achievement in the Arctic, there was a commitment to modernisation at *any* human cost. A host of bureaucratic structures were created and linked to the state's internal security apparatus, and there was an increasing focus on security. The Stalinist agenda represented a fundamentally autarkic vision of modernising the Far North.

Mikhail Gorbachev's Murmansk Declaration of 1987 foreshadowed change within a broader model of development for the Far North. Rather than the centralised plan and the ruthless Arctic schemes of the 1930s, modernisation has been more fragmented. The early 1990s brought free-for-all take-overs of state industries by Russian entrepreneurs who became the new oligarchs; and the transition to operating within the global marketplace brought new levels of accountability and demands for environmental regulation. The Putin era reasserted central control in order to curb the power of the oligarchs and ensure continued western investment in oil and gas. The 1990s has thus given rise to a diverse set of modernisers – foreshadowed in Gorbachev's Declaration– whose rivalries and collaboration have been evident in both regional and national politics.

Modernisation of the Russian Far North is presented in two key periods: the Stalinist era of industrialisation, collectivisation and militarization; and the post-Soviet era of collapse and regeneration. The comparison offers a window onto the regimes' priorities in the 1930s and the 1990s. Despite the difficulties in comparing modernisation across time periods, there is the opportunity to ask why and how development proceeded as it did. Moreover, the comparison contributes to the debate about what is distinctive about Russian / Soviet modernisation, including questions of autarkic development versus Westernisation, repression and statism, and alternative strategies for the Far North.

Arctic Sovereignty as a First Step to Modernisation

The clarification of sovereignty claims in the polar regions – and recognition of those claims by the international community – was arguably the starting point for any modernisation to occur. All circumpolar states sought to clarify the boundaries of their territorial and maritime space given the valuable resources and the measure of security provided by these regions. The claims in turn produced debates internationally about the polar regions in both the 1930s and the 1990s.

The central question was what particular areas each circumpolar state claimed and how conflicting claims were to be resolved. As the state with the largest polar area, the Russian Imperial regime first published its claims in 1915 in a *note diplomatique* circulated to European and North American capitals. The claims were reiterated by the Bolshevik state in 1926 and 1932 and defined the Russian / Soviet North as:

> all lands already discovered, as well as those which are to be discovered in the future ... north of the coast of the USSR up to the North Pole, with the limit of 32° east of Greenwich ... and 168° west from Greenwich to come under Soviet jurisdiction.[2]

In short, the Imperial and Soviet regimes claimed a sector extending up to the North Pole. The 'sector claims' provoked an acrimonious and prolonged international debate about sovereignty in the Arctic regions. The international jurist Hopper summed up that debate in 1937: 'the former "doctrine of discovery, effective occupation and notification" had been replaced by the "sector theory" and the "doctrine of region of attraction."'[3] Leading jurists warned of possible confrontation and there were proposals for an international conference to resolve conflicting territorial claims.[4] The claims nevertheless were accepted and the USSR achieved its goal – recognition of its sovereignty extending to the North Pole. The maritime claims, i.e., all islands and Arctic seas, would have to wait for international recognition until the late Soviet era when the Law of the Sea Conventions (UNCLOS) were negotiated in the 1980s. Following the collapse of the Soviet Union, the Russian Federation ratified UNCLOS in 1994, a clear signal that it is wanted to work within an international framework.

The claims by Imperial, Soviet and post-Soviet regimes in the polar regions can be viewed as an important component of all modernisation programmes. The earlier claims of the 1920s and 1930s were fundamentally about securing the state in order for the resource potential to develop far from the western or eastern borders where threats were building. In the post-Soviet period of the 1990s the issue for the Russian Federation was both securing the NSR and opening it 'for business.' Thus, all regimes have repeatedly identified the boundaries of the Russian Far North for the international community and for modernisation to proceed.

Modernising in the 1930s: Consolidation, Commitment and Confidence

The advent of the Five-Year Plans forged a new Stalinist model of state-building which required input from a variety of sectors: engineering and construction specialists, scientists and technical experts, budgetary and finance person-

2   B. Hopper, 'Sovereignty in the Arctic', *Research Bulletin on the Soviet Union* II (8) 1937, 81; V. L. Lakhtin, 'Rights Over the Arctic', *American Journal of International Law* 10 1930. T. A. Taracouzio, *Soviets in the Arctic*. New York: Macmillan 1938, 320–366.

3   B. Hopper, 'Sovereignty in the Arctic', *Research Bulletin on the Soviet Union* II (8) 1937, 83.

4   O. A. K. Aktivist, 'Imperializm na Polyarnom Severe i Interesy SSSR', *Sovetskii Sever* 1–2 1932. B. Hopper, 'Sovereignty in the Arctic', *Research Bulletin on the Soviet Union* II (8) 1937, 81; T. A. Taracouzio, *Soviets in the Arctic*. New York: Macmillan 1938, 320–366.

nel, internal security staff including political administrators, and a large labour force. Socialist state-building required large centralised institutions to plan, co-ordinate, manage and propel the projects forward. Initiated from above, state-building projects like Dnieper, Magnitogorsk and Belomor combined what Rees and others have called a "command-administrative system" with mass mobilisation campaigns.[5] Kotkin's work on Magnitogorsk emphasises what Moshe Lewin, R. W. Davies and others earlier noted about the period:

> Gigantism, immoderation, refusal of realism ... a state of profound disequilibrium, a circumstance that strongly coloured the emerging authoritarian apparatus ... pursuing an endless search for workable administrative structures through endless decrees ... At the same time, party leaders fought ... to assert control over the operation of the gigantic industrial-administrative complex ... Planning was a world to be discovered.[6]

There was a genuine belief that the state's mobilisation of manpower and resources could produce the 'catch up and overtake' (*dognat' i peredognat'*) transformation Stalin talked about as early as 1925, that Kaganovich referred to in a 1929 speech to Magnitogorsk and that began with the First Five-Year Plan.[7]

The utopian goals of industrial modernisation, articulated for Dnieper and Magnitogorsk, were proclaimed even louder for the Far North. Against the backdrop of these '*grand projets*,' all completed by 1933, the Main Administration of the Northern Sea Route or Glavsevmorput' was established.[8] Within the climate of 'gigantism and immoderation,' the attempt was made to consolidate all previous Arctic operations under a single authority. The language of the Arctic became that of overcoming all technical, logistical and even climatic difficulties – *osvoenie* – mastery over the polar regions. Personnel on polar expeditions were granted hero status, popularised in the press and awarded medals as they published their expeditionary logs, research and even autobiographies.[9]

5   E. A. Rees, 'Stalinism: The Primacy of Politics', in J. Channon (ed) *Politics, Society and Stalinism in the USSR*. London: Macmillan Press Ltd 1998, 65.
6   S. Kotkin, *Magnetic Mountain*. Berkeley and Los Angeles: University of California Press 1995, 41.; R. W. Davies, M. Harrison, et al., eds, *The Economic Transformation of the Soviet Union, 1913–1945*. Cambridge: Cambridge University Press 1994, 143.
7   S. Kotkin, *Magnetic Mountain*. Berkeley and Los Angeles: University of California Press 1995, 42.
8   The Main Administration of the Northern Sea Route was known by its acronym GUSMP or Glavsevmorput' for *Glavnoe Upravlenie Severnogo Morskogo Puti*.
9   P. Horensma, *The Soviet Arctic*. London: Routledge 1991, 57–61; J. McCannon, 'Positive Heroes at the Pole: Celebrity Status, Socialist-Realist Ideals and the Soviet Myth of the Arctic, 1932–1939', *Russian Review* 56 1997, 347; K. E. Bailes, *Technology and Society under Lenin and Stalin: Origins of the Soviet Technical Intelligentsia, 1917–1941*. Princeton: Princeton University Press 1978, 388–394.

Modernisation of the Arctic would begin with a transport project that lay entirely within Soviet polar space, i.e., the Northern Sea Route. The NSR was to serve as the initial focus for developing the mineral wealth of the Far North. The *Sibiryakov's* through-passage between Murmansk and Vladivostok in a single navigational season between June and October 1932 provided the stimulus for a new commitment to the North. Stalin's enthusiasm was clearly demonstrated on the front page of *Pravda* and in articles bestowing heroic status on the *Sibiryakov's* crew and their leader Otto Yulevich Shmidt.[10] In the largest sense, the NSR passage represented the triumph of science and technology over a hostile environment and *socialist* planning to conquer the last frontier. According to John McCannon, consolidating northern development coincided with the *Sibiryakov's* passage:

> ...That a ship could cross the Northern Sea Route in the course of one navigational season was the best indication to date that the route could indeed be transformed into the regular, operational sea-lane ... unlocking the material potential of Siberia and the Arctic finally seemed within reach ... Shmidt left for Moscow soon after the *Sibiryakov* lowered anchor in Vladivostok ... he conferred with the Council of Peoples' Commissars and, by all accounts, with Stalin himself.[11]

Thus, the new development scheme was initiated by personalities who would push for the expansion of GUSMP's work in the Far North.[12]

According to Molotov, Stalin was acutely aware of the economic potential of the Far North and the need for urgent state-building.[13] The project for the Far North would be ideologically driven by those who believed socialist planning would propel the Soviet Union towards industrial and military power equal to that of the West. Within two years, the project grew as did its array of bureaucratic affiliates. GUSMP personnel included bureaucrats, NKVD officials, scientists, engineers, pilots and ships' captains – nearly 30,000 people in all.[14] Projects utilising forced labour were scattered throughout the North, but in the main were controlled by other enterprises such as Dal'stroi and Noril'sk. Public campaigns to popularise polar heroes and their achievements served to add 'Arctic chic' to a regime which increasingly faced challenges on the domestic and international front.

There had already been an ambitious Soviet Arctic agenda devised for the International Polar Year (1932–1933).[15] This agenda set the stage for

10 *Pravda* Through Six Seas: Historic Success of the Through-Passage along the Arctic Ocean in a Single Navigational Season, No. 337, 7 December 1932.
11 J. McCannon, *Red Arctic: Polar Exploration and the Myth of the North in the Soviet Union, 1932–1939*. Oxford: Oxford University Press 1998, 33
12 RGAE, f. 9570, op. 2, d. 72, ll. 1–35 1936; RGAE, f. 9570, op. 2, d. 75, ll. 180–222 (or 1–43) 1936; O. Y. Shmidt, 'Nashi Zadachi po Osvoeniyu Arktiki', (ed) *Za Osvoenie Arktiki*. Leningrad: Izdatel'stvo Glavsevmorputi 1935, 10.
13 V. Molotov, *Sto sorok besed c Molotovym - (translated Molotov Remembers - Inside Kremlin Politics – Conversations with Felix Chuev)*. Moscow 1993, 211.
14 RGAE, f. 9570, op. 2, d. 72, ll. 1–35 1936.
15 IMO (1930). *Compte Rendu des Travaux de la Commission pendant sa Première*

consolidating polar development especially with regard to the scientific tasks required for NSR development: establishing meteorological and navigation stations, and researching drifting ice, magnetism, polar geology, hydrology and climatology. The significance of Soviet work was highlighted in *Pravda* by the first President of the Academy of Sciences and polar geologist, A. P. Karpinskii, who had taken an active role in planning the International Polar Year.[16] He pointed to the lead taken by the USSR and placed the *Sibiryakov*'s achievement in the context of other work done by the Academy of Sciences, and the Arctic, Oceanographic, Hydrographic and Reindeer Institutes.[17]

Another driving force in consolidating a programme for the Arctic was Sergei S. Kamenev, who had directed the Central Committee's Arctic Commission from 1928. His ties to Otto Shmidt and to leading Arctic scientists such as R. L. Samoilovich, George Ushakov and others, were forged on the Arctic Commission.[18] More importantly, his post as Deputy Director of the Narkom for the Army and Navy (NK VMF) and his position on the Military Council may have helped shape Glavsevmorput's agenda. His links to the defence organs injected a focus on strategic concerns in the Far North and along the maritime route. At the very least, he would have recognised the importance of the final development of the NSR's naval potential as well as the importance of territorial claims.[19]

While the Dnieper, Belomor or Magnitogorsk mandates were large from the outset, the decree of the Council of Peoples' Commissars on 17 December 1932 established modest parameters for the new institution:

> GUSMP is charged with the final development of the Northern Sea Route from the White Sea to the Bering Strait, fully equipping this route, maintaining it in proper condition and ensuring the safety of navigation.

Année de Travail, Procès-Verbaux des Séances de la Réunion à Leningrad. Commission de l'Année Polaire, 1932–1933, Leningrad, Secrétariat de l'Organisation Météorologique Internationale; IMO (1931). *Compte Rendu des Travaux de la Commission pendant sa Première Année de Travail, Procès-Verbaux des Séances de la Réunion à Innsbruck.* Commission Internationale de l'Année Polaire, Innsbruck, Secrétariat de l'Organisation Météorologique Internationale; IMO (1933). *Compte Rendu des Travaux de la Commission, Procès-Verbaux des Séances de la Réunion à Copenhague.* Commission Internationale de l'Année Polaire, Copenhague, Secrétariat de l'Organisation Météorologique Internationale.

16 A. P. Karpinskii, *Pravda V Klub' Arktiki*, 18 November 1932. A P. Karpinskii was the first President of the Academic of Sciences after the Revolutions of 1917, and was a prominent geologist.

17 Ibid.

18 V. N. Bulatov, 'Arkticheskaya Komissiya', *Voprosy Istorii* 8–9 1992, 148.

19 Ibid; R. W. Davies, M. J. Ilič, et al., eds, *Soviet Government Officials, 1922–1941: A Handlist*. Birmingham: Centre for Russian and East European Studies, University of Birmingham 1989, 307. The Military Council, or *Voennyi Sovet*, was established in November 1934 taking over the work of the Revolutionary Council. It reported to the Peoples' Commissariat for Defence (NKObor). S. S. Kamenev served on both as a high-ranking deputy chair.

> To GUSMP is transferred all existing meteorological and radio stations located on the coast and islands in the Arctic.[20]

Thus, Glavsevmorput's initial mandate focused on the maritime areas between the White and Bering seas. The firm anchoring of the project to the Transport Commission of the SNK and later the Transport Department of the Politburo, emphasised GUSMP's strategic role as well as its key economic tasks. Shmidt's eleven meetings with Stalin between 1932 and 1938 frequently included members of the economic commissariats and the security organs, highlighting its role in state-building and state-securing.[21]

The modernisation plan for the Far North – embodied in Glavsevmorput' – reflected many of the features of Stalinist state-building institutions between 1932 and 1939. GUSMP rapidly expanded to include highly centralised structures and a personalised style of leadership under the charismatic Shmidt. GUSMP's operations were circumscribed the Party and the state's internal security organs. Like Fitzpatrick's description of Rabkrin as a 'rather ineffectual agency with ... no special interest in industry ... burrowing its way into the economic life of the country,' GUSMP was also a somewhat 'ineffectual agency' that 'burrowed' its way into Soviet economic spheres of the mid-1930s.[22]

Within three months of its creation, Glavsevmorput's mandate was enlarged to include a host of extractive coal industries as well as new port enlargements at Igarka, Dikson, Tiksi and Provideniya. Whatever the impetus to GUSMP's creation in December 1932, the task of maximising and transporting the coal, nickel, copper, graphite, gold and timber of the Far North became paramount: these were resources urgently required for expanding Soviet industries which were increasingly tied to war preparations. As Davies

20 Decree, 'Ob Organizatsii pri Sovete Narodnyx Komissarov Soyuza SSR Glavnogo Upravleniya Severnogo Morskogo Puti', *SZR Sobranie Zakonov i Rasporyazhenii S.S.S.R.* 84 1932.
21 Y. A. Gor'kova, *Kreml' Stavka Genshtab.* Tver' 1995; Y. A. Gor'kova, 'Posetiteli Kremlevskogo Kabineta I. V. Stalina (1932–1933)', *Istoricheskii Arkhiv (Journal of the Arkhivo Nauchno-Informatsionnoe Agenstvo, or AIA)* 1 1995; Y. A. Gor'kova, 'Posetiteli Kremlevskogo Kabineta I. V. Stalina (1934–1935)', *Istoricheskii Arkhiv (Journal of Arkhivo Nauchno-Informatsionnoe Agenstvo, or AIA)* 3 1995; Y. A. Gor'kova, 'Posetiteli Kremlevskogo Kabineta I. V. Stalina (1936–1937)', *Istoricheskii Arkhiv (Journal of Arkhivo Nauchno-Informatsionnoe Agenstvo, or AIA)* 4 1995; Y. A. Gor'kova, 'Posetiteli Kremlevskogo Kabineta I. V. Stalina (1938–1939)', *Istoricheskii Arkhiv (Journal of Arkhivo Nauchno-Informatsionnoe Agenstvo, or AIA)* 5 1995. While the issues discussed during the meetings are not revealed, members in attendance are listed. Often these included members of the internal security organs, the NKVD and the GUGB, as well as members of the air force and key pilots; less often the meetings Shmidt attended included members from the economic commissariats.
22 S. Fitzpatrick, 'Ordzhonikidze's Takeover of Vesenkha: A Case Study in Soviet Bureaucratic Politics', *Soviet Studies* XXXVII (No. 2) 1985, 155. Orzhonikidze took over responsibility for Rabrkin in 1926, and headed it together with the Central Control Commission (TsKK) until 1930, after which he was appointed Chairman of Vesenkha in November 1930. Vesenkha became the All-Union Commissariat for Heavy Industry in 1932.

and Cooper point out, the 'establishment of a modern armaments industry … was more demanding in materials … The industry … swallowed up high-grade fuel, high quality steel, non-ferrous metals …'[23] GUSMP also inherited the assets of the Committee of the Northern Sea Route (Komseveroput' or KSMP), set up in the early 1920s a 'joint-stock agency' with some 40,000 employees and a net worth of nearly 93 million rubles.[24] According to KSMP reports, it had become wasteful, inefficient and incompetent, charges that would again be levied against Glavsevmorput' in the late 1930s.[25]

Glavsevmorput's mandate was further widened in July 1934 due to the 'great success in the scientific study of the Soviet Far North and in the foundations for economic development.'[26] Thus Stalinist modernisation consolidated an ever-increasing range of projects including fisheries, timber trusts, polar aviation, icebreaker repairs, port development at Noril'sk and river transport along the Ob', Yenisey and Lena.[27] According to one source, Spitsbergen coal increased from around 20,000 tons mined in 1932 to some 400,000 tons under GUSMP's control.[28] The vulnerability of Spitsbergen coal as it crossed the White Sea was, however, a key reason for developing other coal production sites to meet the demands of increased shipping. Glavsevmorput's began turning to the Pechora, Noril'sk and Sangarsk mines – all well within the territory of the Soviet Union and in closer proximity to the Northern Sea Route. In some instances GUSMP 'take-over' plans were contentious such as in Yakutia.[29] Yet, 'gigantism' won out and Glavsevmorput's initial NSR work was soon overshadowed by its economic tasks.

23 R. W. Davies, 'Industry', in R. W. Davies, M. Harrison and S. G. Wheatcroft (ed) *The Economic Transformation of the Soviet Union, 1913–1945*. Cambridge: Cambridge University Press 1994, 145.

24 J. McCannon, *Red Arctic: Polar Exploration and the Myth of the North in the Soviet Union, 1932–1939*. Oxford: Oxford University Press 1998, 30; Y. Slezkine, *Arctic Mirrors: Russia and the Small Peoples of the North*. Ithaca, New York: Cornell University Press 1994, 266.

25 STO-SSSR, Postanovlenie STO – "O Rabote 'Komseveroputi' i Peredache ego Glavnomu Upravleniyu Severnogo Morskogo Puti", SZR SSSR, I, No. 21, Para. 124 1933.

26 Postanovlenie SNK SSSR i TsK VKP (b) – "O Meropriyatiyakh po Razvitiyu Severnogo Morskogo Puti i Severnogo Khozyaistva", KPSS v Resolyutsiyakh i Resheniyakh S''ezdov, Konferentsii i Plenumov TsK, 1898–1986, 6, 170–175 1934. Taracouzio cites this extract from *Izvestiya*, 3 August 1934.

27 Ibid. Map A-1 in Appendix A is useful in identifying key coal and oil reserves T. Armstrong, *The Northern Sea Route Soviet Exploitation of the North East Passage*. Cambridge: Cambridge University Press 1952, 80.

28 R. Vaughn, *The Arctic: A History*. Phoenix Mill, Gloucestershire: Sutton Publishing Ltd. 1994, 250–252. Although Spitsbergen (Svalbard) was under Norwegian sovereignty from 1920 onwards, there were several Russian coal concessions. The Spitsbergen trust Artikugol' included two mines, Grumant and the adjacent Barentsburg, bought from the Dutch in 1932. The figure for 1936 included production at both mines. T. Armstrong, *The Northern Sea Route Soviet Exploitation of the North East Passage*. Cambridge: Cambridge University Press 1952, 82.

29 RGAE, f. 9570, op. 2, d. 33, ll. 153–154 1934; RGAE, f. 9570, op. 2, d. 33, ll. 155–156 1934.

Glavsevmorput' also expanded by taking control of the polar scientific institutes in Leningrad. These highly-respected research bodies included the internationally known All-Union Arctic Institute (VAI), the Hydrographic Administration (GU), the Reindeer Institute, the Bureau for Ice Forecasting and the Meteorological Bureau.[30] Not surprisingly, GUSMP's absorption of these scientific research institutes took place against the backdrop of the Kirov assassination in December 1934 and the subsequent transfer of scientific control from Leningrad to Moscow. According to Krementsov, the subordination of scientific institutes was part of a broad policy of 'centralisation, concentration and stratification to liquidate so-called parallel institutes.'[31] Although GUSMP's authorities in Moscow were given 'jurisdiction' over polar research centres, the Arctic Institute and the Hydrographic Institute remained in Leningrad and attempted to carry on as before.[32] This was an anathema to Moscow's attempts to monitor and control polar scientific output. The growing rivalry between the Leningrad affiliates and GUSMP's Moscow-based bureaucrats would spiral downwards into disastrous expeditions and the targeting of Arctic institute personnel during the purges of 1937–1938.

There was one aspect of modernising the Far Northern regions which particularly appealed to Stalin: the development of polar aviation. GUSMP's aviation projects such as flights to the North Pole were sent directly for Stalin's approval.[33] There were direct communiqués between GUSMP pilots and Stalin himself and continual updates on rescue missions including the *Chelyuskin* in the spring of 1934, the over-wintering ships of 1937–1938 and the drifting ice station *Severnyi Pol'yus I* in 1938.[34] Aviation disasters notwithstanding, Glavsevmorput' could point to spectacular rescue efforts and to the culminating event in the spring of 1937: the landing of the crew of four men and equipment on the North Pole. They would then drift on an ever-decreasing ice floe as they conducted research for the next eleven months. The drifting ice stations continued throughout the Soviet period with the thirty-first ice station completing its work in 1991.[35]

The disastrous navigation season of 1937–1938 and the increasing number of air disasters were highlighted in the purge of GUSMP officials.[36] The restructuring and curtailing of GUSMP's operations in 1939 signalled the

30 SNK-SSSR, Postanovlenie SNK SSSR ob organizatsii Glavsevmorputi – "O strukture Glavnogo Upravleniya Severnogo Morskogo Puti", SZR SSSR (Sobranie Zakonov i Rasporiyazhenii S.S.S.R.), I, No. 7, 61–62, Para. 59 1935.
31 N. Krementsov, *Stalinist Science*. Princeton, New Jersey: Princeton University Press 1997, 37.
32 A. V. Kol'tsov, *Leningradskie Uchrezhdeniya Akademii Nauk SSSR v 1934–1945 gg.* Sankt-Peterburg: Nauka 1997, 11–12.
33 RGASPI, f. 475, op. 1, d. 2, ll. 1–4 1935.
34 RGAE, f. 9570, op. 2, d. 33, l. 124 1934; RGAPSI, f. 475, op. 1, d. 15, ll. 130–134 1938; RGASPI, f. 475, op. 1, d. 15, ll. 117–125 1938.
35 F. Giardini, E. Garrou, et al., *Isole di Ghiaccio alla Deriva Storia Postale e Vita delle Stazioni Flottanti Sovietiche nell'Oceano Glaciale Artico (Drifting Ice Islands from a Postal History and Life of Soviet Floating Stations in the Glacial Arctic Ocean).* Leumann, Torrino, Italy: Gribaudo – Associazione Grande Nord 1998.
36 RGAPSI, f. 475, op. 1, d. 15, ll. 85–122 1938.

demise of the Stalinist agency and the waning of the commitment to economic modernisation in the North. In the end, Glavsevmorput' was judged to have failed to fulfil the state's strategic goal of fully developing the maritime route, aviation and scientific triumphs notwithstanding.[37]

Costs of Stalinist Modernisation: The Far North of the 1930s

There were formidable costs in developing the Far Northern resource potential and making the NSR operational by the end of the 1930s. While some costs were related to the intractable challenges of the polar regions – survival in a harsh and unpredictable climate, the vagaries of ice floes and their impact on shipping and aviation, and the little-understood impact of polar magnetism – they were not solely the result of these challenges. As John Westwood noted, there were good reasons for why 'hydrophobia proved very long-lasting.'[38]

A catalogue of mounting air disasters in the May 1938 report to Stalin was but one indication that Arctic development was in trouble. The mounting losses of trained personnel, including prominent aviators such as Chkalov and Levanevsky, were largely due to faulty aircraft equipment, faulty navigation systems and unsafe landing strips. The losses were also attributable to the bureaucratic morass of plans and insufficient investment. Not only had there been accidents and breakages – with charges of sabotage – the incidents also reflected poor training and preparation of pilots as well as the inherent dangers of polar aviation.

The costs of developing the Stalinist Arctic extended to those in leadership posts. As the purges descended on Glavsevmorput', Shmidt as Head of GUSMP was accused of attempting to 'hide GUSMP's catastrophes from the TsK and the SNK.'[39] According to the *Otchet* sent to Stalin in June 1938, Shmidt's agency had failed to coordinate reconnaissance and provide reliable aircraft.[40] The price paid by Shmidt was a transfer from his post as Head of Glavsevmorput'; for others the costs were much higher.

The scientific community based in Leningrad suffered the most. Many teams of geologists, hydrographers and hydrologists, meteorologists and ice specialists had contributed to developing Arctic maritime and mineral resources. Their contributions to the modernisation project were then ruthlessly ended during the great purges of 1937–1938. Melanie Ilič's study of the Great Terror in Leningrad confirms the targeting of scientists among other

37 RGAE, f. 9570, op. 2, d. 33, ll. 153–154 1934; RGAE, f. 9570, op. 2, d. 33, ll. 155–156 1934; RGAPSI, f. 475, op. 1, d. 15, ll. 130–134 1938; RGASPI, f. 475, op. 1, d. 15, ll. 117–125 1938.
38 J. N. Westwood, 'Transport', in R. W. Davies, Mark Harrison and S. G. Wheatcroft (ed) *The Economic Transformation of the Soviet Union, 1913–1945*. Cambridge: Cambridge University Press 1994, 176.
39 RGASPI, f. 475, op. 1, d. 15, ll. 117–125 1938.
40 Ibid.

groups.[41] GUSMP's purges follow a pattern described by Oleg Khlevnyuk:

> The Stalinist leadership always considered terror as its main method of
> struggle with a potential 'fifth column.' The cruel repression of 1937–38
> was above all determined by biographical particulars. The basis for
> shooting or dispatch to the camps might be an unsuitable pre-revolutionary
> past, participation in the civil war on the side of the Bolsheviks' enemies,
> membership of other political parties or opposition groups with the CPSU,
> previous convictions, membership of 'suspect' nationalities (Germans,
> Poles, Koreans, etc.), finally family connections and associations with
> representatives of the enumerated categories.[42]

Khlevnyuk's notion of 'biographical particulars' holds especially true for
GUSMP's Arctic scientific community: most trained as scientists in the Tsarist period and had foreign connections, publishing in international scientific
journals and receiving invitations to speak abroad.

The split between Moscow and Leningrad perhaps reflected older realities:
that of Leningrad's standing throughout the Imperial and Soviet periods as an
academic centre extending back to Peter the Great. While Leningrad looked
outwards, Moscow looked inwards. Throughout the 1930s, Moscow's intense
distrust of Leningrad was reflected in the targeting of GUSMP's scientists.
The Moscow-Leningrad rivalry was less about settling old scores and more
about ensuring the security of Leningrad in a period of increasing threats.

As war approached the earlier commitment to modernisation in the Far
North waned. There were urgent and changing priorities, particularly with
regard to iron and steel production and armaments production and this defence modernising was concentrated well south of the polar regions. As the
maritime route had not been made operational, it had to at least be controlled.
And GUSMP as a development agency was hardly in a position to carry out
a task which was profoundly a military one.

Modernising in the 1990s: Fragmentation and Pragmatism

The post-Soviet era of modernisation in the Far North was foreshadowed
in Gorbachev's Murmansk Declaration of 1 October 1987, which above all
highlighted strategic concerns. At a ceremonial presentation of the Order of
Lenin and the Gold Star Medal to the city of Murmansk, the speech warned
of the possibility of the Arctic and North Atlantic becoming the site for nuclear confrontation: 'One can feel the freezing breath of the Arctic strategy
of the US Pentagon …militarization is assuming threatening dimensions.'[43]

41 M. Ilič, 'The Great Terror in Leningrad: a Quantitative Analysis', *Europe-Asia
   Studies* 52 (8) 2000.
42 O. V. Khlevnyuk, "The First Generation of Stalinist 'Party Generals'", in E. A. Rees
   (ed) *Centre-Local Relations in the Stalinist State, 1928–1941*. Basingstoke: Palgrave
   Macmillan 2002, 60; RGAPSI, f. 475, op. 1, d. 15, ll. 202–206 1938.
43 M. S. Gorbachev, 'Appendix 1 Excerpt from Speech in Murmansk given on 1 October

Among the new threats were: a new American radar station in Greenland which violated the ABM Treaty; the testing of US cruise missiles in northern Canada; and NATO's encroaching presence in Norway and Denmark.

The Murmansk speech reflected the pressures for a change in Soviet policy. There was a focus on Soviet security, but also 'a willingness to divorce matters of security from other affairs ...with an indication that dual use of the NSR may be acceptable.'[44] The USSR was willing to consider opening its maritime route and 'pool efforts ... inviting, for instance, Canada and Norway to form mixed enterprises for developing oil and gas deposits on the shelf of our northern seas.'[45] The speech even proposed an international conference of circumpolar states and the creation of an Arctic Council for facilitating dialogue. Modernisation was to include international collaboration as the late Soviet regime sought to reduce the threat of confrontation and recognised the costs of developing the resource potential of its Far North.

Subsequent to Murmansk in January 1990, Soviet officials sought contact with the Fridtjof Nansen Institute in Norway (FNI). An international research project, the International Northern Sea Route Programme (INSROP), was set up between FNI and the Central Marine Research and Design Institute (CNIIMF) in St. Petersburg and was later joined by Japan, Canada and Finland. The aim was a feasibility study of the Northern Sea Route for shipping between the Far East and Europe. International cooperation and scientific collaboration would be required to investigate the economic potential of the NSR, the exploitation of Russia's natural resources and environmental concerns of all circumpolar states. INSROP also investigated climate change confirming warming trends first noted by GUSMP scientists in the 1930s. The five-year project completed its work in 1998, having brought together Russian, Norwegian, Canadian, Finnish and Japanese collaboration. During this process the Arctic Council met to address environmental concerns for the entire polar region.

Unfortunately, by the mid-1990s, modernisation in the Far North had moved away from openness and cooperation and become increasingly fragmented and at times, anarchic. Control over extractive industries such as nickel, oil and gas concerns has meant uneven development and criminal activity on a grand scale. Lucrative profits have been made by a few Russian entrepreneurs-turned-oligarchs in some regions, while most of the wealth has failed to trickle down to other areas such as the gold and mineral-rich

1987', in L. Brigham (ed) *The Soviet Maritime Arctic*. Cambridge: Belhaven Press in association with the Scott Polar Research Institute 1991, 309; W. Ostreng (1999). 'The Challenges of the Northern Sea Route: Interplay between Natural and Societal Factors – Working Paper 167', Oslo, Norway: *The Fridtjof Nansen Institute, Norway; Central Marine Research and Design Institute, Russia; Ship and Ocean Foundation, Japan.*

44 A. Jorgensen-Dahl and W. Ostreng, 'Military / Strategic Aspects of the Northern Sea Route', *International Challenges* 12 (No. 1) 1992, 114.

45 M. S. Gorbachev, 'Appendix 1 Excerpt from Speech in Murmansk given on 1 October 1987', in L. Brigham (ed) *The Soviet Maritime Arctic*. Cambridge: Belhaven Press in association with the Scott Polar Research Institute 1991, 310.

region of Chukotka.[46] Not unlike the Stalinist era, the indigenous peoples of the North have been again marginalised. Given the complete lack of tax and property regimes state assets were seized – albeit crumbling assets – and then drained of their profitability by oligarchs such as Mikhail Khordorkovsky in 'the murky swamp of Russian legislation.'[47]

The regimes of Yel'tsin and Putin have had to take a more pragmatic view of modernising given the collapse of state enterprises, the lawlessness of the oligarchs and the impoverishment of the northern regions. Foreign investment was seen in some quarters as a panacea, requiring strict legislation in order to satisfy western companies. Recent foreign initiatives on Sakhalin, to take but one example, also illustrate several continuities with modernisation in earlier periods: the introduction of western techniques for drilling and transporting oil and gas; foreign training of Russian experts in prospecting, drilling and environmental protection; and western technology to process oil and gas production.[48] The recent praise by US energy officials for Russian oil transhipment complexes, welcomed by the Russian government eager for continued foreign investment, also illustrates the extent to which Russia seeks to work with the west.[49] This pragmatism has been tinged with lingering suspicions vis-à-vis the West, as seen with the *Kursk* disaster in the summer of 2000, when 'Putin's pragmatic policy … of working with, rather than against, the West,' which had benefited Russia's economic modernisation, was sadly not evident.[50]

Costs of Post-Soviet Modernisation: The Far North of the 1990s

The costs of modernisation at the end of the 20th century were in large measure related to the legacies of the Stalinist era of the 1930s. A Russian journalist starkly summed up that legacy: 'The north was developed not by economic considerations but by ideological ones … Conquering the north was a feature of the Soviet man. And what we see now is the payment.'[51] The large industrial complexes and urban centres in the North – all begun in the 1930s – have become increasingly difficult to sustain. The state-owned industrial complexes such as Noril'sk and Vorkuta have left enormous human and environmental costs, and the reality of the 1990s is the grim picture described by a longstanding Russian Arctic watcher, James Meek:

46 M. R. Gordon, *New York Times* Forsaken in Russia's Arctic: 9 Million Stranded Workers, 6 January 1999.

47 A. Brown, 'Evaluating Russia's Democratization', in A. Brown (ed) *Contemporary Russian Politics*. Oxford: Oxford University Press 2001, 562.

48 A. Panteleyev (2003). 'Drilling Begins on Sakhalin-1 Oil Project in Russian Far East', Moscow: *BBC Monitoring International Reports*.

49 K. Yekaterina (2003). 'US Specialists Praise Russian Oil Transshipment Complexes', Moscow: *ITAR-TASS News Agency*.

50 P. Truscott, *Kursk: Russia's Lost Pride*. London: Simon and Schuster 2002, 195, 197.

51 S. L. Myers, *New York Times* Siberians Tell Moscow: Like It or Not, It's Home.

> Whether it is the miners in Vorkuta being paid in sandwiches, or the former slave labour camp inmates, now pensioners, who are still economic prisoners in Noril'sk sixty years after the Soviets kidnapped them from western Ukraine, or the alcoholism and tuberculosis among the native Evenks … or the gold mine which doesn't receive its subsidies …. There are too many reasons to be miserable in the Russian north.[52]

Fiona Hill and Clifford Gaddy of the Brookings Institution argue that the Russian North is simply unsustainable, overpopulated and in need of transformation. However, their proposed strategy of *de*population promotes a highly insensitive and patronising policy of modernisation that fails to take account of the plight of the older generation who arrived during the Stalinist era or in the boom of the 1950s, and who intend to stay – sandwiches or not.[53]

Some costs of modernising are a direct consequence of the transition to a market economy in the 1990s. The industrial closures and rising unemployment have been predominant features of modernisation in remote towns such as Noril'sk. The workforce in Noril'sk was cut by half in 1997 when one of Russia wealthy oligarchs Vladimir O. Potanin purchased its mines and factories.[54] In turn many of the city's services were forced to close. Yet the irony of a free-market economy is that while the majority lack basic services, there has been an influx of younger workers seeking the few jobs with the relatively higher salaries at Noril'sk Nickel; the company pays $900 compared to the national average of $150, and new cafes and clubs have even opened up.[55]

There are other costs associated with the collapse of the Soviet Union. With the transition came expectations that life in the Far North would improve. Such expectations were found among the older populations who had previously come to work in the mines and industries, their children who hoped that the market economy would generate investment and jobs, and the Arctic indigenous peoples who had suffered throughout the Soviet era. There was then growing resentment as the profits from state-owned assets flowed out of the country to fund 'villas in the South of France, private jets and English football clubs' instead of funding improved health, housing, heating and transport.[56]

Conclusions

There have been important continuities in terms of how successive Imperial, Soviet and Russian regimes approached modernisation of the Far North. All regimes have recognised the potential economic gain from the region's rich

52   J. Meek, 'Reasons to be Miserable', *London Review of Books* 26 (13) 2004.
53   C. Gaddy and F. Hill, *The Siberian Curse: How Communist Planners Left Russia Out in the Cold*. Washington D.C.: Brookings Institution Press 2003.
54   S. L. Myers, *New York Times* Living Today in Siberia, 26 January 2004.
55   Ibid.
56   J. Meek, 'Reasons to be Miserable', *London Review of Books* 26 (13) 2004.

resources and Northern Sea Route development as a necessary corollary. All Arctic development has been underpinned by strategic concerns and modernising has included bolstering security in the northern frontiers. Finally, as each regime faced the same harsh challenges of the vast polar landscape it has attempted to control modernisation from the centre.

The Russian Federation has become somewhat more risk-averse than the Stalinist regime of the 1930s, largely because it has had to contend with new levels of accountability to the Russian public and to the international community. Rather than the confident display of utopian goals for the Far North, the regimes of Yeltsin and Putin have been more muted, and the Russian Federation of the nineties has been less confident regarding their polar development agenda.

Modernisation in the Russian Far North of the 1990s has introduced new debates. The increased foreign involvement in Russia's Far North provokes a degree of ambivalence on the part of the Russian Federation. While the international community is eager to bring Russian resources to the global marketplace and to realise profit in these lucrative regions, it also seeks to exact costs. Those include environmental clean-up, a pre-requisite for energy investment from abroad. Development also necessitates a degree of transparency in an historically secret frontier. The *Kursk* disaster was a case in point, as the Russian regime had to contend with demands for transparency from both its domestic and international audiences. Other costs loom. In a global marketplace, Russia needs to enact predictable tax regimes and formulate responsible legal regulations, and these have to be reconciled with Russia's security interests.

Whatever transpires over the course of the new century, the legacies of the Stalinist era and the Cold War necessarily remain part of Russian policymaking for the NSR and the Far North. The environmental and security concerns remain constraints on full progress in modernising the last frontier. In spite of formidable challenges, the Far North continues to resonate for Russians as it presents possibilities for future development. The final word might be given to Gorbachev: 'The main thing is to conduct affairs so that the climate here is determined by the warm Gulf Stream of the European process and not by the Polar chill of accumulated suspicions and prejudices.'[57]

57 M. S. Gorbachev, 'Appendix 1 Excerpt from Speech in Murmansk given on 1 October 1987', in L. Brigham (ed) *The Soviet Maritime Arctic*. Cambridge: Belhaven Press in association with the Scott Polar Research Institute 1991, 309.

STEFANIE HARTER

Modernising Public Administration in Russia[1]

Introduction

Like most of the transition countries, Russia has inherited a public administration and a civil service which were built on the principle of full
political subordination to the political structures of the Communist party and
the establishment of a parallel bureaucracy of Party and State Administration.
Despite considerable efforts which were undertaken over the last five years
or so to reform the organs of state bureaucracy, Russian state institutions are
still considered inefficient and corrupt.[2] The administration is perceived as
a 'half-abandoned structure, characterised by fragmentation and duplication
undisciplined by a unified chain of command.'[3] The majority of civil servants are neither sufficiently skilled nor motivated; many of the better educated and experienced civil servants have left the state apparatus for better
pay, more promising career prospects and a better reputation in the private
sector.[4] Thus, it is generally acknowledged that the Russian public services,
both the services themselves and their delivery, are of low quality. Services
are difficult to access, and obstacles range from omni-present queues to
artificial administrative barriers. Statutory provisions are complemented by
new non-statutory requirements and burdens.

In performing their duties to exercise state functions, state organisations,
institutions and their officials impose various paid services on individuals
and entities which are perceived by, and often sold to, users as lawful civil

---

1   The following text contains the personal views of the author and does not necessarily
    reflect the official views of the European Commission.
2   Cf. e.g. *Transparency International Corruption Perceptions Index 2004*, http://www.
    transparency.org.
3   Stephen Holmes, 'Potemkin Democracy', in Theodore Rabb & Ezra Suleiman (eds),
    The Making and Unmaking of Democracy, New York and London: Routledge, 2003,
    109–133, 124.
4   M. V. Parshin and M. V. Kirsanov, 'Sotsiologicheskii portret gosudarvstvennogo
    sluzhashchego', in Institut problem gosudarvstevnnogo i munitsipal'nogo upravleniya
    (ed.), *Reforma gosudarstvennogo upravleniya v Rossii: Vzglyad iznutri*, Moscow:
    Institut problem gosudarvstevnnogo i munitsipal'nogo upravleniya, 2004, 41–47,
    42 and 48.

services. Standards of state services, i.e. a systematic compilation of requirements for the order of delivery of state services by state institutions, are to a large extent missing. Equally, the standards which should apply to service delivery, such as being independent from individual services, general rules regarding the co-operation between state and citizen, and general applicability to the state organs and institutions, are absent.[5]

The draft federal law 'On Administrative Regulations in Executive Agencies of the Russian Federation'[6] in its March 2004 version clearly admits that among the major problems causing the low-level performance of state institutions are: excessive state functions, lack of performance indicators; an unreasonable high degree of discretion in exercising state powers; over-complicated and non-transparent administrative procedures which are closed to citizens and public service consumers; lack of clear criteria and mechanisms for effective internal control over the quality of administrative actions and procedures. This leads, on the one hand, to a low-level accountability of executive agencies and officials, inefficient performance, corruption, and administrative abuse, and, on the other, to violation of individual rights and freedoms, overburdens and excess costs for citizens and organisations.[7]

Since March 2004, this was supposed to change. Rather noisily, an overall administrative reform was announced, cutting the number of ministries, civil servants and administrative processes. Laws were passed, decrees written, name plates of government buildings, departments and directorates changed. What used to be a ministry, a state commission or a state committee may have stayed a ministry or became an agency or a service, or was merged with another organisation. Spring and summer of 2004 were times of troubles for many state employees: they did not know, whether, where and under whom they would work, and often did not receive their salaries since previous budget lines were closed while those for the new state organ were not yet opened.

Eight months after the presidential decree, though, Mikhail Dmitriev, a former deputy minister of economy, admitted that reforms did not even pass the Moscow Garden ring, and were implemented to a level of 15 percent of what was planned.[8] One of the problems was that one reform step was not completed, before the next one started, thereby locking in deficiencies and internal difficulties. One example is the intended liquidation of inefficient or duplicating state functions. A first functional analysis and assessment of the federal state apparatus revealed that about 1,200 of 5,600 analysed state

5   Conception to the draft Federal Law 'On Public Service Standards', Moscow, October 2004.
6   Work on the law was preceded by a Conception of the Federal Laws 'On Administrative Regulations in the Bodies of Executive Authority of the Russian Federation' and 'On Public Service Standards' which was approved on 20 October 2004 by the Russian Government.
7   Concept of the Draft Federal Law 'On Administrative Regulations in the Bodies of Executive Agencies of the Russian Federation', Moscow: Tsentr Strategicheskhykh Razrabotok, 19 March, 2004.
8   Vedomosti, 15.10.2004.

functions are sub-optimally allocated and thus can be either abolished, decentralised, privatised or transferred to other entities.[9] In order to do so, however, more than 300 laws and legal regulations were required to be changed. This change has started but is far from complete in 2006. Without a clear functional review and subsequent restructuring, however, it is not very useful to have the regulations and service standards for the newly created state organs fixed. Work on this step has already begun, though.[10] Individual regions have started reform processes and are at times even ahead of the modernisation effort at the federal level. Other subjects of the Russian Federation, though, are lagging significantly behind the restructuring of the state organs. This bears the risk of widening administrative, and hence economic and social differences within the country.

While the expected success of administrative reform does not set in as fast as expected, Russian reform forces analyse, *inter alia*, Soviet modernisation techniques for potential borrowing. Increased political centralisation is viewed as an opportunity to implement administrative reforms swiftly from above. The next section briefly summarises the reform process up to December 2005. It will predominantly focus on administrative reform, only lightly touching upon the equally important and closely related areas of civil service reform and state budget reform. The difficulties of implementation and their causes are lined out in section two. The recent turn to Soviet modernisation mechanics is assessed in section three, by singling out the Soviet space programme. A final assessment follows.

Administrative Reform in Russia

In general, five main areas can be subsumed under a comprehensive administrative reform: modernisation of state power, i.e. of the legislative, the executive and the judiciary; secondly, reform of the administrative-territorial setting of the state; thirdly, the delineation of the functions of federal, regional and municipal organs; fourth, the reform of the civil service and, finally, the reform of structures and functions of the executive. However, it is mainly the last point that should be understood as administrative reform in its narrow sense.[11] Intransparent state procurement habits, for example, or the untargetted allocation and management of public funds are less a result of the territorial delineation of tasks but are rather due to functional and structural deficits of the Russian bureaucracy.

Since the mid-80s, a number of industrial countries have initiated admin-

---

9   The internal Worldbank report, *Increasing Government Effectiveness*, Moscow: Worldbank 2004, mentions that a meeting of the Commission for Administrative Reform on 13 January 2004, singled out 800 state functions as being redundant, 250 as duplicating and another 500 functions as being too broadly formulated.

10   *Online Vremya Novostei*, No. 194, 22 October 2004.

11   A. V. Sharov, 'Ob osnovnykh elementakh administrativnoi reformy', *Reforma gosudarstvennogo upravleniya v Rossii,* 5–13, 5.

istrative reforms. The scope and impact of these reforms has varied widely. While some countries undertook to remedy punctual short-comings, such as, e.g. the Netherlands, others have embarked on an all encompassing reform path, such as, e.g. Brazil.[12] However, despite the variety of objectives, countries with different traditions, organisational cultures and economies have adopted public sector reforms.[13] In Russia, an all-encompassing reform of the public sector is perceived as being indispensable to accompany the wide-ranging changes in the economic, social, and political environment of the country. A functioning bureaucracy is a prerequisite to implementing reforms in the health, education and utilities sector. Reforms of local self-government, the pension system, and the housing system rely directly on a knowledgeable and professional state administration. Policies cannot be implemented by a state administration that is unfamiliar with modern administrative management techniques and is, in addition, badly equipped with information, data, and communication technologies. The asymmetric relationship between state regulators and the subjects of state regulation, expressed by the lack of complaint and sanctioning mechanisms has to be overcome in order to reach the objectives formulated by those proponents of administrative reform,[14] whose conviction follows Schumpeter's dictum that a professional bureaucracy is crucial for a democratic society to develop or preserve itself. "Democratic government in modern industrial society must be able to command (...) the services of a well-trained bureaucracy (...) endowed with a strong sense of duty (...)."[15]

Common to most public sector reform programmes, in Russia and elsewhere, is the aim that the government becomes more accountable. Therefore, emphasis is placed on outcome criteria – efficiency, effectiveness and public satisfaction – which shall complement criteria such as process consistency, rule-adherence, and detailed hierarchical control. In Russia, performance-orientation is stressed, for example, in the mid-term performance-oriented budgeting approach, which is currently implemented – albeit with great difficulty – in the Russian executive.[16] The current strategy for implementing administrative reform in the Russian Federation is a mix of three different approaches which are reflected in the different policy measures taken by the president and the government:

12 Nick Manning and Neil Parison (2003), *International Public Administration Reform: Implications for the Russian Federation,*, Worldbank: Poverty Reduction and Economic Management Unit, Europe and Central Asia Region 2003, 6.

13 Ezra Suleiman, *Dismantling Democratic States*, Princeton and Oxford: Princeton University Press 2003, 121.

14 Mikhail Dmitriev, *DFID conference 'Realizatsiya administrativnoi reformy v 2006–2008 godakh na federal'nom i regional'nom urovnakh'*, 17 February 2006, Moscow.

15 Joseph Schumpeter, *Capitalism, Socialism and Democracy*, 3rd edition, New York: Harper 1949, 206.

16 The relevant conception has been approved by a government resolution on 19 May 2004.

1. Market-driven reform: the delivery of state services and the fulfilment of state functions shall rely on competition, prices and contracts. The privatisation of a considerable number of state-owned enterprises, for example, is foreseen up to 2008 and the number of state-owned institutions which provide state services is to be reduced considerably. The introduction of contracts, public-private partnerships, and the development of standards to make the supply of state services comparable are all components of a market-driven reform process.

2. Managerial reforms: the public sector shall rely on professionalism, skill and a public service ethic. Russia intends a broader role for public government but wants it with less bureaucratic rules and to be more recipient-sensitive. The idea is to manage the country and to monitor the country's economic, political and social progress through a well-educated, skilled and professional bureaucracy. The focus on training of civil servants supports the managerial reform approach.

3. Programme review: relies on policy analysis and evaluation to reallocate resources and redesign programmes. In Russia, federal programmes are currently under review and the transition from input-oriented towards performance oriented budgeting is another step that reflects this approach. Russia envisions a state that produces the desired social outcome within resource constraints and which designs its federal programmes to focus exactly on resources and outcomes.[17]

The first plans to reform the Russian administration were already developed in 2000. Since then, a range of official documents appeared which have prepared and complemented the current reform steps: in April 2002, and later in November 2002, the Russian government adopted a strategy for civil service reform which was published by Presidential Decree "On the Federal Programme 'Reform of the Civil Service of the Russian Federation 2003–2005'" (hereinafter 'Federal Programme').[18] This medium-term Federal Programme lined out a set of measures aimed at improving the legal, organisational, financial, and methodological framework of the civil service of the Russian Federation for the period 2003–2005. However, the relevant subordinate legislation, implementation mechanisms, and the financial means to implement the reform proposals proved to be insufficient which is why no immediate impact could be felt after the publication of the policy papers. An additional decree was signed on 23 July 2003, setting out the priorities for administrative reform for 2003–2004. It reflected a broader conception of administrative reform and put emphasis on the re-definition of government functions and a review of the structure of the federal government itself. The elimination of excess government functions and the reduction of state interference in the economy was also foreseen.[19]

17 For the categorisation of reforms see e.g. Alan Altshuler 'Public Innovation and Political Incentives', in *Innovation in American Government Programme at Harvard University, John F. Kennedy School of Government*, fall 1997, 1st Paper, 13.
18 *Presidential Decree No. 1336*, 19 November 2002.
19 *Presidential Decree No. 824 "O merakh po sovershenstvovaniyu gosudarvstennogo*

In November 2003, the Russian government started to reform the budget process. In accordance with the 'Conception of performance-oriented budgeting', adopted by the government in May 2004, the main principle guiding the future work of the state organs shall be the management-by-results and the state's main task shall consist in the delivery of concrete results. Under the aegis of the "Government Commission to Enhance the Effectiveness of Budget Expenditure", the so-called Zhukov Commission, the government plans to formulate the 2006 budget already following the new performance-oriented principle. In order to implement these principles into practice, though a strict and transparent system of objectives and indicators for the activity of each ministry, institution and department has to be established which is directed towards the fulfilment of the institution's mission. Such a system shall not only increase the possibility of monitoring the government's activities and the activities of individual bureaucrats on a permanent basis but also improve the transparency of the state apparatus as a whole. In August 2004, and again in August 2005, all federal organs were required to submit their proposed indicators to the government. This exercise was very difficult, in view of the fact that not all internal charters (*polozehniya*) for the individual ministries, agencies and services were approved, and consequently, the functions and tasks were not yet fixed. Unsurprisingly, a number of institutions refused to take responsibility for some developments and plans as reflected in the proposed indicators. By December 2005 it seemed that the political will to support this transition weakened.

On 9 March 2004, the Presidential Decree 'On the System and Structure of the Federal Executive Authorities' was published. The Russian administration was transformed into a three-tier system. This reform was the first step in implementing the results of the functional review completed on a basic level by the end of 2003. The number of Ministries was reduced, and services and agencies were introduced. The line ministries were left with the task of redesigning their internal structure and defining the relationship with the newly established – or renamed – services and agencies. The number of ministries was, initially, cut from 23 to 15, while the overall figure of federal state organs increased to 72. Since the process proved to be rather dynamic and subject to political lobbying, by December 2005, a total of 18 ministries and 69 federal state agencies and services existed. Ministries are in charge of developing strategic objectives, legal work, and elaborating financial and human resource planning. Services (*Zluzhby*) will monitor and control policy implementation and agencies (*Agenstvo*) implement politics.[20] In general, agencies and services are subordinate to a ministry. Excluded are a total of 12 institutions, e.g. the Russian Space Agency, which are directly subordinate to the Prime-Minister. The President presides over five ministries, and another 14 agencies and services.[21]

upravleniya", 16 July 2004.

20   Sharov, A. V. "Ob osnovnykh elementakh administrativnoi reformy", 11.

21   Worldbank, *Russian Economic Report,* 8, June 2004, Moscow: Worldbank, www.worldbank.org.ru, Neil Parison, *Increasing Government Effectiveness,*

The expected results of administrative reform in Russia are summarised in the federal target programme "Administrative Reform (2005–2010)", which was elaborated in October 2004 and finally approved in October 2005. The results include, *inter alia*, an improved investment climate, higher living standards for the population, increased efficiency of state spending, facilitated social dialogue and a better managed state.[22] The 'Main guidelines of the Russian government until 2008'[23] signalled a correspondence of presidential and governmental objectives and suggested a broad political backing for reform endeavours. In October 2004, it was agreed that the commission of administrative reform will also deal with the State unitary enterprises and federal state institutions (*federalnye gosudarvstennye uchrezhdenie*) – of 25,000 of such organs which are on the one hand under state control or supervision and on the other hand are involved in commercial activities, only 1000 unitary enterprises and 9,500 institutions will remain under state ownership. The rest shall be handed over to the regions or liquidated.[24]

Yet, more detailed work on "institutional reform", involves the writing of administrative regulations (*administrativnye reglamenty*), the enactments establishing instructions and standards for the performance of state functions. Administrative regulations are one precondition for making the reform operational. Ideally, they are formulated when a functional review has revealed the appropriateness of the new structure, functions, staffing levels and performance objectives. Otherwise weaknesses are locked into the new system and are difficult to eradicate. The subsequent establishment of additional ministries in case of political emergencies (such as the creation of the Ministry of Nationalities and Regional Affairs in September 2004, after the hostage taking of Beslan) or the division of the former Agency for Tourism, Physical Education and Sports under the Ministry for Health and Social Development into two agencies which are now directly subordinate to the government as a result of political lobbying[25] will definitely complicate the establishment of a sound administrative structure and make the operational ability of the state apparatus more difficult.

To ensure that citizens benefit from administrative reform, there are plans to overcome the lack or, perhaps, obvious shortage of clear-cut statutory standards of state services as well. So far, there are no generally accepted civil service quality and accessibility standards applicable to the entire nation. Exceptionally, some standards are implemented on an experimental basis. The Federal Migration Service, for example, announced in January 2006 that passports will be issued within a pre-determined timeframe. In selected mu-

Moscow:Worldbank October 2004, 8; Stefanie Harter, *Russlandanalyse No 36/2004*, www.ruslandanalysen.de.

22 *O federalnoi tselevoi programme "Administrativnaya Reforma (2005–2010)"*, Moscow, October 2004. The new version of the conception and the action plan can be found at http://ar.economy.gov.ru

23 *Osnovnye napravleniya deyatel'nosti pravitel'stva Rossiskoi Federatsii na period do 2008 goda*, 28 July 2004. See also http://ar.economy.gov.ru

24 *Online Vremya Novostei*, No. 194, 22 October 2004.

25 See e.g. www.prime-tass.ru, 19 November 2004.

nicipalities, offices will have longer opening hours to accommodate citizens' needs. However, officials are not liable for a failure to render a service, nor can they be brought to liability for a lack of timeliness, accessibility, quality or excessive burden in the rendering of civil services. The general prosecutor is the only state organ which can reprimand an official for misuse of office. The inability of citizens to challenge excessive administrative civil service requirements or burdens or poor civil service quality paves the way for corruption, improper administrative charges, and, subsequently, excessive expenditures for individuals and entities.

Beside the legal and organisational work to be conducted on administrative reform, Russia also intends to modernise the informational and communication infrastructure of the state. Some experts urgently advise the technological modernisation of the Russian state apparatus. Otherwise, Russia will find itself within five to ten years amongst the outsiders in a globalised world. Furthermore, the gap between the efficiency of the private sector and the state sector is considered as a source of asymmetry which hampers innovation, and thus competitiveness of the Russian economy as a whole.[26] It has, however, also been noted that investment into information and communication technology in the state sector has increased significantly, while the efficiency of state organs has either stagnated or even been reduced.

In general, there is no accepted methodology of measuring e-government in differing countries. In 2003, the International Telecommunications Union (ITU) included three indicators to measure ICT-infrastructure development which directly focused on the involvement of governments: 1. percentage of governmental bodies which have access to the Internet; 2. percentage of government bodies which have web-sites; 3. percentage of public officials who have access to the Internet at their work places.[27] Regarding the use of IT systems and approaches, the public service in Russia lags behind the private sector in the country but also behind other developed countries.[28] Although selected federal services, such as the Federal Tax Service, the Federal Customs Service and the Russian Agency for Patents and Trademarks offer interactive service via the Internet, the number of state organisations and departments involved in direct interaction with business and citizens is limited. Besides under-computerization, there is no government-wide Intranet to speed up internal business processes. No unified protected area for interdepartmental information and document exchange exists. As a consequence, "richer" state organs such as the Central Bank and the Pension Fund established individual information spaces with a high level of data security.[29]

---

26 A. V. Klimenko, 'Elektronnye administrativnye reglamenty', in Institut problem gosudarstvennogo i munitsipal'nogo upravlenie (ed.), *Sostoyanie i mekhanizmy modernisatsii possiiskogo gosudarstvennogo upravleniya,* Moscow: Epifaniya 2004, 128–143, 128–9.

27 V. I.Drozhzhinov, *E-government state-of-the-art in Russia*, Moscow: E-government Competence Centre 2004 www.e-govcompetence.ru, 2.

28 Ibid.

29 Ibid, 8.

As late as 2006, no structured approach to managing ICT development projects throughout the federal government existed to synergise on financial means. The Federal Targeted Programme 'Electronic Russia' and the Programme for Modernisation of the Federal Civil Service addressed the issue but did not make a real difference early on.[30] Nevertheless, the programme "Electronic Russia (2002–2010)"[31] is a significant step towards promoting informatisation. It foresees a total investment of about $ 2.4 bn. The programme was initiated by the Ministry of Economic Development and Trade (MEDT) in February 2001 and was intended to work on a normative basis to regulate the IT market, the implementation of new technologies into state and private organs, setting up an educational programme in order to increase computer literacy and the creation of a larger communication infrastructure. The conception of "Electronic Russia" foresees changing the relationship between state, citizen and business by, for example, extending the amount of information that the state makes available to society and business, also via the Internet. Subsequently, on December 26, 2002, the RF government approved the resolution "On the access of Citizens to Information concerning Government Authority and Local Authority". Draft laws shall be published on the Internet, statistics, as well as procurement tenders, as shall the formulation and spending of the budget and even results of the work of the Accounting Chamber and other control organs.

On 27 September 2004, Resolution No.1244-r of the Russian Government has approved the 'Concept on the Use of Information Technologies in the Work of Federal Executive Authorities until 2010', as well as accepting an Action Plan on the Concept Implementation. The Concept clearly states that a country-wide application of information technologies in the area of state governance shall raise the effectiveness of inter-institutional collaboration, of delivering public services to citizens and organisations and of individual and group work of government officers. The priorities in the area of state governance include development of information systems for raising effectiveness of (1) law-making functions of the state, (2) law-enforcement activities of executive authorities, (3) control and supervision, and finally (4) development of information systems for reducing administrative costs of the government apparatus and for increasing the efficiency of resource management by federal executive authorities.[32]

---

30   V. I. Drozhzhinov, *E-government in Russia, Year 2002*, Moscow: E-government Competence Centre February 2003, 6–9, http://www.e-govcompetence.ru

31   The first step to introduce the programme "Electronic Russia" (www.e-rus.ru) consisted of an analytical part (2002), where infrastructure, legal basis and the level of informatisation were analysed. Furthermore, the first projects within the realm of electronic document turn-over should have been scrutinised in that year. The second step (2003–2004) continues by, inter alia promoting a unified IT- infrastructure. From 2005, large-scale dissemination of information technology in the real sector will start. The preconditions for access to information for citizens will be set up and the standardisation of electronic document turn-over both within state institutions but also between institutions is set.

32   http://www.government.gov.ru/data/news_text.html?he_id=103&news_id=15377

Difficulties in Implementation

Successful administration reform is an amalgam of opportunity (country-specific conditions that may facilitate or retard reform components), strategy (policies and actions that set goals for governments) and tactics (methods used to mobilise support or overcome obstacles to reform).[33] At the beginning of 2004, with the election results of both the Duma elections in December 2003 and the Presidential elections in March 2004, the combination of all three components – opportunity, strategy and tactics – appeared to be conducive to reforming the Russian public sector. Vladimir Putin, already in 2000, backed administrative reform and continued to stress the political will to rid the Russian state machinery of corruption and to transform it into an institution that efficiently complements economic reform and provides state services. Experiences gained over the last decade, especially in the area of civil service reform, made it possible to devise a suitable reform strategy,[34] while the methods of implementing administrative reform were outlined.

In December 2004, state officials involved in the reform programme acknowledged that the effectiveness of state authorities was reduced after the implementation of the reform measures in March 2004 rather than increased.[35] Only over the course of 2005, the bureaucracy settled, albeit slowly, in the new administrative system. Superfluous or inefficient state functions were not eliminated as planned, and the system that state institutions can take over additional state functions or create new administrative barriers has not yet been abolished.[36] Some indicators were developed to measure both the work of the administration and the progress made in the area of reform. Citizens' supply with state services has not really improved. Responsibilities were not delineated, which bears the danger that duplication at the different administrative levels will increase rather than decrease. The number of civil servants at the federal level was indeed reduced by 24,000 civil servants, of which 2000 had left the federal organs and another 22,000 territorial branches.[37] However, over the same period of time, the number of civil servants in the regions has increased. New territorial branches of federal administrative structures have appeared, which increases the danger of duplicating the work of already existing regional authorities.[38] There are signs that on the regional level, responsibilities between regional and federal authorities have to be re-negotiated.[39]

33　Allen Schick, *Opportunity, strategy, and tactics in reforming public management*, paper delivered at the symposium "Government of the Future: Getting from here to there", 14–15 September 1999, Paris, 1.
34　Cf. e.g. Neil Parrison, (ed), *Civil Service Reform in Russia, 1992–2003*, Moscow: World Bank 2004.
35　*Vedomosti*, 17 December 2004.
36　*Kommersant*, 25 October 2004.
37　cf. e.g. "Reformu vernut avtoram, *Vedomosti*, 22 October 2004.
38　*Izvestiya*, 22.10.2004, http://www.izvestia.ru/politic/article560073.
39　Ibid.

A governmental report issued by the Ministry of Information Technology and Communication states that despite recent efforts to improve the equipment of state authorities with IT, levels of IT use in the Russian executive actually fell. The budget earmarked for introducing information technologies was reduced by 50 percent and amounted in 2004 to nine billion Rubles. Due to administrative restructuring, the gap between advanced and lagging state authorities has widened: 80 percent of all funds spent on IT were allocated to the ten most advanced authorities.[40] For the introduction of e-government, in particular, the lack of, or unclear definition of, a final objective, priorities and other selection criteria when assessing the projects of informatisation of the state and administrative organs appears to be an important cause for the inefficient modernisation of the governmental IT infrastructure. Weak unification and standardisation as a basic methodological approach for establishing an effective system is also missing – for both the introduction of e-government and administrative reform in general.[41]

The factors which hamper the targeted and efficient implementation of information and communication technologies in the Russian public sector are similar to those that impede the efficient implementation of public sector reform as a whole: functions of administrative organs and the division of functions within the organs are highly volatile and are still duplicated by various administrative organs; transparency and control of functions is weak, which is closely related to the fact that the activities of the state organs are insufficiently oriented toward the needs of the citizen. The high barriers between state institutions and administrative organs regarding information exchange in particular, but also regarding decision making in general are enormous, which means that managerial and administrative costs are extremely high. Finally, regional diversity hinders the development of a common administrative space. For IT, for example, regional diversity of computerisation and informatisation is mostly dependent on the economic strength of the region.[42] Closely related to these problems is the fact that the Russian Federation is still suffering from under-developed domestic legislative procedures and processes that govern the functioning and performance of executive authorities. Functions and objectives of state organs are not optimised, i.e. tasks and functions of individual institutions, directorates of departments are not aligned to each other. The legal regulations guiding the procedural aspects of the activities of the executive authorities are not systematic and often contradict each other.

However, while legal work is progressing at impressive speed, implementation lags significantly behind. Managerial and financial aspects of laws are often neglected. External control plays a negligible role. The first draft Law 'On the administrative regulations' did not include provisions concerning the relation between state administration and business and the

---

40 http://www.government.gov.ru/data/structdoc.html?he_id=102&do_id=171.

41 V. I. Drozhzhinov and E. Z. Zinder, *Elektronnoe pravitel'stvo: rekommrndatsii po vnedreniyu v Rossisskoi Federatsii*, Moscow: Eko-Trends 2004, 2.

42 Ibid., 1.

citizens. Rules concerning, for example, citizens' applications submitted to the administration, time frames for their examination and submission of the reply and consequences for the administration in case of non-compliance, motivations for the decisions adopted, access to administrative cases, right to be listened to prior to the announcement of an unfavourable decision, the guarantee of inviolability of personal data, were, in the initial state of the law, not foreseen.

Despite these difficulties, one should not overlook that firstly, public sector reform takes time everywhere and cannot be achieved within a year and, secondly, that some success was already achieved. A functional analysis, on the federal level, but also in selected regions, was conducted and the subsequent re-organisation was carried out. Ministries and subordinate institutions have formulated their objectives and have elaborated indicators to measure their achievements. A significant number of normative acts were prepared. However, change at the lower levels of hierarchy has not yet taken place.[43] Control of reform implementation is also only possible at the level of state agencies (*vedomstva*), but not at department or even individual level. Albeit monitoring and on-line control of each step within the administrative process and even to correct processes at an early stage – which would significantly reduce corruption – is expected to be possible in the future, legal, technological and human preconditions are not yet in place.[44]

In order to implement public sector reforms, Russian reform 'technocrats' analyse the suitability of, e.g. the Soviet Space programme, to borrow from its modernisation mechanics. Unlike the Soviet space programme, it was proclaimed, however, that today's administrative reform programme shall be a public exercise rather than be secret, allow for both positive and negative incentives and shall not rely on coercion, and be cheaper, due to the availability of new information technologies.[45]

Innovation and Soviet modernisation techniques: Implications for the Russian public sector

The concept of modernisation in contemporary Russia is rooted in Soviet experiences. Modernisation – here represented by Soviet success in space technology – extended the limits of the industrial sector, which was built up to provide the basis for military power and economic growth, and radiated into society. It demonstrated technological and scientific might and social progress. The Soviet space flight programme was a visible sign af the Soviet state's striving for technological and industrial – and, as a consequence, social – modernisation. Indeed, the space industry and space engineering were

43 *O federaln'noi tselevoi programme "Administrativnaya reforma"*, Moscow: Tsentr strategicheskikh razrabotok, unpublished ms, October 2004.

44 M. Dmitriev, 3 November 2004, Workshop at the Tsentr Strategicheskikh Razrabotok, Moscow.

45 Ibid.

those fields where the Soviet Union did not need to catch up and overtake the United States but felt at the technical edge of scientific art and engineering. Unsurprisingly, the Soviet space programme had – and has until today – an almost mystical notion. Equally, today's orientation towards technological achievements when looking for role-models for the modernisation of the Russian state also reflects a traditional belief in centralised, objective-oriented modernisation from above.

Russia has, since Peter the Great and on the model of the reforms following the Crimean War, demonstrated a pattern where the state acted as the main agency of change in society. Rivalry with other, economically more powerful states provided the stimulus for domestic change.[46] For a branch like the space industry, where even in economically more developed countries the state is the predominant actor in the area, the Soviet Union had for once an advantage – due to the organisation of its industry. The hierarchical and functional structures of the Soviet organisation of research and development (R&D) followed the structure of the governmental organisation. The concentration of power to arbitrate or to prescribe choices of economic, cultural and social development implied – at least in the short run – great efficiency in making decisions on R&D and the ability to quickly mobilise scientific and other resources for any high-priority task, as was the space programme in the 1960s and 1970s.[47] The inauguration of the space programme since the mid 1950s was, for example, reflected in the expansion of professional personnel, which has been rapid, especially concerning the number of engineers. In the space sector, the increase of engineers amounted to about 20 per cent in R&D, while the whole economy counted 11 per cent growth of the number of graduates employed.[48]

In the Soviet past, branch ministries – for the space programme, the Ministry for General Machine Building was responsible – controlled from above their research institutes (which were responsible for applied research) and their design bureaux (which designed and developed products, major subsystems, and production technology). Each ministry had its own branch network of management and operational organisations.[49] The organisational structure, together with the concept of planning technological progress, regulated and channelled the information flow. Furthermore, financial resources went directly and automatically to either the research organisations, higher education institutes or scientific branch establishments.[50] Ministries also had their own central standardisation institutes, which were again supervised by the standardisation and quality departments of the technical administration.

46 David Holloway, *The Soviet Union and the Arms Race*, New Haven and London: Yale University Press 198, 14.

47 Alexander Korol, *Soviet Research and Development. Its organisation, Personnel, and Funds*. Cambridge, Mass: The MIT Press 1965, 4.

48 Ibid., 229.

49 Stephen Fortescue, *Science Policy in the Soviet Union*, London and New York: Routlege 1990, 60–1.

50 *Finansovye Izvestiya*, 18 December 1997, viii.

Standardisation and quality control instruments were thus predominantly developed for a single branch.[51]

Geographical proximity also proved conducive to the mobilisation effort the Soviet Union undertook in its Space programme: 40 percent of the research facilities of the space sector, for example, were located in Moscow.[52] Despite the extraordinary concentration of research, however, a survey of the scientific potential in the Russian Federation came to the conclusion that research duplication was widespread in the past, which would not have been the case if scientific exchange had been possible on a wider scale.[53] The explanation for this remarkable outcome lies in the hierarchical organisation of the R&D process and the connected dependencies between ministerial units and employees. It resulted in a situation in which bureaucratic loyalty took preference over the demands of technological progress, which hindered cooperation between various ministries on both a sectoral and a regional level.[54]

The advantageous situation of the Soviet space sector was reflected in its superior research and scientific achievements. This was – besides the extraordinary financial and political backing it received – due to the exposed role of general designers who had direct access to the Military Industrial Commission and who were often members of the scientific-technical councils of the ministries and also some superior, mainly Communist Party, organs. In their 'political' function, the designers had access to more information and to fellow general designers from other branches than other researchers. They were thus likely to be, at least in theory, in a position to overcome administrative boundaries and facilitate inter-branch projects. Yet, the chief designer Korolev, who was the leading figure behind the Soviet space programme, was successful only as long as he had the political and financial backing of the ruling elite – which could also defend him from dominant military demands which focused on weapons only.[55]

The central planning system, which was so successful in mobilising resources for the development of a space sector within a short period of time, was, however, also responsible for organisational fragmentation and compartmentalisation, functional specialisation and organisational isolation of the various components of the R&D system. As a consequence, the innovation process in the Soviet Union was inefficient and its performance poor.[56] Knowledge generated in the various organisations was not systematically exploited in the productive system. The price system provided no incentive for innovation. Technological change was not customer-oriented. Produc-

51 Fortescue, *Science Policy in the Soviet Union*, 68–9.
52 D. Solopov, and D. Osmolovskii, 'Kosmagoniya', *Kommersant*, No.43, 25 November 1997, 44–46, 46.
53 *Finansovye Izvestiya*, 18 December 1997, viii.
54 Fortescue, *Science Policy in the Soviet Union*, 71.
55 James Harford, 'Korolev, Mastermind of the Soviet Space Program' in http://www.cosmos-club.org/journals/1998/harford.html
56 Julian Cooper, 'Innovation for Innovation in Soviet Industry', in R. Amann, and J. Cooper (eds.), *Industrial Innovation in the Soviet Union*, New Haven and London: Yale University Press 1982, 453–513, 455.

tion and R&D proved inflexible to adjust to new technological developments, hence, no feedback-loops increased efficiency. There was no banking system in place to channel financial means to the most promising technologies. No insurance system cushioned the risks attached to implementing product and process innovation. High costs and a waste of resources were the result of an inefficient production process. In general, only sectors which were generously granted material, financial and human resources, and which were exposed to international competition, like the space and missiles industry, could mitigate the effects that insufficient technological change had on economic performance, and in fact produce out-standing high-technology products.[57]

Thus, the Soviet space programme was indeed impressive for its short-to mid-term achievements up to the mid 1980s. However, even an exclusive and preferentially treated branch like the space industry had to face the by now well known problems of the socialist modernisation system, i.e. the focus on fundamental research created obstacles for implementing research results, an ill-developed incentive system for the institutions and engineers involved, a sub-optimal allocation of resources to jurisdictionally distinct but substantively similar research organisations, and, above all, the absence of lateral informal links and communication and realistic budgeting.[58] The lessons learned from the Soviet innovation system should therefore be carefully studied when attempting to borrow its mechanics for contemporary reform of the administrative structure. Especially the short-comings attached to hierarchically organised innovation and information channels, typical for militarised economies and societies, that appear to exert some attraction for today's reformers, may result in unwanted side-effects. Short-term gains are traded against mid- and long term losses and public sector reform might thus not prove to be sustainable, after all.

Assessment

Until recently, most of the literature of transition has left aside the organisation of the state and has neglected the intimate connection between a professional bureaucratic apparatus on the one hand and democratisation and economic modernisation on the other.[59] However, it has mostly been recognised that 'governmental authority cannot be exercised without professional state structures', and democratic legitimacy cannot be attained without a functioning public sector.[60] At issue is which role the future state

---

57 Stefanie Harter, 'The Military-Industrial Complex, Technological Change and the Space Industry', in: David Lane (ed.), *The Legacy of State Socialism and the Future of Transformation*, Lanham et al: Rowman & Littlefield 2002, 147–169, 148.

58 Korol 1965: 4–5.

59 Ezra Suleiman, *Dismantling Democratic States*, Princeton and Oxford: Princeton University Press 2003, 37.

60 Suleiman, *Dismantling Democratic States*, 279.

has to play and which will be the sources of its legitimacy. If the objective is to set up a democratic state, it cannot 'be consolidated without an effective instrument at its disposal and such an institution cannot be created by a non-democratic regime'.[61] So far, the concurrence of 'technocratic' and 'political' interests has bestowed the Russian public sector reform process with sufficient momentum to enact a range of legal documents and implement reform measures.[62] The technocratic supporters of administrative reform are oriented towards the model of adopting the practices or techniques of business management, or 'new public management'. They seem to have accepted a variety of values such as self-interest, competition, the sanctity of the market and respect for entrepreneurial spirit. At issue is the revision of government *functions*. Their approach is embedded in the debate of privatisation or contracting-out of government functions.[63] The aim is also to reduce opportunities for corruption by eliminating conflicts of interest. The overall objective of reform – from this perspective – is to strengthen internal accountability and to stimulate a system-wide focus on performance delivery. More accountability and responsiveness to society will thus contribute to the strengthening of the democratic state, which depends on a competent, legally based, accountable, and professional bureaucratic structure.[64]

A 'politically-guided' approach, by contrast, supports administrative reform through the building of a strong, centralised state and the strengthening of a top-down approach. Internal discipline is expected to increase the ability to better monitor and control the activities of state institutions. Subsequently, structural and social reforms will be implemented effectively in order to generate continuing public support for the current administration.[65] However, this approach is not necessarily guided by the wish to establish a democratic state, in which state activities are rewarded or sanctioned via regular elections but by the conviction that 'administratively weak states prove incapable of implementing reform'.[66]

Common to both strands of reform is, interestingly, the reliance on theoretical, technical, and, above all, legal considerations. This approach follows the traditional understanding of administrative reform, where it is often assumed that changing formal rules suffices to alter the actions and performance of managers.[67] Both strands are also guided by a linear understanding of innovation, i.e. following the sequencing of basic research, development of

61 Suleiman, *Dismantling Democratic States*, 6.
62 Worldbank, *Russian Economic Report,* 8, June 2004, Moscow:Worldbank, www.worldbank.org.ru.
63 Robert Denhardt, 'The Future of Public Administration', in: *Public Administration & Management: An Interactive Journal*, 4 (2) 1999, 279–292, 283.
64 Stephen Holmes, 'Potemkin Democracy', in: *The Making and Unmaking of Democracy*, Theodore Rabb and Ezra Suleiman (eds.), New York and London: Routledge 2003, 109–133, 119. Suleiman, *Dismantling Democratic States*, 304.
65 Worldbank, *Russian Economic Report,* 8, June 2004, Moscow:Worldbank, www.worldbank.org.ru.
66 Suleiman, *Dismantling Democratic States,* 304.
67 Schick, O*pportunity, strategy, and tactics in reforming public management,* 6.

procedures adjusted to Russian circumstances and then, finally, the implementation. Thus, the approach to administrative reform stands in the light of a long Soviet and Russian modernisation tradition. The prominent inclusion of research institutions into the elaboration of public sector reform concepts and laws, and the predominant focus on legalistic issues provide ample evidence for this approach. However,

> [t]he presumption [of traditional administrative reform, SH] is rooted in the command and control model of public administration, in which central authorities promulgate and enforce rules and subordinates comply. But a succession of failed reforms and new theories and evidence in business management, institutional economics, organisational theory, and related fields have driven home the message that informal rules and managerial incentives must be changed in order for a high-performance managerial ethic to take hold. Changing the formalities does not make much of a difference if the self-interested behaviour of managers sabotages organisational objectives.[68]

Furthermore, both empirical and theoretical research on Western innovation show that external and internal networks of information and collaboration are important for successful innovation and thus have to be changed or modified accordingly. Personal relationships at the formal and informal level are crucial and pluralistic patterns of collaboration are the rule rather than the exception. Informal networks play an analogous role to 'tacit knowledge', and due to the difficulties in communicating 'tacit knowledge' through formalised channels, the movement of people involved in the innovation process is equally essential to technology communication and development as is the movement of physical or written material. Such an understanding of innovation – and the changes in the Russian public sector under way present without doubt a large-scale and comprehensive innovation! – has to take into consideration the moulding of the respective national innovation system. In Stan Metcalfe's words a national innovation system is

> that set of distinct institutions which jointly and individually contribute to the development and diffusion of new technologies and which provides the framework within which governments form and implement policies to influence the innovation process. As such it is a system of interconnected institutions to create, store and transfer the knowledge, skills, artefacts which define new technologies. The element of nationality follows not only from the domain of technology policy but also from elements of shared language and culture which bind the system together, and from the national focus of other policies, laws and regulations which condition the innovative environment.[69]

68 Ibid.
69 Stan Metcalfe, 'Technology systems and technology policy in an evolutionary framework', in Daniele Archibugi and Jonathan Michie (eds.) *Technology, Globalisation and Economic Performance*, Cambridge: CUP 1997, 268–296, 285.

One of the major shortcomings of the Soviet National Innovation System was that it was determined by the weakest link, i.e. the low ability to provide basic consumption goods and state services at a minimal level of quality, reliability and efficiency.[70] This has still not been overcome to a satisfactory degree. Similarly, a structural coherence of the administrative system which would be capable of co-ordinating the complex processes of public sector change, but also facilitating the 'transition from each product vintage to the next'[71] has not yet been reached. A policy which aims 'at generating collective learning for cumulativeness in the restructuring process'[72] in order to provide state institutions that lag behind in adjusting mechanisms with an applicable body of knowledge would therefore be advisable.

The transformation of the administrative system of the Soviet Union therefore has to take into account the legacies of the past regime but also the permanent changes that occur in society, in the economic structure, in the priorities as laid out by the new government and the way these elements are interrelated.[73] Of particular importance for successful administrative reform in Russia is to increase transparency. It has been argued elsewhere that the focus on "state-building capacity" and deliberate reduction of transparency is aimed at 'increasing the public's ignorance of state action' and thereby inadvertently magnifying 'the corporate irresponsibility of public officials'.[74] Analogous to the Soviet space programme,[75] superior political importance *and* public support are the driving forces for successful mobilisation for the modernisation of any sector of society – even in a more centralised system. Public administration is the instrument by which the Russian state can strengthen or weaken its legitimacy. Whatever role the the state is supposed to play in the economy and society in the future, it has to be backed by a bureaucracy, which is able to implement policies.

---

70 Dominique Foray, *The Creation of Industry-Specific Public Goods: New Insights into the Technology Policy Debate*, paper delivered at conference 'The Economics of Industrial Structure and Innovation Dynamics', Lisbon, 16–17 October 1998, 2.

71 Ibid.

72 Morris Teubal, *Enterprise Restructuring and Embeddedness – An Innovation Systems and Policy Perspective*, paper delivered at "The Economics of Industrial Structure and Innovation Dynamics", Lisbon, 16–17 October 1998, 3.

73 Harter, 'The Military-Industrial Complex, Technological Change and the Space Industry', 158–9.

74 Stephen Holmes, 'Potemkin Democracy', 112.

75 *Literaturnaya gazeta*, 22 January 1992, 12.

JULIAN COOPER

The Internet as an Agent of Socio-Economic Modernisation of the Russian Federation

Introduction

The development of the Internet began at the very time when the USSR entered its final stage. While the first electronic mail was exchanged in the United States as early as 1971, the breakthrough that made possible the mass diffusion of the Internet, the invention of the World Wide Web by Tim Berners-Lee, took place in 1989–90. The domain 'su' was officially registered in September 1990, and was used at first for e-mail only. During the failed attempted coup of August 1991, e-mail played an important role in diffusing information about events in Moscow. It has been argued that these developments were not unconnected: the Soviet system, according to Manuel Castells, was unable to meet the challenge of the emergent 'information society'.[1]

The development of the Internet on a worldwide scale has been an extraordinarily rapid process affecting almost all spheres of life in modern society. According to the International Telecommunication Union, by March 2006 the worldwide Internet population reached over one billion, over 15 per cent of the world's population.[2] It has been a process in which national states have played a limited role. To a large extent the impetus has been provided by countless non-state actors, from multi-national businesses to individual households. It is striking that those countries in which the Internet has developed most strongly in terms of the number of users and providers tend to be those with liberal economic orders and governments which have

1   'The more communication technologies made the outside world accessible to the imaginary representation of Soviet citizens, the more it became objectively disruptive to make such technologies available to the population....Thus at its very essence, Soviet statism denied itself the diffusion of information technologies in the social system. And, without this diffusion, information technologies could not develop beyond the specific, functional assignments received from the state, thus making impossible the process of spontaneous innovation by use and networked interaction which characterises the information technology paradigm.' Manuel Castells, *The Information Age: Ecoomy, Society and Culture*, vol. 3, Oxford: Blackwell, 1998, 36.
2   http://www.internetworldstats.com/stats.htm, 1 May 2006.

a laissez faire attitude to the diffusion of information and communication technologies (ICT). This is confirmed by the latest Network Readiness Index: the world's top five countries in 2005 (of 115 included in the index) are the USA, Singapore, Finland, Denmark, and Iceland; with Estonia in twenty-third place as the leading former communist country.[3] From this perspective, the development of the Internet in Russia provides an interesting case study.

The traditional Russian approach to modernisation, as set out in the other chapters, generally involved deliberate action by the state to narrow the developmental gap between Russia (USSR) and the developed countries of the world. It also often involved the imitation of foreign, usually 'Western', models. But the Internet, by its very nature, is not an innovation suited to state-led development, and it is also global in character, not easily characterised as 'Western'. Given Russia's historical record, it would appear that the Internet presents a new challenge, a case of post 'modernisation' modernisation. This chapter is devoted to an examination of how Russia has performed in meeting this challenge. Does it provide evidence that post-communist Russia may be able to adapt successfully to the globalised information society of the 21st century?

The Development and Diffusion of the Internet in Russia

The initial development in the Soviet Union of networked computers leading to the use of electronic mail and then the Internet was the work of a small band of youthful enthusiasts in the 1980s, probably aided by the relaxation of the system under Gorbachev. The initial pioneer was the Kurchatov Institute of Atomic Energy, which developed a system for linking computers, wittily termed UNAS in contrast to UNIX developed in the United States. In 1989 this evolved into DEMOS, later to become one of the main actors on the Russian Internet scene. Another pioneer at this time was Relcom, Russian electronic communications, which again became prominent. In the summer of 1990 the first real electronic link was established by three individuals in Moscow, Estonia and Finland, launching long distance electronic mail. As noted above, in September 1990 the domain name 'su' was registered by Vadim Antonov, one of the early pioneers of the Russification of UNIX. By the end of 1991 the pioneer Relcom network was a reality and the firm registered as a joint stock company in July 1992. The official registration of the domain name 'ru' in December 1993 was the effective launch of what became known popularly as 'Runet', the Russian language zone of the global Internet galaxy.[4]

---

3   http://www.weforum.org/pdf/Global_Competitiveness_Reports/Reports/gitr_2006/ rankings.pdf In this ranking, published by the World Economic Forum, Russia appears in a lowly 72nd place (but 62nd in 2004), behind India 40th, China 50th, and Brazil 52nd.

4   There is an excellent website devoted to the history of the Internet in Russia: http:// www.nethistory.ru

As can be seen from Table 1, the estimated number of regular Internet users expanded rapidly from approximately 1,000 in 1992 to 500,000 by 1996–97, 1.5 million by 1999, 10 million by 2003 and an estimated 16 million in 2004. Taking the widely used indicator of number of users per 10,000 population, Russia reached 15 by 1995, 50 by early 1998, 100 in 1999, 400 in 2002 and 1,110 by 2004. Preliminary data suggest that more than 1,5000 per 10,000 may have been reached by the end of 2005.[5] In this respect, as shown in Table 2, Russia has far outstripped most other CIS member countries and from this viewpoint could be considered to have been successful, although Moldova has been catching up rapidly and, if data reported by the ITU are to be believed, since 2000 Belarus has forged ahead.[6]

However, when this performance is put into a broader perspective, questions are immediately posed. By 2000 the diffusion of the Internet in Russia in terms of regular users lagged far behind the three Baltic countries and all the ex-communist countries of Central and Eastern Europe. In turn, with the notable exception of Estonia, one of the Europe's front runners, and more recently the Czech and Slovak Republics, these countries lagged to a significant extent behind the most developed countries of Western Europe. Given the disparity in levels of development, e.g. in terms of per capita GDP, this could be considered an inappropriate comparison. In Russia today comparisons are sometimes made with Brazil, a country of similar population and overall level of economic development. Until about 1995 the Internet diffused at roughly similar rates in both countries, however by 2002 Brazil had more than twice the number of Internet users per 10,000 population. However since then diffusion in Russia has accelerated and the gap has narrowed. Finally, it is worth considering the case of China: after an initial slow start, Internet use had overtaken Russia's level by the end of 2002, but by 2004 Russia had regained the lead. Now India is also catching up rapidly but still has some distance to travel. The relative progress of Russia in relation to Brazil, China, India and some other comparator countries is shown in Chart 1.[7]

The measurement of Internet audiences is an imprecise art. Much depends on the definition of a 'user'. How frequently does a person have to access the Internet during a given period of time to qualify as a user? For this reason, estimates of the scale of the audience made by different agencies can exhibit considerable variation. One method now becoming widely cited is that of Nielsen/NetRatings, now adopted for regular surveys by the Foundation for Public Opinion (FOM) in Moscow. According to their latest survey, in the autumn of 2005 there were 21.7 million users in all, 20 per cent of the pop-

---

5   http://www.minsvyaz.ru, 18 January 2006.
6   In the author's view the estimated number of Internet users in Belarus reported by the ITU, presumably based on information supplied by the country itself, are implausibly high and cannot be reconciled with data on other dimensions of information technology.
7   Russia's comparative performance in information and communication technologies is explored more fully in Cooper, Julian (2006), 'Of BRICs and Brains: Comparing Russia with China, India and Other Populous Emerging Economies', *Eurasian Geography and Economics*, 47, No.3, 241–270.

ulation aged 18 or over, defined as those using the Internet at least once in the preceding six months; however, users on a weekly basis comprised 12.9 million, or 12 per cent.[8] The rate of growth has been quite rapid: in autumn 2002 the equivalent figures were 8.7 and 4.6 million respectively.

There is an alternative measure for assessing Internet development, namely the number of service providers, or hosts, located in each country. This provides an indication of the extent to which there is domestic activity in the provision of Internet services and for that reason may provide a more accurate picture of the overall level of development. Is a country well-developed in Internet terms if its audience only views sites provided by providers in other countries? Again, there are difficult problems of measurement. In the early years when most providers used the registered national domains such as '.ru', '.uk' and '.ee' (Estonia), it was relatively easy to establish the approximate number of hosts in each country. However, with the proliferation of new domains of the type 'com', 'org' and 'net', this has become much more difficult and during recent years the measurement problems have mounted. However, the data provided twice a year by the Internet Domain Survey of the Internet Software Consortium (http://www.isc.org) are still valuable in establishing the overall picture, and they are used by the ITU in its database of telecommunications indicators. The number of Internet hosts per 10,000 population for Russia and other countries is shown in Table 3. This shows that Russia's lead over fellow CIS countries has been much more pronounced than indicated by the number of users alone, and more comparable with the less developed CEE countries, Romania and Bulgaria. In Belarus, where the Internet is subject to state control, the number of hosts now lags far behind Russia, but Moldova and Ukraine are beginning to catch up. The table once again shows the extraordinary strength of Estonia, and the fact that Russia was on a similar level to Brazil until about 1998, since when the latter has forged ahead (see Chart 2). China's position vis-a-vis Russia is put into perspective: the Internet in China, subject to state control, has been much less successful as a provider than in terms of use, and in the number of hosts per 10,000 people has now been overtaken by India.

In considering the diffusion of the Internet, two elements of infrastructure are important. Firstly, the level of development of telecommunications in general. Space does not permit detailed consideration of this dimension, but Russia does still lag considerably behind most West European countries in the provision of telephone land lines and sets. Internet delivery via mobile phone is still at an early stage, but here also, notwithstanding a very rapid rate of diffusion, Russia, while leading in the CIS, until 2002 lagged far behind the Baltic and CEE countries in terms of the number of mobile phone subscribers per 100 people (see Table 5). In this respect, Russia also began to lag behind not only Brazil, but China. However, very rapid diffusion of mobile phones in recent years has produced a marked improvement in Russia's relative standing (see Chart 3).

---

8   http://bd.fom.ru/report/map/projects/internet/internet13/d051060 ('Internet v Rossii', issue 13, Autumn 2005).

Another important enabling technology is the personal computer (Table 4). The level of Internet use in a country does relate quite closely to the number of PCs available, both at places of work and, for mass diffusion, at home. In this respect Russia is relatively strong, by number of PCs per 1,000 people far ahead of other CIS members and not far behind CEE countries. Indeed, by this indicator alone, Russia still leads Brazil and runs far ahead of China. However, a relatively large share of the total stock of PCs are in use at places of work and study; the further diffusion on the Internet in Russia depends now on the rate of growth of home ownership of computers and the rapidity with which they can be linked by modem to the network. In another respect, Russia's lag behind leading nations is chronic: broadband provision is only at a very early stage and the proportion of Internet users with broadband access is now substantially less than in Brazil and China.

That there may now be technical and social obstacles to further rapid growth of the Internet audience has been hinted by Russian analysts in recent months. According to Petr Zalesskii, director of 'Komkon-media', a leading Internet analytical centre, there is evidence of a slowdown in the rate of growth in large and medium sized towns. He believes that here the majority of those wanting to get on line, given the present state of the technological possibilities of Internet access and the prevailing tariffs, have probably done so.[9] If true, this means that future progress may be heavily dependent on improvements to the telecommunications infrastructure, including the provision of broadband access, and rising incomes of the urban population.

The Demographics of the Internet in Russia

In the early period of Internet development in Russia, users were predominantly male, young, highly educated and likely to live in Moscow or St Petersburg. It was this same social group that was responsible for the creation of the first Internet Service Providers and such companies as Relcom, Demos and Rambler. However, over time the Internet audience has broaden, both socially and geographically and, as Castells has observed, in this respect Russia is following the same path of development, although with some delay, as the United States and other high income countries.[10] The latest FOM survey, autumn 2005, revealed the following demographics.[11] Taking the total audience of 21.7 million, 57 per cent were male; 43 per cent female. In this respect Russia is catching up with Western Europe: in May 2003 women accounted for 45 per cent of the total UK Internet audience and 41 per cent of the German, but 51 per cent of the audience of the USA.[12] Unfortunately,

9   http://www.ng.ru/internet, 21 March 2003.
10 Castells (2001), 254–5. See also Manuel Castells and Emma Kiselyova, *Russia and the Network Society*, 1998.
11 http:// bd.fom.ru/report/map/projects/internet/internet13/d051060 ('Internet v Rossii', issue 13, Autumn 2005).
12 http://www.nielsen-netratings.com, 24 June 2003.

the FOM survey ignores the under eighteens (now experiencing rapid Internet growth in developed countries), but the audience is still predominantly young: 40 per cent 18–24 years of age, 27 per cent 25–34; 18 per cent 35–44; 12 per cent 45–54 and 3 per cent over 55. This means that almost 45 per cent of 18 to 24 year olds were Internet users but only 2 per cent of the over 55s; however, for those resident in the city of Moscow, the shares were 81 per cent and 15 per cent respectively. Russia is slow in following international trends: in the USA there has been rapid diffusion of Internet use among pensioners in recent years. Educational standards are high: 39 per cent of users have higher education and 31 per cent specialised secondary education. Forty-six per cent of people with higher education are Internet users, including 68 per cent of those resident in the capital. There is a steady increase in the extent of Internet access from home: 53 per cent of users in autumn 2005, compared with 32 per cent in spring 2000, but a consistent 41 per cent have access from work. Fifteen per cent of users have access at places of study, while about 11 per cent use Internet cafes and other public provision.[13]

The geography of the Internet in Russia is a topic in its own right; here some general trends only will be indicated. In the early years, Internet use and the creation of service providers (ISPs) was virtually confined to Moscow. Over time, provision and use gradually spread, initially to St Petersburg, then other important regional capitals, followed by increasingly remote regions and smaller centres of population. Now the regional distribution has stabilised. The FOM surveys for autumn 2002 and autumn 2005 both show that almost half of all users were located in the Central and North Western federal districts, with the Moscow city share constant at 20 per cent of total 16, while the North Western district's share remained at 13–14 per cent. There was strong growth in the Volga region, but the share of users in Siberia declined from 13.5 to 11 per cent, in the Urals from 8 per cent to 7 per cent, and in the Far East from 4.5 to 4 per cent. The Southern district shares remained relatively constant at 12 per cent.[14] In autumn 2005 half the population of Moscow aged 18 or over used the Internet and 29 per cent in the North West region, but only 15–17 per cent in the rest of Russia. The Russian Internet specialist Yurii Perfil'ev of Moscow University has undertaken a detailed analysis of the regional dimension of the Internet and has established a typology, shown in Table 6.[15] This suggests that the most developed regions, apart from Moscow and St Petersburg, are those with dynamic economic development, including the extraction of oil, gas and other minerals, some border and coastal regions, and some inland regions with relatively developed science and high technology industry. Some of the regions which Perfil'ev

13 Some users have multiple means of access, so the shares total more than 100. In addition, 18 per cent gain access through friends. The first Internet café in Russia, 'Tetris' in St Petersburg, opened in January 1996.

14 http:// bd.fom.ru/report/map/projects/internet/internet13/d051060 ('Internet v Rossii', issue 13, Autumn 2005).

15 See also Perfil'ev's chapter in I. Semenov *Internet i Rossiiskoe obshchestvo* Moscow: Gendaif, 2002 on the territorial dimension of Russia's Internet.

characterises as 'information deserts' give rise to no surprise, in particular poor and strife ridden republics in the North Caucasus, but it is curious to find in the same category regions in Central and North Western Russia, namely Orel, Smolensk and Leningrad oblasti. This is an issue that merits further research. The results of Perfil'ev's analysis correspond quite well to data provided in a recent Goskomstat RF report on the use of ICT, including the Internet, by organisations in Russia.[16] Again, this requires further research.

Uses of the Internet in Russia

Research into the use of the Internet shows that Russian practice is not dissimilar to that of other countries. It is used for e-mail (the principal use), as a source of information, in particular news, entertainment, contact with interest groups, job seeking, education, and commerce. The first newspaper to publish an Internet version was *Uchitel'skaya gazeta*, in March 1995 (*http://www.ug.ru*), since when almost all national and many regional papers have developed full or partial on-line versions. There are now many Internet only news publications and all the main TV and radio services have web pages. Specialist on line services for the business community have featured from an early stage, one of the best, *http://www.rbc.ru*, being established in May 1995. Diffusion to politics was quite rapid and now every political party and movement of any significance has its own Internet presence.[17] The first politician to create his own website was Boris Nemtsov in March 1998, quickly followed by other well know figures of a liberal orientation and then more slowly by others in the centre and left. The fact that liberal politicians took the initiative is not surprising if account is taken of the political views of active Internet users. The pattern has been consistent and confirmed by polls of voting intentions of Internet users. In advance of the 2003 Duma elections, for example, 20.5 per cent of users opted for the Union of Right Forces, compared with only 4 per cent in a national opinion poll taken at the same time, 15.7 per cent for Yabloko (4 per cent), 10.4 per cent the principal 'party of power' Edinaya Rossiya (20 per cent), 6.4 per cent for the Communist Party (17 per cent), a surprisingly large 5.9 per cent for the new Rodina bloc (1 per cent), and 5.2 per cent for Zhirinovskii's Liberal Democratic Party (4 per cent). However, the survey also revealed that many Internet users appear to be apolitical: 17 (7) per cent intended to vote 'against all' and 12 (21, including 'don't knows' excluded from Internet poll) per cent declared they

16 Gosudarstvennyi komitet Rossiiskoi Federatsii po statistike (2003). I am grateful to Professor Michael Bradshaw of Leicester University for making available this report.
17 For an excellent overview of the Internet and politics in Russia, see the chapter by G. Belonuchkin and E. Mikhailovskaya in Semenov (2002), 70–90. See also March, Luke 'Russian Parties and the Political Internet', *Europe-Asia Studies*, vol. 56, no. 4, May 2004.

would not vote at all.[18] This orientation is perhaps not surprising given the relative youth and educational level of the Internet community.

However, in some fields Russia is still relatively under developed, in particular electronic business. Before the financial crisis of August 1998 there was considerable optimism that a thriving e-commerce sector would soon be developed in Russia and some foreign investors began to show an active interest. The crisis, followed later by the collapse of the world wide 'dot. com' boom, put paid to these over optimistic expectations. In a quiet way economic uses of the Internet have steadily expanded in recent years, including Internet shopping, or B2C (business-to-consumer), banking, and B2B (business-to-business) activities. However, the scale of Internet shopping is still modest: a survey of Internet users in the first half of 2001 revealed that only 0.5 per cent of 'Runet' users had made a purchase on the web; 38 per cent bought books, 17 per cent computers and accessories and 13 per cent, CDs.[19] Since then the volume of sales has grown but there precise data are lacking. According to the National Association of Participants in Electronic Trade (NAUET), the volume of B2C reached between $1.0 and $2.6 billion in 2005, and of B2B $1.3 billion.[20] A major factor holding back the development of e-commerce is the limited use of credit cards in Russia – most payments for purchases made from websites are made in cash, frequently conveyed to the seller by courier service. As elsewhere, there is also distrust of the security of the medium. An inadequate legislative framework is also a factor. A law 'On the electronic digital signature' came into force in January 2002, but has proved to be unworkable and in need of additional measures for its practical implementation.[21]

Since Putin came to power, Russia has addressed more seriously the question of using the Internet as an aid to effective government, above all as a means of providing more timely and comprehensive information on the work of government departments. Putin himself has taken an interest in the Internet and held his first Internet conference, answering questions submitted by the public, in March 2001. On this occasion, he acknowledged that the presidential website was not the best and initiated a competition for its redesign: the extent to which the new site (*http://www.kremlin.ru*) is an improvement on the old is, however, open to debate. A major breakthrough was the adoption by the government in February 2002 of an ambitious programme, 'Elektronnaya Rossiya, 2002–2010', with investment over nine year of some $2.4 billion.[22] This provides for an extensive programme of measures for boosting the development of the information and communications technologies in Russia, including the Internet, with particular emphasis on

18 *Nezavisimaya gazeta*, 10 October 2003, 9. Data of Analytical Service 'VTsIOM': http://www.vciom-a.ru/press/009.html, 10 October 2003.
19 http://www.iworld.ru/magazine, (*Mir Internet*, no.9, September 2002). The typical customer was aged 25–34.
20 *Vedomosti*, 31 March 2006.
21 http://www.rg.ru, 15 October 2003.
22 The programme has its own informative website: http://e.rus.org

so-called 'electronic government', with the use of the Internet by agencies of government at all levels. By the autumn of 2002 all federal government ministries, state committees and agencies were obliged to have their own websites: this was achieved, although for a while there were a number of 'Potemkin' sites – first pages only with no content. Some of these sites are now highly informative and updated on a daily basis, setting a standard commendable in international terms. However, this government initiative to support ICT is being hampered by inadequate funding: according to the Minister of Communications and Informatisation, Leonid Reiman, actual spending on the government programme in 2002 was only 14 per cent of planned.

Russia has been rather slow in diffusing the Internet throughout the educational system. While considerable progress has been made in higher education, in part an outcome of a programme funded by the Soros Foundation, at the school level the introduction of computers and provision of network access is only now becoming a government priority. In November 2001 it was reported that only 2 percent of Russian schools were linked to the Internet, compared with more than 65 per cent in the USA in 1996.[23] The diffusion of the Internet within the educational sector is a priority of the 'Elektronnaya Rossiya' programme: the goal was to provide access to the Internet for all higher educational establishments and 60 per cent of schools by 2005. It is not know whether this goal was achieved as inadequate funding was hampering progress in the early years: as of September 2003, some 20–25 per cent of schools had connection to the Internet.[24] A major role in the school Internet programme is being played by the Federation of Internet Education (FIO), which is establishing centres in many regions for training teachers and also creating regional centre for distance learning. The FIO was originally provided with generous funding by the 'Yukos' oil company, but its activities do not appear to have been affected by the company's takeover and the imprisonment of its chief executive, Mikhail Khodorkovskii.

Problems and Limits of the Internet in Russia

Given the nature of the Internet, one of the most significant potential threats to its development arises from the state itself. The past experience of Russia is such that it could be considered a country unusually vulnerable to attempts by the state to control this new form of modernisation. In some countries of the world governments have indeed attempted to restrict and control Internet development. Approaches have varied, but typically governments have sought to maintain state control over ISPs, restrict access to certain providers considered undesirable, monitor e-mail and other traffic, or limit the access of citizens to modems or other enabling technologies. This applies to a number of ex-USSR countries, notably Turkmenistan, Uzbekistan and Belarus.[25]

23 *Nezavisimaya gazeta*, 6 November 2001.
24 *Novaya gazeta*, 11 September 2003, 19.
25 These three countries are on the list of 'Enemies of the Internet' maintained by the

However, in none of these countries have the methods used been as extreme as, for example, Myanmar (Burma), where the mere possession of a modem renders a citizen liable to 7 to 15 years in gaol. At various times fears have been raised that the Russian government will travel down the same path. In 1995 the FSB secured the adoption of SORM-1 ('system of operational-investigative measures') in relation to telecommunications, extended to the Internet as SORM-2 in July 1998. This measure requires ISPs to provide access to the security services in pursuit of investigations. However, by law ISPs are not obliged to install on a permanent basis the monitoring equipment required by the FSB. The Internet community in Russia has been very alert to the dangers of state intervention. The very first Russian language website devoted to social and political matters was 'Moscow Libertarium' (*http://www.libertarium.ru*), founded in August 1994. The activists responsible to this site, committed to liberalism, have from the outset closely monitored any threats to freedom on 'Runet'. With the accession to power of Vladimir Putin, fears once again mounted. However, he showed an active interest in the Internet during his brief term as prime minister, meeting with leading representatives of the Internet community in December 1999, and at the end of that year issued his first extensive policy statement via the web. No new restrictive measures have been adopted, although the SORM system remains in force. Just as Putin has on the whole backed the government's pursuit of a relatively liberal economic policy and kept the security interest at bay, so he has also favoured a non-interventionist approach to the Internet.[26] According to Balzer, citing an informed private source in Russia, in September 2000 at a closed meeting to discuss information policy, the security ministries argued for the right to monitor flows of information, but were opposed by representatives of the business, science, education and the Internet provider communities. They favoured open networks on the grounds that the country's economic development would be slowed by measures inhibiting information flows. Putin opted to keep the monitoring technology in place but not to implement it.[27]

The author suspects that the real reason why the Russian security services have done little to interfere with the development of the Internet is not any lack of desire to do so, but technological incapability. The USSR KGB appears to have been very slow in realising the potential of the Internet, and in the new Russia, by dispersed private initiative, it rapidly reached a scale rendering control and monitoring extremely difficult in technical terms. With a poorly developed Internet in a relatively isolated country such as Turkmenistan, state control is possible, but once the Internet has grown beyond a certain critical

organisation 'Reporters Without Borders', which monitors media freedom. Control is facilitated by state monopoly telecommunication networks and pressure exerted by security services on ISPs.

26 See the author's 'The Rise and Fall of Economic Securitization', in Edwin Bacon, Bettina Renz and Julian Cooper, *Securitising Russia: The Domestic Politics of Putin*, Manchester University Press: Manchester, 2006

27 H. Balzer 'Managed Pluralism: Vladimir Putin's Emerging Regime', *Post-Soviet Affairs*, Vol. 19, no. 3, 204.

point, it becomes virtually uncontrollable. In Russia today, the leading ISPs have foreign links and partners and any attempt to control their activities would probably result in a rapid transfer of their activities abroad, with no change in access to their sites for Russian citizens. This is a major reason why attempted control in China has had such a limited impact. In addition, the security services in Russia probably have inadequate technical skills in the latest ICTs. Tacit acknowledgement of this may be the decision in 2003 to establish a new higher educational establishment, the Moscow Institute of New Information Technologies of the FSB.[28] It is probably the case that the very dynamism of the technologies associated with the Internet, and the dispersed, disparate and mobile nature of the activities associated with it, that provide the best guarantee that the Russian state will not seek to control the evolving information society.

There are other real and potential obstacles facing Russia in seeking to narrow the gap which has emerged in the level of Internet development in comparison to more developed countries, not only in Western Europe, but also in the ex-communist countries of Central and Eastern Europe. But there is also now the challenge of keeping up with the rate of development in countries of a similar level of per capita income, such as Brazil, not to speak of Russia's neighbouring emergent great power, China. It will first of all be essential to maintain a high rate of growth of investment in the telecommunications infrastructure, and this will require an openness to foreign capital. In recent years the growth of investment has been impressive: according to the minister, Reiman, during the years 2001–05 the telecommunications market of Russia grew at an annual rate of 40 per cent, and total investment has exceeded $7 billion. One obstacle to foreign investment has been the Russian government's reluctance to end the monopoly of 'Rostelekom' in the sphere of long distance telephone provision. This stance arose because the military and security services insisted on guaranteed access to telecommunications networks in the event that new private operators were allowed to enter the market. The intransigence of Russia on this issue became an obstacle to early accession to the World Trade Organisation. In early 2006 relevant legislation was adopted and the 'Rostelekom' monopoly finally came to an end.[29] A second factor is the relatively unfavourable social structure of present-day Russia, in particular the modest size of the 'middle class', the section of society which in developed countries has been the central to a rapid take up of the Internet.[30] With rising living standards and continuing social change the potential Internet audience in Russia should grow steadily, but the signs of a slowdown in the rate of diffusion in urban centres hint that some limits to

28   http://e-rus.org/comments, 15 October 2003.
29   http://www.moscowtimes.ru/stories/2005/10/26/044.html, 27 October 2005; *RBC Daily*, 17 February 2006.
30   According to Tat'yana Maleva, editor of the study, *Srednie klassy v Rossii: ekonomicheskie i sotsial'nye strategii*, Moskovskii Tsentr Karnegi, Moscow, Gendal'f, 2003, in Russia today about 20 per cent of households can be considered middle class and she forecasts a slow rate of growth of this share (http://www.opec. ru, 24 September 2003, interview with Maleva).

the country's absorptive capacity are now being reached.[31] Finally, the available evidence provides strong support for the proposition that the Internet develops best in open, liberal and democratic countries, with developed civil societies. The still weak civil society in Russia with its hesitant development is a potential obstacle to further rapid advancement, in part because, if the state were to seek to control Internet provision or access, the forces able to oppose such a move would face greater obstacles to effective mobilisation.

Conclusion

The collapse of communism created favourable conditions for the early development of the Internet in Russia. A cohort of young enthusiasts was able to lay the foundations of 'Runet' with a minimum of interference from the state. By the late 1990s the Internet in Russia had reached an impressive scale, diversity and geographical spread, rendering it a not insignificant agent of socio-economic modernisation. In comparison to other CIS member countries Russia's performance has been more dynamic, but the rate of development has been such that there is now a quite substantial gap between Russia's level of Internet development and that of the Baltic, Central and East European countries, not to speak of Western Europe. Furthermore, Russia is now falling behind some countries of a similar developmental level and population, in particular Brazil. The example of the Internet indicates that post-'modernisation' modernisation is by no means impossible for Russia, but it also suggests that both the 'providers' and 'users' of the emergent 'network society' have no grounds for complacency that the rate of progress to date will be maintained. Vigilance will be required to keep at bay forces that may wish to control provision and access, and the best hope for future progress is the consolidation of a flourishing economy, democracy and civil society.

31   In this context it is interesting to note that in the USA, as of spring 2003, a comprehensive survey revealed that 52 per cent of users were categorised as suburban, 26 per cent urban and 21 per cent rural. (http://cyberatlas.internet.com/big_picture/ demographics, 16 April 2003. This survey also revealed another phenomenon of potential significance, a growing number of 'net dropouts' – the 17 per cent who once used the Internet but lost interest, up from 13 per cent in 2000.

*ables

able 4. Estimated number of Internet users (000)

	1992	1993	1994	1995	1996	1997	1998	1999	2000	2001	2002	2003	2004
RUS	1.0	20	80	220	400	700	1200	1500	2900	4300	6000	10000	16000
UKR	..	0.4	7	22	50	100	150	200	350	600	900	2500	3750
BLR	..	..	0.05	0.3	3.0	5.0	7.5	50.0	182	422	891	1607	2461
MDA	..	..	0.036	0.15	0.2	1.2	11	25.0	53	60	150	288	406
ARM	..	..	0.3	1.7	3.0	3.5	4.0	30	50	50	60	140	150
AZE	..	..	0.11	0.16	0.5	2.0	3.0	8.0	12.0	25	300	350	408
GEO	..	..	..	0.6	2.0	3.0	5.0	20.0	23	47	74	117	176
KAZ	..	..	0.08	1.8	5.0	10	20	70	100	150	250	300	400
KGZ	..	..	..	..	..	..	3.5	10.0	52	151	152	200	263
TJK	..	-	-	-	-	0.011	0.074	2.0	3.0	3.2	3.5	4.1	5.0
TKM	..	-	-	-	-	0.003	0.263	2.0	6.0	8.0	.	20	36
UZB	..	..	..	0.35	1.0	2.5	5.0	7.5	120	150	275	493	880
EST	1.0	4.5	17	40	50	80	150	200	392	430	444	600	670
LTA	..	..	..	..	20	50	80	105	150	170	310	936	810
LTU	..	..	..	..	10	35	70	103	225	250	500	696	968
BGR	..	0.2	1.7	10	60	100	150	235	430	605	630	1545	1234
CZE	..	60	130	150	200	300	400	700	1000	1500	2600	3100	5100
HUN	5.0	20	50	70	100	200	400	600	715	1480	1600	2400	2700
POL	20	50	150	250	500	800	1581	2100	2800	3800	8880	8970	9000
ROU	..	0.85	6	17	50	100	500	600	800	1000	2200	4000	4500
SVK	..	7	17	28	50	100	145	293	507	674	863	1376	2276
CHN	..	2.0	14	60	160	400	2100	8900	22500	33700	59100	79500	94000
BRA	20	40	60	170	740	1310	2500	3500	5000	8000	14300	18000	22000
GBR	150	300	600	1100	2400	4310	8000	12500	15800	19800	25000	34400	37600
DEU	350	375	750	1500	2500	5500	8100	17100	24800		28000	33000	35200
FIN	95	130	250	710	860	1000	1311	1667	1927	2235	2529	2560	3286

ource: International Telecommunication Union, *World Telecommunication
indicators Database,* 9th edition, 2005.

No Internet users .. insignificant number . data not available

Table 5. Estimated number of Internet users per 10,000 population

	1992	1993	1994	1995	1996	1997	1998	1999	2000	2001	2002	2003	2004
RUS	0.1	1.3	5.4	14.9	20.3	47.5	81.5	102	197	293	409	683	1110
UKR	..	0.1	1.3	4.3	9.8	19.6	29.5	40	69	119	187	525	779
BLR	..	..	..	0.3	2.9	4.9	7.3	49	90	432	899[a]	1628	2498[a]
MDA	..	..	..	0.3	0.5	2.8	25.1	57	120	137	415	[a]	952
ARM	..	..	0.8	4.5	7.9	9	11.3	85	132	132	158	798	395
AZE	..	..	0.1	0.2	0.7	0.9	1.2	10.4	15.5	31.3	369	368	489
GEO	..	..	..	1.1	3.7	5.5	9.2	37	45.8	93.5	149	423	346
KAZ	..	..	0.1	1.1	3.0	6.1	12.2	43.0	61.6	93.2	157	239	260
KGZ	..	..	..	..	..	..	5.4	20.6	106	302	303	189	516
TJK	-	-	-	-	-	..	0.1	3.3	4.9	5.2	5.0	397	8.0
TKM	-	-	-	-	-	..	0.6	4.6	13.5	16.6	.	6.0	73
UZB	..	..	..	0.1	0.4	..	2.1	3.1	48.7	60.1	109	41 192	332
EST	6.5	29.7	113	270	340	549	1034	1387	2721	3005	3277		5122
LTA	..	..	..	..	160	282	407	430	619	723	1331	4441	3543
LTU	..	..	..	..	27.0	108	216	278	609	679	1439	4036 2014	2809
BGR	..	..	2.4	11.9	71.8	120	180	283	528	746	803		1590
CZE	..	58.1	126	145	194	291	389	682	973	1467	2549		4997
HUN	4.8	19.4	48.7	68.3	98	197	294	597	715	1484	1578	3039	2674
POL	5.2	13.0	39.0	64.8	129	207	408	542	725	984	2300	2372	2335
ROU	..	0.4	2.6	7.5	22.1	44.3	66.7	268	357	447	1010	2324	2076
SVK	..	13.1	31.7	52.2	186	353	930	1112	939	1253	1604	1845	4227 2557
CHN	..	..	0.1	0.5	1.3	3.2	16.7	70.3	174	257	460		723
BRA	1.33	2.64	3.90	10.9	47	82	151	208	294	466	822	615 1020	1218
GBR	25.8	51.5	102.7	187.9	408	732	1357	2101	2644	3296	4231		6288
DEU	43.0	46.1	92.0	183.3	305	609	914	1753	3015		3392	5782	4267
FIN	188	256	490	1371	1676	1943	2855	3227	3723	4302	4857	3998	6300

Source: Calculated from International Telecommunication Union, *World Telecommunications Indicators Database,* 9th edition, 2005.

a. Note: these figures derived from the ITU source appear to be implausibly high.

Table 6. Number of Internet hosts per 10,000 population

	1992	1993	1994	1995	1996	1997	1998	1999	2000	2001	2002	2003	2004
RUS	0.004		0.44	1.48	3.94	10.4	12.4	19.8	22.2	24.0	27.9	42.2	59.2
UKR	..	0.097	0.001	0.016	0.25	0.70	1.05	0.88	2.03	3.30	14.9	19.2	27.0
BLR	..	..	0.10	0.47	1.29	2.75	3.89	5.72	7.09	11.6	4.06	5.03	7.01
MDA	..		..	0.011	0.014	0.56	3.13	2.98	4.03	4.00	6.05	33.2	31.2
ARM	..	0.035	..	0.46	0.46	1.16	2.50	6.08	7.00	6.21	7.50	5.47	4.99
AZE	..	..	0.012	0.021	0.040	0.45	0.57	0.78	1.97	1.64	1.40	0.69	0.43
GEO	..	..	..	0.11	0.39	0.76	1.43	1.74	3.46	4.18	6.15	10.1	12.4
KAZ	..	..	0.004	0.11	0.49	0.74	0.90	3.51	4.55	6.80	10.4	13.5	14.7
KGZ	..	..	..	..	..	0.32	0.46	7.29	8.43	9.14	11.8	11.3	11.0
TJK	..	..	..	..	..		0.12	0.84	0.45	0.48	0.47	0.11	0.24
TKM	..	..	..	..	..	0.018	0.61	1.94	2.76	3.35	4.16	1.12	1.21
UZB	..	..	..	0.015	0.053				0.11		0.11	0.41	1.11
		..				0.007	0.098	0.082		0.085			
EST	0.43	..	7.70	24.2	54.3				284		468	474	486
LTA	0.027		2.04	5.22	23.1	0.042	167	209	108	357	152	178	259
LTU	..	2.88	0.34	1.23	4.67		58.3	77.4	48.2	106	158	192	274
		0.23				109	26.5	38.4		95.5			
BGR	..	..	0.16	1.25	3.97	28.6			22.6		42.0	64.1	84.7
CZE	..		10.1	21.1	39.6	10.9	12.3	19.2	155	33.2	222	271	377
HUN	0.47		6.64	15.4	29.2		84.0		104	210	192	365	479
POL	0.41	0.019	2.79	5.98	13.7	8.22	94.1	118.9	87.9	168	170	204	
ROU	..	4.32	0.23	0.77	3.46	55.2	33.7		18.5	127	18.8	21.9	22.6
SVK	..	2.96	2.64	5.43	14.8	66.7	10.5	119.1	70.2	20.7	160	212	227
		1.27				22.9	40.9	44.2		135			
CHN	..		0.005	0.017	0.16	6.01		16.2	0.54		1.22	1.24	1.25
BRA	0.13	0.029	0.38	1.29	4.89	26.9	0.14	55.2	51.6	0.68	129	179	193
		0.96					13.0			95.7			
GBR	8.59		38.7	75.0	122	0.13		0.57	281		485	533	698
DEU	7.57	..	24.4	58.0	84.4	7.33	245	26.6	248	371	314	315	366
FIN	36.7	0.24	134	417	612		177		1022	294	2343		
						167	891	292		1707		2437	2215
		19.1				138		199					
		13.7				946		894					
		65.2											

Source: Calculated from International Telecommunication Union, *World Telecommunications Indicators Database,* 9th edition, 2005.

Table 7. The number of Personal Computers per 1000 people

	1992	1993	1994	1995	1996	1997	1998	1999	2000	2001	2002	2003	2004
RUS	6.4	7.9	11.5	17.6	23.7	30.0	34.6	37.4	63.3	75.0	88.7	105	132
UKR	3.8	5.7	6.9	8.3	10.0	11.8	14.0	15.8	17.6	18.3	19.7	23.6	27.6
MDA	.	.	.	2.1	2.5	3.9	6.4	8.0	14.5	15.9	21.3	23.6	26.3
ARM	.	.	.	.	.	2.4	3.9	5.3	6.6	9.2	15.8	27.1	52.6
AZE	.	.	.	.	.	.	.	.	.	.	.	14.9	17.8
GEO	.	.	.	.	.	.	.	19.3	22.3	28.7	31.6	35.2	37.8
KGZ	.	.	.	.	.	.	.	.	.	12.8	12.9	14.9	17.1
EST	.	.	.	.	68.1	96.0	114	135	153	175	210	440	474
LVA	.	.	3.1	7.9	20.0	40.3	61.0	82.0	140	153	172	188	219
LTU	.	.	5.4	6.5	27.0	33.7	54.0	59.5	65.0	70.6	109	130	155
BGR	10.5	11.8	14.2	16.6	19.1	21.7	24.0	26.6	44.3	46.9	51.6	55.4	59.4
CZE	24.2	29.0	43.5	53.2	67.9	82.5	97.1	107	122	147	177	206	216
HUN	19.3	27.2	34.1	39.0	44.1	58.0	64.8	74.7	87.0	95.3	109	126	146
POL	13.0	17.7	22.1	28.5	31.1	38.8	49.1	62.0	69.1	85.4	106	142	191
ROU	6.6	8.8	11.0	13.2	15.5	17.7	21.4	26.8	31.8	35.7	82.6	96.9	113
SVK	.	.	28.0	41.0	46.5	69.6	87.2	109	137	149	188	236	296
CHN	0.9	1.2	1.7	2.3	3.6	6.0	8.9	12.2	15.9	19.0	27.6	39.0	40.8
BRA	6.4	8.6	11.7	17.3	21.5	26.3	30.1	36.3	50.1	62.9	74.8	88.7	107
GBR	145	165	170	201	216	239	268	303	338	366	406	439	600
DEU	109	125	151	178	209	239	279	297	336	382	431	485	
FIN	129	142	159	232	273	311	340	360	396	424	442	461	482

Source: Calculated from International Telecommunication Union, World Telecommunications Indicators Database, 9th edition, 2005.

Note: There are no data for Belarus and some other CIS countries.

Table 8. Number of Cellular Mobile Phone subscribers per 100 people

	1995	1996	1997	1998	1999	2000	2001	2002	2003	2004	% total 65.3
RUS	0.06	0.15	0.35	0.5	0.92	2.22	5.28	12.1	24.9	51.6	65.3
UKR	0.03	0.06	0.11	0.2	0.43	1.62	4.42	7.66	13.7	28.5	53.1
BLR	0.06	0.06	0.08	0.1	0.22	0.49	1.39	4.67	11.3	22.7	41.4
MDA	-	0.02	0.05	0.2	0.39	3.17	5.13	9.35	13.2	18.5	47.7
ARM	-	0.01	0.16	0.2	0.23	0.46	0.67	1.88	3.10	5.35	25.9
AZE	0.08	0.22	0.52	0.9	2.34	5.44	9.38	9.75	12.8	17.4	58.7
GEO	-	0.04	0.55	1.1	1.88	3.88	6.06	10.2	14.5	16.6	55.2
KAZ	0.03	0.06	0.07	0.2	0.30	1.22	3.62	6.43	8.40	17.9	52.5
KGZ	-	-	-	-	0.06	0.18	0.54	1.06	2.75	5.17	38.7
TJK	-	-	0.01	-	0.01	0.02	0.03	0.21	0.73	2.14	35.5
TKM	-	-	0.05	1.0	0.09	0.17	0.17	0.17	0.19	1.01	11.8
UZB	0.02	0.04	0.07	1.0	0.17	0.22	0.25	0.74	1.25	2.05	24.1
EST	2.05	4.73	9.87	17.0	26.8	38.7	45.5	65.0	77.4	96.0	73.9
LTA	0.59	1.14	3.11	6.81	11.3	16.6	27.9	39.4	52.6	67.2	70.3
LTU	0.40	1.37	4.46	7.23	8.97	14.2	27.7	47.2	62.8	99.3	80.7
BGR	0.25	0.32	0.84	1.52	4.23	9.06	19.1	33.1	44.9	60.9	63.4
CZE	0.47	1.94	5.11	9.4	18.9	42.3	68.0	84.4	95.2	106	75.9
HUN	2.59	4.63	6.94	10.5	16.2	30.8	49.8	67.9	78.5	86.4	70.9
POL	0.19	0.56	2.10	4.98	10.2	17.5	25.9	36.0	45.1	59.9	65.3
ROU	0.04	0.08	0.89	2.86	6.05	11.1	17.2	23.5	32.5	47.1	69.9
SVK	0.23	0.53	3.72	8.77	12.3	20.5	39.9	54.4	68.4	79.4	77.4
CHN	0.29	0.55	1.06	1.90	3.42	6.58	11.0	16.0	20.9	25.8	51.8
BRA	0.83	1.5	2.85	4.4	8.9	13.7	16.7	20.1	26.3	36.3	60.8
GBR	9.80	2.32	15.0	25.1	45.7	72.7	77.0	83.3	91.4	102	64.4
DEU	4.55	6.72	10.1	17.0	28.5	58.6	68.2	71.6	78.5	86.4	56.6
FIN	20.1	29.3	42.0	55.2	63.4	72.0	80.4	86.7	91.0	95.6	67.8

Source: International Telecommunication Union, World Telecommunications Indicators Database, 9th edition, 2005.

Note: in 2004 the world leaders in mobile phones per 100 inhabitants were Luxembourg – 138, Hong Kong (China) – 119 and Sweden – 108. Leader for percentage of telephone subscribers as mobile phone users: Democratic Republic Congo – 99.5%!

Table 9. A typology of Russian Regions by level of development of the Internet, 2001

Level of development (% population using Internet)	Number of regions	Subject of Federation
Very high (8+)	2	Moscow, St Petersburg
High (4-8)	12	Krasnodar krai, Karelia Rep, Primorksii krai, Novosibirsk obl, Sverdlovsk obl, Khanty-Mansiiskii AO, Irkutsk obl, Kaliningrad obl, Perm obl, Kaluga obl, Samara obl, Rostov obl.
Average (2-4)	34	Arkhangelsk obl, Novogorod obl, Stavropol obl, Tyumen obl, Tomsk obl, Moscow obl, Krasnoyarsk obl, Tatarstan Rep, Chelyabinsk obl, Kamchatka obl, Magadan obl, Komi Rep, Vologda obl, Murmansk obl, Nizhegorodsk obl, Khabarovsk krai, Pskov obl, Sakhalin obl, Bashkortostan Rep, Kurgan obl, Buryatiya Rep, Voronezh obl, Marii El Rep, Tula obl, Kirov obl, Tver obl, Tambov obl, Kostroma obl, Udmurt Rep, Amursk obl, Ryazan obl, Mordova obl, Saratov obl, Omsk obl.
Below average (0.9 – 2)	16	Lipetsk obl, Altai krai, Sakha Rep, Orenburg obl, Ivanovo obl, Yamalo-Nentskii AO, Khakasiya Rep, Yaroslavl obl, Kemerovo obl, Belgorod obl, Ulyanovsk obl, Chuvash Rep,. Adygeya Rep, Vladimir obl, Kursk obl, Volgograd obl.
Very low (<0.9) ('information deserts')	25	Chita obl, Astrakhan obl, Bryansk obl, Penza obl, Smolensk obl, Orel obl, N. Osetiya-Alaniya Rep, Aginskii Buryatskii AO, Altai Rep, Dagestan Rep, Evreiskaya AO, Ingushetiya Rep, Kabardino-Balkarskaya Rep, Karachaevo-Cherksesskaya Rep, Komi-Permyatskii AO, Leningrad obl, Tamyrskii AO, Tyva Rep, Ust'-Ordynskii Buryatskii AO, Chechen Rep, Chukotskii AO, Evenkiiskii AO.

Source: Yurii Perfil'ev, *Rossiiskoe internet prostranstvo: razvitie i struktura,* Moscow: Gardarik; 2003, 249–50

302

Figure 9. Internet users per 10,000 population.

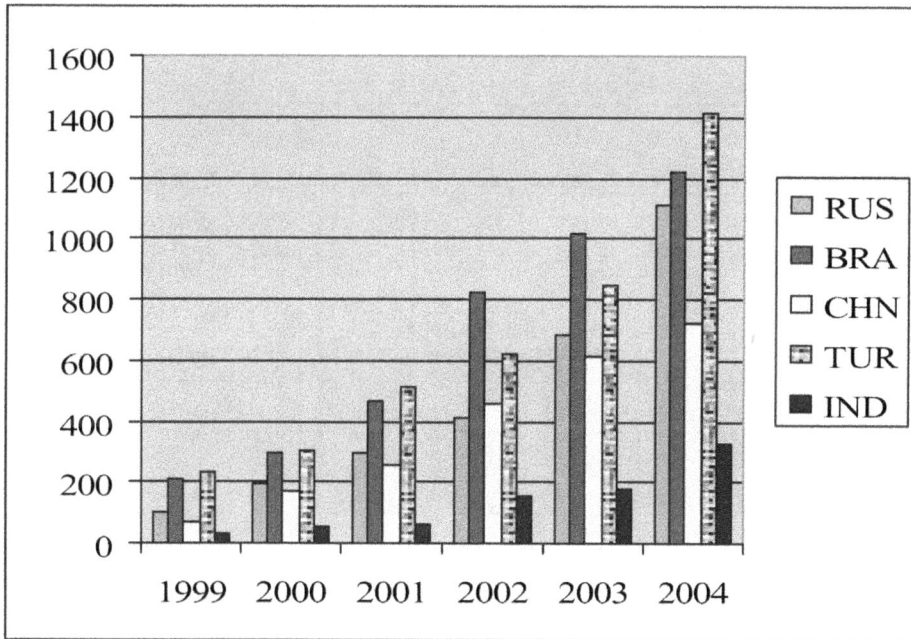

Figure 10. Internet hosts per 10,000 inhabitants.

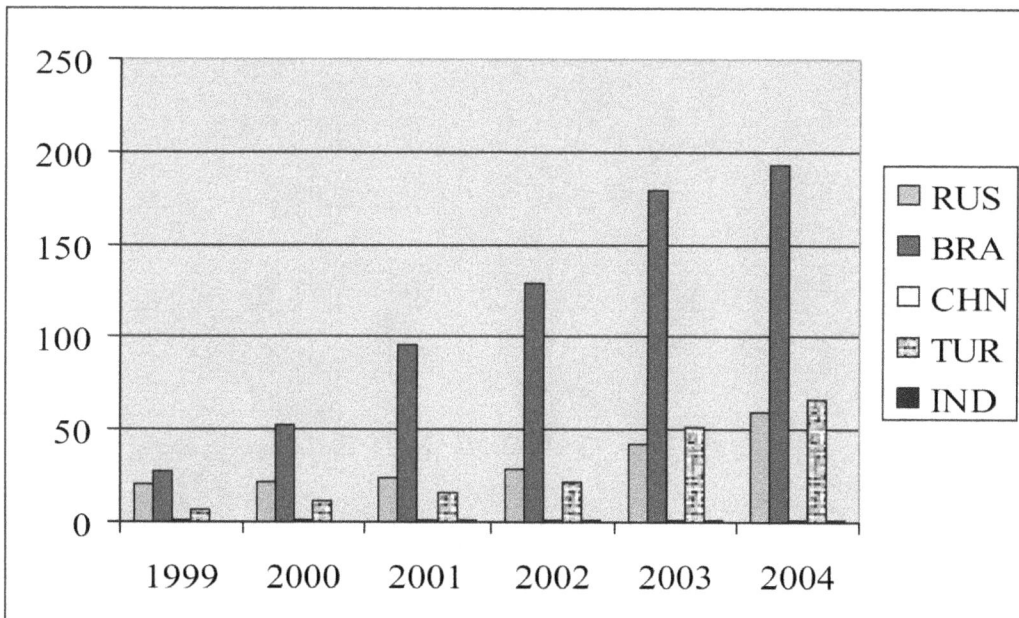

Figure 11. Number of Mobile Phone subscribers per 1,000 inhabitants.

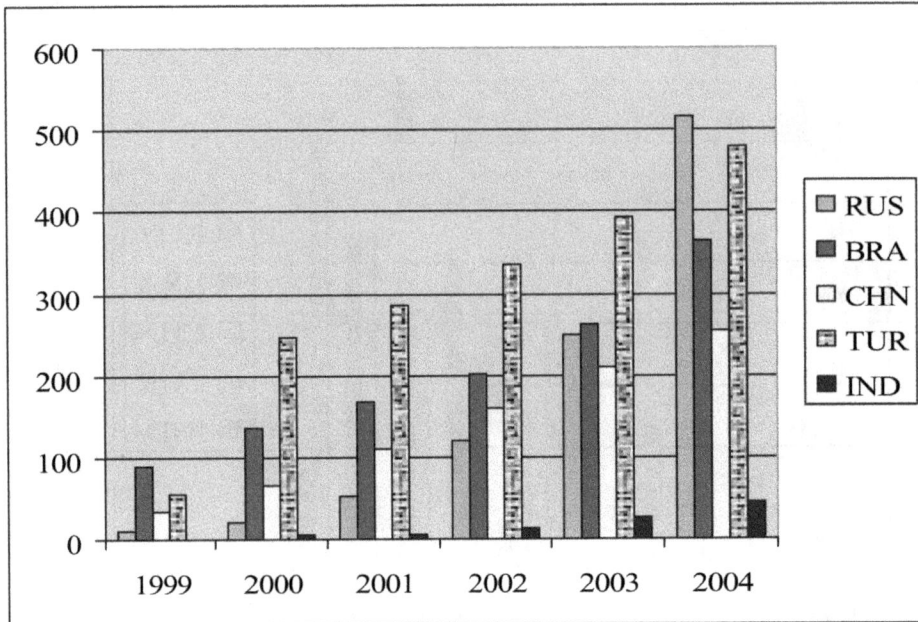

Bibliography

PRIMARY SOURCES

The Archives of the Ministry for Foreign Affairs in Finland, Helsinki (MFA).
Commission of the Finnish-Soviet Scientific-Technical Cooperation (STC).
Gosudarstevennyi Arkhiv Rossisskoi Federatsii (GARF).
Rossiskii Gosudarstvennyi Arkhiv Ekonomiki (RGAE).
Rossiskii Gosudarstvennyi Arkhiv Sotsial'no-Politicheskoi Istorii (RGASPI).

PUBLISHED MATERIAL

Aktivist, O. A. K. Imperializm na Polyarnom Severe i Interesy SSSR, *Sovetskii Sever* 1–2 (1932).

Alexander, G. and Nurina, F. (comps.), *Women in the Soviet Union*. London: Modern Books 1929.

Castells, M. and Kiselyova, E. Russia and the Network Society, Paper of Conference, Russia at the End of the 20th Century, Stanford University, November 1998b. (Later published in revised form, Kiselyova, E. and Castells, M. Russia in the Information Age, in Bonnell, V. and Breslauer, G. (eds.), *Russia in the New Century*, Boulder, Co.: Westview Press 2000.)

Chatham House Roundtable on Using Tax Administration to Advance Russian Statistic Goals: The Impact on Economic and Democratic Reforms, 17 November 2004.

Chislennost' i sostav naseleniya SSSR 1984.

Davis, C. Health crisis: The former Soviet Union, *RFE/RL Research Report* Vol. 2, No. 40, 8 October 1993b.

Decree, Ob Organizatsii pri Sovete Narodnyx Komissarov Soyuza SSR Glavnogo Upravleniya Severnogo Morskogo Puti, *SZR Sobranie Zakonov i Rasporyazhenii S.S.S.R.* 84:(1932), 828.

Dmitriev, M. *DFID conference Realizatsiya administrativnoi reformy v 2006–2008 godakh na federal'nom i regional'nom urovnakh.* 17 February 2006, Moscow.

Eijbergen, B. – Thompson, L. – Carruthers, R. – Gwilliam, K. – Podolske, R., Russia: the Transport Sector. *World Bank Policy Note* August 2004.

IMO, *Compte Rendu des Travaux de la Commission pendant sa Première Année de Travail, Procès-Verbaux des Séances de la Réunion à Leningrad.* Commission de l'Année Polaire, 1932–1933, Leningrad: Secrétariat de l'Organisation Météorologique Internationale.

IMO, *Compte Rendu des Travaux de la Commission pendant sa Première Année de Travail, Procès-Verbaux des Séances de la Réunion à Innsbruck.* Commission Internationale de l'Année Polaire, Innsbruck: Secrétariat de l'Organisation Météorologique Internationale.

IMO, *Compte Rendu des Travaux de la Commission, Procès-Verbaux des Séances de la Réunion à Copenhague.* Commission Internationale de l'Année Polaire, Copenhague: Secrétariat de l'Organisation Météorologique Internationale.

Increasing Government Effectiveness (The internal Worldbank report), Moscow: Worldbank 2004.

International Telecommunications Union, *World Telecommunications Indicators Database,* 9th edition, 2005.

Johnson's Russia List (JRL): (JRL 7186/1), (JRL 7233), (JRL 7462), (JRL 8170).

Law on the Presidency, *Vedemosti S"ezda narodnykh deputatov RSFSR i verkhovnogo Soveta RSFSR*, No. 17 (1991).

Narkhoz v 1979g 1980.
Narkhoz v 1984g 1985.
Narkhoz v 1989g 1990.
Narkomzdrav, *Otchet Narkomzdrav k 8-mu S"ezdu Sovetov*. Moscow 1920.
Narodnoe obrazovanie v SSSR. Moscow: Akademia pedagogicheskikh nauk 1957.
Narodnoe obrazovanie v SSSR. Sbornik dokumentov 1917–1973 gg. Moscow: Pedagogika 1974.
Naselenie SSSR 1983.
Nironen, E. *Teknologian siirto Suomen ja Neuvostoliiton välillä. SEV-kaupan tutkimusprojekti*. Tutkimusraportti 22. Lappeenrannan teknillinen korkeakoulu, tuotantotalouden osasto. Lappeenranta 1980, 5–10.
Nironen, E. *Neuvostoliitto läntisen teknologian tuojana*. Tutkimusraportti 39. Lappeenrannan teknillinen korkeakoulu, tuotantotalouden osasto. Lappeenranta 1991.

OECD, *OECD Economic Surveys. The Russian Federation 1995*. Paris: OECD 1995.
O federalnoi tselevoi programme Administrativnaya reforma. Moscow: Tsentr strategicheskikh razrabotok, unpublished ms, October 2004.
O federalnoi tselevoi programme Administrativnaya Reforma (2005–2010). Moscow, October 2004.
On Administrative Regulations in the Bodies of Executive Agencies of the Russian Federation. Moscow: Tsentr Strategicheskhykh Razrabotok, 19 March 2004.
On Public Service Standards. Moscow, October 2004.
O planirovanii razvitiya narodnogo khozyaistva SSSR. Moscow 1928.
Osnovnye napravleniya deyatel'nosti pravitel'stva Rossiskoi Federatsii na period do 2008 goda, 28 July 2004.
Ostreng, W. The Challenges of the Northern Sea Route: Interplay between Natural and Societal Factors – Working Paper 167. Oslo, Norway: The Fridtjof Nansen Institute, Norway; Central Marine Research and Design Institute, Russia; Ship and Ocean Foundation, Japan. 1999.

Panteleyev, A. Drilling Begins on Sakhalin-1 Oil Project in Russian Far East, Moscow: BBC Monitoring International Reports 2003.
Postanovlenie o sozdanii Glavsevmorputi – Ob organizatsii pri Sovete Narodnyix Komissarov Soyuza SSR Glavnogo Upravleniya Severnogo Morskogo Puti, 17 December 1932, SZR SSSR (Sobranie Zakonov i Rasporiyazhenii S.S.S.R.) I, No. 84, 828, Para. 522 1932.
Postanovlenie SNK SSSR i TsK VKP (b) - O meropriatiiakh po razvitiyu Severnogo Morskogo Puti i Severnogo Khoziaistva, 20 July 1934, KPSS v resoliutsiiakh i resheniiakh S"ezdov, konferentsii i plenumov TsK, 1898–1986 6, 170–175 1934.
Postanovlenie SNK SSSR ob organizatsii Glavsevmorputi – O strukture Glavnogo Upravleniya Severnogo Morskogo Puti, 28 January 1935, SZR SSSR (Sobranie Zakonov i Rasporiyazhenii S.S.S.R.) I, No. 7, 61–62, Para. 59 1935.
Postanovlenie STO – O Rabote Komseveroputi i Peredache ego Glavnomu Upravleniyu Severnogo Morskogo Puti, 11 March 1933, SZR SSSR I, No. 21, Para. 124 1933.
Pravda, Through Six Seas: Historic Success of the Through-Passage along the Arctic Ocean in a Single Navigational Season. No. 337, 7 December 1932.
Presidential Decree No. 1336, 19 November 2002.
Presidential Decree No. 824 *O merakh po sovershenstvovaniyu gosudarvstennogo upravleniya*, 16 July 2004.
Press release of the Parliamentary Association of the Council of Europe (PACE), Strasbourg, of 18 November 2004.

Pribylovsky, V. Oligarchs, True and False, *Russia and Eurasia Review* 10 (2003).
Pyatiletnii plan narodno-khozyaistvennogo stroitel'stva SSSR. Moscow: Planovoe khozyaistvo 1930.

Raionnoe planirovanie: Materialy. Leningradskaia oblastnaia planirovania komissia: Leningrad 1933.
Ryzhkov, A. *Neuvostoliiton taloudellisen ja sosiaalisen kehityksen perussuunnat vuosina 1986–1990 ja vuoteen 2000*. APN Helsinki 1986.

Schick, A. *Opportunity, strategy, and tactics in reforming public management*. Paper delivered at the symposium Government of the Future: Getting from here to there, Paris, 14–15 September 1999.
Sharov, A. V. Ob osnovnykh elementakh administrativnoi reformy, *Reforma gosudarstvennogo upravleniya v Rossii*, 5–13.
Soviet Legislation on Women's Rights: Collection of Normative Acts. Moscow: Progress Publishers 1978.
Suomen ja Neuvostoliiton välinen tieteellis-tekninen yhteistoiminta 30 vuotta. Helsinki 1985.
Suomi-SNTL, Tieteellis-teknisen ja taloudellisen yhteistyön vuorovaikutus. Raportti Suomen ja Neuvostoliiton välisen yhteistyön metodologiaa koskevasta tutkimuksesta, osa 1. Helsinki 1980.
Suomi-SNTL, Tieteellis-teknisen ja taloudellisen yhteistyön vuorovaikutus. Raportti Suomen ja Neuvostoliiton välisen yhteistyön metodologiaa koskevasta tutkimuksesta, Sanasto. Helsinki 1980.

Technology and East-West Trade. Report. Office of the Technology Assessment, Congress of the United States, November 1979.
Teubal, M. *Enterprise Restructuring and Embeddedness – An Innovation Systems and Policy Perspective*, paper delivered at The Economics of Industrial Structure and Innovation Dynamics, Lisbon, 16–17 October 1998.
Trud v SSSR 1988.

Verkhovny Sovet SSSR 1974.
Vneshnyaya torgovlya SSSR za 1918–1940gg.: statisticheskii obzor. Moscow: Vneshtorgizdat 1960.

Worldbank, *Russian Economic Report,* 8 June 2004, Moscow: Worldbank.
World Investment Prospects. Comparing Business Environments Across the Globe. London: EIU 2001.
World Resources Institute et al., *World Resources 1987*. New York: Basic Books 1987.
World Resources 1994–95. New York: Oxford University Press 1994.

1918 RSFSR Constitution.
1936 'Stalin' Constitution.
1977 'Brezhnev' Constitution.

SECONDARY LITERATURE

Ades, D. *Photomontage*. London: Thames & Hudson 1996.
Akiner, S. Between Tradition and Modernity: the Dilemma Facing Contemporary Central Asian Women, in M. Buckley (ed.), *Post-Soviet Women: From the Baltic to Central Asia*. Cambridge: Cambridge University Press 1997, 261–304.
Altshuler, A. Public Innovation and Political Incentives, in *Innovation in American Government Programme at Harvard University, John F. Kennedy School of*

Government, fall 1997, 1st Paper.

Amann, R. Technical Progress and Soviet Economic Development: Setting the Scenes in *Technical Progress and Soviet Economic Development*. Oxford: Basil Blackwell 1986, 5–30.

Amann, R. The Soviet Chemicalisation Drive and the Problem of Innovation, in Ronald Amann and Julian Cooper (eds.), *Industrial Innovation in the Soviet Union*. New Haven: Yale University Press 1982.

Amann, R., Cooper, J. M. and Davies, R. W. (eds.). *The Technological Level of Soviet Industry*. New Haven and London: Yale University Press 1977.

Ananich, N. I. Iz istorii zakonodatel'stva o krestianakh, in *Voprosy istorii Rossii XIX-nachala XX v*. LGU 1983, 34–45.

Andrle, V. *Workers in Stalin's Russia. Industrialisation and social change in a planned economy*. Sussex, New York: Harvester Wheatsheaf: St. Martin's Press 1988.

Antsiferov, A. N. *Russian Agriculture during the War*. New Haven: Yale University Press 1930.

Appelbaum, A. *Gulag, A History*. London: Penguin Books 2003.

Armstrong, T. *The Northern Sea Route Soviet Exploitation of the North East Passage*. Cambridge: Cambridge University Press 1952.

Arnold, D. *Famine: social crisis and historical change*. Oxford: Basil Blackwell 1988.

Ashwin, S. (ed.). *Gender, State and Society in Soviet and Post-Soviet Russia*. London: Routledge 2000.

Åslund, A. Russia's Economic Transformation under Putin, *Eurasian Geography and Economics*, XXXXV: 6 (2004), 397–421.

Atkinson, D. *The End of the Russian Land Commune, 1905–1930*. Stanford: Stanford University Press 1083.

Augé, M. *Non-places. Introduction to an anthropology of supermodernity*. London – NY: Verso 1995.

Autio, S. *Suunnitelmatalous Neuvosto-Karjalassa 1928–1941. Paikallistason rooli Neuvostoliiton teollistamisessa*. Bibliotheca historica 71. Helsinki: SKS 2002.

Backström, C. *Tulevaisuuden topparoikka. Muistiinpanoja Baikalin-Amurin ratatyömaalta*. Espoo: WSOY 1979.

Bacon, E., Renz, B. and Cooper, J. *Securitising Russia: The Domestic Politics of Putin*. Manchester: Manchester University Press 2006.

Bailes, K. E. *Technology and Society under Lenin and Stalin: Origins of the Soviet Technical Intelligentsia, 1917–1941*. Princeton: Princeton University Press 1978.

Balzer, H. Managed Pluralism: Vladimir Putin's Emerging Regime, *Post-Soviet Affairs* 19: 3 (2003), 189–227.

Balzer, H. D. (ed.), *Russia's Missing Middle Class: The Professions in Russian History*. Armonk, N.Y.: M. E. Sharpe 1995.

Baranskaya, N., Nedeliya kak nedeliya, *Novyi mir* (1969).

Baranskaya, N. *A Week Like Any Other* London: Virago 1989.

Barber, J. and Dzeniskevich, A. R. (eds) *Zhizn' i smert' v blokirovannom Leningrade: Istoriko-meditsinskii aspect.*. St. Petersburg: Dmitrii Bulganin 2001.

Barnett, V. *Kondratiev and the Dynamics of Economic Development*. New York: St. Martin's 1998.

Barsukov, M. I. and Zhuk, A. *Za sotsialisticheskuyu rekonstruktsiyu zdravookhraneniya*. Moscow 1932.

Barsukov, M. I. *Velikaya oktiabr'skaya sotsialiticheskaya revoliutsiya i organizatsiya sovetskogo zdravookhraneniya (oktiabr' 1917g – iiul 1918g)*. Moscow: Medgiz, 1951.

Bazin, A. *What is Cinema?* Berkeley: California University Press 1972.

Belinsky, V. G. *Selected Philosophical Works*. Moscow: Foreign Languages Publishing House 1956.

Bel'skii, K. S. O funktsiyakh ispolnitel'noi vlasti, *Gosudarstvo i pravo* 3 (1997), 14–21.

Berdyaev, N. *The Origin of Russian Communism*. The University of Michigan Press: Ann Arbor Paperbacks 1960.

Bereday, G. Z. F., Brickman, W. W. and Read, G. H. (eds.) *The Changing Soviet School.*. London: Constable and Company 1960.

Berliner, J. R. The Harvard Project and the Soviet Interview Project, in Fleron, F. J. Jr. and Hoffmann, E. P. (eds.*), Post-Communist Studies and Political Science*. Boulder and Oxford: Westview Press 1993, 177–182.

Berliner, J. S. *The Innovation Decision in Soviet Industry,* Cambridge, Mass., and London: MIT Press 1976.

Berliner, J. S. *Soviet Industry from Stalin to Gorbachev Essays on Management and Innovation*. Aldershot: Edward Elgar 1985.

Bertsch G. Technology Transfers and Technology Controls: a Synthesis of the Western-Soviet Relationship in: *Technical Progress and Soviet Economic Development*. Oxford: Basil Blackwell 1986, 115–134.

Beyond State Crisis? Post-Colonial Africa and Post-Soviet Eurasia in Comparative Perspective. Beissinger, M. R. and Young, C. (eds.). Washington D.C.: Woodrow Wilson Center Press 2002.

Bilinsky, Y. The Soviet education laws of 1958–59 and Soviet nationality policy, *Soviet Studies* 14: 2 (1962), 138–57.

Bisha, R. et al. (eds) *Russian Women, 1698–1917: Experience and Expression*. Bloomington, IN: Indiana University Press 2002.

Black, C. The modernisation of Russian society, in Black, C.E. (ed.), *The Transformation of Russian Society: Aspects of Social Change since 1861*. Cambridge: Harvard University Press 1960, 661–80.

Blagov, S. BAM railway to become export route, *Eurasia Daily Monitor* 2: 116 (2005).

Blum, J. *Lord and Peasant in Russia from the Ninth to the Nineteenth Century*. New York: Atheneum 1969.

Bogdanov, A. *Red Star*. Bloomington: Indiana University Press 1984.

Bozóki, A. Hungary's Social-Democratic Turn, *East European Constitutional Review* 11: 3, (2002), 80–86.

Bremya gosudarstva i ekonomicheskaya politika: liberal'naya al'ternativa. Yasin, E. (ed.). Moscow: Fond Liberal'naya missiya 2003.

Breslauer, G. W. *Gorbachev and Yeltsin as Leaders*. Cambridge: Cambridge University Press 2002.

Brezhnev, L. *Puheita: Helsingin ETY-kokouksesta Urho Kekkosen vierailuun Moskovassa*. Helsinki: Otava 1977.

Bridger, S. The Cold War and the Cosmos: Valentina Tereshkova and the First Women's Space Flight, in Ilič, M., Reid, S. E. and Attwood, L. *Women in the Khrushchev Era*. Basingstoke: Palgrave 2004, 222–237.

Brigham, L. W. (ed.). *The Soviet Maritime Arctic*. Cambridge: Belhaven Press in association with the Scott Polar Research Institute 1991.

Brik, O. T.n. formal'nyi metod. *Lef*, 1 (1923), 214.

Brooks, J. *When Russia Learned to Read: Literacy and Popular Culture 1861–1917*. Princeton: Princeton University Press 1985.

Brower, D. Urban revolution in the late Russian empire, in Hamm, M. F. (ed.), *The City in Late Imperial Russia*. Bloomington: Indiana University Press 1986, 319–53.

Brower, D. *The Russian City between Tradition and Modernity, 1850–1990*. Berkeley: University of California Press 1990.

Brown, A. Evaluating Russia's Democratization, in Brown, A. (ed.), *Contemporary Russian Politics*. Oxford: Oxford University Press 2001.

Browning, G. The zhensovety revisited, in Buckley, M. (ed.), *Perestroika and Soviet Women*. Cambridge: Cambridge University Press 1992, 97–117.

Buckley, M. *Women and Ideology in the Soviet Union*. Hemel Hempstead: Harvester Wheatsheaf 1989.

Buckley, M. Political Reform, in Buckley, M. (ed.), *Perestroika and Soviet Women*. Cambridge: Cambridge University Press 1992, 60.

Buck-Morss, S. *Dreamworld and Catastrophe. The Passing of Mass Utopia in East and West*. Cambridge, Mass. – London: the MIT Press 2002.

Bulatov, V. N. Arkticheskaya Komissiya, *Voprosy Istorii* 8–9 (1992), 148–150.

Bulgakova, O. L., Montazh v teatral'noi laboratorii 1920-h godov, In: Raushenbakh, B. V. (ed.), *Montazh: literatura, iskusstvo, teatr, kino*. Moskva: Nauka 1988, 99–100.

Busse, E. *The Formal and Informal Workings of Russian Taxation*. Cambridge University PhD dissertation 2001.

Carr, E. H. *The Bolshevik Revolution, 1917–1923*, vol. 2. London: Macmillan 1952.

Carr, E. H. *Socialism in One Country, 1924–1926*, vol. 1. London: Macmillan 1958.

Carr, E. H. *Socialism in One Country 1924–1926*. Harmondsworth: Penguin Books 1970.

Carr, E. H. and Davies, R. W. *Foundations of a Planned Economy, 1926–1929*. London: Macmillan 1969.

Castells, M. *The Information Age. Economy, Society and Culture, Vol. 1: The Rise of the Network Society*. Oxford: Blackwell 1996.

Castells, M. *The Information Age: Economy, Society and Culture, Vol. III End of the Millennium*. Oxford: Blackwell 1998.

Castells, M. *The Internet Galaxy; Reflections on the Internet, Business and Society*. Oxford: Oxford University Press 2001.

Chayanov, A. V. *The Theory of Peasant Economy*. Madison: University of Wisconsin Press 1986.

Chubarov, A. *Russia's Bitter Path to modernity. A History of the Soviet and post-Soviet Eras*. New York-London: Continuum 2001.

Civil Service Reform in Russia, 1992–2003. Parison, N. (ed.). Moscow: World Bank 2004.

Clark, M. G. *The Economics of Soviet Steel*. Cambridge, Mass.: Harvard University Press 1956.

Clements, B. E. *Daughters of Revolution: a History of Women in the USSR*. Illinois: Harlan Davidson 1994.

Clements, B. E., Engel, B. A. and Worobec, C. D. (eds.). *Russia's Women: Accommodation, Resistance, Transformation*. Berkeley, CA: University of California Press 1991.

Cohen, S. *Rethinking the Soviet Experience. Politics and History since 1917*. Oxford: Oxford University Press 1986.

Conquest, R. *Harvest of Sorrow*. Oxford and New York: Oxford University Press 1986.

Conroy, M. S. *In health and in sickness: Pharmacy, pharmacists and the pharmaceutical industry in late Imperial, early Soviet Russia*. New York: Columbia University Press 1994.

Cooper, J. M. The Development of the Soviet Machine-Tool Industry, 1917–41, unpublished Ph. D. thesis. University of Birmingham 1975.

Cooper, J. Innovation for Innovation in Soviet Industry, in Amann, R. and Cooper, J. (eds.), *Industrial Innovation in the Soviet Union*. New Haven and London: Yale University Press 1982, 453–513.

Cooper, J. Of BRICs and Brains: Comparing Russia with China, India and Other Populous Emerging Economies, *Eurasian Geography and Economics*, 47: 3 (2006b), 241–270.

Coopersmith, J. *The Electrification of Russia 1880–1926*. Ithaca: Cornell University Press 1992.

Counts, G. S. *Khrushchev and the Central Committee Speak on Education*. Pittsburgh: University of Pittsburgh Press 1959.

Crafts, N. and Kaiser, K. Long Term Growth Prospects in Transition Economies: A Reappraisal, *Structural Change and Economic Dynamics*, forthcoming.

Crang, M. Time: Space, in Cloke, P. and Johnston, R. (eds.), *Spaces of Geographical Thought*. London, Thousand Oaks, New Delhi: Sage Publications 2005.

Crisp, O. *Studies in the Russian Economy before 1914*. Basingstoke: Macmillan 1976.

Davies, C. M. The health sector in the Soviet and Russian economies: From reform to fragmentation to transition, in *The former Soviet Union in Transition*, Vol. 2, JEC, US Congress, Washington 1993, 855–858.

Davies, R. W. *Crisis and Progress in the Soviet Economy, 1931–1933*. Basingstoke and London: Macmillan 1996.

Davies, R. W. Industry, in Davies, R. W., Harrison, M. and Wheatcroft, S. G. (eds), *The Economic Transformation of the Soviet Union, 1913–1945*. Cambridge: Cambridge University Press 1994.

Davies, R. W. *Soviet Economic Development from Lenin to Khrushchev*. Cambridge: Cambridge University Press 1998.

Davies, R. W., Ilič, M. J. et al. (eds). *Soviet Government Officials, 1922–1941: A Handlist.* Birmingham: Centre for Russian and East European Studies, University of Birmingham 1989.

Davies, R. W., Harrison, M., et al. (eds.). *The Economic Transformation of the Soviet Union, 1913–1945*. Cambridge: Cambridge University Press 1994.

Davies, R. W. *The Soviet Economy in Turmoil. The Industrialisation of the Soviet Union 3*. Basingstoke: Macmillan Press 1989.

Davies, R. W. & Wheatcroft, S. G. *The Years of Hunger: Soviet Agriculture, 1931–1933*. Basingstoke: Palgrave 2004.

Dawidoff, N. *The Fly Swatter: How My Grandfather Made His Way in the World*. New York: Pantheon Books 2002.

Denhardt, R. The Future of Public Administration, *Public Administration & Management: An Interactive Journal* 4: 2 (1999), 279–292.

Denisova, L. H. *Ischezaiushchaia derevnia Rossii: Nechernozem'e v 1960–1980-e gody*. Moscow: Institut rossiiskoi istorii RAN 1996.

Devereux, S. *Fieldwork in developing countries*. Boulder, CO: Lynne Rienner 1993.

Dezhina, I. and Graham, L. Russian Basic Science After Ten Years of Transition and Foreign Support. *Working Papers* 24 (2002), *Russian-and Eurasian Program*. Carnegie Endowment 2002, 6.

Dodge, N. T. Trends in Labor Productivity in the Soviet Tractor Industry: A Case Study in Industrial Development, unpublished Ph. D. thesis. Harvard University 1960.

Dohan, M. Foreign trade, in Davies, R. W. (ed.), *From Tsarism to NEP*. Basingstoke: Macmillan 1990.

Donskoi, M. Ocherednye zadachi planirovaniia zdravookhraneniia, *Voprosy zdravookhraneniia* 1 (1928), 11.

Dore, R. *Stock Market Capitalism: Welfare Capitalism. Japan and Germany versus the Anglo-Saxons*. Oxford: Oxford University Press 2000.

Drozhzhinov, V. I. *E-government in Russia, Year 2002*. Moscow: E-government Competence Centre 2003.

Drozhzhinov, V. I. *E-government state-of-the-art in Russia*. Moscow: E-government Competence Centre 2004.

Drozhzhinov, V. I. and Zinder, E. Z. *Elektronnoe pravitel'stvo: rekommrndatsii po vnedreniyu v Rossisskoi Federatsii*. Moscow: Eko-Trends 2004.

Duncan, P. J. S. *Russian Messianism. Third Rome, revolution, Communism and after*. London and New York: Routledge 2000.

Dunlop, J. et al. Profiles of the newly independent states: economic, social and demographic conditions, in Kaufman, R. F. and . Hardt, J. P (eds.), *The former Soviet Union in Transition*. New York: M. E. Sharpe 1993, 1021–1187.

Dunstan, J. *Paths to Excellence and the Soviet* School. Windsor: NFER 1978.

Dutton, J. C. Causes of Soviet adult mortality increases, *Soviet Studies* 33: 4 (1981), 548–559.

Dyer, G. *Class, State, and Agricultural productivity in Egypt: A Study of the Inverse Relationship between Farm Size and Land Productivity*. London: Frank Cass 1997.

Eckstein, H., Fleron Jr F. J., Hoffmann, E. P., and Reissinger, W. M., *Can Democracy Take Root in Post-Soviet Russia? Explorations in State-Society Relations*. Lanham, MD: Rowman & Littlefield Publishers 1998.

Economy of the USSR, The. A study undertaken in response to a request by the Houston Summit. Summary and Recommendations. Washington, DC, Paris and London: IMF, IBRD, OECD and EBRD 1990.

Edgar, A. L. Emancipation of the Unveiled: Turkmen Women under Soviet Rule,

1924–1929, *Russian Review*, 62 (2003), 132–149.

Edmondson, L. H. *Feminism in Russia, 1900–1917.* London: Heinemann 1984.

Eizenshtein, S. M. Montazh attraktsionov. *Lef* 3 (1923), 70–1.

Eizenshtein, S. M. *Izbrannye stat'i.* T.2. Moskva: Nauka 1964.

Eklof, B. et al. (eds.). *Russia's Great Reforms 1855–1881.* Bloomington: Indiana University Press 1994.

Engel, B. A. *Between the Fields and the City: Women, Work, and Family in Russia, 1861–1914.* Cambridge: Cambridge University Press 1994.

Engel, B. A. *Women in Russia, 1700–2000.* Cambridge: Cambridge University Press 2004.

Engels, F. *Herr Eugen Dühring's Revolution in Science (Anti-Dühring).* New York: International Publishers 1939.

Engels, F. *The Origin of the Family, Private Property and the State.* London: Lawrence and Wishart 1940.

Engelstein, L. *The Keys to Happiness: Sex and the Search for Modernity in Fin-de-Siecle Russia.* Ithaca: Cornell University Press 1992.

Ericson, R. E. The Russian Economy: Market in Form but "Feudal" in Content? in Cuddy, M. and Gekker, R. (eds.), *Institutional Change in Transition Economies.* Burlington, VY: Ashgate 2002, 3–35.

Evans, J. The CPSU and the "Woman Question": the Case of the 1936 Decree "In Defence of Mother and Child", *Journal of Contemporary History* 16 (1981), 757–775.

Ewing, E. T. *The Teachers of Stalinism: Policy, Practice and Power in Soviet Schools of the 1930s.* New York: Peter Lang 2002.

Ezhegodnik Bolshoi Sovetskoi entsiklopedii. Moskva: Sovetskaja Entsiklopedija 1985.

Falkus, M. E. Russia's national income in 1913: a re-evaluation, *Economica* 35 (1968), 52–73.

Ferguson, J. *Expectations of Modernity: Myths and Meanings of Urban Life on the Zambian Copperbelt.* Berkeley: University of California Press 1999.

Field, D. Mothers and Fathers and the Problem of Selfishness in the Khrushchev Period, in Reid and Attwood, *Women in the Khrushchev Era.* Basingstoke: Palgrave 2004, 96–113.

Field, M. G. *Soviet socialised medicine: An introduction.* New York: Free Press, 1967.

Field, M. G. *Social Consequences of Modernisation in Communist Societies.* London and Baltimore: Johns Hopkins Press 1976.

Filtzer, D. *The Khrushchev Era: De-Stalinisation and the Limits of Reform in the USSR, 1953–1964.* Basingstoke: Macmillan 1993.

Fisher, H. H. *The famine in Soviet Russia, 1919–1923; the operations of the American Relief Administration.* New York: Macmillan 1927.

Fitzgerald, D. *Every Farm a Factory.* New Haven: Yale University Press 2003.

Fitzpatrick, S. Ordzhonikidze's Takeover of Vesenkha: A Case Study in Soviet Bureaucratic Politics, *Soviet Studies* XXXVII : 2 (1985), 153–172.

Fitzpatrick, S. *Stalin's Peasants.* New York: Oxford University Press 1994.

Fitzpatrick, S. *The Russian Revolution.* New York: Oxford University Press 1994.

Foray, D. *The Creation of Industry-Specific Public Goods: New Insights into the Technology Policy Debate*, paper delivered at conference The Economics of Industrial Structure and Innovation Dynamics, Lisbon, 16–17 October 1998, 2.

Fortescue, S. *Science Policy in the Soviet Union.* London and New York: Routlege 1990.

Frank, A. G. Economic ironies in Europe: a world economic interpretation of East-West European politics, *International Social Science Journal, UNESCO,* vol. XLIV, no. 1 (1992).

Freeze, G. L. The *soslovie* (estate) paradigm and Russian social history, *American Historical Review* 91 (1986), 11–36.

Freyfogle, E. T. *The New Agrarianism: Land. Culture, and the Community of Life.* Washington, D.C.: Island Press 2001.

Gaddy, C. and Hill, F. *The Siberian Curse: How Communist Planners Left Russia Out in the Cold*. Washington D.C.: Brookings Institution Press 2003.

Gaddy, C. and Ickes, B. W. Russia's Virtual Economy, *Foreign Affairs* 77: 5 (1998).

Gaddy, C. and Ickes, B. W. An Evolutionary Analysis of Russia's Virtual Economy, in Cuddy, M. and Gekker, R. (eds.), *Institutional Change in Transition Economies*, op. cit., 2002, 72–100.

Gatrell, P. *The Tsarist Economy 1850–1917*. London: Batsford 1986.

Gatrell, P. *Russia's First World War: An Economic and Social History*. London: Pearson Longman 2005.

Gerovitch, S. *From Cyberspeak to Newspeak. A History of Soviet Cybernetics*. Cambridge: The MIT Press 2001.

Gerschenkron, A. *Economic Backwardness in Historical Perspective*. Cambridge: Harvard University Press 1961.

Gerth, H. H. and Wright Mills, C. (eds.). *Max Weber: Essays in Sociology*. Oxford and New York, Oxford University Press 1946.

Giardini, F., Garrou, E., et al., *Isole di Ghiaccio alla Deriva Storia Postale e Vita delle Stazioni Flottanti Sovietiche nell'Oceano Glaciale Artico (Drifting Ice Islands from a Postal History and Life of Soviet Floating Stations in the Glacial Arctic Ocean)*. Leumann, Torrino, Italy: Gribaudo – Associazione Grande Nord 1998.

Goldman, W. Z. *Women, the State and Revolution: Soviet Family Policy and Social Life, 1917–1936*. Cambridge: Cambridge University Press 1993.

Goldman, W. Z. *Women at the Gates: Gender and Industry in Stalin's Russia*. Cambridge: Cambridge University Press 2002.

Goldthorpe, J. On the Service Class, its Formation and Future, in Giddens, A. and Mackenzie, G. (eds.), *Social Class and the Division of Labour*. Cambridge: Cambridge University Press 1982, 171–2.

Golkin, A. T. *Famine, a heritage of hunger: a guide to issues and references*. Claremont, Calif.: Regina Books 1987.

Golod 1932–1933 rokiv na Ukraini: ochima istorikiv, movoiu dokumentiv. Kiev: Vid. Politichnoi literatury Ukrainy 1990.

Gomulka, S. *Growth, Innovation and Reform in Eastern Europe*. Brighton: Harvester Press 1986.

Gönenc, L. *Prospects for Constitutionalism in Postcommunist Countries*. The Hague: Kluwer 2001.

Gorbachev, M. *Perestroika: New Thinking for Our Country and the World*. London: Collins 1987.

Gorbachev, M. Appendix 1 Excerpt from Speech in Murmansk given on 1 October 1987, in Brigham, L. (ed.) *The Soviet Maritime Arctic*. Cambridge: Belhaven Press in association with the Scott Polar Research Institute 1991.

Gordon, M. R. Forsaken in Russia's Arctic: 9 Million Stranded Workers. *New York Times* 6 January 1999.

Goricheva, L. Natural conditions of development of national economies in Russia and Western Europe, *Mirovaja Ekonomika I Mezhdunarodnye otnoshenija* 2 (2004), 58.

Gor'kova, Y. A. *Kreml' Stavka Genshtab*. Tver' 1995.

Gor'kova, Y. A. Posetiteli Kremlevskogo Kabineta I. V. Stalina (1932–1933), *Istoricheskii Arkhiv* 1 –5 (1995).

Gosudarstvennyi komitet Rossiiskoi Federatsii po statistike, *Statisticheskii byulleten'*, No.1 (94), May 2003 Moscow.

Granick, D. *Soviet Metal-Fabricating and Economic Development: Practice versus Policy*. Madison, Milwaukee and London: University of Wisconsin Press 1967.

Greenleaf, M., Tynjanov, F. Pushkin and the Fragment: through the lens of montage. In: Gasparov, B. et al. (eds.), *Cultural Mythologies of Russian Modernism: from the golden age to the silver age*. Berkeley etc.: University of California Press 1993, 268–269.

Gregory, P. R. *Russian National Income 1885–1913*. London: Cambridge University Press, 1982.

Gregory, P. R. *Before Command: An Economic History of Russia from Emancipation to*

313

the First Five-Year Plan. Princeton: Princeton University Press 1994.

Gregory, P. and Stuart, R. *Soviet and post-Soviet economic structure and performance.* New York: HarperCollins 1994.

Gribanov, Ye. D. *Vserossisskie s"ezdy zdravotdelov I ikh znachenie dlia praktiki sovetskogo zdravookhraneniia.* Moscow 1966.

Griffiths, F. Arctic in the Russian Identity, in Brigham, L. (ed.) *The Soviet Maritime Arctic.* London and Cambridge: Belhaven in association with the Scott Polar Research Institute 1991, 84–86.

Grigg, D. *The Harsh Lands.* London: MacMillan 1970.

Grinevetskii, V. I. *Poslevoennye perspektivy russkoi promyshlennosti.* Khar'kov: Vserossiiskii tsentral'nyi soiuz potrebitel'nykh obshchestv 1919.

Grubler, A. *The Rise and Fall of Infrastructures. Dynamics of Evolution and Technological Change in Transport.* Laxenburg: Physica-Verlag Heidelberg 1999.

Guroff, G. The legacy of pre-revolutionary economic education: St. Petersburg Polytechnic Institute, *Russian Review* 31 (1972), 272–81.

Hahn, G. M. *Russia's Revolution from Above, 1985–2000: Reform, Transition, and Revolution in the Fall of the Soviet Communist Regime.* New Brunswick, NJ: Transaction Publishers: 2002.

Häikiö, M. *Sturm und Drang. Suurkaupoilla eurooppalaiseksi elektroniikkyritykseksi 1983–1991. Nokia Oyj:n historia.* Helsinki: Edita 2001.

Hans, N. *The Russian Tradition in Education.* London: Routledge and Kegan Paul 1963.

Hanson, P. *Trade and technology in Soviet-Western Relations.* London: Macmillan 1981.

Hanson, P. Long Run Barriers to Growth in Russia, *Economy and Society*, 31: 1 (2002), 62–84.

Hanson, P. *The Rise and Fall of the Soviet Economy. An Economic History of the USSR from 1945.* London: Longman 2003.

Hanson, S. E. Can Putin Rebuild the Russian State?, *Security Dialogue* 32: 2 (2001).

Hare, P. G. Institutional Change and Economic Performance in the Transition Economies, UN ECE, *Economic Survey of Europe* 2 (2001), 77–94.

Harter, S. The Military-Industrial Complex, Technological Change and the Space Industry, in: Lane, D. (ed.), *The Legacy of State Socialism and the Future of Transformation.* Lanham et al. Rowman & Littlefield 2002, 147–169.

Harter, S. *Russlandanalyse* 36 (2004).

Harvey, D. *Spaces of Capital. Towards a Critical Geography.* Edinburgh: Edinburgh University Press 2001.

Hausmann, R., Pritchett, L. and Rodrik, D. Growth Accelerations. National Bureau of Economic Research working paper 10566, June 2004.

Hayden, R. *Blueprints for a House Divided: The Constitutional Logic of the Yugoslav Conflicts.* Ann Arbor: University of Michigan Press 1999.

Hietala, M. *Innovaatioiden ja kansainvälistymisen vuosikymmenet. Tietoa, taitoa, asiantuntemusta. Helsinki eurooppalaisessa kehityksessä 1875–1917.* Historiallinen arkisto 99:1. Helsinki 1992.

Hill, F. and Gaddy, G., *The Siberian Curse. How Communist Planners Left Russia Out in the Cold.* Washington: Brookings Institution Press 2003.

Hoffman, E. and Laird, R. *"The scientific-technological revolution" and Soviet foreign policy.* New York: Pergamon Press 1982.

Holliday, G. *Technology transfer to the USSR 1928–1937 and 1966–1975: The role of western technology in Soviet economic development.* Boulder and Oxford: Westview Press 1979.

Holloway, D. *The Soviet Union and the Arms Race.* New Haven and London: Yale University Press 1983.

Holmes, S. Cultural Legacies or State Collapse? Probing the Post-Communist Dilemma, in Mandelbaum, M. (ed.), *Post-Communism: Four Views.* New York: Council for Foreign Relations 1996, 50.

Holmes, S. Potemkin Democracy, in Rabb, T. & Suleiman, E. (eds.), *The Making and*

Unmaking of Democracy. New York and London: Routledge 2003, 109–133.

Hopper, B. Sovereignty in the Arctic, *Research Bulletin on the Soviet Union* 2: 8 (1937), 81.

Horensma, P. *The Soviet Arctic*. London: Routledge 1991.

Huntington, S. P. *Political Order in Changing Societies*. New Haven, CT: Yale University Press 1968.

Huskey, E. *Presidential Power in Russia*. Armonk, NY: M. E. Sharpe 1999.

Hutchinson, Sir Joseph. *Farming and Food Supply*. Cambridge: Cambridge University Press 1972.

Hutton, M. J. Russian and West European Women, 1860–1939: Dreams, Struggles and Nightmares. Oxford: Rowman and Littlefield 2001.

Ilič, M. Women Workers in the Soviet Interwar Economy: From 'Protection' to 'Equality'. Basingstoke: Macmillan 1999.

Ilič, M. The Great Terror in Leningrad: a Quantitative Analysis, *Europe-Asia Studies* 52: 8 (2000), 1515–1534.

International Research and Exchanges Board (IREX), *The Internet in Russia: On the Eve of Great Change* (2000).

Internet i Rossiiskoe obshchestvo. Semenov, I. (ed.). Moscow: Moskovskii Tsentr Karnegi; Gendal'f 2002.

Ivanov, V. V., Lotman, Yu. M., Pyatigorskii, A. M., Toporov, V. N., Uspenskii, B. A. *Theses on the Semiotic Study of Cultures* (= Tartu Semiotics Library 1). University of Tartu 1998.

Jackson, I. *The Economic Cold War. America, Britain and East-West Trade, 1948–1963*. New York: Palgrave 2001.

Jauho, P. Tieteellis-teknistä yhteistoimintaa Suomen ja Neuvostoliiton välillä kolmekymmentä vuotta, in *Suomen ja Neuvostoliiton välinen tieteellis-tekninen yhteistoiminta 30 vuotta*. Helsinki 1985, 4.

Jensen, P. A. Art-Artifact-Fact: the set on "reality" in the prose of the 1920s, in: Nilsson, N. Å. (ed.), *The Slavic Literatures and Modernism*. Stockholm: Almqvist & Wiksell 1987, 117–123.

Jones, T. *The Dark Heart of Italy*. London: Faber and Faber 2003.

Jorgensen-Dahl, A. and Ostreng, W. Military / Strategic Aspects of the Northern Sea Route, *International Challenges* 12: 1 (1992), 108–115.

Kaganskii,V. *Kulturnii landchaft i Sovetskoe Obitaemoe Prostranstvo*. Moskva: Novoe Literaturnoe Obozrenie 2001.

Kaje, M. and Niitamo, O. Scientific and Technical Cooperation between a Small Capitalist Country and Big Socialist Country in Möttölä, Bykov and Korolev (eds.) *Finnish-Soviet Economic Relations*. London: Macmillan Press 1983, 143–144.

Kak lomali NEP: Stenogrammy plenumov TsK VKP(b) 1928–1929 gg. Danilov, V. P. et al. (eds.). Moscow: Rossiia XX Vek 2000.

Kapitsa, P. L. *Teoriya, eksperiment, praktika*. Moscow: Izd-vo znanie 1968.

Karpinskii, A. P. V Klub' Arktiki. *Pravda* 18 November 1932.

Kasvin, G. A. and Shibanov, A. A. The reform of the schools in the Czechoslovak Republic, *Soviet Education* 1: 4 (1959), 65–70.

Kayden, E. M. An economic study of Russia before and during the war, War Trade Board, Washington D.C., manuscript, 1919.

Keller, S. Trapped Between State and Society: Women's Liberation and Islam in Soviet Uzbekistan, 1926–41, *Journal of Women's History* 10: 1 (1998), 20–44.

Kenez, P. *Civil War in South Russia, 1919–1920 : the defeat of the Whites*. Berkeley: Published for the Hoover Institution on War, Revolution, and Peace: University of California Press 1977.

Kharkhordin, O. *The Collective and the Individual in Russia. A Study of Practice*. Berkeley: University of California Press 1999.

Khenkin, E. M. *Ocherki istorii bor'by sovetskogo gosudarstva s golodom : 1921–1922*.

Krasnoiarsk : Izd-vo Krasnoiarskogo universiteta 1988.

Khlevnyuk, O. V. The First Generation of Stalinist Party Generals, in Rees, E. A. (ed.) *Centre-Local Relations in the Stalinist State, 1928–1941*. Basingstoke: Palgrave Macmillan 2002.

Khlevnyuk, O. et al. (eds.). *Stalin i Kaganovich: perepiska, 1931–1936*. Moscow: Rosspen 2001.

Khrushchev, N. S. Regarding the strengthening of ties between school and life and the further development of the public education system, *Soviet Education* 1: 2 (1958), 3.

Khrushchev Remembers: The Last Testament. Boston: Little, Brown and co., 1974.

Khrushchev, S. N. *Nikita Khrushchev and the Creation of a Superpower*. Philadelphia: Pennsylvania University Press 2000.

Kierkegaard, S. *Toisto*. Jyväskylä: Atena Kustannus Oy 2001.

Kirkow, P. *Russia's Provinces. Authoritarian Transformation versus Local Autonomy?* London: Macmillan Press 1998.

Klimenko, A. V. Elektronnye administrativnye reglamenty, in Institut problem gosudarstvennogo i munitsipal'nogo upravlenie (ed.), *Sostoyanie i mekhanizmy modernisatsii possiiskogo gosudarstvennogo upravleniya*. Moscow: Epifaniya 2004, 128–143.

Klyamkin, Ig. and Shevtsova, L. *This Omnipotent and Impotent Government: The Evolution of the Political System in Post-Communist Russia*. Washington, DC: Carnegie Endowment for International Peace 1999.

Kochergin, I. G. Osnovye voprosy teorii sovetskoi meditsiny i zdravookhraneniia v trudakh N. A. Semashko, *Sovetskoe zdravookhranenie* 5 (1965).

Kohn, H. *Pan-Slavism: Its History and Ideology*. New York: Vintage Books 1960.

Kol'tsov, A. V. *Leningradskie Uchrezhdeniya Akademii Nauk SSSR v 1934–1945 gg.* Sankt-Peterburg: Nauka 1997.

Konstantinova, N. P., Stakanova, O. V., Shkaratan, O. I. Peremeny v sotsial'nom oblike rabochikh v epokhu razvitogo sotsializma, *Voprosy istorii* 5:11 (1978).

Korol, A. *Soviet Research and Development. Its organisation, Personnel, and Funds.* Cambridge, Mass: The MIT Press 1965.

Korollev, I. The mechanisms of the Multilateral Economic Cooperation between CMEA and Finland in Möttölä, Bykov and Korolev (eds.) *Finnish-Soviet Economic Relations*. London: Macmillan Press 1983.

Kotkin, J. The Withering of Rural America, *Washington Post Weekly*, July 29–August 4 (2002).

Kotkin, S. *Magnetic Mountain. Stalinism as a Civilization*. Berkeley – Los Angeles – London: University of California Press 1995.

Kotsonis, Y. *Making Peasants Backward: Agricultural Co-operatives and the Agrarian Question in Russia, 1861–1914*. Houndmills, Basingstoke, Hampshire New York: Macmillan Press: St. Martin's Press 1999.

Kotsonis, Y. and Hoffmann, D. (eds.), *Russian Modernity: Politics, Knowledge, Practices*. Houndmills: Macmillan 2000.

Kotsonis, Y. "Face-to-Face": the state, the citizen, and the individual in Russian taxation, 1863–1917, *Slavic Review* (2004).

KPSS v rezolyutsiakh, vol. ii. Moscow 1954.

Krasnov, M. Konstitutsiya Rossii: zapovednaya territoriya ili sreda obitaniya?, *Konstitutsionnoe pravo: vostochnoevropoeiskoe obozrenie* 4: 29 (1999), 138.

Krementsov, N. *Stalinist Science*. Princeton, New Jersey: Princeton University Press 1997.

Krug, P. Russian public physicians and revolution: The Pirigov Society, 1917–20, PhD in History, University of Wisconsin-Madison 1979.

Krupskaia, N. K. O trudovom vospitanii i politekhnicheskom obuchenii, *Sovetskaia Pedagogika* 12: 2 (1958).

Krzhizhanovskii, G. M. *Sochineniya*, vol. 2, *Problemy planirovaniya*. Moscow 1934.

Krzhizhanovskii, G. M. *Izbrannoe*. Moscow: Gosizdat 1957.

Kuleshov, L. *Sobranie sochinenii*. Moskva: Iskusstvo 1988.

Lakhtin, V. L. Rights Over the Arctic, *American Journal of International Law* 10 (1930), 703–717.

Land Commune and Peasant Community in Russia. Bartlett, R. (ed.). Houndmills: Macmillan 1990.

Lane, D. and O'Dell, F. *The Soviet Industrial Worker: Social Class, Education and Control.* Oxford: Martin Robertson 1978.

Lane, D. The Roots of Political Reform, in Merridale, C. and Ward, C. (eds.), *Perestroika in Historical Perspective.* London: Edward Arnold 1991.

Lapidus, G. W. *Women in Soviet Society: Equality, Development, and Social Change.* Berkeley, CA: University of California Press 1978.

Lavrukhin, I. M. On the crisis in US education, *Soviet Education* 1: 2 (1958), 49.

Lawton, A. *Vadim Shershenevich: from Futurism to Imaginism.* Ann Arbor: Ardis 1981.

Leach, G. *Energy and Food Production.* Guildford: IPC Science and Technology Press 1976.

Ledeneva, A. *Unwritten Rules. How Russia Really Works*, London: Centre for European Reform, 2001.

Lenin, V. I. O "levom" rebyachestve i o melkoburzhuaznosti, in V. I. Lenin, *Sochineniya* vol. 27. Moscow: Partizdat 1931.

Lenin, V. I. A Great Beginning, in *Women and Communism: Selections from the Writings of Marx-Engels-Lenin-Stalin.* London: Lawrence and Wishart 1950, 50–57.

Lenin's Speech at the Non-Party Conference of Women Workers' in 1919 in *Women and Communism: Selections from the Writings of Marx-Engels-Lenin-Stalin.* London: Lawrence and Wishart 1950.

Lenin, V. I. *The Development of Capitalism in Russia.* Moscow: Progress Publishers 1977.

Levada,Y. *Sovetskii prostoi chelovek.* Moscow: Intercentr 1993.

Levin, E. *Sex and Society in the World of the Orthodox Slavs, 900–1700.* Ithaca: Cornell University Press 1989.

Lewin, M The Kolkhoz and the Russian Muzhik, in Lewin (ed.), *The Making of the Soviet System.* New York: Pantheon 1985, 184–86.

Lewis, R. *Science and Industrialisation in the USSR.* Basingstoke: Macmillan 1979.

Lieven, D. *Empire. The Russian Empire and Its Rivals.* New Haven and London: Yale University Press 2000.

Lih, L. *Bread and authority in Russia, 1914–1921.* Berkeley, CA : University of California Press 1990.

Lipovskaya, O. New Women's Organisations, in M. Buckley, *Perestroika and Soviet Women.* Cambridge: Cambridge University Press 1992, 72–81.

Lipset, S. M. Some Social Requisites of Democracy, Economic Development and Political Legitimacy, *American Political Science Review* LIII (1959).

Lipton, M. *Why Poor People Stay Poor: Urban Bias in World Development.* Cambridge: Harvard University Press 1977.

Lisitsyn, Iu. *Health protection in the USSR*, Moscow, Progress publishers 1972.

Litoshenko, L. N. *Sotsializatsiia zemli v Rossii.* Novosibirsk: Sibirskii khronograf 2001.

Long, R. E. (ed.). *The Farm Crisis.* New York: Wilson 1987.

Lotman, Yu. M. *Universe of the Mind: a semiotic theory of culture.* London: I. B. Tauris 1990.

Lotman, Yu. M. *Izbrannye stat'i. II.* Tallinn: Aleksandra 1992.

Lukin, A. Putin's Regime: Restoration or Revolution?, *Problems of Post-Communism* 48: 4 (2000), 47.

Machiavelli, N. Discourses on the First Ten Books of Titus Livius, in Max Lerner (ed.), *The Prince and the Discourses*, translated by Christian E. Detmold. New York: Modern Library 1950.

Maistrakh, K. V. *Organizatsiya zdravookhraneniya.* Moscow 1956.

Maksimova, M. Economic Relations between the Socialist and the Capitalist Countries: Results, Problems, Prospects, in Möttölä, Bykov and Korolev (eds.) *Finnish-Soviet Economic Relations.* Hpundmills: Macmillan Press 1983.

Male, D. J. *Russian Peasant Organization before Collectivisation.* Cambridge: Cambridge University Press 1971.

Mamonova, T. *Russian Women's Studies: Essays on Sexism in Soviet Culture.* Oxford: Pergamon Press 1989.

Mamonova, T. (ed.). *Women and Russia: Feminist Writings from the Soviet Union.* Oxford: Blackwell 1984.

Manning, N. and Parison, N. *International Public Administration Reform: Implications for the Russian Federation.* Worldbank: Poverty Reduction and Economic Management Unit, Europe and Central Asia Region 2003.

March, L. Russian Parties and the Political Internet, *Europe-Asia Studies* 56: 4 (2004).

Margolis, J. *Texts without Referents. Reconciling Science and Narrative.* Oxford: Basil Blackwell 1989.

Mariengof, A. *Cynics.* In *Glas. New Russian Writing*, 1 (1991).

Marx, K. *Capital*, vol. 1. London: Allen and Unwin 1946.

Mason, D. S. Attitudes toward the Market and Political Participation in the Postcommunist States, *Slavic Review* 54: 2 (1995).

Massell, G. *The Surrogate Proletariat: Moslem Women and Revolutionary Strategies in Soviet Central Asia.* Princeton, NJ: Princeton University Press 1974.

Mau, V. and Novikov, V. Otnosheniya Rossii i ES: prostranstvo vybora ili vybor prostranstva?, *Voprosy ekonomiki* 6 (2002), 133–45.

McCannon, J. Positive Heroes at the Pole: Celebrity Status, Socialist-Realist Ideals and the Soviet Myth of the Arctic, 1932–1939, *Russian Review* 56 (1997), 346–365.

McCannon, J. *Red Arctic: Polar Exploration and the Myth of the North in the Soviet Union, 1932–1939.* Oxford: Oxford University Press 1998.

McCauley, M. *Khrushchev and the Development of Soviet Agriculture: the Virgin Land Programme 1953–1964.* Basingstoke: Macmillan 1976.

McDaniel, T. *Autocracy, Capitalism and Revolution in Russia.* Berkeley: University of California Press 1988.

McFaul, M. *Russia's Unfinished Revolution: Political Change from Gorbachev to Putin.* Ithaca and London: Cornell University Press 2001.

McKay, J. P. *Pioneers for Profit: Foreign Entrepreneurs and Russian Industrialisation 1885–1913.* Chigaco: University of Chicago Press 1970.

Medushevskii, A. Konstitutsionnyi perevorot ili konstitutsionnaya reforma: popravki k Konstitutsii 1993 goda kak instrument bor'by za vlast', *Konstitutsionnoe pravo: vostochnoevropoeiskoe obozrenie* 3: 28 (1999), 154–67.

Medushevskii, A. Bonapartistskaya model' vlasti dlya Rossii?, *Konstitutsionnoe pravo: vostochnoevropeiskoe obozrenie* 4:33 / 1:34 (2001), 28.

Medvedev, A. – Shaburov, Yu. *Moscow port of five oceans.* Moscow: Moskovskii Rabotsii 1985.

Medvedev, S. Post-Soviet Developments: a Regional Interpretation (a Methodological Review), in Klaus, S. – De Spiegeleire, S. (eds.), *Post-Soviet Puzzles. Mapping the Political Economy of the Former Soviet Union.* vol II, *Emerging Geopolitical and Territorial Units, Theories, Methods and Case Studies.* Baden-Baden: Nomos Verlagsgesellschaft 1995.

Medvedev, Z. *Soviet Agriculture.* New York: Norton 1987.

Meek, J. Reasons to be Miserable, *London Review of Books* 26: 13 (2004), 1–8.

Megill, A. *The Burden of Reason. (Why Marx rejected Politics and the Market).* Lanham – Boulder – NY – Oxford: Rowman and Littlefield Publishers, Inc. 2002.

Mellor, R. E. H. The Soviet concept of unified transport system and the contemporary role of the railways, in Symons, L. and White, C. *Russian Transport. A Historical and Geographical Survey.* London: G. Bell and Sons Ltd. 1975.

Melnikov, M. A. The content of education in the eight-year school, *Soviet Education* 1: 5 (1959), 9–14.

Mel'nikov, V. I. *Istoricheskaia subd'ba krest'ianstva i melkotovarnogo proizvodstva: polemiki i diskussii perioda NEPa (1921-konets 20-kh gg.).* Nizhnii Novgorod 1999.

Metcalfe, S. Technology systems and technology policy in an evolutionary framework, in Archibugi, D. and Michie, J. (eds.) *Technology, Globalisation and Economic Performance*. Cambridge: CUP 1997, 268–296, 285.

Michelson, A. M. *Russian Public Finance during the War*. New Haven: Yale University Press 1928.

Millar, J. R. History, Method and the Problem of Bias, in Fleron and Hoffmann (eds.) *Post-Communist Studies and Political Science: Methodology and Empirical Theory in Sovietology*. Boulder: Westview Press 1993, 187.

Mints, L. E. *Trudovye resursy SSSR*. Moscow: Nauka 1975.

Mints, Z. G. *Aleksandr Blok i russkie pisateli*. St. Petersburg: Iskusstvo SPb 2000.

Mironov, B. The Russian peasant commune after the reforms of the 1860s, *Slavic Review* 44 (1985), 438–67.

Mixter, T. and Kingston-Mann, E. (eds.), *Peasant economy, culture, and politics of European Russia, 1800–1921*. Princeton: Princeton University Press 1991.

Molotov, V. *Sto sorok besed c Molotovym*. Moscow: Terra 1993.

Moore, T. *The Slaves We Rent*. New York: Random House 1965.

Mote, V. BAM, Boom, Bust: Analysis of Railways past, present and future. *Soviet Geography* 5 (1990), 326.

Muckle, J. *A Guide to the Soviet Curriculum: What the Russian Child is Taught in School*. London: Croom Helm 1988.

Mukhin, A. A. *Piterskoe okruzhenie prezidenta*. Moscow: Centre for Political Information 2003.

Mukhin, A. A. and Kozlov, P. A. *"Semeinye" tainy ili neofitial'nyi lobbizm v Rossii*. Moscow: Centre for Political Information 2003.

Myers, S. L. Living Today in Siberia. *New York Times* 26 January 2004.

Myers, S. L. Siberians Tell Moscow: Like It or Not, It's Home. *New York Times* January 2004.

Neuberger, E. and Duffy. *Comparative Economic Systems. A Decision-making Approach*. Boston: Allyn & Bacon 1976.

Neumann, I. B. *Russia and the Idea of Europe. A study in identity and international Relations*. London and New York: Routledge 1996.

Nichols, T. M. *The Russian Presidency: Society and Politics in the Second Russian Republic*. Basingstoke: Macmillan 2000.

Nikonov, A. A. *Sprial' mnogovekovoi dramy: agrarnaia nauka i politika Rossii (XVII–XX vv.)*. Moscow: Entsiklopediia rossiiskikh dereven' 1995.

Nironen, E. Transfer of Technology between Finland and the Soviet Union, in Möttölä, Bykov and Korolev (eds.) *Finnish-Soviet Economic Relations*. London: Macmillan 1983.

Nironen, E. Teknologisen kehityksen nopeuttaminen SEV-maissa. *Ulkopolitiikka* 4 (1986).

Nironen, E. Lännen embargopolitiikka murrosvaiheessa. *Ulkopolitiikka* 3 (1990).

Northrup, D. Veiled Empire: Gender and Power in Stalinist Central Asia. Ithaca: Cornell University Press 2003.

Nove, A. *An Economic History of the USSR*. Harmondsworth: Pelican Books 1976.

Nove, A. *Soviet Agriculture: The Brezhnev Legacy and Gorbachev's Cure*. RAND/UCLA Center for the Study of Soviet International Behavior 1988.

Nove, A. *Economic History of the Soviet Union, 1917–1991*. New York: Penguin books 1992.

O'Donnell, G. Delegative Democracy, *Journal of Democracy* 5: 1 (1994), 55–69.

Ofer, G. *Soviet Economic Growth: 1928–1985*. RAND/UCLA Center for the Study of Soviet International Behaviour 1988.

Ordzhonikidze, G. *Stat'i i rechi*, vol. 2. Moscow: Gosizdat 1957.

Paperny, V. *Kultura "Dva"*. Ann Arbor: Ardis Publishers 1985.

Paperny, V. *Architecture in the age of Stalin. Culture Two*. Cambridge: Cambridge University Press 2002.

319

Parison, N. *Increasing Government Effectiveness*. Moscow: Worldbank 2004.

Parkkinen, P. The Impact of the Trade with the Soviet Union on Finnish Economy, in Möttölä, Bykov and Korolev (eds.) *Finnish-Soviet Economic Relations*. London: Macmillan Press 1983.

Parshin, M. V. and Kirsanov, M. V. Sotsiologicheskii portret gosudarvstvennogo sluzhashchego, in Institut problem gosudarvstevnnogo i munitsipal'nogo upravleniya (ed.), *Reforma gosudarstvennogo upravleniya v Rossii: Vzglyad iznutri*. Moscow: Institut problem gosudarvstevnnogo i munitsipal'nogo upravleniya 2004, 41–47.

Parsons, T. *Societies: Evolutionary and Comparative Perspectives*. Englewood Cliffs, NJ: Prentice-Hall 1966.

Pasternak, Y. et al. (eds.). *Letters: Summer 1926, Boris Pasternak, Marina Tsvetaeva, Rainer Maria Rilke*. New York: New York Review of Books 2001.

Patterns of European Industrialisation. Sylla, R. and Toniolo, G. (eds.). London: Routledge 1991.

Perfil'ev, Y. *Rossiiskoe internet-prostranstvo: razvitie I struktura*. Moscow: Gardariki 2003.

Perheentupa, O. (ed.). *Suomen ja Neuvostoliiton välisen tiedeyhteistyön kanavat*. Suomen ja Neuvostoliiton välisen tieteellis-teknisen yhteistoimintakomitean julkaisusarja 11. Helsinki 1981

Pound, M. Lacan, Kierkegaard, and Repetition, *Quadlibet Journal* 7: 2 (2005).

Pitt, J. and Pavlova, M. Pedagogy in Transition: from Labour Training to Humanistic Technology Education in Russia, in Stephen Webber and Ilkka Liikanen (eds.*), Education and Civic Culture in Post-Communist Countries*. Basingstoke: Palgrave 2001.

Poety-Imazhinisty. St. Petersburg: Peterburgskii pisatel' 1997.

Polyakov, Yu. A. V. B. Zhuromskaya and I. I. Kiselev, Polveka Molchaniya, *Sotsiologicheskie issledovaniya* 7 (1990), 67.

Popov, V. P. Golod I gosudarstvennia politika (1946–47gg.), *Otchestvennaya istoriya* 6 (1992), 36–60.

Przeworski, A. *Democracy and the Market*. Cambridge: Cambridge University Press 1991.

Pushkareva, N. L. *Women in Russian History: From the Tenth to the Twentieth Century*. New York: M. E. Sharpe 1997.

Putin, V. V. *Razgovor s Rossiei: Stenogramma "Pryamoi linii s Prezidentom Rossiiskoi Federatsii V. V. Putinym"*, 19 December 2002. Moscow: Olma-Politizdat 2003, 14.

Putnam, R. *Making Democracy Work*. Princeton, NJ: Princeton UP 1994.

Raffalovich, A. *Russia: Her Industries and Trade*. London: P.S.King 1918.

Ransel, D. L. *Village Mothers: Three Generations of Change in Russia and Tataria*. Bloomington, IN: Indiana University Press 2000.

Rantanen, P. The Development of the System of Bilateral Agreements between Finland and the Soviet Union, in Möttölä, Bykov and Korolev (eds.) *Finnish-Soviet Economic Relations*. London: Macmillan Press 1983, 43–44, 52.

Reddaway, P. and Glinski, D. *The Tragedy of Russia's Reforms: Market Bolshevism against Democracy*. Washington, DC: The United States Institute of Peace Press 2001.

Rees, E. A. *Stalinism and Soviet Rail Transport 1928–41*. London: Macmillan Press 1995.

Rees, E. A. Stalinism: The Primacy of Politics, in Channon, J. (ed.) *Politics, Society and Stalinism in the USSR*. London: Macmillan Press Ltd 1998.

Reinikainen, V. and Kivikari, U. On the Theory of East-West Economic Relations in Möttölä, Bykov and Korolev (eds.) *Finnish-Soviet Economic Relations*. London: Macmillan Press 1983, 8–9.

Remington, T. F. *The Russian Parliament: Institutional Evolution in a Transitional Regime*. New Haven, CT: Yale University Press 2001.

Rieber, A. J. Sedimentary society, in Clowes, E. et al. (eds.), *Between Tsar and People*. Princeton: Princeton University Press 1990, 343–66.

Romanov, A. Suomen ja Neuvostoliiton välisen tieteellis-teknisen yhteistyön tuloksia, in Möttölä, Bykov and Korolev (eds.) *Finnish-Soviet Economic Relations*. London:

Macmillan Press 1983, 8.

Roosa, R. A. *Russian Industrialists in an Era of Revolution: The Association of Industry and Trade 1906–1917*. Armonk, N.Y.: M.E.Sharpe, 1997.

Rose, R. Getting things done in an anti-modern society: social capital networks in Russia, University of Strathclyde, *Studies in Social Policy* 304 (1998).

Rose, R. Living in an Antimodern Society, *East European Constitutional Review* (1999).

Rostow, W. W. *The Stages of Economic Growth: A Non-Communist Manifesto*. Cambridge: Cambridge University Press 1960.

Rowbotham, S. *A Century of Women: a History of Women in Britain and the United States*. London: Penguin 1999.

Ryan, M. *Contemporary Soviet society: A handbook*. Edward Elgar: Aldershot 1990.

Rykov, A. I. Na puti k usoichivomy krest'ianskomy khoziaistvu, in Rykov (ed.), *V bor'be s zasukhoi i golodom*. Moscow: Gosizdat 1925.

Saharov, A. *Muistelmat*. Juva: WSOY 1991.

Sajó, A. *Limiting Government: An Introduction to Constitutionalism*. Budapest: Central European University Press 1999.

Sakwa, R. *Gorbachev and His Reforms, 1985–1990*. London: Philip Allan 1990.

Sakwa, R. The Soviet State, Civil Society and Moscow Politics: Stability and Order in Early NEP, 1921–24, in Cooper, J., Perrie, M. and Rees, E. A. (eds.), *Soviet History 1917–1945: Essays in Honour of R. W. Davies*. London: Macmillan 1995, 42–77.

Sakwa, R. The Struggle for the Constitution in Russia and the Triumph of Ethical Individualism, *Studies in East European Thought* 48: 2–4 (1996), 115–57.

Sakwa, R. The Regime System in Russia, *Contemporary Politics* 3:1 (1997), 7–25.

Sakwa, R. *Russian Politics and Society*. London and New York: Routledge 2002.

Sandle, M. *A Short History of Soviet Socialism*. London: UCL Press 1999.

Schatzki, T. Practice mind-ed orders, in Schatzki, T., Knorr Cetina, K., von Savigny, E. *The Practice Turn in Contemporary Theory*. London and New York: Routledge 2001, 42–43.

Scheide, C. 'Born in October': the Life and Thought of Aleksandra Vasil'evna Artyukhina, 1889–1969, in Ilič, M. (ed.), *Women in the Stalin Era*. Basingstoke: Palgrave 2001, 9–28.

Schleifer, R. *Modernism and Time. The Logic of Abundance in Literature, Science, and Culture, 1880–1930*. Cambridge: Cambridge University Press 2000.

Schlesinger, R. *The Family in the USSR. (Changing Attitudes in Soviet Russia)*. London: Routledge and Kegan Paul 1949.

Schumpeter, J. *Capitalism, Socialism and Democracy*. New York: Harper 1949.

Semashko, N. A. *Des'yat let Oktiabria i sovetskaya meditsina*, Moscow, Izd. NKZdrava RSFSR 1927.

Semashko, N. A. *Health protection in the USSR*, London: Gollancz 1934.

Semi-presidentialism in Europe. Elgie, R. (ed.). Oxford: Oxford University Press 1999.

Sen, A. *Poverty and famines : an essay on entitlement and deprivation*. Oxford: Clarendon Press 1981.

Seppänen, J. *Tieteellis-tekninen informaatio Neuvostoliitossa*. Suomen ja Neuvostoliiton tieteellis-teknisen yhteistoimintakomitean julkaisusarja 2. Helsinki 1978.

Shaffer, H. G. (ed.). *Soviet agriculture: an assessment of its contributions to economic development*. New York: Praeger 1977.

Shanin, T. *Russia as a 'Developing Society'*. Basingstoke: Macmillan 1985.

Shapiro, J. The Industrial Labour Force, in M. Buckley (ed.), *Perestroika and Soviet Women*. Cambridge: Cambridge University Press 1992, 14–38.

Sharlet, R. Russian Constitutional Change: An Opportunity Missed, *Demokratizatsiya: The Journal of Post-Soviet Democratization* 7: 3 (1999), 437–47.

Sharlet, R. Russian Constitutional Change: Proposed Power-Sharing Models, in Clark, R., Feldbrugge, F. and Pomorski, S. (eds.), *International and National Law in Russia and Eastern Europe*. Amsterdam: Kluwer Law International 2001.

Shebaldin, Iu. N. Gosudarstvennyi biudzhet tsarskoi Rossii v nachale XXv., *Istoricheskie zapiski* 65, 163–90.

Shepelev, L. E. *Tsarizm i burzhuaziia v 1904–1914gg.* Moscow: Nauka 1987.

Shershenevich, V. *2x2=5: Listy imazhinista.* Moscow: Imazhinizm 1920.

Shevtsova, L. Power and Leadership in Putin's Russia, in Kuchins, Andrew (ed.), *Russia after the Fall.* Washington, D.C.: Carnegie Endowment for International Peace 2002.

Shlapentokh, V. A Normal Totalitarian Society. How the Soviet Union Functioned and How it Collapsed. New York: M. E. Sharpe 2001.

Shmidt, O. Y. Nashi Zadachi po Osvoeniyu Arktiki, in *Za Osvoenie Arktiki.* Leningrad: Izdatel'stvo Glavsevmorputi 1935.

Shreeves, R. Sexual Revolution or "Sexploitation"?: the Pornography and Erotica Debate in the Soviet Union, in Rai, S., Pilkington, H. and Phizacklea, A. (eds.), *Women in the Face of Change: the Soviet Union, Eastern Europe and China.* London: Routledge 1992, 130–146.

Shturman, D. *The Soviet Secondary School.* London: Routledge, 1988.

Shugart, M. S. and Carey, J. M. *Presidents and Assemblies: Constitutional Design and Electoral Dynamics.* Cambridge: Cambridge University Press 1992.

Slezkine, Y. *Arctic Mirrors: Russia and the Small Peoples of the North.* Ithaca: Cornell University Press 1996.

Smele, J. *Civil war in Siberia : the anti-Bolshevik government of Admiral Kolchak, 1918–1920.* Cambridge: Cambridge University Press 1996.

Smelyakov, N. Industrial Cooperation and Joint Production in Soviet-Finnish Economic Ties in Möttölä, Bykov and Korolev (eds.) *Finnish-Soviet Economic Relations.* London: Macmillan Press 1983, 101.

Smirnov, V. I. Osnovy 5-letnogo perspektivnogo plana zdravookhraneniia Leningradskoi oblasti, *Zdravookhranenie* 1 (1929).

Smith, J. *The Bolsheviks and the National Question 1917–1923.* London: Macmillan 1999.

Smith, J. Popular Opinion under Khrushchev: A Case Study of Estonian Reactions to Khrushchev's School Reform, 1958–59, in Timo Vihavainen (ed.), *The Soviet Union – a Popular State? Studies on Popular Opinion in the USSR.* St. Petersburg: Evropeiskii dom 2003, 318–337.

Smith, R. E. F. *The Enserfment of the Russian Peasantry.* London: Cambridge University Press 1968.

Snell, P. Soviet Microprocessors and Microcomputers, in *Technical Progress and Soviet Economic Development.* Basil Blackwell 1986.

Sokol'nikov, G. *Finansovaya politika revolyutsii,* vol. 3. Moscow 1928.

Solzhenitsyn, A. *Ensimmäinen Piiri.* Toinen nide. Helsinki: Suuri Suomalainen Kirjakerho 1973.

Stalin, I. V. *Sochineniya* Moscow: Gosizdat 1946–51.

Stalin, I. V. *Problems of Leninism.* Peking: Foreign Languages Press 1976.

Stites, R. The Women's Liberation Movement in Russia: Feminism, Nihilism and Bolshevism, 1860–1930. Princeton, NJ: Princeton University Press 1978.

Suleiman, E. N. Presidential and Political Stability in France, in Linz, J. J. and Valenzuela, A. (eds.), *The Failure of Presidential Democracy: Comparative Perspectives.* Baltimore: Johns Hopkins University Press 1994, 137–62.

Suleiman, E. *Dismantling Democratic States.* Princeton and Oxford: Princeton University Press 2003.

Susiluoto, I. Deritualization of political language: the case of the Soviet Union, in Hänninen, S. and Palonen, K. *Texts, contexts, concepts. Studies on Politics and Power in Language.* The Finnish Political Science Association. Jyväskylä: Gummerus 1990.

Sutela, P. Uuden tekniikan haaste neuvostotaloudelle, *Ulkopolitiikka* 4 (1986).

Sutton, A. *Western Technology and Soviet Economic Development 1945 to 1965.* Stanford Ca: Hoover Institution Press 1973.

Swindler, A. What anchors cultural practices, in Schatzki, T., Knorr Cetina, K., von Savigny, E. *The Practice Turn in Contemporary Theory.* London – NY: Routledge 2001, 76–87.

Tansey, G. and Worsley, T. *The Food System: A Guide*. London: Earthscan 1996.

Taracouzio, T. A. *Soviets in the Arctic*. New York: Macmillan 1938.

Tauger, M. B. The 1932 Harvest and the Famine of 1933, *Slavic Review* 50:1 (1991), 60–79.

Tauger, M. B. *Natural Disasters and Human Action in the Soviet Famine of 1931–1933*. Pittsburgh: Carl Beck Papers in Soviet and East European Studies, University of Pittsburgh 2001.

Tauger, M. B. *Statistical Falsification in the Soviet Union*. Seattle: Donald Treadgold Papers in Russian, East European, and Central Asian Studies, University of Washington 2001.

Tauger, M. B. Soviet Peasants and Collectivisation, 1930–1939: Resistance and Adaptation, *Journal of Peasant Studies* 31: 3–4 (2004), 427–456.

Tauger, M. B. Stalin, Soviet Agriculture, and Collectivisation, in Just, F. and Trentman, F. (eds.), *Food and Conflict in Europe in the Age of the Two World Wars*. London: Palgrave MacMillan 2006.

Taylor, R. & Christie, I. (eds.). *The Film Factory: Russian and Soviet cinema in documents 1896–1939*. London & New York: Routledge 1988.

Thompson, W. J. *Khrushchev: A Political Life*. Basingstoke: Macmillan 1995.

Timasheff, N. S. Overcoming illiteracy: public education in Russia 1880–1940, *Russian Review* 2 no.1 (1941), 80–88.

Tipps, D. C. Modernisation theory and the comparative study of societies: a critical perspective, *Comparative Studies in Society and History* 15 (1973), 199–226.

Tolstov, V. A. *Chronicles of Noril'sk*. Moscow 2004.

Tolz, V. *Russia: Inventing the Nation*. London-New York: Arnold 2001.

Truscott, P. *Kursk Russia's Lost Pride*. London: Simon and Schuster 2002.

Tsetkov, L. A. Chemistry course in the eight-year and secondary school, *Soviet Education* 1: 8 (1959), 8–13.

Tsivyan, Yu. "Chelovek s kinoapparatom" Dzigi Vertova – k rasshifrovke montazhnogo teksta, in: Raushenbakh (ed.), *Montazh*. Moscow: Nauka 1988, 78.

Tsivyan, Yu. *Istoricheskaya retseptsiya kino: kinematograf v Rossii 1896–1930*. Riga: Sinatne 1991.

Tsyganov, V. B. *Formirovanie administrativno-komandnoi sistemy upravleniia kolkhozami Urala (1933-iiun' 1941)*. Sverdlovsk: Urals University Press 1991.

Tuck, R. Grotius and Selden, in Burns, J. H. (ed.), *The Cambridge History of Political Thought, 1450–1700*. Cambridge: Cambridge University Press 1991, 529.

Tudge, C. *The Famine Business*. London: Faber 1977.

Tupitsyn, M. *The Soviet Photograph 1924–1937*. New Haven and London: Yale University Press 1996.

Van Zon, H. Neo-Patrimonialism as an Impediment to Economic Development: The Case of Ukraine, *Journal of Communist Studies and Transition Politics* 17: 3 (2001), 73–74.

Varlamova, N. Konstitutsionnaya modernisatsiya: igra v terminy, igra v reformy ili igra s ognem?, *Konstitutsionnoe pravo: vostochnoevropoeiskoe obozrenie* 2 :31 (2000), 122–5.

Vasil'ev, N. *Transport Rossii v voine 1914–1918gg*. Moscow: Voen. izdatelstvo 1939.

Vaughn, R. *The Arctic: A History*. Phoenix Mill, Gloucestershire: Sutton Publishing Ltd. 1994.

Verkhovskii, A., Mikhailovskaya, E. and Pribylovskii, V. *Rossiya Putina: pristrastnyi vzglyad*. Moscow: Tsentr Panorama 2003.

Vile, M. J. C. *Constitutionalism and the Separation of Powers*.Oxford: Oxford University Press 1967; second edition, Indianapolis: Libery Fund 1998.

Vinogradov, N. *Health protection in the Soviet Union*. Moscow: Foreign Languages Publishing house 1956.

Viola, L. *Peasant Rebels Under Stalin*. New York: Oxford University Press 1996.

Virilio, P. *Speed and Politics. An Essay on Dromology*. New York: Semiotext(e) 1986.

Volkov, I. V. The drought and famine of 1946–47, *Russian Studies in History* 31: 2 (1992), 31–60.

Von Laue, T. A secret memorandum of Sergei Witte, *Journal of Modern History* 26 (1954).

Von Laue, T. *Sergei Witte and the Industrialisation of Russia*. New York: Columbia University Press 1963.

Voznesenskaya, J. *The Women's Decameron*. London: Quartet books 1986.

Walder, A. *Communist Neo-Traditionalism: Work and Authority in Chinese Industry*. Berkeley: University of California Press 1986.

Walicki, A. *A History of Russian Thought from the Enlightenment to Marxism*. Stanford, California: Stanford University Press 1979.

Ward, C. Selling the "project of the century": Perceptions of the Baikal-Amur mainline railway (BAM) in the Soviet Press 1974–1984, *Canadian Slavonic Papers* (2001).

Waters, E. Restructuring the "Woman Question": *Perestroika* and Prostitution, *Feminist Review* 33 (1989), 3–19.

Waters, E. The Modernisation of Russian Motherhood, 1917–1937, *Soviet Studies* 44: 1 (1992), 123–135.

Waters, E. Victim or Villain: Prostitution in Post-Revolutionary Russia, in Edmondson, L. (ed.), *Women and Society in Russia and the Soviet Union*. Cambridge: Cambridge University Press 1992, 160–177.

Wegren, S. (ed.). *Rural Adaptation in Russia*. London: Routledge 2005.

Weiner, D. R. The Genealogy of the Soviet and Post-Soviet Landscape of Risk, in Rosenholm, A. and Autio-Sarasmo, S. *Understanding Russian Nature: Representations, Values and Concepts*. Aleksanteri Papers 4/2005, 212–3.

Wells, H. G. *Russia in the Shadows*. London: Hodder and Stoughton Limited 1920.

Westwood, J. N. *A History of Russian Railways*. London: G. Allen and Unvin 1964.

Westwood, J. N. The railways, in Davies, R. W. (ed.), *From Tsarism to NEP*. Basingstoke: Macmillan 1990, 172–5.

Westwood, J. N. Transport, in Davies, R. W., Harrison, M. and Wheatcroft, S. G. (eds.) *The Economic Transformation of the Soviet Union, 1913–1945*. Cambridge: Cambridge University Press 1994.

Westwood, J. N. *Soviet Railways to Russian Railways*. New York: Palgrave 2002

Wheatcroft, S. G., Davies, R. W. and Cooper, J. M. Soviet Industrialization Reconsidered: Some Preliminary Conclusions about Economic Development between 1926 and 1941, *Economic History Review* (2nd ser.) 39: 2 (1986).

White, S. The Presidency and Political Leadership, in Lentini, P. (ed.), *Elections and Political Order in Russia*. Budapest: Central European University Press 1995, 202–25.

Willerton Jr, J. P. The Presidency: From Yeltsin to Putin, in White, S., Pravda, A. and Gitelman, Z. (eds.), *Developments in Russian Politics*. Basingstoke: Palgrave 2001, 29.

Williams, C. War, medicine and revolution: Petrograd doctors, 1917–20, *Revolutionary Russia* 4: 2 (1991), 259–288.

Williams, C. The 1921 Russian famine: Centre and periphery responses, *Revolutionary Russia* 6: 1 (1993), 277–314.

Williams, C. The Revolution from above in Soviet medicine, Leningrad 1928–32, *Journal of Urban History* Volume 20: 4 (1994), 512–540.

Williams, C. Health care in transition, in Williams, C., Chuprov, V. and Staroverov, V. (eds.), *Russian Society in transition*. Aldershot: Dartmouth Publishing 1996, 186.

Winslow, C. E. A. Public health administration in Russia in *Public Health Reports* 28 Dec. 1917, US Public Health Service: Washington Government Printing House 1918, 3.

Woman and Russia: First Feminist Samizdat. London: Sheba Feminist Publishers 1980.

Women and Children in the USSR. Moscow: Foreign Languages Publishing House 1963.

Women and Communism: Selections from the Writings of Marx-Engels-Lenin-Stalin. London: Lawrence and Wishart 1950.

Women in the USSR: Brief Statistics. Moscow: Foreign Languages Publishing House 1960.

Yakovlev, A. *Tsel' zhizni*. Moscow: Izd-vo politicheskoĭ lit-ry 1967.

Yantzov, A. I. The content of education in the schools for the worker and rural youth,

Soviet Education 1: 5 (1959), 19.

Yekaterina, K. US Specialists Praise Russian Oil Transshipment Complexes. Moscow: ITAR-TASS News Agency 2003.

Yurev, D. *Prezidentskie vybory.* Moscow 1991.

Yurovskii, L. N. *Denezhnaya politika sovetskoi vlasti.* Moscow 1928.

Yuskovich, V. F. Content of Physics courses in first and second stage schools, *Soviet Education* 1: 6 (1959).

Zaleski, E. et al. *Science Policy in the USSR.* Paris: OECD 1969.

Zamyatin, E. *We.* Moscow: Raduga Publishers 2000.

Zaslavskaya, T. *The Second Socialist Revolution: An Alternative Socialist Strategy.* London: Tauris 1990.

Zelenin, I. E. Politotdely MTS (1933–1934 gg.), *Istoricheskie zapiski* 76 (1965).

Zhenshchina v SSSR (published annually).

Zima, V. F. Zasukha, golod, 1946–47, *Istoriya SSSR* 4 (1991), 3–19.

Zima, V. F. Golod v Rossii 1946–1947 godov, *Otchestvennaya istoriya* 1 (1993), 35–52.

Zubok, V. and Pleshakov, C. *Inside the Kremlin's Cold War. From Stalin to Khrushchev.* Cambridge, Mass. and London: Harvard University Press 1996.

NEWSPAPERS AND JOURNALS

Aamulehti (AL) 22.10.2003.
Aamulehti (AL) 23.10.2003.
Argumenty i fakty 11 December 2002.
Asia Times 16 May 2003.

Byulleten' Gipromeza no. 7–8 1929.

Demokraticheskaya gazeta 12–19 September 1991.

Economist 16 August 2003.
Eurasia Daily Monitor June 15 2005.

Finansovye Izvestiya 18 December 1997.
Finansovye Izvestiya 13 October 2004.

Helsingin Sanomat (HS) 22.10.2003.

Izvestiya 3 August 1934.
Izvestiya Ts.K. KPSS, No 2, 1989.
Izvestiya 5 May 1989.
Izvestiya 6 May 1989.
Izvestiya 2 and 4 November 1991.
Izvestiya 12 February 1998.
Izvestiya 9 September 2003.
Izvestiya 22 October 2004.

Kommersant 25 November 1997.
Kommersant 25 October 2004.

Literaturnaya gazeta 22 January 1992.

Monitor 9 June 2000.
Moscow News 16 April 1989.

Moscow News 23 June 1991.
Moscow News 12 July 2004.

Newsline 25 February 2000.
New York Times 6 January 1999.
New York Times 26 January 2004.
Nezavisimaya gazeta 9 November 1993.
Nezavisimaya gazeta 24 February 2000.
Nezavisimaya gazeta 2 March 2000.
Nezavisimaya gazeta, 14 December 2000.
Nezavisimaya gazeta 8 July 2003.
Nezavisimaya Gazeta April 29 2005.
Novaya Gazeta 28 Feb 2005.
Novaya Gazeta 14 March 2005.

October, Fall 1984.
Online Vremya Novostei 22 October 2004.

Partiynaya zhizn' no. 4 1986.
Partiynaya zhizn' no. 21 1987.
Planovoe khozyaistvo no. 2 1926.
Planovoe khozyaistvo no. 3 1930.
Pravda June 18 1930.
Pravda 7 December 1932.
Pravda 18 November 1936.
Pravda 16 November 1958.
Pravda 29 June 1988.
Pravda 29 April 1989.
Predpriyatie no. 6 1928.

Rossiiskaya gazeta 31 October and 1 November 1991.
Rossiiskaya gazeta 27 December 2002.
Rossiiskaya gazeta 26 March 2003.
Russian Mirror 6 August 2003.

Sovetskaia Pedagogika 1958.
Sovetskaia Pedagogika 1959.
Soviet Education 1: 1 (1958), 61–63, 86.
Soviet Education 1: 2 (1958), 51–52.
Soviet Education 1: 3 (1959), 19–26.
Soviet Education 1: 4 (1959), 3–14.
Soviet Education 1: 6 (1959).
Soviet Education 1: 7, 8, 9, 10 (May – August 1959).

USSR in Construction 1937 (no. 9–12).

Vedomosti 23 July 2003.
Vedomosti 30 July 2003.
Vedomosti 31 July 2003.
Vedomosti 6 August 2003.
Vedomosti 31 December 2003.
Vedomosti 15 October 2004.
Vedomosti 22 October 2004.
Vedomosti 17 December 2004.
Versiya 9–15 June 2003.

Washington Post Weekly July 29–August 4 2002.

INTERNET SOURCES

Agentstvo ekonomicheskoi informatsii (www.prime-tass.ru).
American Enterprise Institute *Russia Outlook* (www.aei.org).

BBC Monitoring, 16 May 2003 (http://www.president.kremlin.ru/text/
appears/2003/05/44623.shtml).

Castells, M. and Kiselyova, E. Russia and the Network Society. (http://www.stanford.
edu/group/Russia20/volumepdf/castells.pdf).
The Center for Economic and Financial Research (Cefir) (www.cefir.ru).
The Central Bank of Russia website (www.cbr.ru).
The Concept on the Use of Information Technologies in the Work of Federal Executive
Authorities until 2010 (http://www.government.gov.ru/data/news_text.html?he_
id=103&news_id=15377).

Drozhzhinov, V. I. *E-government state-of-the-art in Russia* (www.e-govcompetence.ru).
Drozhzhinov, V. I. *E-government in Russia, Year 2002* (www.e-govcompetence.ru).

Electronic Russia (www.e-rus.ru).

Governmental report issued by the Ministry of Information Technology and Communication
(http://www.government.gov.ru/data/structdoc.html?he_id=102&do_id=171).

Harford, James, Korolev, Mastermind of the Soviet Space Program (http://www.cosmos-
club.org/journals/1998/harford.html).
Harter, Stefanie. *Russlandanalyse* (www.ruslandanalysen.de).

International Research and Exchanges Board (IREX), (http://www.irex.org/pubs/
russainternet/index.asp).
International Telecommunication Union (http://www.internetworldstats.com/stats.htm).
Internet v Rossii, issue 13, Autumn 2005 (http://bd.fom.ru/report/map/projects/internet/
internet13/d051060).
Izvestiya 22 October 2004 (http://www.izvestia.ru/politic/article560073).

McKinsey Global Institute (www.McKinsey.com).
Ministerstvo informatsionnykh tekhnologii (http://www.minsvyaz.ru).

Nezavisimaya gazeta (http://www.ng.ru/internet).
Novosti kompanii. 5 December 2003, 14:13 MKT. (www.rzd.ru).

O federalnoi tselevoi programme Administrativnaya Reforma (2005–2010), Moscow,
October 2004 (http://ar.economy.gov.ru).
Oktrytie Severo-Muiskogo tonnelja (words of the head of the Russian Railways, Gennadi
Fadeev, at the opening of the North Muisk tunnel on 5 December 2008). (http://www.
rzd.ru/documents/index.html?he_id=892).
*Osnovnye napravleniya deyatel'nosti pravitel'stva Rossiskoi Federatsii na period do
2008 goda*, 28 July 2004 (http://ar.economy.gov.ru).

Semenov, Il'ya. *Internet i Rossiiskoe obshchestvo* (http://pubs.carnegie.ru/books/2002/08is).
Sergei Tsukhlo's monthly surveys of business confidence among large and medium-sized
firms. (www.iet.ru).

Shanin, Teodor. *Russia as a 'Developing Society'* (http://ruralworlds.msses.ru/eng/ shanin-develop/glava2.html).

Sopimus tieteellis-teknillisestä yhteistoiminnasta Suomen tasavallan ja SNTL:n välillä, 16.8.1955. (http://www.finlex.fi/linkit/sops/19550030_2).

The demographics of the Internet in Russia (http://www.nielsen-netratings.com).

The history of the Internet in Russia (http://www.nethistory.ru).

Transparency International Corruption Perceptions Index 2004 (http://www.transparency. org).

Worldbank, *Russian Economic Report,* 8 June 2004 (www.worldbank.org.ru).

World Economic Forum (http://www.weforum.org/pdf/Global_Competitiveness_Reports/ Reports/gitr_2006/rankings.pdf).

Contributors

Sari Autio-Sarasmo is a researcher at the Aleksanteri Institute (Finnish Centre for Russian and East European Studies) at the University of Helsinki. She is also an adjunct professor (dossenti) of general history at the University of Tampere. Her current interest is in Cold War studies, especially scientific and technological developments in the Soviet Union and the Soviet Union's scientific-technical cooperation with the West.

Julian Cooper is Professor of Russian Economic Studies at the Centre for Russian and East European Studies, European Research Institute, University of Birmingham, where he served as Director from 1990–2001. He is author of many works on the Russian economy, including the military sector, science and technology, and the place of Russia in the global economy. Books include *The Soviet Defence Industry: Conversion and Reform* and the co-edited *Technical Progress and Soviet Economic Development, Industrial Innovation in the Soviet Union* and *The Technological Level of Soviet Industry*.

R. W. Davies is Emeritus Professor of Soviet Economic Studies at the Centre for Russian and East European Studies, University of Birmingham. In 1996 he published volume 4 of his history of Soviet industrialisation, *Crisis and Progress in the Soviet Economy, 1931–1933* and volume 5, co-authored with Professor Stephen Wheatcroft, which deals with Soviet agriculture in the same period, was published in 2004. He is now working with Prof. Wheatcroft and Dr Oleg Khlevnyuk on the final volume, dealing with the Soviet economy in 1934–1939. His book on historiography and the public view of the Soviet period of history in Russia during and after the collapse of Communism, *Soviet History in the Yeltsin Era* was published in 1996.

Peter Gattrell is Professor of Economic History at the University of Manchester. His most recent books are *Russia's First World War: A Social and Economic History* and *Homelands: War, Population and Statehood in Eastern Europe and Russia, 1918–1924* (edited with Dr Nick Baron). His other books include *A Whole Empire Walking: Refugees in Russia during the First World War* and *The Tsarist Economy, 1850–1917*. He is currently preparing a book entitled *Refugees in Modern World History*.

Philip Hanson is Emeritus Professor of Economics at the Centre for Russian and East European Studies, University of Birmingham. He has recently published *The Rise and Fall of the Soviet Economy: an Economic History of the USSR, 1945–1991*. Other publications include: *The Consumer in the Soviet Economy; Advertising and Socialism; Trade and Technology in Soviet-Western Relations; Western Economic Statecraft and From Stagnation to Catastroika*; co-author, *The Comparative Economics of Research, Development and Innovation in East and West*. Co-editor, *Regional Economic Change in Russia; Alexander Zinoviev as Writer and Thinker* and

Transformation From Below. Journal articles on technology transfer, economics of transition. He has worked as a consultant on the Russian and Baltic economies for the Economist Intelligence Unit and Oxford Analytica.

Stefanie Harter works for the Delegation of the European Commission to Russia. She is in charge of projects which support the public sector reform process in Russia. She completed her PhD at the University of Birmingham in 1998 on 'The Civilianisation of the Russian Economy: A Network Approach'. She is co-editor of *Shaping the Economic Space in Russia* and author of several articles and reports on the Russian space and aviation industries.

Tomi Huttunen is a Research Fellow and Assistant in Russian Literature in the Department of Slavonic and Baltic Languages and Literature at the University of Helsinki. He has published a textbook on semiotics and numerous scientific and popular articles on Russian literature, art, music and culture, and has translated Russian prose and poetry. He is an editor of the Finnish Review of East European Studies, and is finishing his PhD on Russian Imaginist A. Mariengof and the montage principle.

Melanie Ilič is Senior Lecturer in History at the University of Gloucestershire, and an Honorary Research Fellow at the Centre for Russian and East European Studies, The University of Birmingham. She is author of *Women Workers in the Soviet Interwar Economy: From 'Protection' to 'Equality';* editor of *Women in the Stalin Era* and *Stalin's Terror Revisited*; and co-editor, with S. E. Reid and L. Attwood, of *Women in the Khrushchev Era*.

Markku Kangaspuro is Head of Research of the Aleksanteri Institute, University of Helsinki. He was formerly the Programme Manager of the Research Programme on 'Russia in Flux' of the Academy of Finland, and is Chief Editor of the Finnish Review of East European Studies. He has written extensively on the history of Soviet Karelia in the 1920s and 1930s, and has recently edited *Russia: More Different than Most*. His current research interests are on the political use of history, contemporary Russian politics, and Russia's relation to Europeanness.

Antti Laine is the Head of the Department of Humanities and a Senior Researcher at the Karelian Institute, University of Joensuu. He has published extensively on Russian society and especially on Soviet Karelia.

David Lane is Senior Research Associate in the Faculty of Social and Political Sciences, Cambridge University. He is currently the holder of a Leverhulme research grant on transition in Russia and Ukraine and a British Academy network award on The Enlargement of the EU to the East. Recent publications include *The Legacy of State Socialism and the Future of Transformation*; edited books on *The Rise and Fall of State Socialism: Industrial Society and the Socialist State*; *The Political Economy of Russian Oil*; *Russian Banking: Evolution, Problems and Prospects*; and numerous articles on State Socialism and political elites in the political economy of transformation of the former communist countries.

Katri Pynnöniemi is currently a Visiting Researcher at the Finnish Institute of International Affairs in Helsinki, and is working on a PhD dissertation on 'Russia's European paths. Pan-European/international transport corridors at the conjunction of geography and politics in Russia'.

Richard Sakwa is Professor of Russian and European Politics in the Department of Politics and International Relations at the University of Kent at Canterbury. He has previously taught at the University of California, Santa Cruz, and the University of Essex. His publications include *Soviet Politics: An Introduction* (revised as *Soviet Politics in Perspective* in 1998); *Gorbachev and His Reforms*; *Russian Politics and Society*; *Postcommunism*; and *The Rise and Fall of the Soviet Union, 1917–1991*. His latest book is *Putin: Russia's Choice* (London and New York: Routledge, 2004), a Russian version of which was published in Moscow by Olma-Press in 2006. He has also written numerous articles on contemporary Russian affairs and given many television and radio interviews.

Jeremy Smith is Senior Lecturer in Russian History at the Centre for Russian and East European Studies, University of Birmingham. He is author of *The Bolsheviks and the National Question, 1917–1923* and *The Fall of Soviet Communism, 1985–1991*. His published articles cover the nationalities question in the territory of the former Russian Empire ranging from 1905 to the post-Soviet period, and he has also written on education in the late Soviet period. His current research interests are on ethnic conflict in the Caucasus, Khrushchev's education reforms, and social unrest in the USSR in the 1920s. In 2005 he received awards from the Leverhulme Trust to write a monograph on the nationalities experience in and after the Soviet Union, and from the Arts and Humanities Research Council (with Melanie Ilič and R. W. Davies) for a major research project on the political and economic history of the Khrushchev years.

Mark Tauger is an Associate Professor of History at West Virginia University. He has published numerous articles on Soviet agrarian policy including collectivisation, the political economy of the Soviet countryside, and the Soviet famine of 1932–33. He is currently working on a monograph on the Soviet rural economy.

Linda Trautman has been Head of Humanities at Southbank International School in London in 1989. She completed her PhD in 2005 at the London School of Economics. Her research interests are Soviet and post-Soviet Arctic policies, and the operations of both the U.S.S.R. and the Russian Federation along the Northern Sea Route.

Christopher Williams is Professor of Contemporary History at the University of Central Lancashire. His publications include *Molodezh' v obshchestve riska* (2001) and *Youth, Risk and Russian Modernity* (2003) (both with Vladimir Chuprov and Julia Zubok) and *Sotsial'naia politika: Istoriia i sovremenost'* (editor and contributor with R. Hulme, A. Sargeant and M. Malyshev) (Izd, Udmurtskii gosudarstvennyi universitet, Izhevsk, 2005). He has recently completed *Casualties of Change: The rise and fall of the Russian welfare State* (forthcoming Ashgate, 2006) and is currently working on a monograph entitled *The Politics of Health and welfare in Leningrad, 1917–1941* which will be published in 2007.

www.ingramcontent.com/pod-product-compliance
Lightning Source LLC
Chambersburg PA
CBHW081736270326
41932CB00020B/3287